Perspectives in Cultural-Historical Research

Volume 10

There is growing interest in the work of LS Vygotsky internationally, but also in finding new ways and perspectives for advancing cultural-historical theory for solving contemporary problems. Although Vygotsky has become one of the most influential scholars in education and psychology today, there is still a need for serious studies of his work because so much remains unexamined.

The books in this series draw on the collected works of Vygotsky as a primary source of authority. They go beyond secondary sources and discuss Vygotsky's original ideas in the context of a system of concepts or through the elaboration and theorisation of research findings so that contemporary problems can be addressed in new ways.

This series collectively brings together under one umbrella a more equal representation of works from scholars across both the Northern and Southern continents. In the context of a large volume of contributions to cultural-historical theorisation and the empirical work from North America, there is an urgent need for making visible the works of scholars from countries who reside in countries other than North America.

More information about this series at https://link.springer.com/bookseries/13559

L. S. Vygotsky

L.S. Vygotsky's Pedological Works. Volume 2.

The Problem of Age

Translated with notes and lecture outlines by
David Kellogg and Nikolai Veresov

Springer

L. S. Vygotsky (Deceased)
Moscow, Russia

Translated by
David Kellogg
Sangmyung University
Seoul, Korea (Republic of)

Nikolai Veresov
Monash University
Frankston, VIC, Australia

ISSN 2520-1530 ISSN 2520-1549 (electronic)
Perspectives in Cultural-Historical Research
ISBN 978-981-16-1906-9 ISBN 978-981-16-1907-6 (eBook)
https://doi.org/10.1007/978-981-16-1907-6

This Springer imprint is published by the registered company Springer Nature Singapore Pte Ltd.
The registered company address is: 152 Beach Road, #21-01/04 Gateway East, Singapore 189721, Singapore

Unraveling Some Threads

Surely hanging by a thread is no time to split hairs. In a crisis—and this book is being published in the middle of a crisis that has not only cultural-historical but also political, economic, biological, climatological, and even geological dimensions—it is hard to think of anything but getting "back to normal" or perhaps getting some "new normal" in its place. Why unravel the threads of which the fabric of ordinary life is woven just now?

Such doubts are understandable, necessary—and only implicitly answered in this book. Let's address them explicitly here. For a child, a parent, or even a teacher in the throes of a crisis, or even a crisis within a crisis, it is hard to imagine that a manuscript left unfinished for decades, addressing problems of child development that unfold over years, and centrally concerned with the periodization of growth and development can offer the immediate causes, practicable solutions, or relevant guidance we desperately need. Indeed, for some scholars, it is doubtful whether any science can deal with this kind of complexity (see, e.g., "The Disunity of Psychology as a Working Hypothesis," as expounded by Borsboom et al., 2009: 67). It is somewhat less doubtful for the transdisciplinary developmental science that has developed in our own time (see, e.g., Valsiner, 2005).

For Vygotsky, there was no doubt at all (see the first volume of this series). For Vygotsky, it was precisely the cracks in normality that made segmenting and periodizing the child's history feasible; it would be the "problem of age" that made crises indispensable: not as a way of getting back to the previous developmental period and still less as a way of liquidating them into a "new normal," but rather as revolutionary experiments. For Vygotsky, every crisis was a natural experiment in analysis, just as every analysis of crises was a human experiment in thought.

Here, we will survey just four of these thoughtful experiments with you. First, we will consider how crises distinguish developmental ages from mere calendrical ones. Second, we will analyze the "synoptic" quality of crises and stable periods—the way in which Vygotsky considers them as wholes without destroying their time-dependent quality, as periods which differ and yet still resemble each other. Third, we will think about the way in which healthy and unhealthy development also differ and yet still resemble each other, and we'll see that, here too, the time-delimited quality of the crisis is crucial. Finally, we will attempt a synopsis of the six crises and five stable periods in terms of just one manifest line of development, namely, conversation. We shall put it to you that, as with conversation, we know human development by taking part in it. Perhaps this, more than anything else, will answer the question of why, when the world seems to be hanging by a thread, we must still find the time to splice the strands and to re-weave them into something more substantial and lasting. To do that, we need to unravel them.

The Eponymous "Problem of Age"

To begin with, what exactly is this eponymous "problem of age"? Why did this problem of age take center stage in Vygotsky's interests during the last hectic period of a short busy life? Of course, even to the casual passer-by asking a child "How old are you?", the calendrical, astronomical answer—the number of times the earth has completed a revolution around the sun since the day the child was born—is less interesting than the relationship between this "passport" age and how old the child seems to be, on the basis of the child's stature and behavior and what we can glean of the child's knowledge through his or her speech. To an interested professional like Vygotsky, this problem of age is far more vital in every sense of the word: how does the development of this child compare, in health and in vitality, with the development of other children in his or her age cohort in the class, the school, the community, and the world?

Putting it that way, we can discern two broad and overlapping reasons why the problem of age caught Vygotsky's attention and held his interest even as his own health disintegrated, the professional position of pedology deteriorated, and the revolutionary reconstruction of his country turned to bloody and famished shambles. In the first place, there must have been a keen subjective interest whenever Vygotsky was working interpersonally with individual children, including his own. In the second place, there must have been interests of a more objective sort—contrasting and conflicting social interests—whenever he wished to make verifiable and actionable statements about the developmental potential of large groups of children. Both reasons for interest—more subjective and interpersonal and more objective and sociocultural—must have held true for Vygotsky in his time; both hold true for us today.

For example, during the COVID-19 pandemic, many parents worried that shuttering schools would cause irreparable developmental harm to their children. It is quite possible that thousands of lives were ultimately lost in order to keep schools open and keep parents at work. But here, in the first place, Vygotsky gives us reason to think that child development cannot be reliably time-tabled like this. In the second place, Vygotsky demands that we diagnose child development not with absolute but with relative indicators; that we always consider children in relation to other children and relative to their own development as well. So if all children and teachers in a society are granted an emergency sabbatical until the virus is under control, the underlying relations of development and the relative indicators of development may be largely unchanged. In the third place, crises do not always loom "imminently" in the environment horizon; true developmental crises are always *immanent*—intrinsic—in development itself.

Vygotsky shows us how every higher psychological function—logical memory, voluntary attention, even thinking itself—must make, as it were, two appearances on the developmental stage. The first appearance is as an inter-psychological category, a recitative between real people involved in the drama, but the second is as an intra-psychological category—an aria within. Because we tend to think of logical memory, voluntary attention, and thinking as skills that are learned through practice, we imagine that the transition between the two categories is relatively straightforward and untraumatic—like a singer moving from a duet to a solo in an opera. But just a moment's reflection shows that this cannot be so: just as a recitative has a very different structure from an aria, conversation has a radically different structure from formal presentations; calculation and even mere counting has a very different structure from guesstimation at a glance, and co-translating a book is a very different process from single-authoring one. The same must likewise be true of sociocultural factors such as economics, politics, and language and interpersonal ones like family relations, friendships, and conversations. The very fact that we have far more agency in the latter categories of relationships must make their structure very different, and this by itself can render the transitions between them critical. It also makes it difficult to establish a common relational indicator that includes the categories for socio-cultural and the categories for intra-psychological and physiological development.

Vygotsky rules out the calendrical, astronomical answer to the question "How old are you?"—there is no reason to expect modern children to synchronize their developmental periods to the earth's trajectory around the sun and the four seasons. But Vygotsky also rules out using particular features of development such as dentition, sexuality, or even higher psychological functions as gateway criteria: what is a good criterion for the teething toddler does not work for the teenager and vice versa. Not even an eclectic basket of criteria will do; we cannot "explain" development as swinging from one environmental affordance to another anymore than a child can understand school as swinging from one friendship to another. For Vygotsky, the only real criterion for age periodization is an immanent one: changes in the pace of development itself. Vygotsky then notes that these changes in development do appear to be periodic—there is a regular rhythm of stable periods which alternate with crises, and it is these crises which he takes as his milestones. Just as the transition from inter-psychological to intra-psychological categories must necessarily involve destructuration and revolutionary restructuring, a child's long journey from family to school to community is not simply a matter of meters or even miles. The units for the analysis of this development can only come from development itself.

Synopticon: Social Situation of Development, Central/ Peripheral Lines, and Neoformations

The reader will notice that Vygotsky sometimes repeats himself—and that even when he does not repeat himself, he uses "as we have already said" and "it is completely clear" and even "in previous chapters of this book" or "in previous classes" where it is quite unclear which chapters/classes he is referring to and sometimes even where the point he is referring to has yet to be made. This is hard to follow, but it is easy to explain.

Vygotsky has been compared to Mozart (Toulmin, 1978), and of course both men lived fast, died young, and left behind a beautiful and formidable body of work for us to dissect. But for the purpose of establishing the constellation of key concepts that we started in the first volume, a more useful comparison has to do with Mozart's supposed ability to see each piece of music as a finished whole, with the beginning, the middle, and the ending all in existence synchronically. Legend has it that Mozart could "see" his music before he could hear it, that it existed finished in his head, before he wrote it down as a series of notes, as bars, phrases, and movements which come into existence diachronically. This capability is called synoptic thinking—the capacity for seeing a process that unfolds in time not only from the beginning or the end but at any moment in between and from any angle of observation. Unlike a piece of music or a spoken narrative, we can circumambulate a sculpture or scroll freely around a written text—hence the word "synopsis" for the spoiler at the beginning of a play and the "Synoptic Gospels" for the four differently ordered accounts of the life of Christ in the Greek New Testament.

Vygotsky, like Mozart, was a synoptic thinker. In Chapter Ten, Vygotsky is discussing the method of analysis into units which he first introduced in Lecture 2 of Volume 1 (Vygotsky, 2019). "We often find it necessary," Vygotsky says, "to speak of the unity of the personality and the environment, of the unity of psychological and of physical development, of the unity of speech and thinking." Vygotsky gives three examples of units, and the first is *perezhivanie*, for the study of the unity of the personality and environment. The third is word meaning, for the study of the complex unity of verbal thinking and inner and outer speech. But the second example Vygotsky gives is not named—it is a unit for studying the unity of psychophysiological development.

Vygotsky begins, at the beginning of Chapter Three, with the whole epoch and not with the units for its analysis. The epoch is described synoptically: first, it is detached from any whole temporal process which is not itself development. However tempting and convenient we may find it, the developmental epoch cannot be delimited by the astronomical calendar, analogies with phylogenetic evolution, or even the pedagogical timetable. Next, Vygotsky detaches the epoch from any partial temporal process which explains only one period of development. Teething may or may not explain the "terrible twos" (what Vygotsky calls the crisis at three), but we can be quite certain that the end of adolescence does not coincide with the arrival of wisdom teeth. Conversely, sexual maturation may or may not explain the crisis at thirteen, but we may be quite sure that it can tell us very little about the similarity between teenagers and "threenagers." Nor can the epoch be established by some basket of temporal processes picked up through empirical observation and linked in a haphazard way, for example, by teething for toddlers, then schooling for their older siblings, and finally pubic hair in young adults. Instead, Vygotsky takes the epoch as a cycle, a sinusoidal wave, or a spiral, setting the bounds of each period immanently: the stable epochs are bounded by crises and crises by stable epochs. This allows him to describe each epoch as a structure, a form, whose precise content, the temporal processes, can only be determined, and may therefore only be defined, in relation to the epoch as a whole. We cannot, therefore, begin at the temporal beginning, since at the temporal beginning the epoch as a whole does not yet exist. But where to begin the synopsis of an epoch, if not with some temporal beginning?

Vygotsky says that the "initial moment" is the relationship between the child and the environment, the social situation of development. This social situation of development is not to be found in a physical or mental feature of the child like the brain or the mind, nor is it located in a material or situational fixture of the environment like the school building or the home. Rather, we must seek it out in the analysis of connections that embrace and include both. The relationship is a general one; that is, it is a feature of every epoch, because it is the ultimate source of all development; that is why Vygotsky's "general genetic law" had development proceeding from categories in the environment to categories in the child, in contrast to other genetic laws current in his time, many of which simply boiled down to "bigger is better" (Выготский, 1931, p. 357). The relationship between the child and the environment is also an abstract one, not in the sense of being unreal or nonmaterial or even nonconcrete but rather in the sense of including many different real, material and concrete phenomena in a single relationship. Above all, this general and abstract relationship is a dynamic one; in this, the social situation of development is something like the relationship between the text you are now reading and the context you construe as you are reading it. Although both general and abstract, the relationship is realized in a way that is particular, unique, and specific to each moment.

Within this general, abstract relationship between the environment and the child in which both the child and the environment must always be present, we find different manifestations of the lines of development. Like the relationship itself, none of these lines is ever wholly innate or wholly environmental, but when we unravel the social situation of development into separate lines of development we can still see that some of them run closer to the child's inner life while others have more to do with experience in the world. If we lay the strands of development horizontally across the axis that runs from the child to the environment, we can discern some of the lines from Chapter Seven of *Thinking and Speech* (see Kellogg, 2020): feeling (developing affectively colored sensations and perceptions), thinking (grasping logical links), saying (speech), and doing (play in preschool, schoolwork).

During the periods of crisis, the balancing point of this axis from child to environment seems to shift towards the child pole; hence we find manifestations of the lines of development such as purely instinctive life in the subcortical area of the newborn brain, "autonomous speech" at one, the "seven stars" of misbehavior at three, acting out at seven, and dissociation at thirteen. All of these suggest a more active role for the child, and all of them suggest a crisis. This critical situation cannot last, as it deprives the child of one of the most important means of development, namely, interaction with the ideal forms found in the environment. So, at the end of the crisis, the central line of development becomes peripheral, and—at least in normal development—the transitional neoformation that issues out of it only persists in a subordinated, and more easily mastered, form. Traces of these now-subordinate forms can be discerned in stable neoformations: the shared consciousness between infant and caregiver that Vygotsky calls the *Ur-wir*, or "grand-we," the emotionally colored perception of the toddler, the imaginative play of the preschooler, the complex thinking of the schoolchild, and finally the true concepts of the adolescent. But isn't there a contradiction here? "Neoformations" are new formations, and the central line of development is defined as that which leads to the central new formation of each epoch. How is it possible that an old line of development—one that was peripheral in a previous epoch—culminates in something new and unprecedented in this epoch?

Vygotsky's answer, which will frustrate many, is that these intertwined strands are, in turn переплетены (literally "interwoven" into a single tissue) with the intertwined strands of others in the social situation of development. These other strands provide the "ideal" or "complete" form. Of course, this is metaphor, and not explanation, and the "tissue" metaphor, no matter how loaded with double meanings from anatomy and textiles, cannot explain how the woof of the child's threads are restructured to look more like those of the warp of the interpersonal and social environment. The metaphor can, however, solve our contradiction. It is, after all, the interwoven fabric and not the physiological and neurological tissue of which it is made that is cultural and historical in origin, so it is the pattern as a whole, viewed synoptically, and not this or that line of development that is the new formation. That means that with each new epoch, the design must be picked apart and the old materials reknitted in a new way into a new form. In the transitional epoch—the period which we call adolescence which bridges childhood proper and adulthood—the whole dependency between the child-no-longer and the cultural-historical environment-to-be must be decisively changed, so that children may grow up to be more than mere replicas of their parents, and young people can in turn leave their own mark on the social fabric.

The critical, reader—the kind of reader Vygotsky himself was—will not be entirely disarmed by this tissue analogy; the critical reader can see that its double meaning, in the textile industry on the one hand and in the human body on the other, is not only a strength but also a weakness. On the one hand, it correctly predicts that new patterns will appear both externally as "clothing" (new patterns of behavior) and internally as "organ tissue" (new patterns of feeling and thinking). On the other, it incorrectly suggests that the latter is somehow prior to the former, it cannot explain how the outer layer becomes the inner one, and it utterly ignores speech, which is both clothing and skin, both a behavior and a means of thinking. Let us consider, then, another analogy: the analogy that parents often resort to in a crisis when their children appear to them as if mentally deranged.

Mutatis Mutandis: Crises in Ontogenesis and Pathogenesis

In Chapter Two, Vygotsky is skeptical of parallels between any process that looks like development but is not development. In Chapter Six of *Thinking and Speech*, he reminds us that any heuristic or pedagogical analogy has limits, and the limits may tell us even more about the matter under study than the analogy itself. Yes, there are obvious analogies between the crises and pathologies of development. We pointed these out in "Leaving the Stage" in Volume 1, and we speculated that much of what we call mental illness might be better understood as some nonstandard form of developmental crisis. We even posited three important restrictions which we described in general terms: we said that developmental crises, unlike pathological ones, are restricted to children, that they end in greater vitality rather than in debility or in death, and that they are age specific. Here, with Vygotsky presenting particular crises in particular chapters, we can elaborate those analogies in some detail—and here we can note the limitation of the analogy in each case. In each particular case, we will argue, the most important limit of the analogy is precisely the most defining moment of the crisis: it is always the fact of temporal limitation which sets the ontogenetic crisis apart from the pathogenetic one.

Birth is a crisis. This was a simple fact of life and death in the USSR—it has been estimated that infant mortality was at one point so high that a male child born in the Ukraine in 1933 had an average life expectancy of around 7 years, the same as that of an already 85-year-old man (Vallin et al., 2012). But Vygotsky does not simply mean that, as his colleague Blonsky once put it, there is no other time until the actual end of life that the child is so close to death. What Vygotsky really means by "crisis" is that, first of all, the social situation of development is one in which internal rather than environmental factors appear to be in control. Secondly, and as a consequence, the crisis of birth means that the lines of development are chiefly the innate ones: growth, rather than learning, is the order of the day. And thirdly, the neoformations which emerge at the end of these lines of development are transitional rather than permanent: the "independent, instinctive mental life focused in the lower brain" passes its main functions to the cortex as the cortex becomes operational during infancy. For women undergoing post-partum depression, and even for babies undergoing the "normal" transition from what Ferenczi called the life of an endoparasite to that of an exoparasite, the analogy between ontogenesis and pathogenesis is hardly an analogy at all. But for this very reason, we can see that the analogy between crises and pathogeneses may come to be of more limited heuristic value for mothers coming to terms with motherhood and for children lucky enough to survive the crisis of birth. The key difference between a crisis that is life-giving and one that is death-dealing lies in the temporal limitation of the former and the terminal quality of the latter.

With the crisis at one there is an implicit—and, at the very end of the chapter, quite explicit—analogy with aphasia; Chapter Seven can usefully be read as an elaboration of this analogy. Vygotsky points out, for example, that other critical symptoms such as Kretschmer's "hypobulia" (weak will, i.e., lack of self-control) can be explained by the 1-year-old's frustration at being unable to participate in discourse. But Vygotsky's main elaboration of the aphasia analogy lies within the central neoformation itself. This central neoformation is given, by Eliasberg, the unfortunate name of "autonomous speech," and Vygotsky respects, somewhat reluctantly, Eliasberg's nomenclature. We may more accurately and usefully refer to it here as "proto-speech": it is not, after all, socially, culturally, or even psychologically autonomous in any way, although it is also not the direct product of environmental pressure. But it is most definitely a harbinger of speech proper, albeit an unstable and unarticulated one. First, Vygotsky describes differences in making the sounds of speech: the critical phonological neoformation is a nonstandard articulation that resembles a speech impediment. Second, he describes differences in meaning-making: the critical semantic neoformation of the crisis at one resembles what in Vygotsky's time was called Wernicke's aphasia, where the sufferer babbles fluently but without any clear grasp of word meaning. Third, Vygotsky describes differences in communicative practices—what we call "pragmatics" today; the critical pragmatic neoformation is an inability to contradict the senses or depart from the context which resembles the pathology noted by Cassirer in Parkinson's patients (Выготский, 1931, p. 436). Fourth, he describes differences in grammatical organization of the clause: the critical grammatical neoformation has a certain resemblance to what was called, in Vygotsky's time, Broca's aphasia. But Vygotsky himself points out that in this case much of his data comes in turn from a single anomalous course of development—that of Carl Stumpf's son, in whom the crisis at one persisted until well after the child's third birthday (see Chapter Seven). On the one hand, it is the persistence of the crisis which makes the different organization of word meanings visible, but on the other it is precisely this persistence which makes it atypical of a crisis.

With the crisis at three, analogies with pathology become even more tempting, but even more unmanageable. Parents, as Vygotsky remarks, are often shocked by the sudden changes in the toddler's behavior: negativism, stubbornness, protest-rebellion, defiance, jealousy-despotism, and above all a curious willfulness. But the child's logic is not, as Lawrence Kohlberg stated in his famous studies on moral reasoning in small children, that "good is what I want and like" (1981). On the contrary, Vygotsky points out, the child often wants outcomes that they do not like. Nor is it simply, as Carol Gilligan (Gilligan, 1982; Gilligan & Attanucci, 1988) argued in her response to Kohlberg, that the child's goal is only the love of self and the will to survive. Vygotsky points out that the critical neoformation here is precisely a differentiation between affect and will: sometimes the child wants to have their own way simply because it is their own way, and refuses the ways of others simply because they are those of others. This only becomes a way of surviving and a kind of self-love in the subsequent stable period, with the discovery of true role play. Just as he borrowed "autonomous speech" from Eliasberg, Vygotsky borrows "hypobulia" from Kretschmer as an analogy for the crisis at three; but just as he criticized Eliasberg's terminology, he is unhappy with Kretschmer's term, which implies that free will is already present but somehow enfeebled. For Vygotsky, it is now possible for the first time for the child to oppose affects to volitions. But this is not itself free will: indeed, he refers to it as the antipode of free will since it negates instead of enables the child's active mastery of behavior. In *Pedology of the Adolescent*, Vygotsky mentions the similarity remarked by Blonsky and by others between the crisis at three and cyclothymia, that is, bipolar or manic-depressive personality disorder (Выготский, 1931, p. 154); likewise, they mention the similarity of the crisis at thirteen and schizophrenia. But *Pedology of the Adolescent* is wary of parallels with pathology on three grounds. First, they reproduce Freudian notions of "normal pathology": for Vygotsky, all development, including critical development, is to be characterized by its permanent positive contribution and not by its temporary negative impact on the child's behavior. Second, and as a direct result of the positive contribution, each crisis has an absolutely specific—and unique—inner neoformation, even if some external symptoms may be shared with pathological phenomena. And thirdly, most importantly, development by the very definition Vygotsky gives to it must always involve an increase and not a decrease in the child's potential for higher forms of action: imagination, creativity, consent, and, ultimately, free choice.

But if we cannot understand developmental crises by simple analogies with pathological crises, perhaps we can understand them better by comparison with other developmental crises. In Chapter Nine, Vygotsky is scathing about Kretschmer, who, because he ignored speech and saw all development as a matter of developing will power, could not seem to distinguish between the crisis at one and the crisis at three. Yet in Chapter Ten, Vygotsky himself deals in such comparisons. Of course, the notion of the "terrible twos/teens" and "threenagerdom" is part of our folk concepts of parenting, and Vygotsky shows, in his extensive and in places recursive discussion of what Russian parents call the "seven stars" of negativism in Chapters Nine and Ten, that he is not at all averse to using such folk concepts as "factual material." But this factual material must be refined—that is why, in discussing the crisis at three, Vygotsky is continually focusing on fairly unusual situations where the child must choose between affect and will: the child who does not want to keep playing outside but refuses the order to come in, the child who likes going to the zoo but will not because his mother asks him to, and the child who wants to accompany Vygotsky to a conference but will not because she is being invited by Vygotsky. The crisis at seven, Vygotsky argues, is both similar and different: similar in that some intermediate layer, some prying lever, is inserted between the social situation of development and the child's personality, but different in the very nature of that splitting wedge. For the child at three, the problem is making sense of sensations by definitively dividing affect from active response for the first time. For the child at seven, who has been dividing affect from active response throughout preschool play by subordinating his behavior to roles and then to rules, the problem is very different: making sense out of sensations that have already been internalized as *perezhivanie*—what Edelman (1989) calls the "remembered present," that is, the feeling of what happens taken together with the thoughts about what it all means to the person it is happening to. These internalized *perezhivanie* at first take on a peculiar autism-like appearance: not so much acting, as acting out and acting up with the self as the sole audience. But not only is this acting out volitional, for unlike the 3-year-old the 7-year-old has a robust and even highly mannered will, it is intellectualized: it is not merely a source of falsehoods but of artistic fictions. Vygotsky contrasts this situation with children who are ridiculed but cannot, because of some organic impairment, generalize that ridicule into an inferiority complex. Just as we found with the comparisons between ontogenesis and pathogenesis, we can indeed use one unitary crisis to understand another—that is the whole point of analysis into units such as word meanings, developmental epochs, and *perezhivanie*—but only if we keep the old Latin motto mutatis mutandis firmly in front of our eyes, and we remember that "all things kept the same" never really happens in development. The blunt instruments of comparison must always give way to sharper weapons of contrast.

So the reader shouldn't be too surprised when Vygotsky, in Chapter Fourteen, comes back to the pathogenesis analogy in describing the crisis at thirteen. In *Pedology of the Adolescent*, Vygotsky had treated the transitional age between school age and adulthood in a relatively undifferentiated fashion, although he certainly recognized a negative phase at the outset of the period (Выготский, 1931). Here, 2 years later, he develops this negative phase into a whole critical epoch, with its own critical lines of development and critical neoformations. In *Pedology of the Adolescent*, Vygotsky had developed the theory that adolescence is a human invention dating from the non-coincidence of anatomical, sexual, and sociocultural maturation brought about sociogenetically, that it has no parallel in animals or early humans, who must start new families almost as soon as they are sexually mature, and even that adolescence is experienced very differently by different social classes, because some must leave school and go to work long before anatomical maturation is complete (Выготский, 1929; 1931). Here, 2 years later, he rejects the leading role of anatomical and even sexual maturation and argues that neither can really explain why it is in adolescence and not before that children form realistic interests and true concepts. Vygotsky seeks a "grain of truth" in the finding that schizophrenia often takes hold in adolescence and that a good deal of behavior in the crisis at thirteen involves dissociation, splitting off, and turning away from social life as a whole. On the one hand, this "splitting away" reminds him of the insertion of a mediating "wedge" at three (dividing affect and will) and the insertion of a similar divider at seven (dividing the inner person and the outer persona). On the other, it seems a crucial step in the "splitting and merging" of generalized representations and preconceptual abstractions into the concepts and interests that go into selecting a profession, a partner, and an adult persona. By refining the analogy between ontogenetic crises and those of pathogenesis, by applying the method of analysis into units to the crises as unitary wholes which can be contrasted as well as compared, we can reconcile the view Vygotsky expresses in this lecture with his earlier views on adolescence which stressed the central role of sex and the separateness of "three peaks" of anatomical, sexual, and sociocultural maturation. With sexuality, the child for the first time develops a burning interest and even a distinct concept which is not based on perception, or on any firsthand experience. Interestingly, however, Vygotsky does refer to the adolescent's fantasies about sex as a particular form of *perezhivanie*. The firsthand experience that accompanies this form of fantasy—sex without a partner, which Vygotsky refers to rather quaintly as "onanism"—can be seen as a kind of transitional neoformation, that is, a bound form which persists, but only as a subordinate part of some higher stable formation (given, at any rate, some friendly collaboration).

Two conclusions follow. The first is that higher psychological functions are not, in the end, private matters. Functions like love and speech are still obviously interpersonal in their most developed forms, but even those functions which appear completely internal, such as logical memory and thinking, retain the stamp of their cultural-historical origins and remain interpersonal-social in their immediate and future orientation: they do not end with internalization but instead enable still higher forms of interpersonal, social, and even cultural-historical accomplishments. A function which is purely and solely for internal use is really more like a pathology than a higher psychological function. The second conclusion to follow from this critical analysis of the analogy with pathogenesis is that the "next" or "proximal" epoch of development for any stable period—infancy, early childhood, school age, and even adolescence itself—is always a crisis, and vice-versa—the next or proximal developmental epoch of the crisis is a period of stable accomplishments. This alone would explain Vygotsky's striking final conclusion, at the very end of *Foundations of Pedology*, that it is not growth which enables development but rather development which enables further growth. These conclusions, in turn, bring us to the final concept in the synopsis of concepts we laid out in "Setting the Stage" in the first volume, namely, the zone of proximal development (ZPD).

Hamsa: A Simple Schematic for the Epochs of Development and the Zones that Link Them

In "Leaving the Stage," at the end of the first volume, we laid out a number of outstanding problems with the way in which the ZPD has been interpreted by educational researchers without a pedological understanding of the problem of age: overgenerality, overestimation of the role of assistance, and overvaluation of the child's inner potential (see also Chaiklin, 2003; Veresov, 2017). But we also laid out a number of outstanding problems with the way it was introduced by Vygotsky in his writings outside the pedological texts: a lack of appropriate tasks for diagnosing the ZPD, the offhand way in which Vygotsky refers to means of providing assistance, and the circularity that must occur when we use the same tasks to define developmental years and to diagnose them. We promised that the present volume would include all of the most important pedological references to the zone, as well as a simple schematic that makes it possible to resolve the last three questions, and through them the first three as well.

In many cultures, including the Hindu, the Islamic, and the Hebraic culture to which Vygotsky himself belonged, there is a simple schematic of the human hand, sometimes depicted with a watchful eye in the center of the palm, used as a talisman to attach blessings and ward off evil spirits, either during pregnancy or after childbirth. In the Jewish tradition, this talisman is known as the "hamsa," after the Hebrew word for "five." We can lay out the five stable epochs as fingers and the gaps between the fingers and the edges of the hands in a "hamsa" form, as shown in Fig. 1.

Some of this, particularly towards the bottom, is speculative: as the reader will see in the lectures, although we have clear statements of the manifestations of the lines of development and the neoformations in early chapters (e.g., birth, infancy, the crisis at one), much of the material in later chapters must be inferred. We have adopted the prefix "proto-" to indicate the unstable, transitional, and ultimately transient quality of the critical neoformations, and we have placed the speech forms of all neoformations in bold, to indicate that they are elaborated in Halliday rather than in the present work. But this speculative quality has certain advantages as well as disadvantages; in particular, it allows us to extrapolate a comment Vygotsky makes at the end of Chapter Seven, where he makes the case for speech as the site in which central neoformations after the crisis at one may be best observed. We may, therefore speculate that this might be the place to look for Vygotsky's most celebrated but elusive construct, the zone of proximal development.

The child's speech, recorded in spontaneous everyday use, might provide a variety of appropriate tasks for diagnosing the ZPD. During the crisis at one, for example, we can measure the child's wording along the lines Vygotsky has indicated for

AGE PERIOD	MANIFESTATIONS→NEOFORMATIONS (FEELING, SPEAKING, DOING)
0: nursing, unconditional responses, sleep→undifferentiated innate mental life	
Infancy	smiling, conditional responses, tool use→the "Ur Wir" of shared feeling and doing
1: proto-walking/talking→meaning without wording, **proto-wording**, gesture	
Toddlerhood	perceiving, talking, walking→systemic/semantic consciousness, **wording**, quasi-play
3: "seven stars", negation, tantrums→hypobulia, **proto-dialogue**, wants vs. wishes	
Preschool	role play, games, teacher-led learning→**narrative, dialogue**, rule-governed daily routines
7: cynicism, clowning, mannerism→proto-self-love, **proto-discourse**, fictions vs. falsehoods	
School	meaning-making *perezhivanie*, complexes→intellectualized thinking/**speech**/action
13: dissociation in thinking, speech, and action→"fateful days", **proto-concepts**, proto-interests	
Adolescence	concepts, interests, work→love, **learning speech varieties**, labor
17: school-leaving, coming of age, test-taking→proto-partnering, proto-persona, proto-profession	

Fig. 1 A simple schematic of Vygotsky's five stable periods and six crises for the back of the (left) hand as manifest in conversation (talk). Note that the neoformations in **bold** concerning the growth of child conversation do not come from Vygotsky but from Halliday (2004, pp. 139, 329–369). The manifestations of the lines of development and neoformations for preschool are inferred from Vygotsky 1955/2016 and Выготский, 1936, Vygotski, 1995; all other material can be found in the relevant chapters of the present volume

us (sounding, meaning, communication, and grammatical organization) and it can be evaluated using genetic sections, by comparison with previous versions in infancy on the one hand, and by comparison with adult speech in the child's environment on the other (see, e.g., Kellogg & Ripp, 2020). Alongside these speech tasks, we find appropriate means for providing assistance: on the one hand, as Vygotsky points out in these very pages, the speech of the child is never the creation of the child alone, and on the other, as Vygotsky argues against Piaget, it is precisely in the child's uptake of assistance that we can best observe the specificity of the child's lines of development and their neoformations, and using the system network below this assistance can be made as delicate as we wish. Finally, the tautology of reducing the zone of proximal development to the banal observation that the child is able to learn whatever it is that the child learns next can be eliminated. Speech development is not circular, since at every point it offers the child not one but many possible paths, some of which are simple and others complex, some of which are well-worn, and others tempting but virtually untrodden.

Take, for example, toddlerhood, that is, the period of early childhood from roughly 1–3 years of age. According to these lectures, the child's next epoch is the crisis at three, and the pedological task is then to measure the distance to that milestone using the child's speech. We know that the crisis at three is a crisis of negativity, argumentativeness, and all the "seven stars" Vygotsky enumerates in Chapters Nine and Ten. We know that in English these "seven stars" are typically realized through the system of Mood: "No, I won't", "Won't you?" "I would if I could but I can't so I shan't." Halliday and Matthiessen represent the system of Mood as a system network, as shown in Fig. 2.

With polarity and potential negation, the child is faced with what Halliday calls a "magic gateway," a system which is part of every ordinary clause but which can confer extraordinary powers for regulating behavior; the child has every motive and opportunity to seize it. But, navigating the network, the child can always take either easier "right turns" or more difficult "left turns." For example, at the first gateway, the child may turn right and make a "minor clause" without a verb Predicator (e.g., "No!"), but this will not take the child very far in the face of adult insistence. Or the child could turn left and add a Predicator verb (e.g., "No" plus "go bedtime" "eat

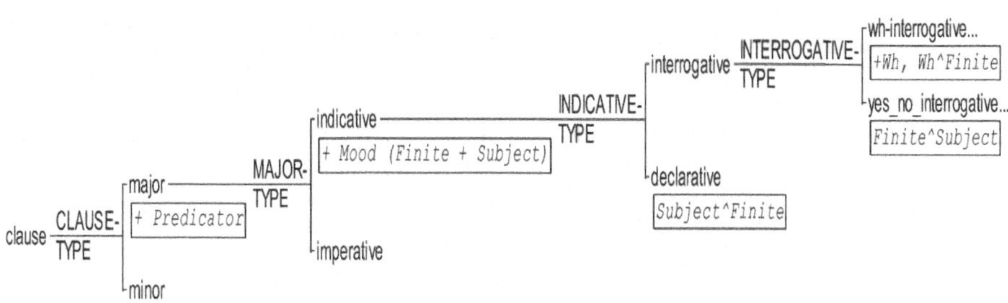

Fig. 2 Halliday's system network for the development of Mood (Halliday & Matthiessen, 2014: 24)

dat," "stay home") and create an imperative—or, with a Mood, the child can create an indicative ("I won't go to bed," "I won't eat this," "You must stay home").

Beyond each gateway, there are new gateways—indicatives may be declaratives ("I won't go to bed") or interrogatives ("Must I go to bed?") and interrogatives can be yes/no questions ("May I…?", "Might I…?") or wh-questions where word order is sometimes even trickier (e.g., the difference between "Who will make me?", which appears to have the Subject-Verb-Object order of a normal declarative and "When can I stay up all night?" which appears to have the Finite-Subject order of a yes/no interrogative!). With this "magic gateway," or rather a network of magic gateways, the child confronts an endless series of tasks that are appropriate to diagnosing the distance to the next great epoch of development, copious and appropriate assistance in the immediate social situation of development, and above all an intricate thread to follow: the child is not only ready to learn whatever the child learns next; the child is also free to fall back on a simpler option (the "right turns" in the system network) or to attempt the magic gateway to a newer, higher, and more potent magic still.

Knots to Untangle

Let us, from the very outset, acknowledge some difficulties—some real conflicts and apparent contradictions in what follows. The lectures in the first volume *Foundations of Pedology* were uniformly short, orderly, and complete. Although *The Problem of Age* is supposed to be a companion course, following on from the foundations, Vygotsky's lectures and notes are often long, frequently discursive, and yet almost always still incomplete in some excruciatingly crucial way. Fortunately, Chapter Two (which is about a third the length of Chapter Four and half the length of Chapter Eight) unexpectedly ends with a tidy, complete list of the six crises and five stable periods, and even a brief account of how the crises can be divided into phases and the stable periods into stages. This turns out to be the key to dividing childhood into periods and therefore to the rest of the book.

Unfortunately, Vygotsky's numbering is not very consistent—sometimes periods overlap by a year (the crisis at three and preschool), and sometimes they seem to abut each other (the crisis at seven and the period of school age); the whole of the promised preschool chapter appears to have gone missing. And then there is the unexplained addition of the crisis at seventeen right in the middle of the supposedly stable period of adolescence! As a consequence of these conflicts and contradictions, all the previous attempts to compile a table of the social situation of development, the central and peripheral lines of development, and the neoformations for all the crises and periods have, by their authors' own admissions, been thwarted by Vygotsky's omissions and apparent inconsistencies (e.g., Blunden, 2008; Léopoldoff-Martin, 2014, as well as the table we presented in Fig. 1).

We dare not pretend that what we have attempted to do here is any more definitive; that is, as Vygotsky said of his own *Thinking and Speech*, the prerogative of the reader to decide (Выготский, 1934: 3). All we can say is that in compiling the text itself we have tried to be inclusive even to the point of being redundant: the reader will find, in addition to the follow-on course to *Foundations of Pedology* based on the Russian edition put together by G.S. Korotaeva (2001/2019), material on the problem of age taken from the Russian language edition of Vygotsky's *Collected Works* (1984/1998); we shall specify in the chapter outlines the provenance of the chapter material. Some readers will find this material exhaustive to the point of being exhausting. For example, the reader will find that Chapter Eleven does not simply pick up where Chapter Ten left off, but instead repeats word for word in places. But it also directly contradicts the previous chapter in at least one place. Since these are transcripts of spoken lectures, we have no way of knowing which of these tangled knots were left by Vygotsky and which were those of the stenographer. So we have confined our own interpretations of the text to this essay at the outset and a pendant piece at the end. We will also give a summary outline at the beginning of each chapter, and provide notes to the text where these can contextualize and illuminate it. In-text notes in brackets are marked "(…–GSK)" when they are those of G.S. Korotaeva, and marked "(…–Trans.)" when they are our own. Elsewhere, we have resisted the temptation to interpret, to paraphrase, or cut at the risk of leaving knots untangled. So we have tried, a little like Penelope at the loom, to remain faithful to the overall pattern without ever quite finishing the task.

To say that *The Problem of Age* was a work in progress when Vygotsky died is to reduce the ideas of this book to the number of paper pages that make it up; it seems as obvious and as obviously wrong as reducing the problem of age to the number of revolutions around the sun since a child was born. What is more to the point is to say that *The Problem of Age* is still a work in progress today. This compilation and this translation—and even your perusal and reconstrual of it—are merely two or three more strands in an intricately tangled, tantalizingly definite, and yet ultimately indefinable web.

Nikolai Veresov
Monash University, Frankston, VIC, Australia

David Kellogg
Sangmyung University, Seoul, Korea (Republic of)

References

Borsboom, D., Kieit, R. A., Cervone, D., & Hood, S. B. (2009). The two disciplines of scientific psychology, or: The disunity of psychology as a working hypothesis. In J. Valsiner, Peter C. M. Molenaar, M. C. D. P. Lyra, & N. Chaudhary (Eds.), *Dynamic process methodology in the social and developmental sciences* (pp. 67–97). Springer.

Blunden, A. (2008). *Vygotsky's unfinished theory of child development.* Manuscript. Laboratory of Comparative Human Cognition.

Edelman, G. M. (1989). *The remembered present: A biological theory of consciousness.* Basic Books.

Gilligan, C. (1982). *In a different voice*. Harvard University Press.
Gilligan, C., & Attanucci, J. (1988). *Two moral orientations*. In C. Gilligan, J. V. Ward, J. M. Taylor, & B. Bardige (Eds.), *Mapping the moral domain: A contribution of women's thinking to psychological theory and education* (pp. 73–86). Harvard University Press.
Halliday, M. A. K. (2004). *The language of early childhood*. Continuum.
Halliday, M. A. K., & Matthiessen, C. M. I. M. (2014). *Halliday's introduction to functional grammar*. Routledge.
Kellogg, D. (2020). Commentary: On the originality of Vygotsky's "Thought and Word". *Mind, Culture, and Activity, 27*(1), 86–91. https://doi.org/10.1080/10749039.2020.1711775
Kellogg, D., & Ripp, A. (2020). The question of questions: Hasan's critiques, Vygotsky's crises, and the child's first interrogatives. *Early Years, 40*(3), 351–369. https://doi.org/10.1080/09575146.2018.1431874
Kohlberg, L. (1981). *The philosophy of moral development*. Harper and Row.
Léopoldoff-Martin, I. (2014). *La science du développement de l'enfant: La conception singulière de Vygotskij*. Université de Genève. These No. 561.
Spinoza, B. (1677/1994). *A Spinoza reader: The Ethics and other works* (Edwin M. Curley, Trans.). Princeton.
Toulmin, S. (1978, September 28). The mozart of psychology. *The New York Review of Books*.
Vallin, J., Meslé, F., Adamets, S., & Pyrozhkov, S. (2012). The crisis of the 1930s. In F. Meslé, & J. Vallin (Eds.), *Mortality and causes of death in 20th-century Ukraine* (pp. 13–38). Demographic Research Monographs. https://doi.org/10.1007/978-94-007-2433-4_2
Valsiner, J. (Ed.) (2005). *Heinz Werner and developmental science*. Springer.
Veresov N. N. (2017). ZBR and ZPD: Is there a difference? *Cultural-historical psychology, 13*(1), 23—36. https://doi.org/10.17759/chp.2017130102
Vygotski, L. S. (1935/1995). Apprentissage et développement a l'âge préscolaire (F. Sève. trad.). *Société française, 52*(2), 36–45.
Vygotsky, L. S. (1966/2016). Play and its role in the mental development of the child (N. Veresov & M. Barrs, Trans.). *International Research in Early Childhood Education 7*(2), 3–25.
Vygotsky, L. S. (2019). *Vygotsky's pedological works. Volume 1. Foundations of pedology* (D. Kellogg & N. Veresov, Ed. and Trans.). Springer.
Выготский, Л.С. (1929). *Педология подростка. Задание 1–8*. Москва: Издание бюро заочного обучения при педфаке 2 МГУ.
Выготский, Л.С. (1931). *Педология подростка. Задание 9–16*. Москва и Ленинград: Государственное учебно-педагогическое издательство.
Выготский, Л.С. (1934). *Мышление и речь*. Москва: Соцэкгиз.
Выготский, Л.С. (1935). Умственное развитие ребенка в процессе обучения. Москва-Ленинград. Государственное учебно-педагогическое издательство.
Выготский Л.С. (2001). *Лекции по педологии*. Ижевск: Удмуртский университет.

Contents

The original version of the book front matter and back matter was revised. The affiliation of David Kellogg has been updated in front matter and the names of the authors have been listed in the back matter of the book.

Chapter 1
The Concept of Pedological Age

Outline of Chapter 1: The Concept of Pedological Age

Vygotsky does not usually begin with a statement of his concept. The concept emerges from the research. But for Vygotsky, that research always includes a critical, dialectical, review of the history of the concept, where each iteration of the concept is good for some purposes but not for others and each researcher solves some of the problems of previous researchers but uncovers new problems for subsequent researchers to tackle.

Here, for example, Vygotsky notes that Alfred Binet saw the importance of history in development, but considered it a simple function of time. Arnold Gesell thought development looked more log-linear, slowing with growth, and that mental development followed physical development like a shadow. In contrast, William Louis Stern thought that periods of child development could be marked off by the appearance of new personality formations like space perception, time perception, color, length, depth, and understanding speech vs. producing it spontaneously, but he had no way of explaining the order of these neoformations. Vygotsky concludes the chapter with the suggestion that child development be periodized according to immanent cycles of self-movement and self-contradiction, of which the neoformations are the culmination.

Let us elaborate these four moments into a four-paragraph outline.

I. **Development takes time, but it is not a simple, linear function of time**. Vygotsky says that even body weight, plotted on a graph, appears as a wave and not as a line. Moreover, the wavelength changes; the period required for, say, a 10% increase in body weight is not constant. So child development is characterized by periodicity—that is, by rhythms, cycles, or (since there is a clear pro-

This chapter is taken from material edited and published by G.S. Korotaeva in 2001.

L. S. Vygotsky, *L.S. Vygotsky's Pedological Works. Volume 2.*, Perspectives in Cultural-Historical Research 10, https://doi.org/10.1007/978-981-16-1907-6_1

gression toward complexity) an ascending spiral. Like the historical developments of which it is a distant echo (e.g., the invention of literacy, compulsory schooling, apprenticeships), child development does not repeat itself, but it does rhyme.

II. **Researchers believe that mental development follows growth**. Gesell believes that personality development follows physical development, slowing with growing. Richter, Froebel, and even Tolstoy apparently believed that the most important lessons in life are learnt even before kindergarten. Vygotsky agrees that a year of physical development is never equal to any other year in physical development, and acknowledges that we might well expect that what is true for physical development might be equally true for psychological development.

III. **Some mental functions seem to precede others.** Vygotsky says that development taken as a whole is a highly complex process, and its changes are qualitative as well as quantitative. Moreover, the means of development itself develops: some functions that were not central lines of development become central and others that were central lines of development become peripheral. Even in general-anatomical growth, the basic organs and basic functions mature quickly and rapidly, while higher organs and higher functions which require this base as a prerequisite necessarily develop later and more slowly. Stern, for example, claims that the child learns to deal with space before time, with length before depth, and with understanding speech before producing it. Vygotsky deduces from this the possibility of defining a pedological age period:

    1. By what comes before and after, and not by calendar time
    2. By its place in the overall process of development
    3. By general laws of development expressed in a way completely specific to child development

IV. **Some of the most important neoformations seem to be cultural and historical rather than merely biological and chronological in their origins and process.** There is one sense in which child development really is like cultural-historical, and even biological and geological, development. Each stage can be characterized by the neoformations that arise in it (e.g., capitalism is characterized by the neoformation of capital, the age of reptiles is characterized by the neoformation of dinosaurs, and the Cambrian period by the neoformation of animal life in the fossil record). Each age period, then, is the history of the rise of a particular neoformation. Although the age periods of child development do not coincide with the calendar years of child age (any more than the periods of cultural history correspond to years BC or AD, or even dynasties of kings), there are nevertheless certain regularities in child development (just as there are in the progress of cultures).

Taken in bulk, these can be correlated to calendar years, so long as we understand the correlation as a statistical probability and not as a simple dependency. When we do this, we discover that age periods vary from one culture to another, which implies that at least some psychic neoformations realize cultural-historical developments (such as speech, literacy, and concept formation), rather than just biological developments (such as the myelinization of the brain cortex, teething, or sexual maturation). On the one hand, this suggests a certain objective similarity in the products of development, at least within a culture. So, for example, almost all children in a culture will learn speech and almost all children in a literate culture will become literate. On the other hand, this suggests uneven processes, because complexes of biological and cultural-historical development cannot possibly occur in lockstep. So, determining the real pedological age of each child and the next zone of development is both a group (objective) and an individual (subjective) task for the teacher.

Chapter 1: The Concept of Pedological Age

Child development is a historical process, one which flows through time. The link between the developmental level of the child and his age, that is, the number of years that have flowed by since the day of his birth, as well as the link between the process of development and the change in the age of the child, is so striking that in a certain sense we may consider child development a function of time. The events that make up the course of the child's development emerge and unfold one after another over time with a robust definiteness and regularity. At a definite age, walking and speech develop; at another, the child attains the capacity for school learning. This link between the changes in the age of the child and the changes in his personality in the course of development is what is meant when it is said that development is not merely accomplished in time but is a function of time (Gesell[1]) or that the properties of childhood are a function of age (Blonsky[2]).

But development is not a simple function of time, nor are the changes proportional to the quantity of years lived by the child. Changes in the course of development do not correspond directly to chronological time. Development is a complex

[1] Arnold Gesell (1880–1961), a medical doctor, Yale professor, and author of many books and even a film on child rearing: *The Mental Growth of the Preschool Child* in 1925. His *Atlas of Infant Behavior* (chronicling typical milestones for certain ages) was published the year Vygotsky died. He pioneered the study of children using one-way mirrors. He was something of a fanatic about developmental schedules, and his work later led to a good deal of diagnostic testing of children for mental underdevelopment. For Gesell, the specifically human functions are derived by the maturation of hereditary potential through adaptation under certain environmental conditions. This is still the mainstream theory of development today, and it is very close to the group of theories that Vygotsky calls biogenetic. According to this theory, child development is a function of biological development, because heredity is the main determinant of a child's potential.

[2] Pavel Blonsky (1884–1941), a Soviet psychologist who began as a specialist in Plato and philosophical idealism but became a founder of "objective, Marxist" psychology (i.e., behaviorism) after the Russian Revolution. He was a colleague and friend of Vygotsky for many years, although they disagreed on important points, for example, on behaviorism. Blonsky, like Gesell, was essentially biogenetic. Blonsky was later severely criticized for his links to pedology and for his advocacy of psychological testing.

function of time, linked to it by extremely peculiar, and highly volatile, complex dependencies. The course of child development in no way resembles the uniform and gradual movement of an hour hand over a clock face, measuring out time's flow. The process of development is exemplified by the **rhythmic** or **cyclical** nature of the course it takes. It does not present itself in a single straight line but is more like a wave form, with ups and downs that may be taken as a symbol of the especial rhythmic character of this process, never flowing at the same tempo, but constantly revealing periods of quickening and slowing, intensifying and slackening, progressive and regressive movement.

Because of this, the temporal organization of child development turns out to be extremely complex; one year of development is never equal in its value to that of another year. The value of each year of development is defined by the place it occupies in the wave-like curve that we discussed previously. The growth in weight and height in the child from birth to 18 years was studied by Minot.[3] He inserted into the diagram 30 vertical lines forming the length of period necessary for each 10% increase in weight. "These lines," said Minot, "were in the beginning very closely adjacent to each other. One ten percent increment was followed by another in quick temporal succession. But eventually the interval indicated by the distance between the vertical lines lengthened. Our diagram is a simple graphic expression of the fact that the older we get, the greater the amount of time required for the growth of a given proportional magnitude will be." (See Fig. 1.1., taken from Minot and Gesell–Trans.).

Gesell did the same in relation to the mental development of the child and established that in this area of development there exists a similar pattern.[4] Comparing the monthly increase in intellectual development in the first year of life with the

---

[3] Note the reference, in the previous sentence, to what Vygotsky discussed previously—clear evidence that this part is part of a course and not the unfinished manuscript of a book. But the next chapter includes clear evidence that it is part of a book and not simply a course.

Charles Sedgwick Minot (1852–1914), an American anatomist and embryologist who later founded the American Society for Psychical Research. He wrote a 1914 treatise on "The Problem of Age, Growth and Death," from which Gesell took the Minot quotation that Vygotsky cites.

This is p. 18 of Gesell's 1925 book. Minot's graph is Fig. 1.1, and Gesell's graph, supposedly based on a wide variety of mental tests, is given below it.

[4] In the beginning of the paragraph, Vygotsky, citing Gesell, writes of умственного развития ребенка, that is, "the mental development of the child," and in Russian this implies higher functions, such as thinking, so it is tempting to translate this as "the intellectual development of the child." But the English word "mental" is in fact what Gesell uses in the table based on Minot's work. At the end, when Vygotsky quotes Gesell directly, he uses the termмесяц интеллектуального возраста and we have chosen to render this literally as "a month of intellectual age." First of all, this represents the fact that two different words are used in the original Russian, and the second is a loan word meaning "intellectual." Secondly, "the mental development of the child" represents the fact that Gesell is trying to establish a kind of parallelism between physical growth and intellectual growth, but that he recognizes that at least at the outset they are not really differentiated: the intellectual life of the child is largely sensation, feeling, and affect rather than logical thinking. Thirdly, "a month of intellectual age" reflects a somewhat different concept, the precursor of what we call today the IQ.

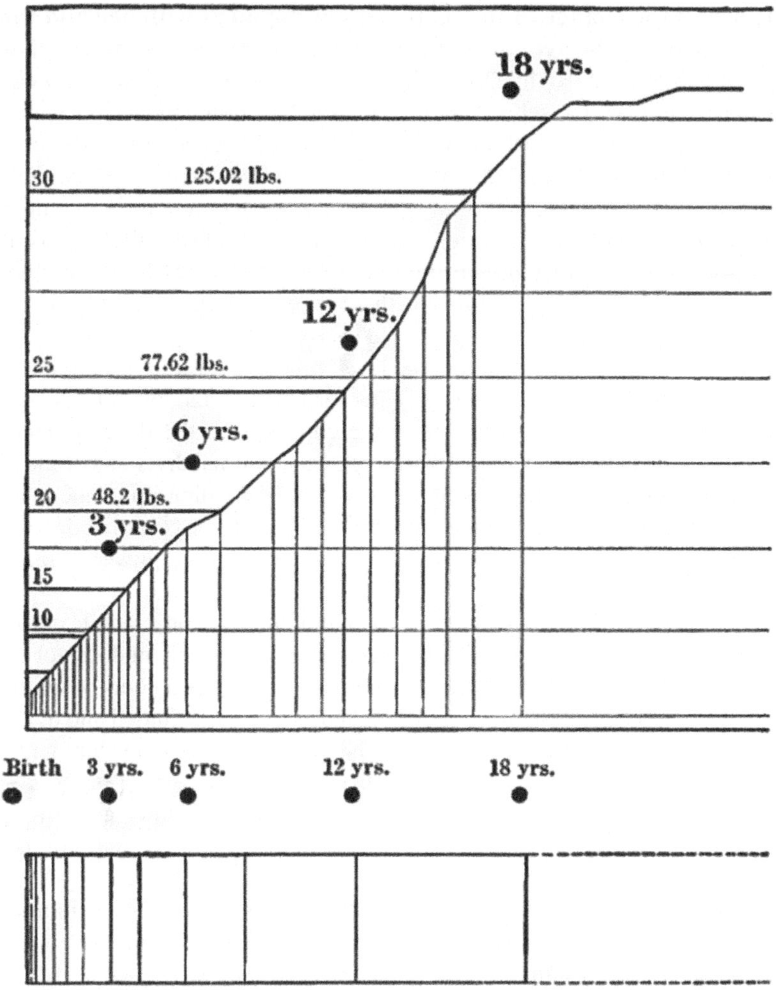

Fig. 1.1 Graphs of physical and mental growth

following annual increments up to 13 years, he found, as shown in the diagram, that one series in growth follows another. This leads us to the conclusion that during the first 12 years of life, any year starting from the second has the same value, in terms of its importance of development, as a corresponding **month** in the first year of life. He says, "In a chronological sense, a month is always equal to a month. But a month of intellectual age is derived from an organic cycle, and this month will vary enormously depending on its position in the developmental cycle, and moreover, the cycle is more like a spiral than a circle or an ellipse. In early childhood, one month may turn out to have been a decisive problem in the further development of the individual."

The fact of **the change of the tempo of development with age and the relative slowdown of the tempo of development with increasing** age has been known for a long time. Richter[5] said that from the infant to the speaking child is a bigger step than from the schoolchild to Newton. The same idea was expressed by Froebel.[6] Tolstoy, the world-famous writer, in his old age spoke of the first years of his life: "Was it not then that I acquired all of which I now live, and gained so much so quickly that in the rest of my life I have not acquired even one hundredth as much? From the child of five to myself, only a step. From the newborn to the child of five, a terrible distance. From the embryo to the newborn, an abyss, and from non-existence to the embryo there is no longer an abyss, but the incomprehensible."

In this way, in the economy of mental development, the value of a month is determined by its position in the cycle of life (Gesell). This same law relates equally to any other aspect of the development of the child and to the development of the personality of the child as a whole. Therefore, these internal divisions of the process of child development do not coincide with a simple dividing up of the process of child development by chronological age, by the quantity of years lived. It is incorrect to suppose that a year of development in any one age is equivalent to a year of development in another age.

In this way, the division into age periods cannot be based on a simple chronological principle. Why is it that the flow of the process of development does not coincide with the flow of time? We have already said, in analyzing problems of child development, that child development cannot be taken as a process guided and determined by some sort of outside forces or factors. The process of child development is subordinate to its own, internal regularities. It flows as a dialectical process of self-movement. These inner regularities determine the circumstance that child development is not equivalent in the tempo, the rhythm, or the sequence of its autonomous movement to the astronomical flow of time.

We have already mentioned above that the process of child development is a process which is complex to the highest degree, which in its progressive movement changes in the intensity and rhythm of its course, which takes place in a disproportionate manner in relation to the various partial processes that make it up.

Some aspects of the personality of the child are developed disproportionately and unevenly. In development, there occurs a constant disruption of proportional progress, in the sense that at any one time a function which thus far has

[5] Jean-Paul Richter (1847–1937) was an art historian who wrote Baedeker tourist guides. Today, he is chiefly remembered as the editor of Da Vinci's notebooks.

[6] Fredrich Froebel (1782–1852) was the founder of early childhood education who emphasized play with solid objects. He founded kindergartens based on this principle which still operate today. This section of text is very close to Vygotsky's preface to K. Gracheva's 1932 book, "The education and instruction of severely retarded children," published in 1932. Ekaterina Konstaninova Gracheva, also known as Auntie Katie, was a popular writer who supported teaching the severely brain damaged, something Vygotsky also vigorously championed.

played in only one isolated area, which may have played only a very minor role, can advance to the first plane. It then remains for the course of a certain time the central point of the child's activity and for a short time there occurs a remarkably rapid **development.** When this tumultuous time is past, a new area of function and interest will perform in the same way. Previously discovered areas, it stands to reason, continue to still develop. However, they do not do so in such a stormy way, but rather slowly within the overall framework of the personality—and, in this way, the child in each phase of his development presents a qualitatively new picture (Stern).

One of the basic laws of child development establishes the earlier maturation of basic organs and functions which alone permit the development of the higher types of activity in the child. "Therefore, the child learns to manage space much earlier than time. Knowledge of spatial forms is acquired before the knowledge of color. An eye for linear distance is acquired earlier than the ability to evaluate the distance of objects from us. Obligatory qualities are mastered earlier than nuances. Articulation in large joints develops earlier than articulation in delicate ones. Understanding speech develops earlier than voluntary speech. All of this is subject to the same law" (Stern).

Like all processes of development, child development is made up of consecutive transitions from one stage to another stage, and, naturally, is divided into a number of separate, relatively closed, but interrelated cycles, epochs, or stages of development. The term "stage" denotes a certain step in a given regular cycle (Gesell). We come, in this way, to the concept of **pedological age** which, as we have seen, must be strictly distinguished from **age in the chronological** or **passport sense**. We might define **pedological age** as **the epoch, cycle, or stage of development**

1. Which is linked **with preceding and with subsequent epochs of development**
2. The value of which is determined by its place in the overall developmental cycle
3. In which **the general laws of development** are at all times **given a unique qualitative expression**

In this sense, the age stages of development may be compared with historical stages or epochs of human development, with evolutionary epochs in the development of organic life, or with geological epochs in the history of development of the earth. In the transition from one age stage to another, there arise new formations that did not exist in preceding periods, restructuring and modifying the course of development itself. In this way, the development of the child consists of nothing but a continuous transition from one age stage to another, linked to the change and construction of the personality of the child. In this sense, it is said that development is subordinate to age, and that in all types of development, even the most unusual, the change of observed phenomena is subject to regularities of age (Gesell). Therefore, to study child development means to study the child's transition from one age stage to another and the changes in his personality within each age period which occur under certain sociohistorical conditions. This is, for the pedology of age, the task at hand.

As we have seen, the division of the whole process of child development into separate age stages according to internal laws of development can never coincide with the partitioning of the child's passport age, with the chronologically defined periods of his life. If we divide the whole period of child development covering the first 10 years of his life into different intervals of 1, 2, 3, years, etc., we will never get real periods of child development. However, there are, determined by internal laws, regularities linking the age level of development and the chronological age of the child. This means that each pedological age happens within chronologically defined boundaries, that is, it covers certain definite years in the life of the child. These chronological boundaries of each age vary depending on the historical epoch, on the social conditions of development, and on the individual characteristics of the child. They, in this way, present in themselves historically conditional values, changing in the course of the historical development of humanity.

We said earlier that the passport, or the chronological age of the child, may not coincide with his pedological age. Children who are the same in their passport age, that is, who have lived the same quantity of years, are at different stages in their age development. Kremiton[7] investigated nearly 4000 boys from a physiological point of view and found that at age 14, only a third of them had already gone through sexual maturation, while another third was just within the period of sexual maturation, and another third was still not in this period. The same thing was found by these researchers in thousands of children with respect to teething. Burt[8] made an analogous study of psychological development in 32,000 children from age three to fifteen. His studies showed that among children with a chronological age of 11, only 30.6% of the cases of 11-year-olds were at their pedological age. Twenty-nine percent were 10 years old, 10.9% at 9 years, 17.7% at 12 years, and 6.2% at 13 years. This discrepancy between the passport and the real age is due in each case to individual variations in development of the child. Children who are born on one and the same day, in one and the same hour, and at one and the same minute, will not develop in strict accordance with each other, like watch mechanisms timed to the minute, due to the fact that highly complex organismic processes of development can determine this or that deviation in individual cases, depending on the totality of the conditions of development. For this reason, some will be ahead of others in their development, while others will be left behind. Therefore, the first and basic task of practical pedology must be the determination of **the real pedological age** of the

[7] "Kremiton" appears to refer to I.U. Kremiton, a Ukrainian physiologist.

[8] Sir Cyril Burt was a British psychologist who specialized in intelligence testing and believed in the inheritance of intelligence. Much of the data he used to demonstrate this, however, appears to have been invented.

child, that is, the stage actually reached in the course of his development, and the degree of deviation between the real age and the passport age of the child determined by the quantity of years that have elapsed from his birth. Knowing the real pedological development of the child aids the pedagogue in implementing an **individual** approach to the pupil.

Reference

Gesell, A. (1925). *The mental growth of the preschool child.* Macmillan.

Chapter 2
The Problem of Age Periodization in Child Development

Outline of Chapter 2: The Problem of Age Periodization in Child Development

In Vygotsky's *Collected Works*, this is not a single chapter but only the first section of a multisection chapter called "The Problem of Age," which, with some substantial alterations, covers roughly the next three chapters of this book. Because some of these alterations (e.g., omission of the word "pedology," cutting references to testing, and the insertion of the word "dynamics" in the title of Chap. 4) seem counterproductive and/or politically motivated, and because we concur with D.B. Elkonin that this material was designed to be part of a book, we will instead follow the divisions given by G. Korotaeva, the editor of *Lectures on Pedology* (2001), and present this material as a separate chapter.

It is a lengthy one. So as we did in the last outline, we first present it as a short summary of four "moments" and then expand each of these points into a more detailed outline. First, Vygotsky argues that there are many ways of periodizing childhood, but they are all metaphoric, metonymic, or eclectic. A truly scientific periodization of childhood will require new concepts, and Vygotsky proposes the rather algebraic terms "neoformation" and "social situation of development" to describe novel structures in the child's patterns of feeling, thinking, and doing on the one hand and the relationship between the child and the environment on the other.

Vygotsky then argues that crises must be considered valid periods of childhood in their own right, because they have age-specific neoformations (even though these

---

This chapter is translated from material edited and published by G.S. Korotaeva in 2001.

This chapter was published in abridged form in the Russian journal *Вопросы Психологии* (Выготский, 1972), and there is a version in the Russian (1984: 244–268) and English (1998: 187–196) *Collected Works* which was apparently taken from the Vygotsky family archive. But the most complete version seems to be the chapter found in the *Lectures on Pedology* (Выготский, 2001). This version is the basis of our translation. Where there are differences between this version and the one to be found in the *Collected Works*, we will explain the differences in footnotes.

L. S. Vygotsky, *L.S. Vygotsky's Pedological Works. Volume 2.*, Perspectives in Cultural-Historical Research 10, https://doi.org/10.1007/978-981-16-1907-6_2

are not long-lasting) and because they involve unique forms of relation with the environment: any historical crisis is part of history and not outside it. Finally, Vygotsky proposes his own scheme of periodization, one that can historicize each crisis and reveal the uniqueness of each period of childhood.

I. **There are many ways of periodizing childhood, but they are all metaphoric, metonymic, or eclectic**. Vygotsky divides extant theories of periodization into three groups, but there are really four groups, if we include the Binet theory of simply counting off calendar time from birth, as parents and children themselves do when giving their age in years and months. This folk theory he dismisses at the very outset of the chapter.

The first group of theories that Vygotsky considers worth criticizing, however, is a group we may call "metaphoric" theories, because they compare child development to some external process which is not child development but which is more or less comparable to it. For example, there are theories that compare child development to phylogenesis or sociogenesis, as well as some more adequate theories that compare child development to the periods we find in public schooling. Vygotsky points out that all of these theories are not simply wrong theoretically (because they impose external time categories on what is essentially a process of internalization) but they put the cart before the horse in practice (because instead of giving teachers guidelines for when certain forms of cultural behavior should be taught, they instead trail along behind the guidelines that parents and teachers already have).

The second group of theories that Vygotsky considers worth criticizing is a group we may call "metonym" or "synecdoche" theories, because they compare child development to some internal process which is a small part of child development itself. For example, there are theories that compare child development to teething, to puberty, or to psychosocial activity. Vygotsky points out three flaws common to all of them:

1. They are subjective: they choose a single criterion, often simply because it is suggestive to the researcher of some more important function (e.g., eating or sexuality or labor), or because it is conveniently observed (dentition or puberty or social behavior), or because it is objectively measurable. Although the criterion itself may be objective, the selection of the criterion is not, because it is up to the observer. Vygotsky notes that observers tend to choose criteria that are easy to observe rather than intrinsically important; a little like looking for a lost object where the light is better rather than where it is likely to be found.
2. They are monosymptomatic: they try to explain the whole complex process by a single line of development. But, as Vygotsky points out, the meaning of any line of development will change a lot as the child matures: eating is a central line of development for a newborn but not for an adolescent, while friendships with the opposite sex may be highly charted for the adolescent in a way they are not for the toddler.
3. They are empiricist, and they dwell on the visible symptoms of development rather than the hidden causes.

The third group of theories that Vygotsky considers worth criticizing are a group of theories we may call "eclectic," because they try to get around the weakness of the metaphorical theories by choosing a basket of different factors both internal and external, and to get around the weakness of the metonymic theories by switching from one symptom to another as the child grows. In this way, teething can be held to be important for the infant but not the adolescent and other-sex friendships can be important for the adolescent but not the infant. Vygotsky applauds the idea that each period has its own central line of development and its own age-specific symptom. But he notes that some scholars (e.g., Gesell and Kroh) who have taken this road tend to find that development slows down after the first year, while other scholars (e.g., Bühler) still depend on empirically measurable symptoms and as a result find it hard to explain moments when development apparently comes to a halt.

II. **Scientifically periodizing childhood requires new concepts: the neoformation and the social situation of development.** Vygotsky now sums up the lessons learned from his critical review of theories of periodization. First, he notes that all theories must conceptualize development as:

    1. Nondevelopment: the metaphysical realization of some whole potential given in its entirety, once and for all, at birth (e.g., Nazi theories of racial psychology, Pearson's biological determinism, Stern's theory of personalism, and, in our own time, Steven Pinker's "language instinct").
    2. Self-development: the partial realization of some partial potential given at birth which in turn creates new, greater psychological potential. Vygotsky further subdivides this idea of self-development into:

        (a) An idealistic conception, where the self-development of the personality is simply self-realization by a vitalistic "life force," just as nondevelopment was the unfolding of a whole potential given "once and for all."
        (b) A materialist conception, where the self-development of the personality is a complex step-by-step unification of the social and the psychological, just as the person is a complex unity of the biological and the psychological.

If we take up the last point of view, we can trace development through changes which define the child's consciousness in relation to the environment, changes which Vygotsky calls "neoformations." Neoformations include new forms of consciousness, and for Vygotsky consciousness explains and is realized by a structure of behavior. Human consciousness is both formed by the environment and forms it in turn. Vygotsky proposes that each period may be identified with a specific neoformation, just as periods of geological development may be identified with rock formations, periods of biological development are identified with the rise of new forms of life, and periods of historical development with the emergence of new relations of production. Vygotsky also proposes that periods of child development may be subdivided into stable and critical periods, just as geological change, biological evolution, and social progress may be either gradual or catastrophic.

III. **A historical crisis is part of history and not outside it.** Vygotsky considers the studies on crises. First, he notices that, unlike stable periods of development, the crisis has not been analyzed, explained, or theorized at all; in theory, many scholars deny that it is a necessary part of development, although they admit it as an empirical fact. Vygotsky then describes a number of features which explain the undertheorized status of the crisis in the literature on development.

1. The crisis often has a clear peak, but the beginning and the end of the crisis are much more difficult to determine.
2. The crisis is often associated with children who are difficult to teach and therefore difficult to study. What is more, some children do not seem to experience a crisis at all, and these children receive a good deal of attention, to the point where they are sometimes considered the rule and not the exception. Vygotsky, however, argues that variations in the environment mask the crises, that crises are intrinsically necessary to development, and that if we make a diachronic, longitudinal comparison rather than a synchronic, cross-sectional one, as Vygotsky suggested in Chapter 2 of *Foundations of Pedology*, we will see immediately that every child in a critical period manifests a certain difficulty in teaching in comparison with his or her noncritical periods.
3. The crisis is characterized by negative content, which masks its positive content; that is, adults tend to focus on what the child is not doing during the crisis rather than what is new and revolutionary (e.g., we notice, when the child produces autonomous speech, that he or she is failing to communicate rather than that he or she is differentiating vowels and consonants, or mastering intonational patterns).

Despite these features, Vygotsky says, there is considerable empirical material that supports the existence of the crisis. However, the material has emerged haphazardly, in no particular order, for the reasons given above: first the crisis at 7–8, followed by the crisis at 3, then the crisis at 13, and finally the crisis at 1. Vygotsky then proposes that birth should also be considered critical (although the peak of birth is clear, the earliest moment of viability for premature infants and the latest safe moment for delivery are still not entirely clear to doctors). With each crisis, Vygotsky shows that although when they were first noted, the negative content alone was remarked, each crisis discloses a certain positive content as well: expanded autonomous discovery at 7, new elements of affect and volition in the personality at 3, a change from visual to conceptual modes of understanding at 13, proto-walking and proto-talking at 1, and physiological independence at birth. As Vygotsky remarks, it is precisely the emergence of these complex forms of consciousness and their competition with the older forms which appear to be responsible for the crisis.

IV. **Pedology needs a scheme of periodization that can historicize each crisis and reveal its uniqueness.** In the final part of this chapter, Vygotsky outlines his proposal. He now has three ways of periodizing childhood that are intrinsic to development, multivariate, and noneclectic, each with both an empirical and a theoretical component. First, he has the various neoformations that emerge in the consciousness with all of their symptoms in behavior, speech, and thinking. Second, he has the relatively stable periods in which these nontransitional, lasting neoformations seem to be formed. Third, he has the crises, in which the child's relationship to the environment, transformed by the emergence of a transitional, nonlasting neoformation, is decisively altered. The stable periods have a two-part (early stage-late stage) structure and crises can be subdivided into prepeak, peak, and postpeak phases. He next lays out four key points in which his own scheme differs from preceding ones.

1. The theorization of crises and their inclusion as an indispensable, immanent, inherent part of development
2. The exclusion of embryology, on the grounds that it is not a moment in the development of a social personality
3. The exclusion of the young adult, on the grounds that young adults are better understood socially as immature adult personalities rather than as senile children
4. The inclusion of puberty as a stable period, on the grounds that the neoformations of puberty (e.g., friendships with the opposite sex) are not transitional but permanent in nature.

This yields the six crises and five stable periods.

Chapter 2: The Problem of Age Periodization in Child Development

We have seen that the development of the child as a historical process is divided into distinct epochs or stages, which we call ages. Self-evidently, a first and basic task in the study of child development is the establishment of the basic periods, or stages, that constitute the process as a whole, or, in other words, the periodization of child development. We have also seen that the basis for the periodization of child development cannot be taken from a simple chronological division of the whole period of childhood into equal intervals of time such as a month, a year, a 3-year span, etc. The periodization of child development must be built upon the basis of the internal division of the process of development according to its own laws. Just as some historical epochs differ not on the basis of randomly selected chronological periods of time—by century or by millennium—but on the basis of the internal laws of their own historical development, so too child development requires, self-evidently, a periodization of the same kind.

Although all of this is firmly established and absolutely indubitable truth, there have remained, nevertheless, some vestiges in pedology of a prescientific stage of development in the shape of attempts to periodize child development in purely **chronological** terms. So, for example, we can still find attempts to study the growth and the organic development of the child as equal chronological periods of time (in years), regardless of ages. This includes one of the oldest but still commonest methods of researching and measuring the mental development of the child, the method of Binet[1] that separates intellectual age into chronological units of time, assuming that one year of development is always equal to another and forgetting that the meaning of each year of development is determined by its position in the cycle of life.

However, pedology has long since rejected attempts of this sort and put forward the problem of periodizing the development of the child on the basis of the study of the course of development itself. There exist a number of attempts to divide the course of child development into separate periods on a variety of traits. All of the proposed scientific schemata of periodization for child development may be divided into three groups if we attend to their theoretical bases.

The **first** group are the attempts at the periodization of childhood not by the path of dividing the course of development of the child itself but on the basis of the step-by-step formation of other processes which are in one way or another closely linked with child development.

By way of example, we might name the efforts to periodize child development on the basis of biogenetic principles. As we have already said in one of the preceding chapters, biogenetic theory claims that there exists a strict parallelism between human development and child development, and that ontogenesis in a short and concise way repeats phylogenesis. It is completely obvious that from the point of view of this theory, it is natural that all childhood may be divided into periods formed not on the basis of the development of the child himself but on the basis of the periods of human history. In this way, the basis of periodizing childhood is taken from phylogenetic development. Into this group of periodizations of childhood fall the works of Hutchison,[2] Stern,[3] and other authors.

---

[1]Alfred Binet (1857–1911), a psychologist who invented the IQ tests we still use today (for Vygotsky's critique of these tests, see 1997, Chapter 14). Binet trained as a lawyer, and then self-educated as a psychologist, working as a researcher in the neurological clinic in Paris, the Salpêtrière (where Charcot and Freud were also working). Under Charcot he became interested in hypnotism. His early work on intelligence involved studying how expert chess players could play chess blindfolded, and his approach to testing mental development was actually quite similar—a good example of the purely descriptive, empirical approach that Vygotsky criticizes in this chapter. These tests were later used by Goddard and others in the USA (e.g., Stanford University) to measure a "general" factor supposedly common to all intelligence. Such was never Binet's intention—his tests were only designed to help teachers place children in mainstream or in remedial classes (see Binet et Simon, 1905, 1907 in the references).

[2]Sir Robert Hutchison (1871–1960) was a Scottish pediatrician, author of many books on diet, childhood diseases, and child development. As a medical student, Vygotsky would have studied *Hutchison's Clinical Methods*.

[3]William Louis Stern (1871–1938), a German child psychologist and founder of the philosophy of personalism, which included the idea that rocks, plants, animals, and humans are born with free will. Vygotsky was a harsh critic of Stern, whom he apparently met in Germany. He created the notation we use for child development today (e.g., "1;6" for one year and six months) and also the notation for IQ (Stern 1924). Along with his wife Clara he carried out one of the first well-documented longitudinal studies of his own children's speech development, and also wrote a mono-

However, not all classifications of this group are untenable in equal measure. In this group are placed, for example, attempts to periodize childhood according to the steps of the enculturation and education of the child, according to the divisions of the public education system adopted in a given country. So in this scheme, the periodization of childhood is done not on the basis of inner divisions of the course of development itself, but on the basis of the stages of enculturation and education.

In this lies the error of these schemata. But since the process of child development is tightly linked to the process of enculturation of the child and the division of enculturation into separate stages is based on vast practical experience fitting the stages of education to the corresponding ages of the child, it is natural that such a division of childhood according to pedagogical principles often brings us extremely close to a true and practical division of childhood into different periods. To this day, pedological periodization has retained the pedagogical designation of individual ages, which are named according to the stages of public education which take place for the child at given ages: preschool age, primary school age, etc.

Nevertheless, such a periodization turns out to be not only false in its theoretical basis, but practically unfeasible, since it does not take into account the differences in grades of public education in different countries, or even within the same country for different classes of the population (under the capitalist regime). To speak of the essence, the levels of enculturation and of education ought to be constructed according to the age periodization of childhood. Pedology, by taking these levels as the basis for the division of childhood into separate ages, not only does not give the clear answer required by pedagogy to a number of pressing pedagogic questions—when teaching-and-learning may commence, what the stages of teaching-and-learning ought to be, etc.—but instead bases itself on current pedagogical practices.

In the **second** group of classifications into ages should be placed the most numerous attempts, which are made on the basis of the selection of one trait or another in some segment of child development as the conditional criterion for dividing development into separate periods. The attempts by Langstein[4] and by Blonsky to divide childhood into epochs on the basis of dentition, that is, the emergence of and replacement of teeth, may serve as a typical example of this group of theories. The trait on the basis of which we distinguish one epoch of childhood from another ought to be (1) very indicative for judging the general development of the child, (2) easily accessible to observation, and (3) objective. All these requirements are satisfied by dentition. Dentition processes are intimately related to substantial

graph on lying and fiction in children (see Stern and Stern, 1909/1999 in the references for this chapter).

[4] Leopold Langstein (1876–1933) was a German pediatrician who founded nonprofit hospitals and nursing homes throughout Germany and wrote extensively on child development. His death a year after Hitler came to power was suspected to be a suicide by his widow (they were Jews). The *Collected Works* version does not mention Langstein, although Blonsky is mentioned in the previous paragraph. Blonsky had a rather physicalist, vulgar-Marxist, view of the periodization problem, and believed that teeth were comparable to means of production. For example, the eating of meat produced a surplus of energy which accounted for crises in childhood.

constitutional features of the growing organism, especially to calcification and to the activity of the glands of internal secretion.

At the same time, they are easily accessible to observation and can be stated in indisputable terms. Dentition is a clear symptom of aging. On the basis of dentition, postnatal childhood is divided into three epochs: toothless childhood, the childhood of milk teeth, and the childhood of permanent teeth. Toothless childhood lasts until the eruption of milk teeth (from 0;0 to 2;0 or 2;6). The childhood of milk teeth lasts until the beginning of tooth change (approximately six and a half years). Finally, the period of permanent teeth ends with the appearance of the third rear rooted teeth (wisdom teeth). In the emergence of milk teeth, in its turn, we may distinguish three stages: absolutely toothless childhood (the first half a year), the stage of teething (the second half a year), and the stage of eruption of the first molar and the canines (the third year of postnatal life) (Blonsky).

Another, analogous, attempt to divide childhood into ages on the basis of one or another facet or trait of development is the schema of Stratz,[5] which selects sexual development in place of dentition as the central qualitative criterion. Stratz distinguishes between the following periods: the age of nursing (0–1 years), (2) the age of neutral or asexual childhood (2–7 years), (3) bisexual childhood (8–15 years), and (4) the period of sexual maturation (15–20 years).

Other schemata constructed by the same principle select **psychological criteria** instead of dentition or sexual development as the criteria for separating childhood into ages. Such a periodization is that of Stern, who differentiates between early childhood, during which the child displays play activity (up to 6 years), (2) the period of conscious entrainment and the division of work and play, and (3) the period of juvenile maturation (14–18 years) and the development of an autonomous personality and plans for subsequent life.[6]

We will not dwell upon a critique of all of these theories but will instead attempt to distinguish the principle common to all of them—according to which they are all constructed—and to determine the limits of its soundness. Already the presence of a plurality of these types of schemata, each not excluding another, many partly

---

[5] Carl Heinrich Stratz (1858–1924) was born in Odessa in Russia but became a German citizen. He trained as a doctor and traveled through Africa, China, and Indonesia treating women and children (he was a gynecologist). He had an extensive collection of photographs of both children and women from many different countries and races. This became the basis for a theory of ideal proportion that is still used in art schools today (unfortunately, a good deal of his collection is now banned as child pornography, although it was seen as entirely innocent in Stratz's own time). Vygotsky uses Stratz's notion of alternating periods of "stretching out" and "rounding out" in child growth in Chapter 5 of *Pedology of the Adolescent*, and this is undoubtedly one of the forerunners of Vygotsky's own theory of crises and stable periods.

[6] Vygotsky earlier placed Stern in the first group of schemata, the ones based on a single external process such as the biogenetic principle; now he places Stern in the second group, the ones based on single trait of growth. Which is it? It is both: the "single trait" selected by Stern is the growth of the personality, but Stern's idea of the growth of personality is seen as biogenetic. We noted earlier that Stern was a philosopher. As a philosopher, Stern was a German idealist: he conceived of the world as a hierarchy of personalities (adult, child, animal, plant, and crystal). The key trait of an adult personality is judgment—that is, the ability to value and be valued.

overlapping with and partly diverging from another, indicates the flaw in all of them: the criterion chosen to divide childhood selected in all of these schemata is chosen quite conventionally and arbitrarily. In essence, it follows from the requirements which are formulated by Blonsky in the passage above—the criterion should be indicative, easily accessible to observation, and objective. But it is obvious that many such traits exist, and therefore the choice of one of them cannot help but be conventional and arbitrary.

In this way, the schemata of this group are purely subjective schemata. Although they put forward an objective trait as the qualitative criterion for dividing into ages, this trait they choose on a subjective basis, depending on which processes seize more of our attention and believing that the milestones which differentiate ages can be placed at various points on the path of life. In this lies the gravest fault of this group of theories.

Child development, like any objective process that exists in reality independent of our consciousness, can be scientifically understood only if we can establish the stage periods of its course as **they exist objectively in the course of its own development**, no matter where we turn our attention to. Age is an **objective category** and not a conditional, arbitrarily chosen, fictitious value. Therefore, the landmarks which delimit age cannot be placed at just any point on the life path of the child, but only at those at which objectively one age ends and another begins.

The second drawback of all of these theories is that they put forward a single criterion consisting of one trait (a monosymptomaticity) in order to outline all ages, forgetting that in the course of development the value, meaning, indicativity, symptomaticity, and importance of the trait changes. A trait, highly indicative and essential for judging the general course of development of the child in one epoch, loses this indicative value in the following, thanks to the basic fact that in the course of development those aspects that were at one stage standing in the first plane or in the center were relegated in the next stage to the second plane. It is not difficult to see, for example, that the trait of sexual maturation is essential and indicative at the age of puberty but does not have this meaning in a preceding stage—in infancy and in early childhood.

It is equally clear that if the teething on the border of infancy and early childhood can be taken as indicative sign for the overall development of the child, the replacement of teeth at about seven years and the emergence of wisdom teeth cannot, in their significance for overall development, be likened to the **first appearance** of the teeth. These theories do not account for the reorganization of processes themselves in their forward progress, by virtue of which the importance and signification of any trait changes continuously from age to age, so as to rule out the possibility of dividing childhood into separate epochs using a single criterion for all ages, if this criterion covers one or another trait or one or another isolated aspect of child development.

In addition, when we attempt to keep any trait, such as the trait of **dentition,** as the unitary quality for distinguishing all the ages, we inevitably come up against the fact that from the point of view of the same processes (chemical and endocrine) some traits may be more important and more indicative, but then projected upon later ages it is necessary for them to undertake a secondary, subordinate role, junior in meaning in relation to this basic criterion, grossly violating the objective hierarchy of traits and delineation of ages. So, sexual maturation, having no doubt infinitely more symptomatic significance from the point of view of the restructuring of the endocrine system, only delineates one **stage** of permanent teeth in the child from another when the replacement of teeth is taken as a boundary separating one age **epoch** from another.

Theories that bring up a broader trait which is more directly linked to the development of the child's personality, such as, for example, the degree of development of the central nervous system (Zalkind[7]) or the delineation of the basic types of activity proper to each age group (Stern) and so on, are richer and closer to the facts, but they fall behind the former theories in the sense of that selected trait's practical applicability, which is often difficult to the highest degree. But the gravest drawback consists in their monosymptomaticity, which is still inherent in them just as it was in the former theories. In place of a narrow trait they bring in a different, broader one. In place of one aspect of development they bring up another. But despite that, they do not go beyond making one single trait of development represent every single aspect of it.

Finally, the third and most important of all of the faults of these theories is the principle of establishing a study of external symptoms of child development and not the inner essence of this process. All sciences at an early stage in their development begin with a static and external approach to the description of phenomena, without analyzing the inner dynamics of the processes under study. Phenomena are systematized on the basis of a purely empirical analysis, and their study is of descriptive or phenomenological character. The scientific study of the inner links of phenomena and their causal relationship is replaced by a classification based on purely external traits. In the biological sciences, this period took place in botany and zoology before Darwin, before the establishment of the evolutionary theory. Such a period in the development of all the medical sciences took place in the period dominated by so-called symptomatic medicine. At the time, diseases were distinguished and classified purely on the basis of external symptoms, so that one group took in all patients suffering from coughs, headaches, fevers, etc. The inner essence of the pathological

[7]Aaron B. Zalkind (1888–1936), a psychiatrist and an earlier Soviet follower of Freud. Zalkind was also the founder editor of the journal *Pedology*, which Vygotsky took over in 1930. Zalkind fell out with Blonsky over the issue of periodizing childhood; Blonsky believed in a scheme that emphasized dentition, while Zalkind was interested in sex education and in group activities. Both of these criteria are essential schemes for periodizing growth and not development in the sense of differentiation. It might be argued that a scheme based on sexuality is at least potentially a scheme that takes in social development.

Zalkind was a party activist, but, as Vygotsky points out, a vulgar materialist rather than a Marxist. In the 1920s, he was criticized for mechanically transferring Freudian theories of sex development into Marxist psychology, and the criticism actually has some truth to it. So, for example, in his "twelve sexual commandments," Zalkind says that falling in love with a member of an enemy class is a sexual perversion like falling in love with a crocodile or an orangutan! He died suddenly, apparently of a heart attack, at the very meeting when the Communist Party abolished pedology. Foul play has not been ruled out.

process was unknown, and the outward signs were mistaken for the essence itself of the disease process. External forms were confused with for the essence proper of things.

In practice, the inner essence of things and their external forms of manifestation do not coincide. "All science would be superfluous if the outward appearance and the essence of things directly coincided (Marx)." Indeed, if things were in fact what they appear to us in direct experience, then simple registration of phenomena, simple empirical establishment of their connection, direct experience, and common sense would be perfectly sufficient for knowledge. Scientific research is therefore a necessary means of understanding reality where forms of manifestation and the substance of things do not directly coincide[8].

Pedology is at the present time undergoing the same transition from a purely descriptive, empirical, phenomenological analysis of the study of phenomena to disclosing their inner essence, just as the biological and medical sciences once did. In the same way that botanists of old used to systematize and classify plants according to the similarity of external traits (the form of the leaf, the color of the flower), pedology not too long ago announced that its main objective was the study of symptoms, of external traits, and of the different individual epochs, stages, and phases of child development. A symptom signifies a trait.

To say that pedology studies the symptomatic complexes that distinguish epochs, phases, and stages of child development (Blonsky) means to say that it studies the traits of child development. If the study of external features directly coincided with the study of child development itself, then pedology, as a science, would be unnecessary. In essence, there can be no science in general which studies traits of a process as such, in themselves. In the end, pedology studies child development, benefitting from the analysis of separate traits, symptoms, and their complexes, but the task of pedology consists of this: exploring what lies under these traits and what causes them, that is, the very process of child development in its inner laws.

In relation to the problem of periodization of child ages that interests us, this means that we should move away from all attempts at symptomatic classification [of age and proceed to classification[9]] based on the inner nature of the process under study.

With this, we may complete the consideration of the second group and proceed to the **third**, which is something like a stage of transition toward a truly scientific periodization of child psychology. The essential trait that distinguishes all of the

---

[8]The *Collected Works* version of this text ends this paragraph with the following sentence: "At present, psychology is moving from a purely descriptive, empirical and phenomenological study of phenomena to disclosing their essence." (Vygotsky, 1998: 189). But in the *Lectures on Pedology*, this sentence appears at the beginning of the next paragraph, and it is about "pedology" not "psychology." It is fairly easy to understand why the Soviet editors of the *Collected Works* would change the banned word "pedology" into "psychology," but it is not easy to see why, having done that, they wished to transfer it to the previous paragraph.

[9]G. Korotaeva, the editor of the *Lectures on Pedology*, adds a footnote: В стенограмме отсутствует, that is, "left out in the stenogramme."

theories in this group is an attempt to break away from symptomatic and descriptive divisions of childhood into separate epochs and to make a division based on the essential characteristics of child development. However, all of these attempts correctly set out the task rather than carry it out. They always appear to hesitate over the decision, never going through to the end with it, and show their inadequacy when they attempt to address thoroughly the problem of periodization. The fateful obstacle in the path turns out to be for them the methodological difficulties that arise from an antidialectical and dualistic conception of child development, which does not allow them to consider the process of child development as a unified process of self-development.

One example is Gesell's attempt to construct a periodization of child development from the changes in the internal rhythm and tempo, from determination of the "current amount of development." Starting from the mostly correct observation outlined above of the changes in the dynamic rhythm of development with age, Gesell proceeds to the division of childhood into separate rhythmical and dynamic **periods or waves of development**, internally united by **a consistent tempo** persisting through this period and delimited from other periods by a clear change in tempo.

Gesell presents the whole dynamics of child development as a process of continuous **slowing** of growth, so that it is joined to that group of modern pedological theories which, in his words, make early childhood the supreme authority for the understanding of the personality and its history. The most important and significant development of the child, for Gesell, is in the early years and even in the first months of his life. All subsequent development, taken as a whole, is not worth the very first act of this drama, rich in content to the utmost extent.

Where does this delusion come from? Evidently, it must arise of necessity from the evolutionary conception of child development upon which Gesell depends. If it is true that in development nothing new appears, that development does not proceed through qualitative changes but only through growth and through increase of what was given at the beginning, then there is no other conclusion to draw than this one upon which Gesell bases his conception. In fact, development is not confined to the scheme of "more or less" but is characterized in the first place by the presence of qualitatively new formations, which are subordinated to their own rhythm and which require their own specific measurements in each case. It is true that in early ages we observe the maximal tempo of development of those premises which bring about all the further development of the child. We know that the basic organs and functions mature earlier than the higher ones, but it would be incorrect to assume that all of development is limited to the further growth of these basic elementary functions constituting the prerequisite for the maturation of higher aspects of personality. If we take the higher aspects of the personality, the result would be the opposite: the rhythm and tempo of their development will be minimal in the first acts of the drama of development and maximal in its finale.

We have brought up the theory of Gesell as one instance of those halfway attempts at periodization which we have assigned to the third group, those which stop halfway in the transition from a symptomatic to an essential separation of ages. Also in this group is a scheme proposed by Kroh, which distinguishes between two main periods of child development (before and after three years of age) from the point of view of the relationship in which the development of child and his upbringing and learning-teaching are found. At three years, the child becomes amenable to teaching, and he enters his first school. The type of child development and its inner structuration depend upon this change. But while Kroh, having doubtlessly put his finger on an essential moment in child development, accepts a change in the very type of the interrelationship between the child and the surrounding milieu in the transition from age to age, he still remains entirely on the ground of evolutionism and therefore turns out to be helpless to solve the problem as a whole, just as throughout the period of child development after three years he cannot find an equivalent value for the changes in the type and internal structure of development which might serve to further periodize child age.[10]

To this group belongs the theory of Bühler,[11] which handles child development as a process which is unified and linked, but divided into phases. What is valuable in this theory is the attempt to distinguish between individual phases from the point of view of something new that occurs in a given period of development and that which cannot be reduced to a simple change from a previous level. In this way in the schema the abstract and formalistic character of the purely quantitative conception of Gesell is overcome. But this theory also divides the phases of child development empirically, mainly on the basis of the statistical evaluation of the various traits which are not present in each phase.

We have not, I think, undertaken this long journey into a critical analysis of the main theories in the periodization of childhood in vain. Our aim was to study the history of the scientific understanding of the problem in pedology, to show how it has unfolded scientifically, and to show how a correct division might be attained.

---

[10] Gesell's periodization was empiricist: it was based on measurable features of the very young child, and that is why it orients so heavily to early childhood. Kroh's periodization is, in some ways, the very opposite: it is teleological, based on the future trainability of the child. But Kroh's trainability is gradualistic and his theory of development is evolutionistic, so he cannot further differentiate the period after the key turning point at three that he has correctly identified. Both Gesell and Kroh are "half-hearted," but their hearts belong to different halves of the child's development.

[11] Karl Bühler (1879–1963) was a student of Oswald Külpe and later a teacher of Karl Popper. He was a major influence on Habermas and also, to a lesser extent, on Halliday. Bühler was a central figure in the Würzburg school of psychologists that arose in rebellion against the idea, of their teacher Wilhelm Wundt, that only lower psychological processes could be studied in a laboratory. The Würzburgers recognized that a successful psychology could not fail to study higher processes, including thinking, and they denied that these higher processes could be reduced to mental images. All this they shared with Vygotsky. However, unlike Vygotsky, the Würzburgers (including Max Wertheimer, Kurt Koffka, and Wolfgang Köhler) saw no special role for language in thinking and no qualitative distinction between verbal thinking and other kinds. Vygotsky says that Bühler's theory divides development into phases, but nevertheless is able to take the process as a unified whole. Even better, it can characterize the phases according to what is qualitatively new, and not simply according to what has quantitatively grown. So, what is missing from Bühler's theory? Vygotsky says that it is empirical—once again, it is based on observations and statistical regularities rather than directly upon comparing the phases and stages of development itself. Because of this, Bühler's theory cannot distinguish between critical and noncritical periods of development.

We can now, summarizing all that has been said, formulate the basic components of the important requirements for a scientific classification of ages.

As we have seen, it cannot be based on a chronological division of child development. Nor is it possible to construct a child development scheme by borrowing from neighboring fields, no matter how closely they may be linked to the development of the child. This classification, moreover, cannot be arbitrary, conventional, or subjective if it is to meet scientific requirements. It must abandon all attempts to secure a single criterion for distinguishing the segments of all ages. It cannot, in general, rely on any single trait. More broadly speaking, it must abandon the principle of symptoms fully and completely. Nevertheless, based on the objective internal laws of the development process itself, it cannot find the correct solution of the problem without abandoning evolutionistic and dualistic conceptions. Otherwise, it will inevitably run the risk of sharing the fate of those theories which we reviewed at the end of our analysis.

What are the basic principles for constructing this classification?

We already know where to find the principal bases of a periodization of childhood. Only the internal changes in the course of development itself, only the breaks and turns in its direction of flow, can give us a sound basis for determining the basic epochs of constructing the personality of the child which we call ages. We have already discussed in the chapter dealing with the problem of development of how all the theories of child development at present may be reduced to two conceptualizations. According to one of them—and this is the metaphysical conceptualization—development is nothing other than realization, modification, and combination of propensities. In development, nothing new emerges. Throughout its duration, there arise only growing, bifurcating, and regrouping of all of those moments that were already given at the beginning.

According to the second conceptualization, development is an unceasing process of self-propulsion, characterized in the first instance by the process of constructing a personality through the unceasing emergence and formation of what is new and did not exist in previously undertaken steps. This point of view includes in development something which is of the utmost importance for the dialectical understanding of this process. In its turn it allows the development of both an idealistic and a materialistic theory of the construction of the personality. In the first case, it finds its incarnation in theories of creative evolution directed by an autonomous, internal, *élan vital* which is committed to the self-development of personality, a will to self-establishment and self-perfection. In the second case, it leads to a materialist understanding of the dialectical process of development characterized by the unity of the physical and psychological aspects of child development, a unity of the social and the personal in the ascent of the child through each stage of his development.

Evidently, with this last point of view, there is and there can be no other criteria for identifying the concrete epochs or ages of child development, besides those **neoformations** that characterize the essence itself of each age as a new epoch or a new stage in child development. By these age **neoformations, we understand a new type of construction of the personality and its activities, the physical and social changes which occur in a given stage for the first time and which in an**

important and basic way define the consciousness of the child in relation to his environment, his interior and exterior life, and the course of his development during a given period.

Applying this criterion, pedology responds to all of the requirements that we have listed above as historically prepared by the course of development of scientific knowledge. It is not difficult to see that in this case the resolution of the problem of dividing the process of development into individual epochs is methodologically solved exactly as it is in other sciences which have as their object one or another form of development. So, each new historical epoch is determined by a new social structure which occurs in this epoch for the first time and which yields up a qualitatively distinct expression by the general laws of historical development (feudalism, capitalism, socialism). So too biology defines each epoch of evolutionary development from the point of view of an organic species that first arose in this period.

But for the scientific definition of the principles of periodization of child development this was not enough by itself. Included as well must be the dynamics of development, the dynamics of the transition from one age to another. Going by the path of purely empirical investigation, pedology established that age-related changes can take place acutely and critically, or they can also take place gradually and lytically. We shall use the terms epochs and stages for times of the child's life separated from each other by crises which are either more (epochs) or less (stages) acute. We shall likewise use the term phases for the times of the child's life that are separated from each other one from each other in a diffusive way (Blonsky). [12]

In reality, the factual study of child development and the observation of its course inevitably lead to the conclusion that development in different periods takes on different characteristics. In not a few epochs or ages, development is characterized by a slow, incrementally evolutionary, diffuse course. These ages are predominantly those of smooth, gradual, often imperceptible, and internal changes in the child's personality, brought about by way of accumulating apparently insignificant "molecular" motions. Here over a more or less extended period of time usually lasting several years, no fundamental or catastrophic shifts or alterations reconstruct the whole personality of the child. More or less significant changes in the child's

[12] The term Vygotsky uses here and in the next paragraph is литический liticheskiy ("lytic"). This term comes from the ancient Greek word λυτικός which means a purging of poisons or a laxative for constipation. It is variously used in chemistry to mean soluble or degradable and in biology to mean the breaking up of an organism (e.g., the breakup of a cell which has been attacked by a virus). It is sometimes (e.g., in Vygotsky's English *Collected Works*) translated literally as "lytic." But none of this seems to convey Vygotsky's meaning here.

Vygotsky appears to mean that in some epochs (infancy, preschool, school age, and adolescence) change is diffuse, and changes are diffused throughout the whole system of physical and psychological functions. For this reason, these changes do not appear to have a clear focal moment as they do during a crisis. So for example, infancy does not have a clear peak as the crisis of birth does. Less obviously, preschool does not have a peak like the "terrible twos" we find just before it or the sudden transition to primary school we find after preschool age. Similarly, puberty appears to have a clear critical peak at or around thirteen years of age, but adolescence itself is a more diffuse set of changes involving general-anatomical changes in weight and height, psychosexual maturation, and above all sociocultural coming of age.

personality occur in these ages only through or as a result of an extended course of a "molecular" development process. They emerge and become accessible to direct observation only as the conclusion of an extended process of latent development. "As this process takes place entirely in a hidden form, the moment of detection often produces impressions full of surprise for the observer. The child can do something which does not yet, apparently, fall within the circle of his interests; it simply occurs to him." (Stern)

In these ages, which could be called, due to the inherent character of their development, relatively steady or stable ages, development takes place in the main due to microscopic changes occurring daily in the personality of the child which accumulate to a certain point, and then, in a single leap, appear as a given age neoformation. These ages take up, if we judge purely chronologically, the major part of childhood. This is the age of maturation in the sense that it is in these ages that the child acquires the aspects and properties of his personality that bring him to maturity. If, then, within these ages development goes on as if by some underground path, it is no wonder that when we compare the child at the beginning and at the end of these clearly stable ages, the vast change that has taken place in the personality, the significant progress in its maturation, clearly stands out and even strikes the eye.

These ages and this type of child development have been studied more completely than ages characterized by a different course of child development. These latter were discovered by empirical paths, one by one, in a haphazard manner, and many have still not been shown by the majority of investigators in systems and are not included in the general periodization of child development. Many authors have even doubted the inner necessity of their existence. Many are inclined to take them as "maladies" of development, as deviations of the process from the normal path, rather than as internally necessary periods of child development. Almost none of the bourgeois investigators have realized their theoretical significance, and the attempt in our book at their systematization, at their theoretical interpretation, and at their inclusion in the general scheme of child development for this reason should be seen as perhaps the first attempt of this kind.

However, no researcher can deny the fact of the existence of these unique periods in child development and even the most nondialectically oriented authors acknowledge the necessity of allowing, at least as a hypothesis, the presence of crises in the development of the child, even in early childhood (Stern).

These ages are characterized by a purely factual aspect of the matter, the inverse of the relationship we have just described as steady or stable age. Here, in these periods, in a relatively short time of several months, years, or at most two years, there are sharply concentrated changes and alterations, shifts and breaks in the personality of the child of capital importance. The child changes the main features of his personality as a whole before our very eyes and in a very short period of time. Development takes rapid, speedy, alterations of its course that are sometimes catastrophic in character. There occurs in a short period, a radical and fundamental restructuring of the whole interior aspect of the personality of the child and the whole system of its relationship with the surrounding environment. Development in these periods resembles a revolutionary rather than evolutionary course of events, both in the tempo of changes taking place and in the significance of the events that occur. This—the age of fractures and ruptures—takes place at turning points in the history of child development. The flow of development takes the form of acute crisis.[13]

These ages, which are usually called, because of the intrinsic character of development, critical ages, in contrast to the **stable** ages, have a series of features that make the correct theoretical understanding of them extremely problematic.

The first of these features consists in this: that the borders separating the beginning and the end of the crisis from the ages that are adjacent are delineated in a manner that is vague to the highest degree. The crisis grows imperceptibly; it is difficult to define the precise moment of its beginning and its ending. It simply flows imperceptibly forth or shades into the subsequent age as it did from the preceding one. On the other hand, it is characterized by a sharp intensification of the crisis usually occurring around the middle of the age period. Such a culminating point, at which the critical course of development reaches its apogee, characterizes all critical ages without exception and sharply distinguishes them from the stable epochs of child development.

Next, the second feature of these ages consists in what is the starting point for their empirical study. A significant number of children, undergoing critical periods of development, appear to be difficult to teach. Children are apt to drop out of the system of pedagogical influence which up to now has provided the normal course of enculturation and teaching-and-learning. At the age of schooling, during critical periods, a decline in school performance is apparent, alongside a slackening of interest in school tasks and generally decreased work productivity. With all critical ages, development is often accompanied by more or less sharp conflicts with the milieu. With all critical ages, the inner life of the child is often linked with disorders and painful experiences, with internal conflicts, and with the overcoming of previously unencountered problems. As with teething, crises of child development are often accompanied by pain and not a few general disorders in the life activities of the child.

It is true that it is far from always that this happens. In different children, the critical age will unfold differently. There exists far more variation here in the unfolding of the crisis, even among children who are most similar in developmental type and in the social situation of their development, than in stable periods. In many children, there is never any clearly expressed unteachability or reduction of school achievement at this age. The large range of variation in the unfolding of these ages

[13] There is some disagreement between the Korotaeva version, which we use here, and the version in the *Collected Works*. The Korotaeva version has Это – возраста перелома и перехода, повторные пункты в истории развития ребенка ("This—the age of fractures and ruptures, repeated points in the history of child development," 2001: 172). But the *Collected Works* version is Это поворотные пункты в детском развитии ("These are turning points in child development" 1984: 249). It is quite possible, as the editors of the Soviet *Collected Works* appear to have thought, that there is a transcription error here and that the word повторные ("repeated") should actually be поворотные ("turning"). But it also seems possible that Vygotsky wants to stress the repetitive nature of crises.

in different children and the striking influence of external and internal conditions on the unfolding of the crisis itself are so significant and large that it gives rise to many authors raising the question of whether or not the general crisis of child development is purely the product of adverse external effects upon the child's condition alone and whether or not they should therefore be considered an exception rather than a rule in the history of child development (Busemann, etc.).

External conditions, it stands to reason, determine the concrete character of the appearance and unfolding of critical periods, differing in different children; they are responsible for all of the varied and multiform pictures of the various options in the critical age which we discussed above. But it is not to the presence or absence of any specific external conditions but rather to the internal logic of the process of development itself that the necessity of the critical, crucial periods of child development is due. Of this, we are convinced by the study of comparative indices.

Thus, if we move from an **absolute** standard of unteachability to a relative one, based on a comparison of the ease or difficulty of bringing up the child in the stable period before the crisis or the one after the crisis with the degree of his unteachability during the time of crisis, it is impossible not to see that each child in this age is **relatively difficult** when compared **with himself in the adjacent stable age.** In the same way, if we move from **an absolute evaluation** of school success to a relative one based on a comparison of the tempo of progress of the same child during the course of teaching and learning in different age periods, it is impossible not to see that each child in a period of crisis becomes a **relatively** poor student, that is, reduces the tempo of his progress in school learning in comparison to the tempo which characterized his progress during the stable period. The reliability of these relative indices can hardly be seriously placed in doubt: after all, we can only form a correct appraisal of the changes which come with this or that age if we compare the child at a given age with himself at another segment of his development.

Thirdly, and this is perhaps, the feature of the critical ages that is most important in relation to theory, the most obscure, the most unclear, and therefore the most difficult for the correct understanding of nature of child development during these periods, there is the negative character of the development which distinguishes these ages. All who write about these unique periods of child development have noted in the first place as their most striking and most eye-catching feature the circumstance that development in this period, in contrast to the stable ages, accomplishes more destructive than constructive work. The progressive direction of development, pushing forward the formation of the child's personality, pushing him up the ladder of development, the continuous and unbroken construction of the new which was so distinctly carried forward in all of the stable ages as the basic content of child development, now, in the period of crisis, seems to fade away and be shut off, temporarily suspended, quitting the stage, and disappearing from the sight of the observer. In place of these constructive processes of development in the first plane are processes of dying away, withering, and decay of what was formed in the preceding stage and which distinguished a child of that age. The child in these periods does not so much acquire as discard much of what was previously acquired.

These ages are not marked by the advancing of emerging new interests in the child, new aspirations, new types of activity, and new forms of inner life. The child coming into these periods is instead characterized by the contrary; he loses the interest which yesterday still provided the guiding influence for all of his activities. The very activity that not long ago still absorbed the greater part of his time and attention appears to be frozen: the forms of external relations and inner life established previously appear as if abandoned. Tolstoy referred figuratively but precisely to one of these critical periods of child development as "the desert of adolescence."

All of this is what we have in view in the first place when we speak of the negative character of the critical periods.

By this what is intended is to convey the idea that the development in these periods appears to change its affirmative, positive, constructive meaning, making the observer characterize these periods in a predominantly unfavorable and negative manner. Many authors even hold that this negative content completely exhausts the sense of development in its critical periods. This conviction is expressed by the very names that have been laid down for the critical ages: one—the negative phase; another—the phase of obstinacy, etc.

As was already stated above, the conception of the separate critical ages has been introduced into science in an empirical way, at random, or, rather, in disarray, in isolation from general development and in one form or another. Before all of the others came the discovery and description of **the crisis at 7–8** years. It was noted in practical work and in scientific observation that the seventh year of life in the child consists of a transition between the preschool and juvenile periods. A child of 7–8 years of age is already no longer a preschooler but is not yet a youngster. The seven-year-old is an utterly unique being, distinct from a preschooler and from a school child. In view of this, the seven-year-old is difficult, in relation to enculturation. The negative content of this age is manifest first of all with respect to a disruption in psychological equilibrium, with respect to volatility in volition, and in a reduced ability to defer, and instability of mood (Vasileysky[14]).

Later came the discovery and description of **the crisis at three**, referred to by many authors as the phase of obstinacy and stubbornness. In this period, the child's personality undergoes abrupt and drastic changes in a limited period of time. The child becomes difficult to teach. He displays obstinacy, stubbornness,

[14] Serafim Mikhailovich Vasileysky (Серафим Михайлович Василейский, 1888–1961) was a student of Wilhelm Wundt and the philosopher J. Vokelt (the Nazi psychologist Hans Volkelt's father). Returning to Russia during the war and the revolution, he became a professor in Samara and then in Vitebsk. In the 1920s, he worked in "psychotechnical selection" (that is, looking for gifted children) and thus became involved in pedology, becoming Dean of the School of Education in Nizhny Novgorod Pedagogical Institute. In 1939, he was fired for smuggling "pedological distortions" into courses in child psychology. He went into linguistics instead, and became a professor at the Kirov Pedogogical Institute in Leningrad. In 1941 (i.e., during the war), he was Dean of the Faculty of Languages there. When he later tried to take his Ph.D. examinations, he was failed, probably because of his history in pedology. After the war he continued to work in testing, but when he tried to publish his dissertation on the psychology of scientific invention as a book, it was refused.

capriciousness, and willfulness. Internal and external conflicts often accompany this whole period. A strong emphasis on his own "I" leads to an almost asocial character to this child, and the child may consciously set himself apart from other people and be antagonistic to them (Stern).

Still later, the crisis at **thirteen years**, which was described as the negative phase of the age of sexual maturation, was discovered and studied. As indicated by the very name, the negative content of this crisis appears in this period in the first plane and due to a superficial observation seems to exhaust the sense of development in this period. Achievement decreases, efficiency drops, disharmony in the internal structure of the personality, collapse and death of the established system of interests, negative, protesting character of the whole of behavior—all this was characterized by Kroh as an entire period of disorientation in the internal and external relationships, leading to this: hardly ever in the entire process of development is the human "I" and the world more separated than in this period. This is what gave rise to Tolstoy calling this period "the desert of adolescence."

Finally, what has been theoretically acknowledged comparatively recently is the proposition, which for a long time has been well studied from the factual aspect, that the transition from infancy to early childhood age that occurs around one year of life is, in essence, also a critical period of development characterized by all of the distinguishing features which are familiar to us in the general description of this particular form of development.

In order to obtain a completely finalized chain of the critical ages, we would propose to include in it as the initial link what is, perhaps, the most unique of all the periods of child development, which is known as **that of the newborn**. This long-known and well-studied period stands apart from other ages in the system and is, by its very nature, perhaps, the most striking and indubitable crisis in child development. Catastrophic changes and leaps in the whole course of development in the act of birth, when the newborn, rapidly, enters critically into a completely new environment (Blonsky), transform the whole structure and the course of his life and delimit the beginning period of intrauterine[15] development as one of the most acute and undoubtedly critical ages.

All of the critical ages, listed above, occupy a very specific place in development, strictly regularly located between two stable periods of development and constituting something like epochs of transition between one period and another. The crisis of the neonate divides the embryological period of child development from the period of infancy. The crisis at one year divides infancy from early childhood. The crisis at three years constitutes the transition from early childhood to preschool. The crisis at seven years constitutes a connecting nexus between preschool and school age. Finally, the crisis of thirteen years coincides with the break in development with the transition between school age and the age of puberty.

[15] This appears to be a mistake, either by the stenographer or by Vygotsky himself. Vygotsky appears to mean "extra-uterine," or perhaps he meant to characterize the crisis of birth as the ending period of intrauterine development.

In this way, we have revealed a completely regular, profoundly meaningful, and clear picture. Critical ages are interleaved with stable ages. They constitute watersheds, turning points, once again confirming that the development of the child is a dialectical process in which the transition from one state to another is carried out not in an evolutionary but in a revolutionary way. Even if the critical ages had not been discovered empirically, the concept of them should be introduced into the schema of development on the basis of theoretical analysis. But now it is only left to the theory to acknowledge and interpret what has already been established through empirical research.

Critical ages do not have clear and well-defined borders; they emanate imperceptibly from the preceding age and just as imperceptibly flow into the subsequent one; they most vividly emerge only in the culminating point or peak of the crisis. This is due to the very nature of these age periods, as well as to the circumstance that in these crucial moments of development, the child becomes relatively difficult to teach due to the fact that the change in the educational system applicable to the child has not kept pace with the rapid changes in the child's personality, and the fact that the pedagogy of the critical ages is least developed in practical and theoretical relation to major all science about enculturation.

The negative content of these critical ages comes out very clearly in these periods. We know, however, that there is a general law, according to which any development is closely intertwined with a process of reverse development. In the expression of Bal[dwin],[16] every evolution is at the same time an involution, as all living is at the same time dying (Engels), and so it is precisely development, as one of the very complex forms of life, which must necessarily include in itself the process of decay and dying. Any appearance of a new in development must imply a dying away of the old. The transition to a new age is always marked by the twilight of the former age. These processes of involution and reverse development, and the demise of the old are concentrated precisely at the critical age.

Yet, it would be a colossal delusion to suppose that this exhausts the value of the critical ages. Development never ceases its permanent work of creation nor does it

---

[16] In some places, either the stenographer or Vygotsky himself apparently abbreviates. So, the name of Baldwin in the manuscript appears as "Bal", which is completed by Korotaeva as "Baldwin." Vygotsky refers to *Mental Development in the Child and the Race*, a 1906 book by James Mark Baldwin, in which Baldwin discusses the idea that Vygotsky was later to develop an "analysis into units" in this way:

"Instead of a fixed substance, we have the conception of a growing, developing activity. Functional psychology succeeds faculty psychology. Instead of beginning with the most elaborate exhibition of this growth and development, we shall find most instruction in the simplest activity that is at the same time the same activity. Development is a process of involution as well as of evolution, and the elements come to be hidden under the forms of complexity which they build up."

Vygotsky also refers in passing to a favorite quotation from Engels' unfinished *Dialectics of Nature*, p. 295:

"Life and death. Already no physiology is held to be scientific if it does not consider death as an essential element of life (note, Hegel, *Enzyklopadie*, I, pp. 152–53),[246] the negation of life as being essentially contained in life itself, so that life is always thought of in relation to its necessary result, death, which is always contained in it in germ."

replace it with nothing but destruction and devastation. In the critical periods, we observe not only the constructive work of development but, more than that, the processes of involution, so clearly expressed in this age, are themselves subordinated to the processes of establishing a positive personality, found from them in direct dependency, forming an indivisible whole. The destructive work of development occurs in these periods only in response to the need for and to the extent of the development of new properties and new traits of the personality.

Factual studies show that the negative content of development in these ages constitutes only the reverse, or the shadowy, side of **positive changes in the personality making up the main chapters and the basic sense of each critical age.** Thus, in relation to the seven-year crisis, it has been noted by all researchers that, alongside the negative symptoms of this age there are found a series of great achievements. In this period, the activities of inner construction are found: the child dreams, imagines, and resolves questions about being and the origins of life. What is changed in this period is the internal structure of the child's personality. It is predominantly concerned with works that originate within him, the cause of which is found within the self. The autonomy of the child expands; his relations with other children are transformed. There are increasing instinctual contradictions of direct and immediate impact upon the child, there are new forms of relationships being outlined in his relations to the phenomena of nature, and in his work there begins to prevail study of an independent character and autonomous discovery of truth (Schleger).[17] It is easy to see even from this brief and short list that during the crisis at seven years, there is a complete restructuring of the child's personality, full of positive meaning, and of the relationship to the external reality and to the social environment.

We see the same thing in the crisis at three. The positive meaning of this age in relation to the development of the personality has the effect that during the process of the crisis there arise new characteristics and elements of the personality unseen before. "The child is aware and feels himself a personality in a world of objects." (Köhler). It has been observed and factually established that wherever the crisis at three years is for any reason weak or unexpressed, it leads to a grave delay in the development of the affective and volitional side of the child's personality in subsequent ages. This constitutes another proof of the positive meaning of this crisis.

The same may be said of the crisis at thirteen, in which, as a rule, according to Sterzinger[18] and Kroh, the biggest reduction in the capability and productivity of mental work in the student has its reason in the circumstance that here arises changes

---

[17] Louise Karlovna Schleger (Шлегер, Луиза Карловна. 1863–1942) was a pioneer in early childhood and elementary education in prerevolutionary Russia. She founded popular kindergartens and an experimental primary school in Moscow with E.Y. Fortunatova, which specialized in discovery learning, especially scientific discovery.

[18] Othmar Hugo Sterzinger (1879–1944), an Austrian psychologist, a student of Oswald Külpe. He wrote very widely on subjects as different as right-handedness and left-handedness in amputees, the human response to musical intervals, the ability to create poetic images, and the problems that teachers have teaching 14- and 15-year-olds. Vygotsky mentions his work in *Pedology of the Adolescent* in connection with the decline in productivity in the crisis years.

from the fixation[19] upon visuals to that upon understandings and deductions. This transition to a new, higher form of intellectual activity is accompanied by a temporary decline in performance. What Kroh notes in relation to this decline in achievement is confirmed by all the other negative symptoms of this crisis: in every negative symptom, some positive content is hidden, usually consisting of a transition to some new and higher form.

Finally, no doubts exist about the positive content of development in the crisis at one year. Here, negative symptoms are so obviously and directly linked to positive achievements which the child accomplishes during the crisis—learning to stand on his feet and mastering speech—that pointing out the reductions of all this crisis to only the destructive work of development would be to break down an open door, so obviously do the positive functions of this crisis appear revealed.

The same thing entirely may be attributed to the crisis of the neonate. In this first period, the child is degraded even in relation to his physical development. In the first few days after birth, a physiological decline in the average weight of the neonate is observed. The catastrophe of birth and the difficulty of adjusting to a new form of life make such high demands on the viability of the child and such a complete change in the whole of his life activity that "(n)ever does man stand so close to death as in the hours of his birth" (Blonsky) and in the newborn. Nevertheless, this period, more than any of the subsequent crises, reveals the fact that development is a process of the formation and appearance of the new. We can say without any exaggeration that all with which we meet in human development during these days and weeks is one continuous neoformation.

The very symptoms of an adverse character that characterize the negative content of this period flow from the difficulties arising from the first appearance of new higher, increasingly complex forms of life.

The most significant content in the age of crisis consists of the appearance of neoformations. But the neoformations of critical ages, as the concrete research of each similar individual period reveals, are highly distinctive and specific in their formation. The main and most substantial difference from neoformations in the stable ages consists in their **transitional** character. This means that they are not preserved as they appear, as they emerge in the critical period, in subsequent ages, and are not included as a necessary addendum in the integral structure of the future personality. They are not preserved as such in the next age, not linked by any direct link to subsequent development, and do not constitute a basis for its subsequent direction. As such, they die off, as if subsumed by the neoformations of the

[19]Vygotsky writes changes in установки (ustanovki), which means something like an "installation," or a "fixture." We have chosen to translate it as "fixation," which in English suggests both and can also refer to a focus of attention. Vygotsky probably has in mind the work of his contemporary Uznadze, a Georgian psychologist who he references elsewhere (e.g., Chapter 5 of *Thinking and Speech*). Uznadze was a student of the Leipzig school of Ach and Reimat who returned to Russia to work in pedology: his major contribution was the idea of "fixations" which acted as "determining tendencies" in tasks that had definite developmental value (e.g., the transition from learning by seeing to learning by thinking).

subsequent stable age, included in them as a subordinated instant,[20] not having an independent existence, dissolved in them, altering them and transforming them, so that without a special or profound analysis it often proves impossible to detect the presence of this transformed formation of the critical age in the accomplishments of a subsequent stable age. As such, these critical neoformations die with the beginning of the subsequent age, but continue to exist in a latent form inside it, not living an independent life but merely participating in a subterranean path of development which in the stable age, as we have seen, leads to the sudden appearance of neoformations.

The concrete content filling these general laws of the neoformations of the stable and critical ages is not included in the tasks of the present chapter, as it should constitute the content of each of the subsequent chapters of the present book,[21] devoted to consideration of each individual age. The task of this chapter is only the preliminary sketch and overall scheme of the periodization of child development, an acquaintance with the basic and most general laws of construction, and the unfolding of ages as determinate, concrete epochs in child development. All that has been said above allows us to proceed directly to the exposition of this scheme.

The general features of this scheme have already quite clearly been sketched out before us in the course of our exposition; it is only necessary for us to bring them together in order to then be able to formulate the basic scheme of periods of child development itself. We already know that the neoformation shall serve as the basic criterion of the division of child development into separate ages in our scheme. We know, furthermore, that the sequence of age periods should in this scheme be determined by the alternation of stable and critical periods. We must still point out the defining characteristics of the one and the other. The stable ages possessing a more or less distinct range are defined by moments of commencement and ending; it is correct, as is customary in pedology, to define precisely this range as established by periods of commencement and ending of a given age. Critical ages due to their different character and passing could be more correctly defined by the principle that from the different culminating points or critical peaks we allow for the beginning of the crisis a period of half a year into the previous age and an ending point of around half a year into the subsequent one.

---

[20] A "subordinated instant" means a moment that cannot be separated from the following moment. Take, for example, the independent, but largely instinctual, mental life that is the transitional neoformation of birth; it does not disappear in infancy, when the child begins to learn through imitation. But the feeding instinct which drove behavior in birth are now subordinated moments of a learned routine. Similarly, the proto-speech of the crisis at once does not entirely disappear when the child learns speech properly: it continues as the subordinated instant of intonation and stress. But there is no intonation or stress in speech proper without vocabulary and grammar.

[21] This is a clear reference to the fact that the present text was not simply intended as part of a course of lectures but did indeed form the "problem and approach" chapter of an unfinished monograph. Given the criticisms that Vygotsky has of the extant textbooks on pedology by Blonsky and Zalkind, and his insistence on carrying out positive, constructive work rather than simple negation and destruction, this should not surprise us.

Next, detailed features within the division into stable and critical ages should be pointed out. Whereas the stable ages, as it has been established by empirical research, have a clearly expressed two-part structure, first and second (or early and late stage of a given age), the critical ages, due to the specificity of their course, have a pronounced three-part structure, made up of three logically interconnected transitory phases: precritical, critical, and postcritical.

Finally, the substantial differences, those which distinguish the scheme of ages in child development proposed below from other schemes for determining the basic periods of child development that are near to it, must be pointed out. New in this scheme, in addition to the basic child development concept of using the principle of the emergent neoformations as a criterion for the division into ages, are the following moments: (1) the introduction of critical ages in the scheme for periodization, (2) the exclusion from this scheme of the period of embryological development of the child, (3) the exclusion from the period of development usually called youth, covering the ages from 17 to 18 years of age up until final maturity, and (4) the inclusion of sexual maturation among the number of stable, steady, and not in the critical, ages.

We exclude embryonal child development from our scheme of ages in child development according to the simple principle that it, first of all, cannot be considered of the same order as the extra-uterine development of the child as a social being, as one of the age periods in the history of the development of the child's personality along with the other periods, because it represents in itself a completely distinct type of development subject to completely different laws other than those which begin with the moment of birth and the development of the child's personality; and, secondly, because it is studied by itself in the developed science of embryology, which cannot be regarded as a component chapter in pedology. Pedology must take into account the laws and data of embryological development of the child concerning the course of this period and the way in which they affect the course of postuterine development, but pedology does not include in itself an embryological viewpoint, just as it is necessary to take into account the laws and data of genetics, that is, the science of heredity, but this does not transform genetics into one of the chapters of pedology. Pedology does not study heredity or uterine development as such (these are the subject of special sciences) but only the role and influence of heredity and uterine development in the course of the social development of the child. Therefore, knowledge of elements of genetics and embryology, along with knowledge of the elements of general biology, anatomy, physiology, and psychology, are prerequisites for the study of pedology.

In addition, youth is removed by us from the scheme of age periods in child development on the grounds that a theoretical study has also made us reluctant to extend the period of child development excessively to include the first twenty-five years of life (Blonsky). The age of youth should be seen rather as the infancy of the mature age than as the senility of the childhood periods of development. By the basic laws and by the very sense of the age period from 18 to 25 years, it is, rather, the initial link in the chain of mature ages than the final link in the chain of periods of child development. It is hard to imagine that human development which has reached the age of legal majority may be subject to the laws of child development.[22]

Finally, the inclusion of puberty among the number of stable ages[23] is a necessary logical deduction from all of what we know about this age and what characterizes this period as a period of enormous increase in the development in the adolescent of higher syntheses which occur in the personality at this time. This follows as a necessary logical deduction from the whole critique in Soviet pedology that theories that reduce the period of sexual maturation to "normal pathology" (Homburger[24]) and to a profound internal crisis have been subjected to.

Thus, we may imagine a periodization of age periods in child development in the following form:

A scheme of periodization for child development

1. The Crisis of the Neonate
   (a) Precritical phase
   (b) Critical phase
   (c) Postcritical phase

---

[22] We have seen that Vygotsky has been quite critical in this chapter of the work of his friend and colleague Blonsky. At the period when Vygotsky was writing this, Blonsky was leaving pedology and arguing for a much more biological approach to childhood, as Vygotsky pointed out earlier. At the same time, Blonsky, who was closely allied with Lenin's wife Krupskaya, defended the idea of labor schools, and therefore, the continuity between childhood and working life. Vygotsky was changing too, but in the other direction. For Vygotsky, the great drama of adolescence is a drama of speech and thinking, not simply sexual and work activity. This is why Vygotsky's periodization scheme is much closer to the periods of schooling as it existed in prerevolutionary Russia and in the later USSR of his time (with primary school beginning around 7 years old and high school finishing at 17).

[23] Vygotsky tells us that puberty is a stable period, not a crisis. He has several reasons for this. First of all, the period he is talking about lasts for four years (14–18). Secondly, it is a profoundly constructive period, since it sees the formation of true concepts (the "higher syntheses" that Vygotsky refers to here). But the third reason is the one he stresses in this paragraph, and it is more theoretical. In the early years of the Russian Revolution, Freudian theories were very popular with artists and intellectuals, even at the vanguard of the arts (e.g., Chagall's fascination with Freud's theory of dream) and in the Bolshevik Party (Trotsky was very sympathetic to Freudianism and believed it provided materialist foundations for psychology). Many psychologists, including Luria and Spielrein, became convinced Freudians. Not Vygotsky. Vygotsky found Freud's theories of child sexuality adult-centered—a projection of (male) adult interests back onto childhood. So, the idea that every male child suffered an Oedipal complex or a castration complex or some other form of "normal pathology" was heavily criticized on theoretical grounds: it was teleological, pansexual, and male centered. The justice of these criticisms is widely recognized today, even though hardly anyone remembers that they begin with Vygotsky, Blonsky, and Soviet pedology.

[24] August Homburger (1873–1930) was a German child psychiatrist. Born in Frankfurt, he studied the Babinski reflex and became interested in battle shock during the First World War. After the war, he began to study psychopathology in children. He wrote several books, including *Psychopatholgie des Kindes und Jugendalter*, and he was a theorist of play. Vygotsky credits him with the idea of "serious play."

2. The Age of Infancy (2 months to a year)
   (a) First stage: Early infancy
   (b) Second stage: Late infancy
3. The Crisis at One Year
   (a) Precritical phase
   (b) Critical phase
   (c) Postcritical phase
4. Early Childhood (one to three years)
   (a) First stage
   (b) Second stage
5. The Crisis at Three Years
   (a) Precritical phase
   (b) Critical phase
   (c) Postcritical phase
6. Preschool Age (3–7 years)
   (a) First stage: Early preschool age
   (b) Second stage: Late preschool age
7. The Crisis at Seven Years
   (a) Precritical phase
   (b) Critical phase
   (c) Postcritical phase
8. School Age (8–12 years)
   (a) First stage: Early school age
   (b) Second stage: Late school age
9. The Crisis at Thirteen Years
   (a) Precritical phase
   (b) Critical phase
   (c) Postcritical phase
10. The Age of Puberty (14–18 years)
    (a) First stage: Early age of puberty
    (b) Second stage: Late age of puberty
11. The Crisis at 17 Years
    a. Precritical phase
    b. Critical phase
    c. Postcritical phase

References

Binet, A., & Simon, T. (1905). Méthodes nouvelles pour le diagnostic du niveau intellectuel des anormaux. *L'Année Psychologique, 11*, 191–244. https://doi.org/10.3406/psy.1904.3675

Binet, A., & Simon, T. (1907). *Les Enfants anormaux*. Arnand Colin.

Stern, W. L. (1924). *The psychology of early childhood: Up to the sixth year of age*. Henry Holt.

Stern, C., & Stern, W. L. (1909/1999). *Recollection, testimony and lying in early childhood*. American Psychological Association.

Vygotsky, L. S. (1997). *Collected works* (Vol. 4). Plenum Press.

Vygotsky, L. S. (1998). *Collected works* (Vol. 5). Plenum Press.

Выготский, Л. С. (1972). Проблема возрастной периодизации детского развития. *Вопросы психологии, 2*, 114–124.

Выготский, Л. С. (1984). *Собрание сочинений Т.4*. Педагогика.

Выготский, Л. С. (2001). *Лекции по педологии*. Удмуртский университет.

Chapter 3
The Structure and Dynamics of Age

Outline of Chapter 3: The Structure and Dynamics of Age

In this short chapter, Vygotsky explains the relationship between the lines of development and the neoformation in general terms (i.e., in terms that should apply in each of the subsequent chapters). The chapter, as the title indicates, falls into two parts. In the first part, Vygotsky argues that new structures (neoformations) are both the culmination and the continuation of functional lines of development. In the second part, Vygotsky shows that the social situation of development is dynamic, because a home is not a house, but rather a small community surrounding the child that can and does change as the child changes.

I. **New structures are both the culmination and the continuation of functional lines of development.** In the first part of this chapter, Vygotsky explains the emergence of the neoformation by introducing the lines of development (peripheral and central). Vygotsky begins by reminding us of the relationship between parts and wholes in structural psychology: it is the whole which determines the value of the part rather than vice versa, and consequently, the whole process cannot be understood as a simple sum of the independent partial processes but must instead be taken as a structural whole made up of interdependent processes. We remember that in Lecture 5 of *Foundations of Pedology* (see *Pedological Works, Volume 1*), the relationship between psychological functions at the outset of development was theorized as a system of dominants (Ukhtomsky). For example, in infancy, the dominant function is affective perception, and other functions, for example, memory and thinking, are still dominated by that function, that is, memory and thinking are linked to affective perception and not to each other, and they tend to operate in a manner that is affectively tinged and perception-dependent as a result. This principle now applies to the lines of development of the functions as well: each part of the process of development

---

This chapter is translated from material edited and published by G.S. Korotaeva in 2001.

L. S. Vygotsky, *L.S. Vygotsky's Pedological Works. Volume 2.*, Perspectives in Cultural-Historical Research 10, https://doi.org/10.1007/978-981-16-1907-6_3

depends on its relation to the developing neoformation. Some central lines of development are directly involved with that neoformation. So for example the line of development of affect and perception in infancy that runs through receptive interest, shared activity, and active imitation is directly involved with the emergence of the central neoformation. Other, peripheral, lines of development are not directly involved with bringing this neoformation about. For example, the line of development of memorizing is not directly involved in the formation of the central neoformation. This neoformation is a generalized form of intersubjectivity that Vygotsky calls a "Grandwe," perhaps because it is a "we" that is related to "you and me" in more or less the same way that a grandparent is related to a parent and also because it a kind of proto-"we." (Vygotsky was probably influenced by Goethe's work on the "Ur-phenomenon" in plants.)

II. **The social situation of development is dynamic, because a home is not a house.** In the second part of this chapter, Vygotsky explains the lines of development in turn by referring to the source of development: the environment. Here he must introduce a third key component: the social situation of development, which explains what Seth Chaiklin (2003, p. 51) calls the "objective" zone of proximal development.

Vygotsky begins by defining the social situation of development as the unique relationship that the child has to the environment (physical and then social) at a particular age. So for example at birth the relation is one of physiological separation from the mother, but it is also one of biological dependency. During infancy, it is still one of biological dependency, but it is now one of social contact. Vygotsky reminds us that this social situation of development is the ultimate source of all development: like that of all human beings, the child's consciousness is determined by its social existence rather than the other way around. It follows, therefore, that neoformations, which are structures of consciousness, emerge from the social situation of development at the end of an age period rather than at the beginning.

However, it does not follow that the flow of developmental change is entirely one-way; the child is an actor, and not simply an inert object that is acted on by the environment. Vygotsky says that the child who has changed the very structure of his personality now has a very different relationship to the other personalities in the environment. It is not simply that the child perceives the world differently, the child learns to act in the world and on the world in different ways too. This in turn means that the social situation of development which brought about the neoformation now disappears. For example, the newborn infant who relied on pure instinct to feed and then learned to interact with a mother in order to satisfy its needs finds that instinctive life is all but useless in the learned habits of the feeding routine. Similarly, the infant who relies on wordless social contact to satisfy needs and then learns speech finds that wordless social contact does not actually convey specific needs beyond those that can be shared by affective perception. This destruction and restructuration of the social situation of development constitutes the content of the crisis. Therefore, it is not preventable. But can the destruction be predicted and can parents and teachers intervene in a timely way to help in the process of restructuration? That possibility provides the content of Chap. 4.

Chapter 3: The Structure and Dynamics of Age

The task of the present chapter consists in establishing the most general propositions characterizing the inner structure of the process of development, which we will call **the structure of age in each specific epoch of childhood.**

The most general proposition, which we must point out at the very beginning, is that the process of development in each age epoch, regardless of the complexity of its organization and its make-up, in all the multi-form constituents of the processes that make it up which are revealed with the aid of analysis, presents an altogether unified whole, has a certain strictly regular structure, and that the laws of the whole structure, or the structural laws of the age, determine the structure and the course of each separate process of development that forms a part of the whole. Such structures, known as holistic formations, do not sum up the individual parts, representing, as it were, their aggregate; instead, it is they which determine both the fate and the significance of each of the constituent parts.

Ages represent just such holistic and dynamic formations, the structure which defines the role and weight of each partial line of development. At each given age epoch, development is not accomplished in such a way that individual aspects or parts of the personality of the child's personality are changed with the result that a restructuring of the personality as a whole takes place. In development, there exists precisely the opposite relationship, which can be presented thus: the personality of the child changes as a whole in its inner structure, and the laws of change of this whole determine the movement of each of its parts.

As a consequence of this, at each given age step we always come upon a central neoformation, which appears to lead throughout the entire developmental process as a whole and which characterizes the reconstruction of the whole personality on a new basis. Around this basic, or central, neoformation of the given age are located and grouped together all the other partial neoformations, along with all the other processes of development linked to neoformations of previous and of subsequent ages. The processes of development which are more or less directly linked to this basic neoformation we shall call the central line of development of a given age, and all other partial processes of change taking place at the given age will be called peripheral lines of development. It stands to reason that those processes which are central lines of development during one age will become peripheral lines of development during the following, and conversely—peripheral lines of development in one age will come to the first plane and become central lines of development in another age, as there are changes in their significance and in their relative weight in the total structure of development, and as there are changes in their relation to the central neoformation. So, in the transition from one stage to another, the reconstruction of the whole structure of the age is accomplished. Every age has its own specific structure, unique and proper to it alone.

Let us explain with examples what we have stated. If we focus on the consciousness of the child, understood as his "relation to his environment" (Marx), and we take consciousness generated by the physical and social changes of the individual, for the integral expression of the highest and most substantial features of the structure of the personality, we see that in the transition from one age to another what grows and develops is not only the separate, partial aspects of consciousness, not only its separate functions or ways of activity, but in the first place what changes is the general structure of consciousness which is characterized in each age first and foremost by a system of relations and dependencies that exist between the separate aspects, the separate types of its activity.[1]

It is quite clear that in the transition from one age to another, alongside the overall restructuring of the system of consciousness, the central lines of development change place. So, for example, the development of speech in early childhood in the period of its emergence is so closely and immediately linked to the central neoformation of this age when the social and objective consciousness of a child first emerges in its most tentative outlines that it is impossible that speech development should not be attributed centrality among the lines of development of this age. But at school age the continuation of speech development has a completely different relation to the central neoformation of the age and, consequently, should be considered as one of the peripheral lines of development. In the same way, in the age of infancy, when the form of speech babble occurs, these processes are linked to the central neoformation of the period of infancy in such a way that it should also be considered one of the peripheral lines of development.

We see, in this way, that one and the same process of speech development may act as a peripheral line in the age of infancy, becoming a central line of development in early childhood and once again turning into a peripheral line in the subsequent age. It is quite natural and clear that in direct and immediate dependence on this, the course of speech development, regarded as such, will in itself proceed in completely different ways in each of these three ages.

But the interchange of central and peripheral lines of development in the transition from age to age directly leads us to the second issue of the present paragraphs—the question of the **dynamics** of the emergence of neoformations. We once again, as with the question of the structure of ages, must restrict ourselves to only the most general explanation of this concept, leaving the concrete exposition of the dynamics

[1]Vygotsky (1997) sees consciousness as not merely an external relation with the environment but also a system of internal functions (which are of course linked to the environment). So for example in the infant, attention, perception, and (short term) memory form a definite psychological system, and because this psychological system defines the child's relationship to the environment we may define it as consciousness (2019). For Vygotsky, a central neoformation defines a form of mental life specific to a particular age, and in the infant this form of mental life (the "proto-we" of the child's relationship with the mother) is not yet dependent on speech.

of the age changes to one side as a problem for subsequent chapters reviewing separate ages.

The problem of the dynamics of the age follows immediately on from the problem of the structure of each age. As we have seen, the structure of the age is not a static, unchanging, immobile picture. In each age, there is a transition from a preexisting structure to a new structure. The new structure is composed and emerges in the course of development of the age. The relationship between the whole and the parts, so essential to the concept of structure, is a dynamic relationship that determines change and development as a whole, as well as that of each part. By the dynamics of development, therefore, it should be understood the totality of all the laws that determine the appearance of transitions, changes, and the interconnections of structural neoformations at any given age.

The most basic and essential moment in the general definition of the dynamics of an age is a dynamic understanding of the relations between the personality of the child and the social situation surrounding the child at each given stage of the age. One of the greatest obstacles to theoretical and practical study in pedology as a science consists in the heretofore faulty solution of the problem of the environment and its role in the dynamics of the age. The fault lies in an understanding of the role of the environment in the development of the child in which the environment is considered as something which is external to the child, as the setting of development, a set of conditions that are objective and indifferent to the existence of the child, affecting him by their very existence. One cannot transfer to pedology, to the study of child development, the understanding of the environment which has developed in biology in relation to the evolution of animal species. It should be recognized that at the beginning of each given age period there exists a completely original, exclusive, unique, and unrepeatable relationship between the child and the environment specific to that age alone, which we will call the social situation of development of a given age. The social situation of development of a given age is the starting point for all of the dynamic changes occurring in development during a given period. It determines wholly and entirely the forms and the path by following which the child acquires newer and newer properties of his personality, drawing them from the environment as the main source of his own development, the path by which the social becomes the individual. In this way, the first question which we must address in studying the dynamics of any age consists of clarifying the social situation of development.

The given social situation of development, specific to each age, defines in a strictly regular manner the whole **form of the life of the child**, or his **social being**. From this arises the second question, with which we are confronted in the study of the dynamics of any age—that is, the question of the origins, or the genesis, of the central neoformations of the given age. Having ascertained the social situation of development that has developed at the beginning of this age and is determined by the relationship between the child and the environment, we must then elucidate how **the life of the child in this social situation makes necessary the emergence and development of neoformations** that are appropriate to this age. These neoformations, characterized primarily by the restructuring of the **conscious** personality of the child, do not constitute the prerequisite but the result or the product of age development. **Change in the consciousness of the child arises on the basis of a definite form of his social life, specific to a given age**. That is why the maturation of a neoformation is never at the beginning but always at the end of a given age.

But once there arise neoformations in the conscious personality of the child, this brings about a change in that same personality. This cannot help having the most substantial consequences for the course of subsequent development. If the previous task in the study of the dynamics of the age lay in the task of defining the way that the child's social being moved the new structure of his consciousness forward, now the following task arises: defining the path of the opposite movement from a change in the structure of the consciousness of the child to a restructuring of his being. For the child who has changed the structure of his personality is another child, a social being which cannot help but differ, in its most essential form, from the being of a child of an earlier age.

In this way, the subsequent question before which we shall stand in the study of the dynamics of age consists in the question of the consequences which follow from the fact of the emergence of neoformations of the age. Through concrete analysis of this question, we may come to see that these consequences are so varied and so immense that they cover the entire life of the child as a whole. The new structure of consciousness acquired at a given age inevitably represents a new character of perceiving external reality and of activity in it, as well as a new character of perceiving the inner life of the child himself and the inner activity of his psychological functions.

But to say this means at the same time to say something else that brings us directly to the final moment that characterizes the dynamics of age. We see that as a result of age-related development there emerge at the end of a given age neoformations that lead to the restructuring of the whole structure of consciousness in the child and which in this way change his whole system of relations to external reality and to the self and which in this way change the whole system of relating external reality to the self. The child at the end of the age becomes a being of completely different substance than the one that he was at the beginning of the age. But this means that the social situation of development that has developed in its most basic components at the beginning of this age must also change. For the social situation of development means nothing less than the system of relations between the child of a given age and the environment. So, if a child has been changed in some radical way, this relationship must inevitably be restructured. The former situation of development breaks up to the extent of the course of development of the child and so in proportion to the progress of his development, the main features of a new situation of development, which must constitute the starting moment for the new age, are made up. Research shows that such a restructuring of the social situation of development makes up the important content of the critical ages.

In this way, we come to the elucidation of the basic law of ages, according to which the very forces which move the development of the child at a given age lead inevitably to the rejection and destruction of the foundation of this development during this age, and with an inner necessity determine the annihilation of the social situation of development, the end of an epoch of development and a transition to the subsequent, or higher, age stage.

Such, in very general terms, is the schema of the dynamic development of age.

References

Chaiklin, S. (2003). The zone of proximal development in Vygotsky's analysis of learning and instruction. In A. Kozulin, B. Gindis, V. S. Ageyev, & S. M. Miller (Eds.), *Vygotsky's educational theory in cultural context* (pp. 39–64). Cambridge University Press.

Vygotsky, L. S. (1997). *Collected works, Vol. 4*. Plenum.

Vygotsky, L. S. (2019). *L.S. Vygotsky pedological works Vol. 1: Foundations of pedology*. Springer.

Chapter 4
The Problem of Age and the Diagnostics of Development

Outline of Chapter 4: The Problem of Age and the Diagnostics of Development

Unlike Chaps. 2 and 3, this chapter diverges widely and often from the version which appears in the Russian language *Collected Works* (1984). As a consequence, it is quite different from any version that has previously appeared in English.

These differences begin with the title. The words диагностика развития ("diagnostics of development") which appear in the title of this lecture in the Korotaeva collection of lectures (2001, p. 191) are replaced by the words динамика развития ("dynamics of development") in the *Collected Works* (1984, p. 260). This choice of title all the more surprising because the previous chapter had the word динамика "dynamics" in the title, and this chapter is not a redundancy. The Russian *Collected Works* have two paragraphs which do not occur in the Korotaeva version; we have included these in footnotes. In addition, there are also twelve paragraphs in the Korotaeva version which do not appear in the *Collected Works*. The *Collected Works* version avoids the word "pedology" (the word as well as the discipline was under a cloud in the USSR after Vygotsky's death). Vygotsky, in this spoken lecture, uses the word 32 times.

It is in the context of a pedological diagnostic, not a pedagogic device, that Vygotsky's most famous concept, the zone of proximal development, takes shape in this chapter. Vygotsky first asks how we can know whether children are developing normally. Then he notes that mass studies have yielded three important results—a minimal but also a maximal age for teaching-and-learning; "pedological standards" for particular milestones of development which allow us to distinguish between normal and anomalous development; and the ability to relate the milestones to

This chapter is taken in the main from material edited and published by G.S. Korotaeva in 2001. Divergences from the version in the Russian edition of Vygotsky's *Collected Works* are footnoted throughout.

L. S. Vygotsky, *L.S. Vygotsky's Pedological Works. Volume 2.*, Perspectives in Cultural-Historical Research 10, https://doi.org/10.1007/978-981-16-1907-6_4

coherent structures. Thirdly, Vygotsky argues that these results of mass studies are not enough to answer our question about normal development in clinical settings (and teaching is one of these), and the zone of proximal development is introduced as a diagnostic tool. Vygotsky concludes the chapter by reminding us that diagnosis does not simply mean remarking one symptom after another; diagnosis is only diagnosis when it can rise to the level of diagnosing the underlying cause. We can expand these four points into an outline of the chapter as a whole.

I. **How can we know if children are developing normally?** "Passport age" is no reliable guide to diagnosing the actual level of the development. But having separated "passport age" from "pedological age," Vygotsky then asks how can pedologists can tell whether a child is typical or atypical. He answers that pedology, just like any other clinical science, uses standardized norms based on large populations (rather than experiments on or observations of individual children) and complexes of symptoms (rather than the sort of individual trait schemata criticized in Chap. 2).

II. **Mass studies have yielded three important results, but these are not nearly enough to answer our question about normal development.** Vygotsky considers three important results of such pedological studies:

The first result is that there are not only lower limits of development for teaching-and-learning speech, literacy, and conceptual thinking, there are also upper limits, and if the optimal period passes without teaching-and-learning, as for example when adolescents attempt to master literacy or when adults try to master the pronunciation of a foreign speech, the results are generally poorer than when teaching-and-learning can rely on developing functions rather than already developed ones.

The second result is that normal, typical development may be differentiated from abnormal, atypical development simply by calculating the ratio between the actual level of development and the norm of development for the child's passport age. (Note that this ratio must be combined with the assumption that there is a single underlying factor for intellect before the idea of intelligence quotient or IQ can be obtained; there is no evidence that Vygotsky believed in a single general factor underlying intelligence.)

The third result is that the relations between accomplishments such as speech, literacy, and numeracy can tell us a great deal more than any one of these accomplishments can by itself, just as calculating body mass index from height and weight can tell us more about physical health than either height or weight alone.

Vygotsky then argues that these results, however useful, do not tell us nearly enough. Because the content of development is constantly changing, and because the very means of development itself (e.g., affect, memory, speech, thinking) is developing, the past is no reliable guide to the next zone of development. Vygotsky then suggests that this next zone of development can be diagnosed by using the same standardized norms and complexes of symptoms used to calculate the actual level of development, but allowing children to solve problems in collaboration, or, as he puts it, by allowing imitation. The only reason this has not been allowed, Vygotsky says, is a misunderstanding of the essence of imitation—it has been assumed that imitation tells us only about the mind of the imitated and not about that of the imitator. Köhler's experiments with chimpanzees demonstrated that the only skills that apes could learn from imitation were those they were also capable of performing independently. Vygotsky says that the situation is far more complex with children, because children, with verbal teaching-and-learning, are capable of intelligent solutions that go far beyond visual examples, and far beyond the information they are given; indeed, they are capable of unprecedented behavior they have never seen demonstrated at all.

III. **The zone of proximal development is a diagnostic and not simply a pedagogical device.** In speaking of imitation, Vygotsky does not have in mind a simple copy of behavior without any grasp of its purpose. He has in mind the child's ability to reproduce and even to vary actions with a shared goal firmly in mind, and this is why he equates imitation with collaboration. It is also why he believes that imitation-in-collaboration does not simply show what a child can do with help. Just as the ape's imitations tell us what the ape can do independently, the child's collaboration has the power to show us what a child will be able to do independently in the near future, particularly since collaborative tasks often come to the child in connection with the social situation of development, In this way, the child's ability to solve problems in imitation and collaboration has the power to diagnose the next zone of development, both for the individual child (what Chaiklin [2003] calls the subjective zone of proximal development) and, using the principle of standardized norms, for the population (the objective zone of proximal development). Vygotsky shows how this standardized norm is applied by using two eight-year-olds (i.e., children who are just past the crisis at seven, and in the stable period of school age). Unassisted, they achieve identical and normative scores, but then they are offered problems from the next zone of development (i.e., problems that require conceptual thinking) along with assistance: leading questions, started solutions, or demonstrations for imitation. Under these conditions, one child is able to perform at the level typical of the end of school age (12 years old), but the other is only able to solve the type of problem normal for a 9-year-old. Vygotsky concludes that this is because although the developed functions that enable independent performance are identical, the lines of development of the developing functions which will lead to the neoformation are not the same. It is interesting that although a great deal of attention has been paid to the precise forms of assistance (leading questions, starting solutions, demonstrations), Vygotsky himself does not dwell on them at all, and even remarks that although physical development cannot actually be shared in quite this way, the general principle is the same for all forms of development. This tells us that for Vygotsky, at any rate, the principle is not that children perform better with imitation-in-collaboration, something Vygotsky might consider of only symptomatic interest. Vygotsky has in mind something that is at once more theoretical and more practical; that is, in a clinical diagnosis of the next zone of development, such as the sort a practicing teacher needs to do all the time, we need to consider more than just the symptom of what the child does on his or her own.

IV. **Child development is not simply one symptom after another.** To conclude this chapter, Vygotsky elaborates the theoretical and practical significance of the zone of proximal development and then returns to the problem with which he began: how pedology can move beyond a purely symptomatic approach.

The theoretical significance of the zone lies in the fact that it is the social environment, which is the immediate source of development, even if it is the child himself who is the actual site. It is for this reason that the child's behavior in collaboration can tell us so much about his ability to access the sources of development, and therefore predict the child's next zone of development.

The practical significance of the zone lies in the fact that it diagnoses maximally effective periods for learning-and-teaching. Vygotsky reminds us of the curious fact that a 1-year-old child who has less attention, cognition, and motor control appears to master the pronunciation of the mother tongue as well or even better than a 3-year-old (and far better than a 13-year-old learning it as a foreign language). He concludes that learning and development are so tightly linked that learning builds not on developed neoformations but rather on the still developing ones.

Vygotsky now argues that in order to move beyond a piecemeal, symptomatic approach to development, diagnosis must include the lines of development that are still in progress. Here Vygotsky returns appreciatively to a source he criticized at the outset of the chapter: the eclectic, unreliable Gesell, who had the courage to argue for an immanent theory of development but not the courage to follow it through. He agrees with Gesell that the child must not simply be measured, but interpreted. The actual word that Gesell used was indeed the English word "interpret," but to the Russian speaker Vygotsky this word must have been somewhat imprecise: a heuristic rather than an objective and analytical approach. Unless this interpretation can rise to the kind of explanation, we derive from looking beyond already internalized functions to the very source of learning and development in the environment, the diagnostic power of the teacher is not much more than that of a doctor who tells a coughing child that he is suffering from a cough. Without diagnostic power, the teacher cannot hope to intervene in a timely and effective way.

Chapter 4: The Problem of Age and the Diagnostics of Development

The problem of age constitutes not only a central question in the whole of theoretical pedology, but the key to all questions of pedological practice as well. This problem leads by an immediate and very close connection to the **diagnostics of age development in the child.** The diagnostics of child development conventionally denotes the particular system of devices in pedological research deployed for the task of **defining the real level of development attained by the child**. The real level of development is determined by that age, or stage, or phase inside the given age, which the child is going through.

We know already that the passport age of the child cannot provide a reliable criterion for determining the real level of his development. For this reason, the determination of the real level of development always requires the employment of a specialized pedological inquiry, whose result can establish the pedological diagnosis of development.

Determining the real level of development is vital and indispensable task in resolving all the practical questions related to the area of the enculturation and teaching-and-learning of the child, to the control of his normal physical and mental development, and to the determination of this or that disorder of development disrupting his normal course and discerning all of the processes of an atypical, an abnormal, or in some cases a pathological character. Therefore, to determine the real level of development is one of the first and most basic tasks of the diagnostics of development.[1]

We formerly attempted to show that the scientific research of child development does not commence until that moment when pedology tears itself from the chronological age of the child and sets itself the challenge of studying the sequence and the changes in the age periods of development, as measured by the intrinsic measure proper to itself (real age). But pedology has torn itself away from the chronological age of the child only so as to differentiate the concept of the passport and the real age of the child and then to return once again to the question of what regularity of connection exists between the one and the other. The factual development of the child always proceeds at a definite season of life. Each age epoch is related in a regular way to a definite chronological date. Defined events take place in the development of the child at defined points in time. Pedology would be of no practical use at all in solving any practical task if it, having first distinguished between the real age of the child and his passport age, then failed to return to join both of these ages in a regular, unified link, if it did not know how to answer the question of how the real factual process of child development can be matched to the years of the child's life. We know that between the rhythmical flow of astronomical time and the inner rhythm of child development there is no simple coincidence. It appears that both series are linked in an extremely complex link. Establishing this link, that is, determining the factual allocation of the major or larger and smaller periods of child development by the years of the child's life, therefore constitutes the second moment

[1] In the *Collected Works*, we find the following two paragraphs.

"The study of the symptomology of child ages allows us to identify a series of reliable traits with the aid of which we can come to know what phase and stage of which age the process of the development of the child is now unfolding, just as a doctor on the basis of this or that symptoms establishes the diagnosis of a disease, that is, determines the inner pathological process which is detected in the symptoms."

"By itself the study of some age symptom or group of symptoms or even the precise quantitative measure of them is not yet considered a diagnosis. Between measurement and diagnosis, Gesell says, there exists a vast difference (1925). It consists in this: a diagnosis may be made only in those cases where we are able to disclose the sense and significance of the symptoms we have found." (Выготский, Л.С. [1984]. *Собрание сочинений* T.4, p. 261; Vygotsky, L.S. [1998], *Collected Works* Vol. 5, p. 200)

for solving the problem of defining the real level of development. This challenge has been solved, as we already said, with the aid of standardized age symptoms and symptom complexes.

By **standards of age development,** we refer to **the symptoms that characterize this or that aspect of child development during a definite period, connected by the chronological age of** the mass, the average, the norm, the typical for the given defined group of children to which the child belongs.

Pedology employs such standards, that is, definitions of the constant, typical traits which are associated with definite years of the child's life, just like any other science, by applying standardized benchmarks. Thus, we know, the standard normal temperature for a human is 37 degrees. The degree of deviation from this standard we measure as abnormal, disordered, decreases, or increases in the temperature of the human body. Similarly, pedology employs such typical indicators, norms, or standard as units of measurement, as a means of comparison, as a technique for qualifying and determining the actual level of development of the child.

We know that the teaching-and-learning of the child in this or that subject, skill, or ability is only enabled and made fruitful when it is confined to a flow of definite epoch or age of child development, during which all the necessary preconditions for a given type of learning and teaching ripens in the child. Everyone knows that it is not possible for a 1-year-old to learn reading and writing and that learning literacy at 10 years old is as much too late as learning would be premature at 1 year of life. The child begins to master literacy, given appropriate conditions, at around 6 years. In this way, there exists an optimum time for any kind of teaching-and-learning; that is, there exist most opportune periods for learning-and-teaching particular subjects within child development. It turns out that too late in this respect is just as inopportune as too early. Thus the optimal period for speech teaching-and-learning is the second and third year of the child's life. We know how easily, how without any voluntary effort at remembering and memorizing, the child learns during these years the language of the people around him, and sometimes even two languages, if they are sufficiently differentiated in their application to the child. But the child who takes up the study of a foreign language in the school years of his life will spend incomparably more effort and exertion and learn with far less perfection the analogous forms of foreign language. Overly delayed teaching-and-learning of speech turns out to be the same grievous error as premature teaching-and-learning.

In this way, a practical task of paramount importance emerges, determining the optimal timing for learning-and-teaching and enculturation, and for the fit between the levels of education and enculturation of the child and the levels of his age development. This will yield **standards** of child development that we propose for the establishment of optimal periods for the mass child[2] developing in a definite system of conditions.

[2]The term Vygotsky used here is массового ребенка ("the mass child"), which the English *Collected Works* translates, in a different context, as "the average child" (1998, pp. 66, 326) and supplements with the following note, translated verbatim from the Russian *Collected Works*, (1984, pp. 91, 409). "The term mass child was introduced by P.P. Blonsky: ....pedology prefers to

To identify the symptoms of age-related development in the child, we compare him with standards that temporally match the emergence of these symptoms to a specific year in the life of the average or the population of children. Knowing the passport age of the child, we can determine the degree of deviation above or below the passport age of the child with respect to the standard age at which these symptoms should appear. Suppose, for example, that the child with a passport age of 10 years has the symptoms of mental development which are attributed by the standards to the population of 5-year-old children. We may conclude from this that our child lags in his mental development by 5 years behind his peers, as he at age ten has only reached a level of development that other children reach at age five. The real level of development of the child is defined as **plus or minus the difference between his passport age and the standard of the population of children of his age, corresponding to the level of development which is set for a child with the help of pedological research.** According to how great the discrepancy between the passport age and the standard one is, we may judge the degree of deviation of the development of a given child from the norm. According to the degree of the difference, we may distinguish normal, subnormal, abnormal, and supra-normal children.[3] In our example, the lag of 5 years in the mental development demonstrates a serious and profound mental retardation in the child. In determining the real level of development in pedology we often employ not only the definition given by the difference between the passport and standard age, but also that given by the ratio between them. In the case of complete coincidence between the passport and the standard age, the ratio is equal to one, while in the case of a lag by the child, the ratio is expressed by a fraction, less than one, and in the case of accelerated development, this relationship will be expressed as one plus a fraction. So in our example, the difference between the passport and the standard age consists of 5 years, but the relative index of this level of development is 0.5. This **relative indicator** of the level of intellectual development is usually called in pedology **the coefficient of mental development.**

The use of standards in pedology in relation to the population and to the individual child undoubtedly requires an analytical, distinguishing, approach to the symptoms of age-related development. As we have seen above, no single symptom or group of symptoms that can characterize the whole of the process of development in general exists. Therefore, the study of symptoms of the individual ages, stages, and phases of child development and their standardization, that is, their allocation to

be based on a study not of the individual random child but on the mass of children. Pedology wants to think not in units, but in masses. Its point of departure is the mass child, the mass of children (1930, p. 9)." This point of departure is not easily accessible to us today, and is only poorly conveyed by the term "average child" or the "typical child," neither of which includes the central meaning of a child developing as part of a whole population in a collective institution of some kind. So we have chosen to render it literally, as "the mass child." See also Блонский П. П. (1930). Педология в массовой школе первой ступени, p. 13.

[3] Korotaeva notes that this expression "supra-normal" is "thus in the stenogramme." It is not really an expression used in Russian today, but in context it makes good sense: all the supra-normal children are above average (Выготский, 2001).

specific years of life in the average of a population of children necessitates a differentiated study of singular aspects of child development. In this way, we encounter in pedology standards for physical, mental, speech, motor, and other types of development in the child, which are in turn subdivided into even finer subtypes of standards, for symptoms that characterize this or that partial process of inner area of development. Thus, for the area of physical development, we have differentiated standards for height, weight, circumference of the chest and head, and other symptoms that characterize the growth and development of important organic systems.

But the very presence of such differentiated standards of child development necessarily requires the establishment of links and relations between different groups of symptoms. For this purpose, there are introduced into the diagnosis of development a wide variety **of coefficients or indicators** which are found with the aid **of establishing a relationship between two or several traits and which are more symptomatic in some respects than individual symptoms**. More, for the same purpose, pedological research introduces the establishment of every kind of correlative dependencies or links between separate features of development. These correlations are fixed with the aid of statistical methods and express numerically a stronger or weaker dependency which exists between two or several processes which make up development and which are found in these or those symptoms.

In this way, it is completely necessary and unavoidable from the point of view of the diagnosis of development to differentiate age-related symptoms and with the same necessity to raise the question of integrating the multiple symptoms obtained by way of this differentiated study into a linked and unitary picture characterizing the real level of development of the child as a whole. The pedologist appears, in this case, exactly the same way as the doctor who, investigating separate symptoms then links them, associates them, and systematizes them in order to arrive at a definition of the inner processes of the disease that lies behind these symptoms.

This task of integrating multiple and partial symptoms into a linked picture, allowing them to define the real level of development of the child as a whole, is justified by the above methods for determining specific coefficients of development and correlations between individual groups of traits, is only the lesser part of it. The important and basic way consists in the **interpretation or elucidation of the symptoms found** in the study.

The tasks confronting the diagnostics of development can only be resolved through a fundamental, deep, and broad knowledge of all of the sequence of the course of child development, all of the characteristics of each age, stage, and phase, of all of the basic types of normal and abnormal development, all of the structures and dynamics of child development in all of their variety. In this way, by itself, to determine the real level of development and the quantitative expression of the difference between the passport and the standard age of the child or the relation between them expressed as a coefficient of development is only the beginning step on the path of pedological diagnosis.

To speak of the essence, such a definition of the real level of development does not only not exhaust the whole picture of development but very often occupies only an insignificant portion of it. Stating the presence of this or that symptom in defining the real level of development is factually defining only that part of the general picture of development which covers the processes, functions, and properties which have already matured at that date. Thus, for example, we define the height, the weight, and the other indicators of physical development which characterize the already completed cycles of development. This is the end, the result, the final attainment of development in the period gone by. These symptoms tell us more about how development took place in the past than how it is taking place in the present and what direction it will take in the future. But this by itself has turned out to be utterly inadequate. To speak figuratively, when finding the real level of development we determine only the fruits of development, that is, that which has already ripened and completed its genetic cycle. But we know that the basic law of development consists in the asynchrony of maturation between the different aspects of the personality and its different properties. While some processes of development have already brought forth their fruits and completed their cycles, other processes are only in the stage of maturing. The true diagnosis of development must know how to cover not only the completed cycles of development, not only the fruits, but also the processes which are in their period of maturing. Just as a gardener would have done wrong if, in defining the coming harvest, he had calculated only the already ripened fruits in his garden and was unable to assess the condition of the trees which had not yet born ripened fruit, so too the pedologist who restricts himself to the sole definition of the matured and leaves aside the maturing can never achieve a proper understanding of the internal state of affairs and cannot transcend a symptomatic to a clinical diagnosis.

Determination of the processes which are still immature today but which are in the period of maturing constitutes the second task of the diagnostics of development. This task is solved by finding the zones of proximal development. We explain by a specific example of child mental development this concept, important in the highest theoretical and practical terms.

In determining the real level of intellectual development of the child or the standard intellectual age in pedology for the most part what is used is the method of tests, which consists in this: that the child is asked to solve an increasingly difficult series of tasks that are standardized against the years of life of the child. Each time research identifies where the limit of difficulty that is within the child's grasp lies and what standard age this corresponds to. This determines the mental age of the child. But it is always governed by one common and basic rule: what is considered indicative of the mental development of the child are only those solutions which the child carries out **on his own** without any help from the side. Only and exclusively independent solutions of tasks are considered indicative of the mind. If in the course of solving a task the child is offered a leading question or given a guiding instruction, or shown how to solve the problem, the solution is not counted in determining mental development.

The basis for this rule lies in the belief that the nonindependent solution of a task carries no significance or implications for the child's mind. In fact, this belief is in sharp contradiction with all the data of contemporary psychology. It arose from an old misconception which now has lost all meaning, that the imitation of an intellectual operation can purely be a mechanical, automatic act telling us nothing at all about the mind of whoever is doing the imitating. The original error of this view has been exposed in zoopsychology. Kohler, in his experiments on humanoid primates established the remarkable fact **that animals can imitate only those intellectual actions which lie in the zone of their proper capabilities**. Thus, a chimpanzee can replicate those rational and appropriate actions shown to it only if the operation in its type and degree of difficulty belongs to the same category of rational and appropriate action that the animal can independently perform. Animal imitation is strictly confined to the limits of its own proper capacities. The animal can imitate only what it is capable of by itself.

Much more complicated is the state of the child. On the one hand, the child at different stages of development is also far from being able to imitate everything. And his capacity to imitate in the intellectual field is severely restricted by the level of his mental development and by his age potential. On the other hand, a general law maintains that the child, as opposed to the animal, may extend the area of imitation in intellectual operations to those that are **more or less far beyond what he is capable of in the area of autonomous, conscious, rational actions or intellectual operations**. At the basis of this distinction between the child and the animal is that the animal is incapable of teaching-and-learning in the sense that we apply this word to the child. It lends itself only to **dressage.**[4] It can only gain new skills. It may, by means of practice and recombination, **improve its intellect** but it is incapable of mental development in the proper sense of the word, by means of learning-and-teaching.[5]

In this way, we see that with the help of imitation the child can always carry out in the intellectual field more than that which he is capable of if providing all action

---

[4] Note the distinction that Vygotsky makes between skill dressage and mental development. The Russian term he uses for skills entrainment is дрессировке. This is a term used in lion taming or horse "dressage." This is in contrast to путем обучения, literally, "the path of teaching-and-learning." Unfortunately, English (unlike French, German, and Russian) does not have a term that means both "teaching" and "learning" (e.g., "apprendre" or "lernen" which can be used both for what the teacher does and for what the student does). The English *Collected Works* uses "instruction;" but it seems to us that this places far too much emphasis on teaching and not enough on learning. As the example of imitation makes clear, both teaching and learning is meant. For example, in *Thinking and Speech* Vygotsky emphasizes that the child doing homework at night who "imitates" an example she or he saw done by the teacher during the day is involved in обучение; it would be rather misleading to say that the child is carrying out instruction, or even carrying out instructions. For this reason, we must translate the perfectly graceful Russian term обучение as the somewhat awkward hyphenated form "teaching-and-learning."

[5] The version in the *Collected Works* includes:

"This is why all experimental attempts using instruction to develop in higher animals new intellectual functions not proper to them but specific to man inevitably meet with failure, as did the attempt of R. Yerkes to graft human speech into ape offspring or the attempts of E. Tolman to train and instruct chimpanzee offspring together with human children." (See Vygotsky, 1998, p. 301.)

This is not in the Korotaeva manuscript (Выготский, 2001). Note that in *Thinking and Speech* Vygotsky leaves open the question of whether apes can be taught humanlike language, so if these lines were actually written by Vygotsky and not inserted by the editors, it means that he changed his mind.

only independently. But at the same time, we see that the capability of his intellectual imitation is not without limit, but strictly changed according to the course of his mental development, in such a way that at each age step there exists for the child its own particular zone of intellectual imitation related to the real level of his development.

When we speak here of imitating, we have in mind not mechanically, automatically, and senselessly, but rational imitative performance of a given intellectual operation based on understanding. In this regard, we have narrowed the meaning of this term, using it to refer to an area of operations that are more or less directly linked to the rational activity of the child. On the other hand, we have deepened the meaning of the term by using "imitation" to all sorts of activities of a particular type being performed by a child not independently, but in collaboration with adults or with another child. Everything that a child cannot do independently but which can be **learnt** or which can **be performed under the guidance** or **in collaboration with the help of leading question or with the help of assistance in difficult points**, we will treat as the sphere of **imitation**.

With this definition of the concept, we may at once establish the symptomatic significance of this intellectual imitation widely used in the diagnostics of mental development. It is completely clear that what a child can do by himself, without any aid from outside, may be indicative of already matured capabilities and functions. These are identified with the aid of tests usually employed to determine the real level of mental development, as these tests are based exclusively on solving problems independently.

But, as we have already said, it is always important to define not only the matured processes but also the maturing ones. In relation to the child's mental development, we can solve this task with the help of determining what the child is capable of in the area of intellectual imitation, if we understand this term as meaning the definition given above. Research shows that there exists a strict genetic relationship between what the child is capable of in this area and his mental development. What the child is able to do today in collaboration and under guidance, he will tomorrow become capable of performing independently. This means that by investigating the potential of the child working in collaboration, we define thereby the area of maturing intellectual functions that in the near stage of his development should bear their fruits and thereby move to the level of real mental development.

In this way, by investigating what the child is capable of performing independently, we investigate the development of the bygone day. Exploring what the child is able to perform in cooperation we define the development of the day to come.[6] This whole area of immature but maturing processes makes up the zone of proximal development of the child.

---

[6]Vygotsky says завтрашнего дня, which is literally "the after's day," or "tomorrow's day." As the whole botanical metaphor makes clear, he is not speaking of the next 24 h, any more than when he talks of a child growing a head taller in play he is speaking of a new skull sprouting from the old one. We have tried to render Vygotsky's more figurative meaning—essential to distinguishing between learning and development—by translating the Russian rather literally.

We will explain with a simple example how we determine the zone of proximal development. We assume that as a result of our inquiry we have established with respect to given two children that they are at the same year in their mental age. Let us say that both are 8-year-olds. This means that both of them handle tasks of the degree of difficulty which corresponds to the standard for 8-year-olds by themselves. In this way, we have identified the real level of their intellectual development. However, we do not cease our inquiry with this, but rather continue it. With the help of specifically developed techniques for each given method, we examine how capable both children are in handling tasks which somewhat exceed the standard for 8-year-olds. We show the child how to handle the task, and we see whether he can, imitating this demonstration, manage it; or we begin the solution of the task and allow the child to complete it. Or we offer the child some cases of solutions of problems that go beyond his mental age, in collaboration with other, more developed children, or, finally, we explain to the child the principle of handling the task; we put leading questions to him, we divide the task into parts, etc. In short, we offer to the child various forms of cooperation for handling those tasks that exceed his mental age, and we determine how far the opportunity for intellectual cooperation extends the intellectual sphere for the given child and how far it goes beyond his mental age.

It then turns out that one child can solve in collaboration tasks at, say, the 12-year-old standard. His zone of proximal development exceeds his mental age by 4 years. The other child turns out to advance with cooperation only to the 9-year-old standard age. His zone of proximal development covers only one year of development.

Now ask yourself: are these two children who find themselves at the same age level established by their real level of development the same with regard to the entire picture of their development to the present day as a whole? Obviously, the similarity is only limited to the area of already matured functions, capable of independent application. But in relation to maturing processes, one child went four times as far as the other.

We have explained the diagnostic principle for immature processes and properties using the example of **mental** development in the child.

It is completely clear that in the domain of determining the **physical** development of the child that method of inquiry which we have just described with respect to intellectual development would appear to be completely inadmissible. But in principle, the question stands in relation to this aspect of development, as well as with all the others, completely the same. It is important for us to know not only the limits of growth that the child has already reached but also other processes that contribute to the physical development of the child. It is important for us to know also how the very process maturing which will reveal its accomplishments in later development is proceeding. If we know the proximate causes that affect the growth of the child, we can with the aid of special techniques[7] determine how those not-yet-mature growth processes occur.

We will not dwell upon the definition of the zone of proximal development in relation to other aspects of the growth of the child's personality. We should only explain the theoretical and practical significance of this definition.

The theoretical significance of this diagnostic principle consists in this: it allows us to penetrate the inner causal-dynamic and genetic links that determine the process of mental development itself. As we already mentioned above, the social environment constitutes the source of all the specifically human properties of the human personality progressively acquired by the child, that is, the source of social development in the child taking place during the process of the real interaction of the ideal and the initial forms. The immediate source of development of the individual properties of the personality of the child is a collaboration (understood in the broadest sense of the word) with other people. In this way, when we apply the principle of collaboration for the identification of the zone of proximal development; we thus obtain the opportunity to directly investigate what exactly determines in the most immediate way the mental maturation which should be completed in the immediately following period of his age development.[8]

The practical significance of this diagnostic principle is linked to the problem of learning-and-teaching. A detailed clarification of this problem will be given in

[7] Physical development is obviously different: for example, the principle of imitation and the principle of cooperation do not appear to apply to bodily growth or even body training in the same way it applies to mathematics or science or even fine arts; we do not seem to bulk up merely by watching other people in the gym. But the principle of knowing the maximal period for bone growth is important in knowing what kind of diet and what kind of exercise children need, and of course knowing the developmentally optimal period for sexual maturation is essential to sex education. That appears to be the principle, applicable to all forms of development, that Vygotsky wishes to establish.

Léopoldoff-Martin and Schneuwly (2018, p. 140) note that the phrase с помощью специальных приемов "with the aid of special devices" does not occur in the *Collected Works*, and they believe that this may be because Vygotsky is referring to mass testing, which was banned after his death. Note, however, this is only one of many differences between the paragraph in the Korotaeva version (Выготский, 2001)and that in the *Collected Works*. (1984: 265).

[8] Note the co-presence of the initial and the ideal or final or completed form of development: this is, as Vygotsky remarked in Lecture 4 of *Foundations of Pedology*, *(L.S. Vygotsky's Pedological Works, Volume 1)* what makes child development unlike any other form (and unlike animal development, at least in the all-important area of speech and cultural behavior generally). It is also worth noting that the zone is what we identify. But what actually determines, or delimits, or defines development—the ultimate source for maturation in speech development and in the development of all of cultural behavior generally—is collaboration. The social is therefore not simply one factor but the ultimate source of all development—quite directly in stable periods and somewhat indirectly in critical periods. This is even true for physical development, since the social environment is the ultimate source of our diet and much of our exercise. As the example of physical education should make perfectly clear, it is not the tasks that determine the zone of development, but rather the zone of development which determines what tasks we need to identify it: lifting weights is not the definition of muscle development, but the level of muscle development can certainly be identified by weight-lifting.

another of the subsequent chapters. Now we will focus only on the most important and primary of its moments. It is known that in the development of the child there exists optimal times for each type of learning-and-teaching. This means that only during definable age periods is the learning-and-teaching of a given subject, a given knowledge, a skill, or a mental ability at its most easy, efficient, and productive. This circumstance has for some time now been overlooked. At first only the lower boundary of these optimal learning-and-teaching periods was discovered. It was known that for a 4-month-old infant the learning-and-teaching of speech is not possible nor is literacy for a 2-year-old, because in these periods the child is not mature enough for this learning-and-teaching. This means that he has not yet developed the properties and functions which are required as prerequisites for this type of learning-and-teaching. But if there were only this lower limit for the opportunity of learning-and-teaching at a defined age, we would expect that the later that the appropriate learning-and-teaching commences, the more fruitful it should prove, because in later ages we encounter a greater degree of maturity required as a necessary precondition of learning and teaching.

In fact, this turns out to be untrue. A child who begins the learning of speech at 3 years or of literacy at twelve, that is, too late, also turns out to be in an unfavorable situation. Too late learning-and-teaching turns out to be as difficult and unproductive for the child as too early. Obviously, there is an upper boundary for optimal periods of learning-and-teaching from the point of view of the development of the child. Too late with regard to teaching and learning turns out to be just as bad as too early.

How can the fact be explained that the child of three years of age, in whom we encounter a greater degree of maturity, attention, cognition, motor skills, and other properties which are prerequisites for the learning of speech, undoubtedly assimilates less speech with more difficulty than a child of one year and a half, in whom we undoubtedly encounter to a lesser degree of maturity these same prerequisites?[9] Obviously, the reason lies in the fact that learning-and-teaching is based not so much on the already matured functions and properties of the child as it is upon those which are still maturing. The period of maturation in the corresponding functions constitutes the most favorable or the optimal period for the corresponding type of learning-and-teaching. This is self-evident if we take into account the fact that the child develops in the very process of learning-and-teaching rather than first completing a given cycle of its development, the fact that the teacher instructs the child not in that which the child is already able to do on his or her own but rather in that which he does not yet know how to do but which he can perform with the aid of

[9] Vygotsky is referring to two well-established facts of speech development. First, the sound system is largely in place by age three or so, and after that the sound system itself does not develop so quickly. Secondly, around age three the child begins to show clear "U-shaped curves" in speech development, so for example English speaking children will stop using "ran" as the past tense of "run" and use the incorrect form "runned." Since the child is mostly using the most frequent verbs, and these are the most often irregular, this "U-shaped curve" of development is very conspicuous.

learning-and-teaching and guidance; and, finally, (the fact—Trans.) that the process of learning and teaching always occurs in one or another form of collaboration between the child and an adult and constitutes a special case of the interaction between the ideal and the initial forms which we mentioned above as one of the most general laws of the social development of the child.

In detail and concretely the whole of this problem of the relationship between learning-and-teaching and development will be laid out in one of the later chapters in relation to school age and school learning-and-teaching. But already now it should be clear to us that, as learning-and-teaching depends on nonmature but maturing processes and the whole sphere of these processes is covered by the zone of proximal development of the child, the optimum time for learning for a population of children of a certain age, as well as for each individual child, is determined by the zone of their/his proximal development. That is why the definition of the zone of proximal development is of such great practical significance for pedology.

That which we have described above, that is, the determination of the actual level of development and the proximal zone of development constitutes what is commonly referred to in pedology as **the normative diagnostics of age**. The normative diagnostics of age have as their task the definition with the aid of **age norms or standards a given stage of development characterized by the aspects of matured and also of nonmatured processes**. Unlike **symptomatic** diagnostics based only on the establishment of external traits, a diagnosis which tends to the determination of the internal state of development discovered by these signs is called clinical diagnostics by analogy with medical science.

A general trait of all scientific diagnostics of development consists in the transition from symptomatic diagnostics, based on the study of the symptom-complexes of child development, that is, its traits, to clinical diagnostics, based on the definition of the inner course of the process of development itself. "Normative data should not be approached mechanically or purely psychometrically. We need not only to measure the child; we need to interpret him" (Gesell.). Measurement, definition, and comparison to the standard symptoms of development should be taken only as a means for establishing a diagnosis of development. The diagnosis of development should not be only the reception of data by tests and measurements. The diagnostics of development is a form of comparative study with the assistance of objective rules as points of departure. It is not only synthetic but analytic.

The given tests and measurements constitute the objective basis of comparative evaluation. The schemes of development give a measure of development. But diagnosis in the true sense of the word must be based on a critical and meticulous interpretation of data obtained from different sources. It is based on all of the manifestations and facts of maturation. A synthetic, dynamic picture of these manifestations, the totality of what we call the personality is in its entirety within the scope of research. We cannot, of course, precisely measure the parts of the personality. We find it difficult to define that which is called personality, but from the viewpoint of developmental diagnosis, we are obliged to monitor it, with the make-up and the maturity of the personality (Gesell).[10]

If we limit ourselves to defining and measuring the symptoms of development, we will never be able to transcend a purely empirical statement of what is known by observers of the child. At best we can only clarify and verify their measurements. But we will never be able to explain any of the phenomena observed in the development of the child, nor to point out the future course of development, nor to indicate what means of a practical nature should be taken in relation to the child. This sort of diagnosis, barren of prognostic, explanatory, and practical power in relation to the diagnosis of development in the child, may be compared only to the kind of medical diagnosis which doctors put in the epoch ruled by symptomatic medicine. The patient complains of a cough and the doctor states a diagnosis: the disease is a cough. The patient complains of a headache, and the doctor states a diagnosis: the disease is a headache. This diagnosis constitutes, in essence, an empty diagnosis because the research does not add anything new to that which he knew from observation of the patient and from his own complaints, only providing them with a scientific etiquette (i.e., a scientific label—Trans.). An empty diagnosis that does not explain the observed phenomenon can predict nothing in relation to their fate and can offer no advice in relation to practical measures. A genuine diagnosis must give an explanation, a prediction, and must have scientifically based practical prescriptions.

So too with the symptomatic diagnoses in pedology. If a child is brought for pedological consultation with complaints that he is poor in mental development, that he… […remembers poorly, and after inquiry the psychologist[11] states the diagnosis—a low coefficient of mental development, mental retardation—this likewise explains nothing, predicts nothing and can offer no practical help, like the doctor who states the diagnosis: the disease is a cough. We may say without exaggeration that absolutely all practical actions to protect the child's development, on his learning and upbringing as they relate to this or to that age, necessarily require a diagnosis of development. The use of the developmental diagnostics to solve practical

[10]As Gesell (1925) remarks, we may not be able to define personality, but we must nevertheless reckon with it when we diagnose development.

"The synthetic, dynamic aspect of the behaving individual which we call personality also comes within the scope of observation. We cannot, however, measure personality traits with precision. We can scarcely define what we mean by personality, but from the point of view of developmental diagnosis we are obliged to reckon with the make-up and maturity of the personality." (*ibid*, p. 417).

[11]Léopoldoff-Martin and Schneuwly (2018, p. 142) believe that this word was probably "pedologist" and not "psychologist." This is possible, since this part of the paragraph was inserted from the *Collected Works*, and the *Collected Works* avoids using the word "pedologist." But Korotaeva, who edited the mimeos after the fall of the USSR, must not have thought it was worth changing or even noting, and she had no reason to censor the word "pedologist;" she allows Vygotsky to use the word "pedologist" quite freely in other contexts. Vygotsky argues in the *Pedology of the Adolescent* (1929, pp. 26–27) that pedologists have no other method than those of the psychologist for measuring mental functions, and it is precisely that which is at issue here.

tasks, infinite in number and in variety, is defined in each concrete case by the degree of scientific elaboration of the diagnosis of development itself and by the demands which are made upon it in dealing with any concrete practical problem.][12]

References

Chaiklin, S. (2003). The zone of proximal development in Vygotsky's analysis of learning and instruction. In A. Kozulin, B. Gindis, V. Ageyev, & S. Miller (Eds.), *Vygotsky's educational theory in cultural context* (pp. 39–64).

Gesell, A. (1925). *The mental growth of the preschool child*. Macmillan.

Vygotsky, L. S. (1998). *Collected works* (Vol. 5). Plenum Press.

Блонский, П. П. (1930). *Педология в массовой школе первой ступени*. Работник просвещения.

Выготский, Л. С. (1984). *Собрание сочинений Т.4*. Педагогика.

Выготский, Л. С. (2001). *Лекции по педологии*. Удмуртский университет.

[12] The conclusion to this paragraph, that is, the material in brackets, appears to have been inserted by the editor from Volume Four of Vygotsky's *Collected Works* in Russian (it is the last paragraph of "Problem of Age," which is the shortened version of Chapter One found in the *Collected Works*). It is not clear why the editor inserted it here, as it is largely a restatement of what Vygotsky just said. (Note that in the 2001 edition of Korotaeva's book the first bracket is missing.)

Chapter 5
The Crisis of Birth

Outline of Chapter 5: The Crisis of Birth

In Vygotsky's *Collected Works,* the editors present the next two chapters as a single chapter of Vygotsky's unfinished book on child development and give it the rather misleading name "The Age of Infancy." The editors also stipulate that the first part of the manuscript—including, presumably, the title—is missing, and this is why they begin the material with Section 2 and not (as the English version of the *Collected Works* has done) with Section 1.

For three reasons, we have taken a somewhat different course, dividing what appears as a single chapter in the *Collected Works* into two chapters—the present chapter on the crisis of birth, and Chap. 6, the Age of Infancy. We have also replaced the confusing numbering with subheadings. First of all, the separation and the headers are justified by the plan and periodization scheme given in Chap. 2. Secondly, both measures will help—we hope—to make Vygotsky's lengthy and variegated material easier to follow. But thirdly and most importantly, it seems to us that the separation between critical periods and stable ones, and therefore between birth and infancy, are at the very center of Vygotsky's pedological works.

In this chapter, and in subsequent chapters, Vygotsky pursues a path well-trodden by Hegel, by Marx, and even by Charles Darwin (Blunden, 2017). First he works through a compendium of "factual material" and establishes a concept—in this case, the critical, transitional nature of birth and its neoformation. He then proceeds to reconstruct the factual material in the image of the concepts. This procedure may seem somewhat redundant and even circular, but it has the indubitable advantage of checking facts against concepts, and then concepts against facts. It also has the

As explained in the outline, this chapter was taken from the 1984 Russian edition of Vygotsky's *Collected Works*.

As we said at the outset of the outline, the editors of the Russian *Collected Works* say that the first part of the manuscript is missing, and they begin this section with the number "2." The editors of the English *Collected Works*, in contrast, begin this section with the number "1." It seems less confusing to simply eliminate editorial numbering altogether and use sub-titles.

L. S. Vygotsky, *L.S. Vygotsky's Pedological Works. Volume 2.*, Perspectives in Cultural-Historical Research 10, https://doi.org/10.1007/978-981-16-1907-6_5

advantage of making it easy to outline the chapter in four parts: factual material on feeding and sleeping, factual material from phylogenesis and ontogenesis, the concept of a transitional, critical neoformation at birth (individual psychic and social life), and the reconstruction of data with this concept in mind.

I. **Factual materials on nursing and slumber.** Vygotsky begins with a unique social situation of development: the child is separated from the mother physiologically, but not biologically. The child is entirely dependent on the mother for food, warmth, protection, and even basic mobility. This combination of separation and dependence offers two lines of development. Both are transitional, that is, neither entirely new nor identical to their previous forms:

   1. Nursing. The child is no longer connected by the umbilical cord but still takes food from the mother's body.
   2. Slumber. The child must now breathe independently and distinguish between light and dark, but sleep and waking are not yet clearly differentiated.

II. **Evidence for the transitional status of birth from phylogenesis and from ontogenesis.** Vygotsky argues for the special, critical, status of birth, on two different grounds.

   1. A special state in phylogenesis. As primates, human neonates have certain features shared with other primates but not with non-primates. Unlike marsupials and den-dwelling animals, human children are raised in the open air, but unlike cursorial offspring (running animals such as deer and horses) they depend entirely on the mother for mobility. As a result, they share a number of reflexes with apes having to do with grasping and hanging.
   2. A critical state in ontogenesis. Vygotsky now establishes that birth is not a single event but a whole independent period with its own lines of development and neoformations. To do this, he notes that gestation in humans varies by as much as four months. He also notes that, at least according to Gesell, the physical indicators of development (e.g., weight, height, maturity of the nervous system) in prematurely born babies and in post-maturely born babies seem to more or less coincide if we just consider their calendar age from conception. So whether or not the development is taking place inside the womb (as with postmature babies) or outside it (with premature babies) does not seem to alter the basic "substratum" of mental development. However, Vygotsky rejects the idea that development is continuous and gradual during this critical period. Instead, he argues that birth represents the original moment of something entirely new.

III. **Central neoformation: Autonomous psychic life.** Vygotsky defines this new formation as "individual mental life." Vygotsky emphasizes that, contrary to what Gesell says, this neoformation is not a slow, gradual accumulation of changes: there are two aspects of birth that are entirely new.

   1. Although life, and even its content, is not entirely new, its separate, individual, autonomous form is novel.

2. Although the child may not be conscious of it, this new autonomous mental life is social in nature and therefore psychological in quality.

   Vygotsky notes ironically that reflexologists and behaviorists have tended to ignore the former aspect and treat psychic life as non-autonomous and wholly dependent on stimuli from the environment, while the poets and philosophers have tended to ignore the latter and treat the child as fully endowed with personality and recoiling from the environment. He argues that although the child's cortex is quite underdeveloped, like any other structure, the function of the brain depends on the relationship of its parts, and the subcortical parts of the brain are able to sustain autonomous mental life. And although the child seems oblivious to his or her own social role, the social environment—the family—is not at all indifferent to the child.

IV. **Revisiting the data with the transitional nature of the newborn's individual psychic life in mind.** Stern, it appears, tends to the camp of poets and philosophers: he believes that in addition to reflexes the rudiments of the child's personality are given at birth. Vygotsky points out three moments which clearly distinguish the newborn's mental life from the personality that develops later.

1. Sense and affect are still undifferentiated, and the child's *perezhivanie* is a single whole (rather than as a stimulus located in the environment and a response located in the self).
2. The child and other objects are still undifferentiated, and the child appears to experience whole states rather than objects.
3. Objects and people are still undifferentiated, and the child only slowly learns to contact with others.

   Precisely because these elements are all undifferentiated, Vygotsky holds that the newborn's perceptions are not chaotic, merely diffuse. Vygotsky argues that the child's next zone of development is actually the differentiation of objects and people rather than the distinction between sense and affect or between the child and other objects: the child selectively responds to human voices and faces before the child selectively responds to form, color, or size. The infant's transformation of simple perception into primary intersubjectivity (i.e., mutual attention and interest between a mother and an infant), however, marks the end of the newborn period, and with this the unique forms of individual mental life which are located in the subcortical areas of the brain wither away, definitively demonstrating their transitional character.

Chapter 5: The Crisis of Birth

Child development opens with the critical act of birth and follows on with a critical age, which is called that of the newborn. At the moment of birth, the child is physically separated from the mother, but due to a range of circumstances, there is not yet at this moment a biological separation from the mother. In the basic functions of life; the child remains a biologically dependent creature for a long time. During the whole period under consideration, the livelihood and the very being of the child is of such a specific character that this gives grounds for separating out the newborn period as having all of the distinctive features of a critical age.

If one attempts to characterize the important feature of the age, one may say that it is rooted in the unique situation of development that is created thanks to the fact that the child is at the moment of birth separate from the mother physically but not biologically. As a result, all of the child's existence in the newborn period appears to occupy a middle position between intra-uterine development and subsequent periods of postnatal childhood. Newborns are like a link between uterine and extra-uterine development; they combine in themselves portions of the one and the other. This link is in a true sense a transitional stage from one type of development to another, radically different in form from the first.

The transitional or combined character of the child's life in the newborn period can be traced in several basic features that distinguish its existence.

Let us begin with feeding. Following the birth of a child there is a drastic change in diet. S. Bernfeld[1] says that in just a few hours after birth, the mammalian is transformed from a water-breathing being of variable temperature that eats only osmotically, in the manner of a parasite, into an air-breather with a constant temperature that consumes liquid food. In the words of S. Ferenczi,[2] after birthing the child changes from an endoparasite into an exoparasite. In the opinion of this researcher, the physical environment of the newborn constitutes to some degree a half-way house between the environment of the fetus (the placenta) and the environment of later childhood (the crib), and the communication of the newborn is in part a weakening and in part a modified continuation of the relationship between the fetus and the pregnant woman. The direct physical link between the child and the mother is no longer there, but he still receives food from the mother.

Indeed, we cannot fail to see that the feeding of the newborn is of a mixed character. On the one hand, the child feeds in the way animals do: he receives external stimulation, responds by expedient motions with the aid of which food is taken up

---

[1] Siegfried Bernfeld (1892–1953) was an Austrian psychoanalyst, one of the first followers of Freud. He was a socialist who developed a "Freudian Marxism" that appealed strongly to many in Russia (including Luria). From 1917 to 1921 he worked in a Zionist group with homeless children and then took a strong interest in education. He wrote a book about the psychology of the newborn *(Psychologie des Säuglings)*, and also a work on education through labor: he was one of the very first advocates of the idea that the more cooperation we have in the classroom, the more individuation there is in the child.

[2] Sandor Ferenczi (1873–1933) was a Hungarian psychoanalyst, and at first a close disciple of Sigmund Freud. But he soon fell out with Freud, because he believed that his patients' stories of sexual abuse were true and that sex abuse was traumatic for children (Freud thought stories of sex abuse were child wish fantasies). His ideas were later influential for counseling psychologists like Carl Rogers and theorists like Jacques Lacan. Ferenczi believed that all children had a desire to "return to the womb" and the comfort of the amniotic fluids and placenta; this idea was later taken up by Lacan.

and then taken in. All of his digestive apparatus, and, supporting this apparatus, a complex of sensorimotor functions, play the chief role in feeding. On the other hand, the baby is being fed with the fore-milk (i.e., the colostrum—Trans.) of the mother and later her milk, that is, with an intra-organic product of the maternal organism. In this way, feeding of the newborn takes a transitional form, as it were half way between intrauterine and subsequent extra-uterine feeding.

We uncover without difficulty this same duality and this same intermediate character in the basic forms of the newborn's being, which is distinguished in the first place by insufficient differentiation between sleeping and waking. As studies show, around 80% of the newborn's time is spent sleeping. The main feature of the newborn's sleeping is its polyphasic character. Short periods of sleeping are interspersed with little islands of waking. Most sleeping is not sufficiently differentiated from waking, and therefore what is often observed in the newborn is an intermediate state between waking and sleeping, reminiscent of dozing. Despite the great amount of sleeping, it turns out, according to the observations of C. Bühler[3] and H. Hetzer,[4] that these periods are very short; uninterrupted sleep of nine to ten hours does not occur until the seventh month. The average number of periods of sleep in the first quarter of the year equals twelve.

The most remarkable distinction in the sleep of the newborn is its restless, spasmodic and shallow character. The newborn in sleeping produces many impulsive movements, sometimes even eating without waking up. This once more points to the fact that his sleeping is not sufficiently differentiated from waking. The newborn is capable of falling asleep with partly open eyes and, contrariwise, will often lie

[3] Charlotte Bühler née Malachowski was a pedologist, a psychologist, and a feminist, first in her naïve Austria and then in the US. She was a student of Edmund Husserl and Oswald Külpe; her doctorate, with the latter, was on the psychology of thinking. She then worked with, and eventually married, Karl Bühler, and they founded an influential developmental institute at the University of Vienna. Charlotte wrote some of the very first studies on adolescent development, in addition to many studies on early years. Unlike most developmental psychologists, she gave equal attention to the development of girls. Eduard Spranger complained—quite wrongly—that she was only interested in women. Vygotsky criticized her—with more justice—for equating concepts with word use. Unlike Vygotsky, she ascribed full-fledged concepts to three-year-old children and saw adolescence as a time of emotional development but intellectual stagnation. When the Nazis took over Austria, the Bühlers settled in the USA. They found it difficult to find professorships (there were many other Jewish refugees looking for jobs) and did clinical work instead, but eventually became highly influential with a generation of humanistic and neo-Gestaltist psychologists including Carl Rogers, Fritz Perls, and Abraham Maslow.

[4] Hildegard Hetzer (1899–1991) was working in a kindergarten in Vienna when Charlotte Bühler began her studies of poor and working-class children. She became involved in her work on intelligence, and completed a Ph.D. under Bühler in 1927. In 1931 she became a professor in early years at the University of Vienna. She is credited with creating a set of tests for very young children (one to six years old). Staying in Austria after the German Anschluss, she eventually found work with an agency which specialized in "Germanizing" promising Polish children (i.e., those who looked racially German, although they were Polish speakers). It is possible that she succeeded in saving some children from death at the hands of the Nazis; it is certain that she collaborated with the SS and their system of "relocation camps" (i.e., extermination camps).

awake with the eyes closed, but in a state of dormancy. According to D. Canestrini,[5] the wave of the brain pulses in a newborn does not display distinct boundaries between sleeping and waking. The criterion of sleep that we get from observing an adult or a child older than six months is not yet in force for the first weeks of life.

In this way, the general life condition of the newborn may be characterized as a state of general doziness from which are gradually differentiated states of sleep and wakefulness. For this reason many authors, such as J. Lhermitte[6] and others, have come to the conclusion that the first days of the extra-uterine existence, the child is as if it were continuing its uterine life and retaining its psychological features. If we add to this the fact that the child retains a pose like an embryo during sleep time and often in the time of wakefulness, the intermediate character of this life activity will become completely clear. The preferred position of the child in sleep time remains embryonal. The same position is taken by the child in a time of restful wakefulness. Only in four-month-old children can we observe another position during sleep time.

The sense of this unique life state leaves no manner of doubt as to its nature. In the maternal womb the child's life activity is entirely restricted to autonomic functions and minimal animal functions. But sleep is a condition in which the first plane consists of vegetative processes and a more or less drastic reining in of animal functions. The sleeping newborn shows the comparative predominance of his vegetative system. The abundance and frequency of sleep in the newborn apparently constitutes a continuation of the behavior of the fetus to a certain degree; the usual state is, so far as we may speculate, much like dreaming. Sleep, from the genetic point of view, is the most primitive vegetative behavior. Genetically it precedes wakefulness, which develops from sleep. Thus the slumber of the newborn, as well as its feeding, occupies an intermediate place between the state of embryonic and postnatal development.

Finally, the animal functions of the newborn also leave no manner of doubt as to the fact that the child of this age occupies as it were a position on the border of intra- and extra-uterine development. On the one hand, he already has a series of motor reactions occurring in answer to internal and external stimuli. On the other, he is entirely devoid of the most basic feature of the animal—that is, the capacity for independent displacement in space. He has the capacity for independent motion, but he transports himself through space only with the aid of adults. His mother moves

[5] Silvio Canestrini (not "D. Canestrini"—this appears to be an error on Vygotsky's part) wrote a 1913 monograph on sleeping and waking in infants using a pneumograph (measuring breathing) and also brain pulses. Bernfeld also quotes this monograph, so Vygotsky may be using Bernfeld as his source.

[6] Jean Lhermitte (1877–1959) was the son of a well-known realist painter, Leon Lhermitte (there is a beautiful realist painting of Jean as an infant). Jean studied medicine and became interested in spinal injuries during World War I, which is why many different hallucinations, neck injuries, and neurological diseases are named after him (e.g., Lhermitte's syndrome, Lhermitte-Levy syndrome, Lhermitte-McAlpine syndrome, Lhermitte-Trelles syndrome). He wrote books telling priests how to distinguish between mental illness and demonic possession. Vygotsky is probably referring to his book *The biological foundations of psychology* (1925).

him, which likewise points to how he occupies a position intermediate between a fetus and a child standing on his feet.

The motility of the newborn raises a number of exceptionally instructive biological parallels. F. Doflein[7] divides the young of mammalians into four groups according to their decreasing dependence on the mother during the extra-uterine stage. In the first place should be put the marsupials, whose young are put by the mother in an external womb and who spend the beginning of their childhood in a pouch. Here we have, as it were, a gross anatomical expression of the transitional stage between intrauterine development and independent existence. In the second place are put hibernating animals whose young are often born blind and who carry on the beginning of their childhood in the den, again reminiscent of a transitional environment between the maternal womb and the external world. In the third place are put the nursing young which are carried around by their mother. All of these young have clasping instincts. Finally, in the last place should be placed the cursorial young, born quite developed, who soon after birth begin to run and to feed themselves with plants in addition to nursing.

In the human newborn child we observe a series of motions which are indubitably linked phylogenetically to the grasping reflex in the third group of mammalians. When a monkey offspring is born, it reflexively grasps the hair of the mother's body with all four limbs and hangs under her breasts with the spine downwards. The offspring remains in this state when asleep as well as waking. When the mother moves, it, being firmly connected to her, moves as well. We have in this instance as it were a functional mechanism which is manifested otherwise than in the marsupials, expressing the newborn's new dependency on the mother.

In the newborn human offspring, we likewise observe movements that are related to this reflex. If you put a finger or some long object into the hands of the newborn, the newborn will grasp it so tenaciously that the child can be lifted into the air and will hang in that position for about a minute. The affinity of this reflex with the grasping reflex of the infant ape is obvious. Such is also the meaning of the Moro reaction, known under the name of the grasping reflex and arising as a result of shaking the head.[8] First the hands and feet symmetrically diverge only to link up again in the form of an arc. The same movements of the newborn come in response to any strong and sudden stimulus, giving a well-known fear reaction expressed in

---

[7] Johann Franz Theodor Doflein (1873–1924) was a German zoologist who did extensive fieldwork in China, Japan, and the Far East and created a functionalist zoology, for example, by showing how penguins adapt to the environment in ways that are similar to seals. He was mostly interested in one-celled animals, but, as Vygotsky says, he also developed a taxonomy based on how the young are cared for (Doflein, 1910, 1914).

[8] The Moro reflex typically develops before birth and persists until the middle of infancy. Ernst Moro, the Austro-Hungarian doctor who discovered it, elicited it by slapping the baby's pillow, but it can be elicited by any sudden movement near the baby's head. The baby spreads his or her arms, then clasps them together, and usually starts to cry. Unlike the startle reflex discovered by Peiper, it persists even when you repeat the stimulus many times in a row.

grasping movements. According to A. Peiper,[9] fright reactions are equivalent to grasping reflexes in both humans and apes.

In this way, in these archaic rudiments of motion adaptations, we find the traces shared with all mammals, a unique stage of biological dependence of the newborn upon the mother, a dependence which continues after birth.

Finally, direct and indisputable evidence that the newborn period should be considered as a transitional period between uterine and extra-uterine development consists in the following. The last months of embryonic development can, in the case of premature birth, take place under the conditions of extra-uterine development, just as the first months of the newborn state can take place under uterine conditions of development in cases of delayed and postponed birth.

Sometimes a child is born post-term. If the normal period of pregnancy is ten lunar, or nine solar, months (280 days), it appears that the child who is born either prematurely or postmaturely may deviate from the normal term in one direction or in the other by forty days. A child may be born starting from the 24th and up to the 320th day, counting from the last menstruation. In exceptional cases, pregnancy may be prolonged up to the 326th day. In this way, the time for the birth of a viable child has a window of variation of approximately four months.

What does research indicate about the development of premature and postmature children? Briefly we can say that the extra one or two months of extra-uterine development for the premature child, like the extra one or two months of intra-uterine development in the postmature child, cannot in themselves cause any substantial changes in subsequent development. This means that the last two months of uterine and the first two months of extra-uterine development are so closely linked to each other by the very nature of the processes that take place in these periods that it is as if they were equivalent, the one to the other. In this way, according to Gesell, the postmature baby from the beginning presents an indubitable picture of generally accelerated development. This means that the extra month spent by the child in the womb of the mother also advances this extra-uterine development for a corresponding period. The coefficient of mental development must be worked out by adjusting for the one extra month of his uterine development.

In exactly the same way, a premature child proves to be viable even in that case where it remains in the maternal uterus for merely three quarters the (average—Trans.) period of time. The mechanisms of behavior at seven months are already almost ready for action and during the last two months of fetal life the tempo of development is somewhat slower. In this way the survival is ensured in cases of premature birth. A prematurely born child resembles for this reason a normal newborn to a greater degree than might be expected. However, given the course of development of a premature child, we must once again amend the coefficient of his mental development, counting the circumstance that the first two months of extra-uterine development the child was undergoing the unfinished embryological period.

[9]Albrecht Peiper (1889–1968) was a German pediatrician who studied neural activity in infants (Peiper, 1928). The Peiper Suspension test for reflexes is named after him, and so is the Peiper-Isbert reflex. He became a Nazi party member in 1937.

If we ask whether prematurity brings noticeable changes in mental development, in general the answer to this question must be negative.[10]

Research on premature and postmature children, we believe, confirms without any doubt the transitional character of the newborn period. However, from this fact it seems to us erroneous to draw the conclusion according to which the act of birth, such an indubitable and striking example of saltatory development, should be considered as a simple stage in the evolutionary sequence of uterine and extra-uterine development as has often been done by the partisans of evolutionistic views of child development. Proponents of this view, correctly seeing the sequence and connection between the two steps of development, do not notice the dialectical leap that the child performs, moving from one type of development to another. Gesell says that the most general conclusion we can base on research on premature and postmature children is that the development of behavior is carried out in a regular ontogenetic order regardless of the time of birth. There is, it appears, a solid substratum to development which cannot be particularly affected by birth time. Thanks to this, the general character of the curve of growth is the same for those children born at term and those that are premature. Or, simply put, a premature child, despite the fact that it is prematurely taken from the mother's womb, continues for some time in the development of a fetal type.

Such a conclusion seems to us unfounded. There is undeniably a profound continuity between the last months of intra-uterine development and the first months of the newborn. We have tried to illustrate this by analyzing some of the most important features of the newborn. We can point out as well some of the movements of the fetus in the maternal womb, which also tell us that the development of the embryonic period of the child's life is not restricted wholly to the vegetative processes. However, this indubitable continuity remains no more than the background against which, in the foreground, there appears as the primary basic moment not so much the resemblance as the difference between the embryonal and the postnatal state. Like every transition, the period of new birth is first of all a break with the old and a beginning of the new.

The task of the present paragraphs does not include a detailed description of the genesis and dynamics of the basic neoformation which occurs in the newborn period. For our purposes it is altogether sufficient to name this neoformation, to briefly point out that it has all of the typical features of neoformations of the critical

---

[10] The Russian *Collected Works* (p. 273) adds the following footnote:

"Studies have shown that the earliest conditional reflexes can be formed by the second to third week of life (N.I. Kasatkin, 1951)." (p. 413) The relevance (and even the accuracy) of this footnote to the text is not clear to us. Vygotsky has just said that the "second to third week of life" does not depend on the date of birth, and the date of birth can potentially occur anywhere in a window of nearly four months. Perhaps the Soviet editors were concerned that Vygotsky was understating the impact of the environment on the child and hence underestimating what early educational interventions could accomplish. This was a common criticism of Vygotsky at the time (e.g., Leontiev, 1935?/2005; c.f. van der Veer and Valsiner 1991, pp. 374–381) and remains a major theme today (c.f. prenatal and immediately postnatal programs such as "Baby Mozart" and "Baby Einstein").

ages, and thus to identify the starting point which forms the commencement of the subsequent development of the personality of the child.

If we attempt to define in general terms the central and basic neoformation of the newborn period, appearing first as a product of this step of development and constituting the starting moment of subsequent development of the personality, we may say that it is the individual psychic life of the newborn. Two points should be noted in this neoformation. Life inheres in the child already in the period of embryonic development. What is new in the newborn period is that this life becomes an individual existence, separate from the organism inside of which it was born, a life which, like each individual human being, is intertwined and interwoven into the social life of the people around the child. That is the first moment. The second moment consists in the individual life, being the first and most primitive form of existence of the child as a social being, constitutes at the same time a psychic life, for only psychic life can be part of the social life of the people surrounding the child.

The question of the content of psychic life of the newborn has given rise for a long time to great differences and disputes because the direct study of his psychic life is completely impracticable. Poets, philosophers, and psychologists have been inclined to ascribe to the mind of the newborn an overly complex content. So, Shakespeare lends, in the mouth of Lear, a deeply pessimistic sense to the first cry of the child.

"When we are born, we cry that we are come.

To this great stage of fools."

An analogous sense is attributed to the child's crying by A. Schopenhauer, who saw it as an argument for pessimism, proof that misery prevails at the very beginning of existence. I. Kant interpreted the cry of the newborn as a protest against the imprisonment of the human soul in the shackles of sensuality.

Researchers belonging to the reflexological school are inclined to reject the existence of all psychic life in the newborn, considering it as a living automaton, perceiving and acting entirely because of certain neural connections and devoid of any trace of psyche.

However, at the present time the vast majority of researchers are in agreement in acknowledging two basic propositions: (1) the newborn has to the most primitive degree the beginnings of psychic life, and (2) this psychic life is of a completely unique character. We shall examine both propositions.

Objections to acknowledging psychic life in the newborn are based usually on the fact that most of the centers of brain in the head of the newborn are immature. Particularly immature in the first place is the cerebral cortex, which, as is known, is closely related to the activity of consciousness. It is noteworthy that a neonate without a cerebral cortex is in the most important signs of life not much different from a normal one, at least for the first few days of living.

By itself, the fact of the immaturity of the central nervous system in the newborn seems beyond doubt. However, two moments compel us to recognize this argument as unfounded. We are accustomed to taking the cerebral cortex as the site of all of the manifestations of consciousness, and since in the newborn this organ is not yet functioning, we would have to conclude that no consciousness exists and that it has none. This conclusion would be compelling only if it could be established that all the manifestations of our consciousness are linked to the cerebral cortex. The facts which are at our disposal show that this is not quite true. The cerebral cortex is linked, it appears, only to the manifestations of the higher forms of conscious activity. The life of our drives, our instincts, and our simplest affects, in all likelihood, is linked more directly to subcortical centers which in some measure already function in the newborn.

Further, comparison between normal newborns and anencephalics indicates that merely for the most obvious manifestations of reflexes is there no noticeable difference between the one and the other. A more delicate comparison shows that a child who is born without the higher portions of the brain does not display any expressive motions. Therefore, it seems likely that a normal newborn not only is not merely a purely spinal-medullary being, as defined by R. Virchow,[11] but in general is not a purely paleo-encephalic being, that is, a being whose life is determined only by the ancient brain. There is reason to believe that the new brain is in some way already involved from the very beginning in the behavior of the newborn (K. Koffka).[12] According to some researchers, the greater helplessness of the human child compared to the offspring of animals is due to the fact that the ancient brain mechanisms of the human child are less autonomous in their functioning thanks to their links to still incompletely mature newer parts of the brain (N.M. Schelovanov).[13]

---

[11] Rudolf Virchow (1821–1902) was a founder of modern pathology, social medicine, and medican theorist. He discovered trichonosis, created the methods of autopsy still used today, and formulated the dictum that all cells come from other cells. However, he rejected Darwin (as well as his own student, Ernst Haeckl, who formulated the dictum that ontogenesis recapitulates phylogenesis). He also rejected the germ theory of disease and attributed all diseases to social inequality ("Medicine is a social science, and politics is nothing but medicine on a large scale"). He was elected to the Reichstag, where he was a strident critic of Bismarck's militarism; he supposedly responded to a duel challenge by asking Bismarck to choose from a pair of sausages, one of which was to be infected with the deadly parasites he had discovered. Bismarck, allegedly, declined.

[12] Kurt Koffka (1886–1941) was a Gestaltist; student (and experimental subject) of Max Wertheimer and colleague of Wolfgang Köhler. He believed most early learning is sensorimotor (i.e., rewards and punishment) but distinguished between this and learning through language. Vygotsky uses his work extensively but critically in *Thinking and Speech*, English *Collected Works*, Volume One (1987). Koffka took part in Luria's expeditions to Central Asia in but his conclusions were diametrically opposed to those of Luria. See Koffka, 1983.

[13] The "new brain" vs. "old brain" distinction is both a phylogenetic and an ontogenetic distinction. Phylogenetically, lower animals tend to have relatively small, smooth, and undeveloped "new brain" cerebral cortex, while the "old brain" medulla and the midbrain are relatively large, complex, and developed. Ontogenetically, as Vygotsky says here, the "new brain" remains unmyelinated for a long time after birth, and is therefore not as functional as the "old brain," which is responsible for the instinctive, independent mental life which Vygotsky gives as the neoformation of the neonatal crisis.

Nikolai Matveevich Schelovanov (Николай Матвеевич Щелованов, 1892–1981) was a reflexologist who specialized in brain activity. He was interested in problems of comparative psychology (i.e., comparing the development of humans and animals) and he developed a system of early education for infants still used in Russia today.

In this way, the condition of the nervous system of the newborn does not rule out the possibility of his psychic life but, on the contrary, suggests the rudiments of psyche, although completely different from the developed psyche of an adult or a child of an older age. Psychic life, predominantly linked to subcortical centers and related structurally and functionally to an insufficiently mature cortex, naturally must be quite different from the more serious forms of psychic life possible in the developed and mature central nervous system. The decisive argument in favor of acknowledging the rudiments of primitive psyche in the newborn is the fact that shortly after birth we observe all of the basic processes of life which in older children and adults are linked to psychic states. This is especially true of expressive motions that reveal psychic states of joy or elevated mood, grief and sorrow, anger and fear, surprise and hesitation. Here we should also include instinctive movements of the newborn related to hunger, thirst, satiation, satisfaction, and so on. Both groups of reactions occur in the newborn in such forms that make us acknowledge the presence of primitive psychic manifestations of this age.

However, as we have already said, this psychic life is sharply different in form from psychic life of a more developed type. Let us point out the basic differences.

W. Stern believes that in the newborn, alongside reflexes there must exist the first traces of consciousness, which soon are developed into a rich and multi-faceted psychic life. Of course, we may speak only of a rudimentary state of the psychic life of the newborn, from which it is necessary to exclude all of the intellectual and volitional phenomena which make up consciousness. There are no inborn representations, no valid apperceptions, that is, no understanding of external objects and processes as such, nor, finally, any conscious will or aspiration. All that we can assume with any justification is that there is some vague, unclear state of consciousness in which the sensory and the emotional features are still indivisibly fused in such a way that we can call them sensuous emotional states or emotionally colored states of sensation. There are pleasant or unpleasant emotional states observable already in the first days of life of the child, in his general appearance, in his facial expression, and in the character of his crying.

In a similar way the psychic life of the newborn is characterized by C. Bühler. The first contact of the child with the mother is so tight that we would rather speak of a cohesive existence than of mere contact. In just the way that the child in the act of birth is only physically separated from the mother, so too psychically he only slowly distinguishes the stimuli as coming from individual objects in the external world. If it is possible to formulate in this way the failure to objectify impressions on the part of the infant, he at first seems to experience states rather than objects. It is difficult to say at what age the child accepts movements, changes in place, etc. and at what age he starts to not only accept it all but experience the *perezhivanie* that someone is playing with him. We tend to think that in the first month for the child there does not exist anyone or anything, that he, rather, all stimuli and all the surroundings are experienced only as a subjective state.

We find, in this way, two substantial moments characterizing the uniqueness of the psychic life of the newborn. The first of these relates to the exclusive predominance of unsorted and unseparated *perezhivanie* representing, as it were, an alloy (i.e., a fusion—Trans.) of inclinations, affects, and sensations. The second characterizes the psyche of the newborn as not distinguishing the self and its *perezhivanie* from the perception of objective things, not yet differentiating social and physical objects. What remains is simply to indicate the third moment, which characterizes the psyche of the newborn in relation to the outside world.

It would be incorrect to imagine newborn perception of the world as chaotic, fragmentary, separate sensations: one of temperature, an intraorganic one, an auditory one, a visual one, a tactile one, and so on. Research has shown that the individuation of certain independent and separate perceptions is the product of much later development (K. Koffka). Still later in development emerges the capacity to individuate some components in a whole perception in the form of sensations. The first perceptions of the child present unarticulated impressions of the situation as a whole, where not only are there no separate individual objective moments of the situation, but there is no differentiation between the elements of perception and feeling. It is noteworthy as a fact that the newborn, long before showing the ability to react to separately perceived, disarticulated elements of the situation, begins to respond to the complex, emotionally colored, integrated whole. For example, the face of the mother and her expressive movements will call forth a reaction in the child long before the child is able to separate the perception of form, color, or size. In the initial perception of the newborn, all external impressions make up an indivisible unity with the coloration by affect or sensory tone of the perception. The child perceives a welcome or a threat, that is, expression in general, earlier than objective elements of external reality as such.

The basic law of perception in the newborn can be formulated in the following way: at first an amorphous perception of the situation as a whole is the background on the basis of which there stands out for the child a more or less defined and structured phenomenon which is perceived as a special quality in this background. The law of structuring or separating out the figure and the background constitutes, apparently, the most primitive feature of psychic life, forming the starting point of the subsequent development of consciousness.

In this way, we can build an initial overall understanding of the psychic life of the newborn. It remains for us to point out to what consequences this level of psychic life in the social behavior of the child leads. The newborn, as is easily understood, does not display any specific forms of social behavior. As has been shown in the studies of C. Bühler and H. Hetzer, the first communication of the child with people lies outside the newborn period. For this communication what is required are psychic processes, thanks to which a child becomes "aware" that someone is playing with him, thanks to which a child responds to another person differently than the child does to other surroundings. We may with some confidence speak for the first time of social impressions and reactions regarding the period between two months and three months, that is, beyond the newborn period. In this period the social life of the child is characterized by complete passivity. In his behavior as well as in his consciousness there is nothing which would speak to a social *perezhivanie* as such. This permits us to single out the newborn period, for a long time unanimously identified by biologists, as a unique stage in the social development of the child.

The psychic life of the newborn has all of the typical features of neoformations in the critical ages. As we pointed out, the neoformations of this type never lead to mature formations but are transitory and transitional, disappearing subsequently into a stable age. What is the neoformation of the newborn period? It is a unique form psychic life linked mainly to the subcortical areas of the brain. It is not retained as such, as a distinct, lasting acquisition of the child in later years. It blooms and withers within the narrow time limit that encompasses the newborn state. It does not, however, disappear without a trace, like some evanescent episode in child development. It merely loses, in the subsequent course of development, its independent existence and is included as a subordinate instance in a nervous and psychic formation of a higher order.

The question of the borders of the newborn state is still to the highest degree debatable: some authors consider the newborn period equal to one month (K. Lashley, Troitsky, Hutinel) and others, like K. Vierordt, limit it to one week in all. For the end of this period the scarring of the umbilical cord wound or the obliteration of Botallo's duct and the umbilical vein is usually taken. Finkelstein and Reiss consider the upper limit of this period to be the moment when the child recovers his initial weight after physiological loss (ten to twenty-one days).[14] P.P. Blonsky proposes to consider the seventh postnatal day, when the physiological loss of weight stops and is replaced by an increase in weight, as the borderline for the newborn state. It is impossible, however, to disagree with M.S. Maslov that such formations which are unlikely to be useful, as well as such processes which do not affect the general condition of the child like the discarding of the umbilical cord and the obliteration of Botallo's duct, cannot be considered in any way the limits of the

---

[14] Karl Spencer Lashley (1890–1958) was an American behaviorist psychologist. A student of Watson, he wanted to demonstrate that memories were simple areas of the brain where impressions were recorded by teaching rats to run mazes, and then destroying the parts of the brain where he believed the memories to have been stored. He succeeded in demonstrating exactly the opposite: if part of the brain is destroyed, another part simply takes over its functions.

Matvei Mikhailovich Troitsky (Троицкий Матвей Михайлович, 1835–1899) was a professor of psychology and philosophy at Moscow State University; he was much influenced by English associationist psychology (e.g., Alexander Bain).

Victor Henri Hutinel (1849–1933) was a French pediatrician. He wrote a standard five-volume work on the diseases of childhood, and had liver disease named after him.

Karl von Vierordt (1818–1884) was a German physician who created the first tools for measuring blood pressure. He also studied psychological topics like time sense.

Botallo's duct (the ductus arteriosus) is a blood vessel that allows the fetus's blood to bypass the lungs by connecting the left pulmonary artery (that is, the blood vessel which takes blood to the lungs) with the descending aorta (that is, the blood vessel which takes blood from the lungs). It normally closes at birth, when the baby begins to breathe air.

The umbilical vein is the blood vessel which carries oxygen and food from the mother to the fetus. Like Botallo's duct it is obliterated at birth and like the rest of the umbilical cord it takes about a week to disappear.

Finkelstein may refer to Harry Finkelstein (1865–1939) an orthopedic surgeon who created Finkelstein's test for "mommy's thumb," the pain that many mothers get in their wrists. "Reiss" may refer to the American pediatrician Oscar Reiss, who was an early advocate for immunization.

newborn period. M.S. Maslov believes that if we wish to define this period we need to take the totality of anatomo-physiological traits and features, as well as the whole of metabolism. It has been found that in this period the child is distinguished by a unique metabolism and has a unique condition of the blood, related to features of the immune system and anaphylaxis.[15] All of this, taken together, says that the period of the newborn extends far beyond the discarding of the umbilical cord and in all cases last for not less than three weeks, passing imperceptibly, without a sharp boundary, into the breastfeeding period by the second month.

As we see, there is every basis to consider that the newborn period is characterized by a unique general biological picture, that the newborn lives a completely specific life. But for reasons which we have discussed in detail in the preceding chapter as the criterion for distinguishing any age only the basic and central neoformation that characterizes a given stage in the social development of the personality of the child will serve. Therefore, it seems to us that in determining the boundaries of the neonatal state, what ought to be used is those data which characterize the psychic and social condition of the newborn. The closest match to this criterion is the data regarding the higher nervous activity of the child, most directly linked to his psychic and social life. From this point of view, the research of M. Denisova and N. Figurin[16] shows that by the end of the first or the beginning of the second month, a turning point in the development of the child arrives.

As a symptom of the new period, the authors consider the appearance of a smile to conversation, that is, the first specific reaction of the child to the human voice. The researchers C. Bühler and H. Hetzer showed that the first social reaction of the child, indicating a general change in his psychic life, is observed on the border of the first and second month of life. By the end of the first month, they point out the cry of one child evokes the cry of another. Between the first and second month the child responds to the sound of a human voice with a smile. All this suggests that here is the upper limit of the newborn period, traversing which the child arrives at a new age stage of development.

References

Blunden, A. (2017). The germ cell of Vygotsky's science. In C. Ratner & D. N. H. Silva (Eds.), *Vygotsky and Marx* (pp. 132–145). Routledge.

Bühler, C., Hetzer, H., & Tudor-Hart, B. (1927). *Soziologische und psychologische Studien über das erste Lebensjahr*. Fischer.

[15] Anaphylaxis is an extreme allergic reaction that sometimes results in infant death during the first week of life. It is associated with high levels of histamine in the blood.

[16] M.P. Denisova (М. П. Денисова) and N.L. Figurin (Н. Л. Фигурин), along with Schelovanov were reflexologists—students of Vladimir Bekhterev, Pavlov's great rival. They published articles in *Pedology*, the journal edited by Blonsky and then Vygotsky. This is probably a reference to their 1929 article, "Some results reflexological study of behavioral development of the child from birth to 1 year."

Doflein, F. (1910, 1914). *Tierbau und Tierleben in ihrem Zusammenhang betrachtet*; 2 volumes, (with Richard Hesse). Leipzig and Berlin: Druck und Verlag von B.G. Teubner.
Leontiev, A. N. (1936?/2005). Study of the environment in the pedological works of L.S. Vygotsky. *Journal of Russian and East European Psychology, 43*(4), 8–28. https://doi.org/10.1080/10610405.2005.11059254
Koffka, K. (1983). The Russian-Uzbekistan expedition. In H. Harrower (Ed.), *Kurt Koffka: An Unwitting SelfPortrait* (pp. 143–161). University Presses of Florida.
Lhermitte, J. (1925). *Les fondements biologiques de la psychologie*. Editions Gauthier-Villars. Science et civilisation.
Peiper, A. (1928). *Die Hirntätigkeit des Säuglings*. Springer.
van der Veer, R., & Valsiner, J. (1991). *Understanding Vygotsky: A quest for synthesis*. Blackwell.
Vygotsky, L. S. (1997). *Collected works vol. 4*. Plenum.
Vygotsky, L. S. (1998). *Collected works vol. 5*. Plenum.

Chapter 6
The Age of Infancy

Outline of Chapter 6: The Age of Infancy

As we mentioned in the outline for the previous chapter, this material originally formed part of a single chapter called "The Age of Infancy," in which Chap. 5 was merely a prologue. *The Collected Works* in Russian informs us that the manuscript was found in the Vygotsky family archives but that the first two sections were missing. The editors mention some studies which appear to corroborate Vygotsky's account of infancy, but chide him for underestimating the ability of infants to form conditional reactions. They also remind us of the importance of the influence of the environment on the infant, as if seeking to counteract Vygotsky's own emphasis.

That emphasis is soundly on the emerging influence of the infant on the environment. Vygotsky ended the last chapter with the emergence of interest in the environment and the demise of the passive state of physiological separation and biological dependence that brought about the social situation of development in birth. Vygotsky commences this chapter with a new social situation of development; he continues with the social and neurological factors (backgrounded in birth and now foregrounded in infancy) that bring the neoformation into being; he then defines and delimits the neoformation that solves and dissolves the social situation of development (at least from the child's point of view); finally, he ends this chapter with a critical review of competing theories, from the most environmentalist to the most solipsistic.

I. **The Social Situation of Development in the Age of Infancy**

   1. The apparent asociality of the infant. The infant appears, at least to a superficial empirical eye, to be more of a social object than a social actor: speechless, passive, and preoccupied with simple needs like feeding, sleeping, and positioning. This misleading passivity in social relations gives rise to all of the incorrect theories of infancy to be critically reviewed at the end of the chapter.

This chapter is translated from material in the Russian *Collected Works* of 1984.

L. S. Vygotsky, *L.S. Vygotsky's Pedological Works. Volume 2.*, Perspectives in Cultural-Historical Research 10, https://doi.org/10.1007/978-981-16-1907-6_6

2. The real pansociality of the infant. In fact, the infant is a maximally social being because these simple life needs (food, rest, and comfort) can only be satisfied through being "intertwined" with caring adults.
3. The limitations of infant sociality. But the infant is not yet "interwoven" with the culture because the infant entirely lacks speech. As a result, the scope of the child's sociality is entirely nonverbal and interpersonal.
4. The social situation of development: maximal sociality and minimal speech. This contradiction—between maximal sociality and minimal sociocultural communication—constitutes the child's social situation of development in infancy.

II. **The Genesis of the Basic Neoformation in Infancy.**

1. The dynamics of infancy. Vygotsky commences with a discussion of changes, both between the first two age periods of life and within the second.
2. The genesis of higher brain centres. Vygotsky notes that these inter-age and intra-age changes appear to coincide with important changes in the brain, both quantitative and qualitative.
3. The genesis of instinct, habit, and intellect. Vygotsky now demonstrates that infancy includes at least three qualitatively different relationships between perception and behavior. He first notes two important aspects: their primordial, primitive unity and their potential for complex recombination in a higher structure. Then, Vygotsky suggests three qualitatively different structures for the unity of perception and behavior that can occur in infancy, namely the higher structures of behavior that Bühler proposed: instinct, habit, and intellect.
4. The genesis of social behavior. The higher brain centres and the links between sensory perception and behavior examined in the previous parts are external and internal lines of development which all have to do with the site of development, that is, the child himself. Vygotsky now ends this section with a consideration of the form of behavior that is closest to the source of development, namely social behavior.

III. **The Basic Neoformation of the Age of Infancy.**

1. What is new? In the previous section, Vygotsky stated the prerequisites for the emergence of the basic neoformation in the form of lines of development in the brain and in behavior. In this section, he will sketch the outlines of that basic neoformation. In the next section, Vygotsky will attack the Piagetian view which holds that the child is not fundamentally oriented to real satisfaction of real, physical needs. In this section, however, he begins by arguing that the helplessness of the infant is only overcome thanks the real satisfaction of real needs.
2. The Great We. Vygotsky now defines and delimits the basic neoformation of the child's consciousness, which corresponds exactly to this path through another person. He calls it the "Ur Wir," a German term which means a "proto-We" or perhaps a "Grand-We," by which he means a form of consciousness in

which the child does not differentiate between his own consciousness and that of others; the child simply assumes that just as we share the world of perception and the world of planned activity, we must also share the world of consciousness that subtends perception and activity. It is a "proto-We" in the sense that it is a "we" that exists even before there is an "I" and a "you" or an "I" and a "he": It is a "Grand-We" in the sense that it is the ancestor of the world of individuals voluntarily collaborating which will eventually develop. Vygotsky draws on two researchers to elucidate this concept:

a. Evidence for the differentiation of infant pansociality. Vygotsky now looks for experimental evidence of a "Great We" and finds it in the work of Fajans, a student of Kurt Lewin. We remember that Kurt Lewin found certain objects had "vectors" or "fields of attraction" that suggested activity affordances: for example, a door would attract children to open it, and a rock would attract children to sit on it (but some rocks would actually lose its attraction for very young children as soon as they turned their backs on it to sit!).
b. Evidence against the gradual socialization of infant individualism. To conclude this section—and to introduce the necessity for the next section on the competing theories of infancy—Vygotsky notes critically that most theories of infancy turn the social development of the infant inside out.

IV. **Basic Theories of Infancy.**

1. Reflexology. Vygotsky begins his critical review of theories of infancy at the extreme environmentalist end of the axis environment-child, with the theory he criticized above that interprets the infant's behavior as entirely reducible to reflexes.
2. Three stages. Bühler's theory, which was the origin of his own distinction between instincts, habits, and intellect, takes three steps in the direction of the child's subjectivity. But like the reflexological theory, it fails one of the key tests that Vygotsky sets for any viable theory of infancy: the ability to pinpoint theoretically the distinction between a speechless infant and an animal.
3. Structure. The Gestaltist tradition in psychology correctly notes the starting point of infant development. Once again, however, the theory overgeneralizes a single valid insight; if we reduce the whole of development to structure, we find that the way in which a chimpanzee solves a problem such as fetching a fruit with a stick and the way the same problem is solved by a human is structurally identical, and therefore structural theory also fails the key test. Just as development in the means of development disappears when we reduce all development to the formation of reflexes, there can be no development if all development is reducible to the formation of structures.
4. Subjectivism. Vygotsky now turns to a theory which does recognize the specificity of infant development, but which explains it as the slow extension of the ego through the active expansion of the radius of subjectivity. This means that the child experiences the world as a set of material processes

(i.e., doings) rather than relational processes (i.e., beings). In other words, the child experiences activities with objects as events rather than as things; the child's world is made up of processes rather than participants. This deontic rather than epistemic infancy is interpreted in an even more extreme fashion by Piaget in the final group of theories.

5. Solipsism. Vygotsky concludes this chapter as he began it, with the argument that what has been interpreted as the asociality of the infant is in fact the infant's pansociality. This pansocial Ur Wir consciousness is a true stable neoformation in that it forms an inseparable part of and plays an independent role in many higher social activities. For example, when we sing in chorus, when we dance in groups, when we march in protests, or when we play or even just watch a game of soccer, we can feel that the Ur Wir still exists and exerts a great force in social and in psychological life.

Chapter 6: The Age of Infancy

The Social Situation of Development in the Age of Infancy[1]

At first sight, it might appear easy to show that the infant is an asocial being, either completely or very nearly so. He lacks even the most basic means of social communication—human speech. His life activity is largely limited to the satisfaction of simple life needs. He constitutes to a great degree an object rather than a subject, that is, an active participant, in social relations. This easily gives the impression that infancy is the asocial period of child development, that the infant is a purely biological entity, utterly deprived of specifically human properties, and particularly the most basic among them—sociality. It is this view which lies at the foundation of a series of erroneous theories of the age of infancy, to which we turn below.

For in truth, both this impression and its foundation in this view of an absolutely asocial infant constitute a grave misconception. Careful research shows that we encounter in the child in the age of infancy a completely specific and utterly unique sociality, one which stems from the ineffable and unrepeatable social situation of development, the uniqueness of which is defined by two basic moments. The first of these consists of that which strikes our glance first, out of all of the features of the infant, that which we usually characterize as a complete biological helplessness. The infant is incapable of satisfying a single one of life's needs by himself. The most elementary and basic needs of life for the infant can be met in no other way than with the help of adults who care for him. Neither the feeding nor the movement

[1]As we mentioned at the beginning of the outline of this chapter, the Russian *Collected Works* editors say that the first part of Vygotsky's manuscript is missing, so they begin the section on the newborn with the number "2." The present section on the age of infancy is, accordingly, numbered "3" in the Russian *Collected Works* (and, somewhat confusingly, "2" in the English edition). To avoid confusion, we have simply eliminated the numbers.

of the infant, not even turning him from one side to the other, can be accomplished in any other way than through cooperation with adults. This path through the other, through the adult—this is the basic path of activity for the child of this age. Absolutely everything in the behavior of the infant is intertwined and interwoven into the social. Such is the objective situation of his development. It only remains for us to find what it is that corresponds to this objective situation in the consciousness of the subject of development, that is, of the infant.

No matter what happens to the infant, he always finds himself in a situation linked to caring provided to him by adults. Thanks to this there arises a completely unique form of social relations between the child and the adult persons in his environment. Above all, thanks to the immaturity of the biological functions, none of what will subsequently fall within the sphere of individual adaptations of the child and none of what is to be carried out independently can be done except through others, except through a situation of collaboration. Thus, the child's first contact with reality (even when performing the most elementary biological functions) is entirely socially mediated.

Objects appear and disappear from the child's purview always thanks to the participation of adults. The child always moves through space in someone's arms. Changing his position, even simply turning over, is once again woven into a social situation. Eliminating irritations which annoy the child and satisfying his basic needs always take place (in the same way) through others. Thanks to all of this, there arises a unique and unrepeatable dependency of the child upon the adult which permeates and pervades, as we have said, the most apparently individual biological needs and requirements of the infant. The dependency of the infant upon adults creates the utterly unique character of the relations of the child to reality (and to himself): these relations are always mediated by others, always refracted through the prism of relations with another human being.

In this way, the relations between the child and reality from the very beginning are social relations. In this sense, the infant can be called a maximally social being. Any relationship of the child's, even the simplest, to the outside world always turns out to be a relation refracted through relations with other humans. The whole life of the infant is organized in such a way that in every situation, visibly or invisibly, another human is present. This can be expressed in another way by saying that every relation of the child to things is a relationship carried out with the aid of or by means of other humans.

The second feature which characterizes the social situation of development in the age of infancy is that with this maximum dependency upon adults, with all the infant's behavior being completely intertwined with and woven into sociality, the child still lacks the basic means of social communication in the form of human speech. It is this second aspect in conjunction with the first that lends a peculiarity to the social situation in which we find the infant. The whole organization of life compels maximal communication with adults. But this communication exists as nonverbal communication, often silent communication of an utterly unique order. The contradiction between the maximally social infant (the situation in which the infant finds himself) and minimal possibilities for communication lays the basis for the whole of the child's development during the age of infancy.

The Genesis of the Basic Neoformation in the Age of Infancy

Prior to proceeding with an analytical review of the complex composition of the processes of development in the age of infancy, we wish to preface this with a general summation and a characterization of the dynamics of this age.

The beginning of the age of infancy coincides with the end of the newborn crisis. The turning point is found between the second and the third month in the life of the child. At this time we may observe new manifestations in all areas. With the culmination of the sudden drop in the curve of daily quantity of sleep and the termination of the maximum amount of negative reactions, food intake is no longer done so greedily, so that the child now sometimes interrupts feeding and opens his eyes. There is every precondition for activities that go beyond sleeping, feeding, and crying. In comparison with the neonate, there is a diminishment of the frequency of reactions to individual excitations. There is far less internal interference observed in sleep and wincing when exposed to external excitations. In contrast, the activity of the child becomes more diverse and extensive.

As new forms of behavior at this time, there is the addition of experimental play, babble, the first active sensory organ activity, the first active reactions to positioning, the first coordination of two simultaneously acting organs, and the first social reactions—expressive motions linked to functional pleasure and surprise.

Everything points to this: that the passivity with which the neonate related to the world has now given place to reciprocating interest. The latter becomes most obvious in the new manifestations of perceptual activity in the waking state. As we have said, in place of passivity, out of which the child emerges only when exposed to strong sensory stimulation, there is now a propensity to have an influence over stimuli. What is new here is the impact on attention of sensory stimuli, of the child's own movements, of his own sounds, and of sound in general, and of attention to other humans. Only now does an interest in all of this make possible further development in each separate area (Bühler et al., 1931, p. 219).[2]

---

[2]Vygotsky is referring to the 1931 Russian translation of: Bühler, Charlotte; Hildegard Hetzer und Beatrix Tudor-Hart (1927). *Soziologische und psychologische Studien über das erste Lebensjahr*. Jena: Fischer.

Beatrix Tudor-Hart (1903–1979) was, along with Hildegard Hetzer, a research assistant of Charlotte Bühler in Vienna. She returned to the United Kingdom and taught at the Beacon Hill School founded by Bertrand Russell. She then had a very successful career as a teacher and principal in a number of experimental cooperative schools. In the 1930s she founded the Fortis Green School, which was the first school in Britain owned and run by parents and teachers. Later, she wrote several books on preschool and elementary school education, including *Toys, Play and Discipline in Childhood* (1955) and *Learning to Live* (1963).

H. Wallon[3] also notes that the second month opens a new period in the development of the child, in which a purely affective type of motorics[4] gradually gives way to an activity approaching in character the sensorimotor. At the same time, as established by sensory synergy (the disappearance of strabismus), the face assumes an expression of attentiveness and availability for the perception of external influences. The child begins to take in visual impressions, and soon he begins to listen—at first, it is true, only to sounds that emanate from himself. He reaches for objects and touches them with his hands, lips, and tongue, displaying true activeness. At this time, there is the development of the makings of manual activeness, which has such a major significance for the whole of psychic development. All of these reactions, correctly oriented, are directed to adaptations, and they become positive; so long as there is not too much excitation, they do not descend to the negative or organic forms that prevailed in previous stage.

In this way, at the beginning of this period, the child shows an especial interest in the outside world and the capacity to actively go beyond direct drives and instinctive tendencies. For the child, it is as if the external world has been discovered. This new relationship to reality signifies the beginning of the infant period—or rather of its first stage.

The second stage of the age of infancy is also marked by a drastic change in the relation of the child to the external world. A turning point of the same significance is observed between 5 and 6 months. From that time, sleep and wakefulness occupy equal amounts of time. Between 4 and 5 months, the daily quantity of neutral reactions increases dramatically, along with the duration of positive expressive movements during the daytime. Fluctuations between the preponderance of single

[3] Henri Wallon (1879–1962) was a French psychologist and a Marxist (he served as Minister of Education in the underground Resistance Government formed by the uprising against Nazi rule in 1944). He was a central figure in reestablishing public school education after the war, and remained a central figure in French educational psychology for the whole of the postwar period (although less important in Switzerland because of the influence of Piaget). His periodization scheme is quite close to Vygotsky's (and thus quite distant from Piaget's).

[4] Vygotsky uses the term моторика here. It is tempting to translate this as "motor skills," and that is certainly how we would translate the term if Piaget was using it to describe a stage of infant development. But in the next sentence, Vygotsky includes strabismus, when the eyes do not focus on the same point (e.g., in cross-eyedness). Many infants are born with strabismus, which can interfere with depth perception; this is poorly described as a "motor skill." In fact, the sensorimotor stage about which Piaget wrote is yet to come; instead, Vygotsky is referring to Wallon (e.g., 1943, p. 129, 1949, p. 194), who uses "inquiétude motrice" to describe infant hunger and "connexions motrices" to describe feeding; in English this would be "motoric uneasiness" and "motoric connections" or "motoric links," that is, neurological links and not nascent ability or knowledge. Moreover, Vygotsky is referring to Wallon in Russian, which does have a perfectly good single word for this, a word we have chosen to render as "motorics." This has two disadvantages. First of all, the word is not strictly English (although it could be, since "motoric" is an English adjective). Secondly, it does not seem to describe pathology very well. So when Vygotsky speaks of defective motorics (e.g., persistent strabismus), we will translate моторика as an impaired or degraded "motility." Like the Russian word, "motility" does refer to the self-propulsion faculty of an organism (as opposed to "mobility" which is more generally a capacity for passively being moved as well as a capacity for active motion).

reactions and impulsive movements on the one hand, and that of prolonged processes of behavior on the other, extend up to 5 months. Among the new forms of behavior at this time, we see, *inter alia*, the first assured defensive movements, assured ostension, the first lively outbursts of joy, cries at the failure of intentional movements, and also, possibly, the first wishes, experimental acts, social reactions to peers, and searches for missing toys. All of these forms of behavior speak to a particular activeness which transcends responding to an excitation, an active quest for stimulation, active employment, which becomes evident in the simultaneous growth in the daily quantity of spontaneous reactions. As it appears, these facts largely cannot be explained simply by reciprocating interest. We must assume that its place has been taken by an active interest in the surroundings.

We could add to this summary characterization of the second stage of the age of infancy an essential feature: It consists in the appearance of imitation. In the first stage of the age of infancy, early forms of imitative movements, vocal reactions, etc., as several authors have claimed, do not occur. What has been noted by psychologists as early imitation of movements (opening the mouth—W. Preyer[5]) or sounds (W. Stern) are only apparent imitations. For up to 5 months or even longer, no imitation of any kind can be obtained. Obviously, imitation is possible only when motivated by a conditional reflex.[6]

Proceeding from what was said above with regard to periods, we may in the first year of life distinguish a period of passiveness, a period of receptive interest, and a period of active interest which present a gradual transition to activeness. A noteworthy turning point is the 10th month, when, with the disappearance of aimless movements, we may observe in the making the future development of more complex forms of behavior: the first utilization of tools and the usage of words to express a wish. The child begins a new period, which will end already outside the first year of his life. This period is the crisis at 1, which is a connecting link between infancy and early childhood.

This summary characterization of the basic stages and bordering periods of the age of infancy does not pursue any other aim than to create a very broad presentation of the external picture of development in this beginning stage. To study the basic patterns of development in the age of infancy, we must necessarily divide the complex process of its self-composition, analytically consider its most important

[5] W. T. Preyer (1841–1897) was an English physiologist who studied and worked in Germany (Heidelberg and then Jena). He wrote *Die Seele des Kindes* ("The Soul of the Child"), one of the first books of child psychology. Preyer was a staunch Darwinian, much interested in Fechner's "psychophysics," which constituted the first quantitative study of the relationship between stimulus and sensation.

[6] This appears to contradict the editors of the Russian language *Collected Works*, who argue that conditional reflexes occur in the first or second week of life (see Footnote 11 in Chap. 5). But it also appears to contradict Vygotsky's own statement, at the end of Chap. 5, to the effect that a child at only a month or 2 of age responds to a cry with a cry and smiles at the sound of a familiar voice. Perhaps it is useful to keep in mind that Vygotsky has a definition of "imitation" that includes construing its goal or purpose. Where the sense of an action is not understood, Vygotsky refers to only "apparent" or "seeming" imitation—a mere copy of real imitation.

aspects with complex internal dependencies of one upon another, and in this way find a path which leads to the emergence of the basic neoformation of this age. We must begin with the most primary, the most independent, process—the growth and development of the major organic systems, which constitute the direct continuation of the embryonic period of development and serve as prerequisites for other, more highly placed, aspects of the development of the child's personality.

By the moment of birth, the infant brain has already been formed in its basic components (form, positioning of the separate components, and their mutual links). However, the cerebrum of the brain is also characterized at this moment as profoundly immature, both in its structural and in its functional relations. This immaturity is so eye-catching that it has given rise to the assertion, on the part of R. Virchow, that the infant is a purely spinal-medullary being, with behavior in which the cerebrum does not take any part. This theory was not supported in the light of further research—the basic results of which we now present.

The first and most blatant expression of the immaturity of the cerebrum of the brain we see in the fact of the extremely rapid growth of cerebral substance in the child. According to O. Pfister,[7] by the fourth or fifth month, the weight of the brain doubles. Further increase does not proceed so quickly. According to L.L. Volpin,[8] the brain doubles in weight by 8 months, and by the end of the year, it has increased two and a half times. Later the growth slows, so that by 3 the weight of the brain has tripled compared to the weight of the newborn brain. This indicates that the most enhanced growth in the brain takes place in the first year of life, a time when the increase in brain substance weight is equal to the build-up in all the subsequent years taken together.

However, by itself the sum of brain weight still has little to say about the inner development of the central nervous system. To answer this question it is necessary to turn to the consideration of development of the most important sections and systems of the cerebrum of the brain. The most remarkable feature of the function of the central nervous system in the age of infancy is that the motorics of the child in the first months of life are dominated by primitive motor reactions that in adults are inhibited and revealed only in pathological conditions. By the end of the first year, there still persist significant mechanisms that are characteristic of quadrupeds. With the further development of higher centres these atavistic movements are inhibited, but under conditions of illness they can be disinhibited and discovered at a later age.

In this way, the motorics of the newborn and the infant differ in three quite exceptional features: (1) The movements specific to the infant completely disappear in the course of subsequent development. (2) These movements are in their

---

[7] Oskar Pfister (1873–1956), an early colleague of Sigmund Freud, Eugen Bleuler, and Carl Jung, was a Swiss Lutheran minister who tried to apply psychoanalysis to Christian theology.

[8] L.L. Volpin is listed as the author of a Russian paper published in 1902 on weight data on the growth of the brain in children. Note that all of these claims about brain weight gain have been supported by modern research which is not limited to studying autopsy data: if anything, Vygotsky somewhat underestimates brain growth in the first 2 years of life, which is usually around 350% (Brodal, 2016: 155).

character archaic, atavistic, and ancient in the phylogenetic sense of this word and may be compared to ancient phylogenetic stages of the development of the central nervous system. In this way, it has been suggested, the development of the brain of the child might observe the transitional stages of phylogenesis: from the fishes, which lack the striatum (the striped corpus) and which function only with the pallidium (the pale corpus), to the amphibians, in which the former has already reached a significant stage of development (Maslov[9]). (3) Finally, these specific parts of infant motorics that disappear in the course of development display analogies not only to phylogenetically ancient functions but also to pathological motoric symptoms observed in later ages with organic and functional lesions of the central nervous system. All the descriptions of infant motility are filled with such analogies between the motorics of the infant and pathological motility such as athetosis, chorea, and other nervous disorders.

The three features above may be explained only in the light of basic laws of the history of development and construction of the nervous system. Three of these laws are of paramount significance for the problem that interests us. We present them as formulated by E. Kretschmer.

The Conservation of Lower Centres as Discrete Stages

In the history of development, the lower, older centres and arcs[10] are not simply pushed to one side with the gradual formation of the higher centres, but work on in union with them as subordinate instances, run under the control of higher, historically younger, centres, so that in an undamaged nervous system they cannot usually be independently discerned.

---

[9]This does not refer to the American psychologist Abraham Maslow (who created the idea of a pyramid of hierarchically ordered needs crowned by self-actualization) but rather to the Russian pediatrician, Mikhail Stepanovich Maslov (Михаил Степанович Маслов, 1885–1961). He published clinical lectures on childhood illness in 1924, and Vygotsky cites him in his work on belly button formation in neonates.

[10]The "reflex arc" (and also the "subcortical arc of action" Vygotsky refers to below) refers to the "arc" created by a sensory motor neural impulse which simply "jumps" to a motor nerve without actually entering the brain or the cerebral cortex. It is this which allows a medullar-spinal frog to catch flies, and it is also this which accounts for human reflex actions, such as removing your hand from a hot stove before you even feel pain.

Vygotsky uses the term подчиненные инстанции which we have translated quite literally as "subordinated instances." The word "instance" here means something like "moment": a holistic structure in itself which becomes part of another one (the way that a clause becomes a subordinate clause in a long sentence). A previously independent function becomes a subordinated instant or a moment of a more complex one, the way that the instinctive salivation of a dog is a lower, historically older, and instant in the complex operation of the dog's feeding by a human. Not only the infant's hunger but the whole of the neoformation of infancy, the child's "independent, instinctual" life linked to the midbrain is similar: it lives on, but only as dependent and noninstinctual life now controlled from the cortex.

The transfer of functions upwards. However, the subordinate centres do not retain their original type of functioning in the history of the development, but give up a substantial portion of their previous functions to the higher, new centres being constructed on them. (Foerster, M. Minkovsky, and others).[11] So, the spinomedullar frog, which has been surgically deprived of its cerebral functions and retains only its spinal-medullar centres, can perform very complex and relatively expedient actions, such as the scratching reflex,[12] in such a way that some have spoken outright of a spinomedullar soul. Such developed functions in humans are proper to the brain alone, particularly the cortex of the large brain, and with a rupture in connection they can no longer be implemented by the medulla, which in humans functions only very primitively and fragmentarily as an independently acting body.

The emancipation of the lower centres. If the higher centre is functionally weakened or cut off from the subordinate centres as the result of shock, infirmity, or injury, the overall function of the nervous apparatus does not simply cease but is transferred to a subordinate instance, which becomes independent and displays to us all the surviving elements of the previous type of functioning. We have already seen, as has been said, how a human spinal medulla separated from the brain retains a tonic-clonic reflex phenomenon of a primitive kind.[13] And the same regularities

---

[11] It seems probable that the reference to "M." Minkowski is incorrect (like the previous reference to "D. Canestrini") and that either Eugene Minkowski (1885–1971) or Oskar Minkowski is meant. Eugene was a phenomenologist, close to Bergson, who was a student of Bleuler and who worked on the loss of psychological functions in wartime. But it is more likely that Vygotsky means Oskar Minkowski (1858–1931), who specialized in experiments on dogs in which various organs were destroyed surgically, and is best known for his work on the pancreas. The only "M. Minkowski" who might qualify would be too young and in the wrong profession—the famous conductor Marc Minkowski, who was Eugene's grandson.

Otfrid Foerster (1873–1941) was a German doctor, a student of Wernicke and Babinsky, who did his thesis on typhoid fever. Although he was not trained as a neurosurgeon, during World War I he had patients who suffered epilepsy as a result of gunshot wounds to the head. He would give them local anesthetic and then find the areas of the cortex which caused epilepsy by poking with electrified needles. When he found the area, he would cut it out of the brain, and his cuts were delicate enough not to cause damage. By doing this to many patients, he was able to develop the first "map" of the cerebral cortex.

[12] If you scratch a dog's belly, you often get an apparently sympathetic movement from the hind leg called a "scratching reflex," as if the dog were trying to produce the effect that you are producing. Similarly, a frog, even one whose brain has been destroyed, will scratch with its hind leg if you apply an irritant to its body. Ukhtomsky, who is probably one of the others who Vygotsky refers to here, used this as evidence for his theory of development as the discovery of one "dominant" reaction that is able to overcome others. This theory is related to Vygotsky's own theory of developmental periods that culminate in a central neoformation.

[13] Vygotsky is apparently referring to Virchow's work on the spine and the medulla, in which Virchow speculated that the newborn child is essentially a "spinal-medullar" being, like a frog whose brain has been destroyed. As we saw, Vygotsky rejected this view because consciousness is not simply located in the cortex.

"Tonic" and "clonic" describe two phases of an epileptic seizure—the tonic phase is the first phase, in which the muscles suddenly contract and the person falls, while the clonic phase is the phase of convulsions. Here, Vygotsky apparently just means the kinds of nervous signals that are given by the spinal cord during muscle spasms.

are repeated with the higher, not yet anatomically differentiated, cortical and subcortical arcs of action. We see this especially in hysteria and catatonia when in violation of the higher psychic functions of the intentional will, the patient will often function in a psychomotoric functioning mode, lower from the point of view of historical development, which takes over the leadership mechanism, a mode which we will later consider as a hypobulic mechanism, as a lower layer of higher volitional processes. This general neurobiological law can be formulated in the following way: if within the psychomotor sphere, the action of a higher instance becomes functionally weak, the proximal lower instance becomes independent, with its own primitive laws.

To these three basic laws it is necessary to add yet another law, first formulated by L. Edinger, who in the process of studying animals found that in principle all mechanisms, beginning with the end of the spinal medulla (which relates as well to the initial brain) and ending with the olfactory nerves, are in higher and lower vertebrates structured identically, that, consequently, whether we speak of humans or fish, the basis of all the simple functions is absolutely identical for the whole series.[14]

The regularities we have outlined, appearing in the history of the construction of the nervous system in onto- and in phylogenesis, permit us to explain the main noteworthy features of the functions of the brain in the age of infancy.

If we give up the view according to which the infant has an exclusively spinomedullar existence, it is nevertheless impossible not to admit that the cerebral cortex constitutes in this age the most immature portion of the nervous system. This is evident in the lack of all higher psychological functions doubtless directly related to the activity of the cortex and also in the lack of specific motor actions which are characteristic of mature and developed cortical functions. Research shows that the infant constitutes a being whose behavior is due in large part to the ancient subcortical centres of the brain, a creature of the midbrain.

From the circumstance that the lower, more ancient segments of the brain mature earlier than others and are to a greater degree already mature at the moment of birth, it is very clear and necessary from the point of view of development that it is in these very areas where the apparatuses playing the leading role in the whole economy of organic life that all the basic life directions are concentrated. Here is the concentration of the centres of instinctive and emotional life, which are linked on the one hand to the vegetative nervous system which governs the basic life functions of the organism, and on the other—with the cerebral cortex—, the higher organ of human thinking, will, and consciousness. However, the age we are considering is characterized by the circumstance that, thanks to the immaturity of the cortex and links between the subcortical and cortical centres, the apparatuses of vegetative and

[14]Ludwig Edinger (1855–1918) was a German neuroanatomist who in 1885 discovered the Edinger-Westphal mechanism that controls the size of the pupil and linked it to expressions in human fetuses. He was, as Vygotsky says, very interested in comparative anatomy in both ontogenesis (where he studied ancephalic children) and phylogenesis (where he and his daughter Tilly studied the neuroanatomy of fish, reptiles, and even dinosaurs). But the insight that all neurons have the same basic structure (axon, dendrites, and nucleus) was not original to him.

primitive animal life remain still relatively independent without being subject to regulation, inhibition, and control from the side of higher cortical centres.

That is why the activity of these apparatuses resembles, on the one hand, the motor skills of lower vertebrate animals in which the apparatuses we are considering constitute higher centres, higher centres that do not have hierarchically dominant centres above them, and on the other hand has an affinity with pathological motorics, originating thanks to the emancipation of the lower centres. The emancipation of the lower centres, which is manifested in their activity according to their autonomous, archaic and own primitive laws, is normal for infants and is caused by the immaturity of the higher centres. This explains the atavistic character of infant motorics, as well as their amazing resemblance to pathological motor manifestations of later ages. The key to both can be found in the immaturity of the higher centres and the resulting independence of the lower parts of the nervous system. It is quite natural that, with the functional immaturity of the cortex, a motility should arise that is similar, in the first place, to the motility of animals completely devoid of a new brain, and, in the second place, to the pathological motility arising from the degradation of higher centres and the emancipation of lower arcs of action.

In this is also found likewise the explanation of the third feature of infant motorics. In the course of further development of movements which are proper to the indicated age, it is as if they completely disappear from the inventory of motor acts which are proper to a more mature age. As a matter of fact, the movements of the infant do not disappear with the course of development but, according to the first law we cited, the centres that took charge continue to work in alliance with higher nervous formations, entering to their composition as subordinate instances and transferring a part of their functions upwards to younger and newer centres.

As we have already said, the nervous system undergoes extremely energetic development during the course of the first year of life. This manifests itself not only in the speed of growth in brain weight but also in a series of qualitative changes that characterize the dynamic construction of the nervous system in infancy. Studies have shown that in the first year of life we may distinguish three epochs that succeed each other in the construction of the nerve centres and their functions.

The first one is characterized by the immature cortex and stratium and the predominant significance of the pallidum, which constitutes in this epoch the highest of the independently functioning brain centres. This determines all of the specificity of the motorics of the newborn. In the beginning period of development, the child constitutes a pallidal being. That the motor actions of the newborn are regulated by the thalamopallidal system is shown by the athetoid, worm-like movements of the newborn, their *en masse* (i.e., undifferentiated—Trans.) character, and by the physiological muscle rigidness. Motorics in the newborn are very similar to what is seen in neurological clinics of the motorics of people with damage to the striatum. This centre in the newborn is not yet covered by a myelin sheath. It is responsible for acts of sitting, standing, and walking. But its most important significance lies in that it is a higher centre relative to the globus pallidus (the pallidum), that it takes over a part of its functions, and that it has a regulating and inhibiting influence on pallidal functions.[15]

This is why the underdevelopment of the corpus striatum explains the independent and the disinhibited functioning of pallidum. The same disinhibited pallidal function occurs in adult humans if the striatum is damaged when a lower centre is emancipated and begins to act according to its independent laws. Hence, the athetoid character of the motorics of the newborn. In the phylogenetic line, these motorics remind us more of the motorics of fish, which do not have a corpus striatum and in which the globus pallidus is the supreme nervous centre. The thalamus opticus, directly linked to the activity of the globus pallidus, constitutes the organ which collects all of the excitations from external and internal stimuli that flow into the cerebral cortex, where they are colored with affective hues. The thalamus opticus includes the apparatus which leads gestures of the body and face, as well as all of the expressive movements in general. So along with the thalamus opticus, the globus pallidus is linked from the very beginning with the underlying spinal-medullar centres; the reactions of the newborn more accurately characterize it as a thalamo-optico-pallido-spinal-medullar being. These reactions are expressed in unconditional reflexes and in undifferentiated masses of movements: the first are related to spinal-medullar activity in the newborn, while the second are pallidum functions. The striatum, as we have said, is the organ of sitting, standing, and walking. Based on this, pallidum childhood may be characterized as a nonsitting, nonstanding, and nonwalking, that is, as a recumbent childhood, where mobility is of an automatic-massed character, phylogenetically interpreted by Foerster[16] as the creeping mechanism.

The second epoch in the development of the nervous system in the age of infancy is the maturation of the corpus striatum. Linked to this there are primitive attitudinal mechanisms and synergies necessary for sitting, standing, and grasping. This epoch can be called striatopallidal. The pallidum system is lower reflex centre, and the striatal system is the higher reflex centre with receptive-coordinative functions. The striatal system has no direct link with its periphery. The zone of influence of the striatal system applies only to the pallidum, and it has no direct associative link with

[15] Vygotsky ended *Foundations of Pedology*, Lecture 7, with the unusual suggestion that it is not growth that makes possible differentiation, but rather differentiation that makes growth possible. We might think that the growth of the brain, which makes possible the differentiation of behavior, disproves this. But when we really understand Vygotsky's argument, we see that brain differentiation is a nearly perfect example of what he is talking about.

Humans are born with almost all the brain neurons they will ever have. Nevertheless, as Vygotsky says, the brain's weight doubles in the first year alone. The main growth in the weight of the brain is in the glial cells. Glial cells build coatings of myelin around the long stem fibers of the nerve cells (the "axons"), and it is this insulation which keeps the nerve impulse from spreading to other nerve cells. In other words, the growth of weight in the brain is not in the wiring, but rather in the wiring insulation (the myelin). It is the differentiation and discrimination of brain cells that makes brain weight growth, and it is this growth that makes possible the differentiation and discrimination of signals, enabling further growth.

[16] See Footnote 11.

the cortex, which makes it independent, unless the excitation which emanates from the thalamus is also transmitted to the corpus striatum. The main purpose of the corpus striatum is the simultaneous implementation of static functions of the brain, the regulation of muscular tonus, the inhibition and regulation of functions in the globus pallidus, and the regulation of timeliness in the inhibition and disinhibition of the whole complex of agonist and antagonist, on the synergy of which depends the correctness of all motion. This same system is related to primary automatisms such as facial expressions, gestures, expressive movements, and so on.

The transition to the third epoch is marked above all by the maturation of the cerebral cortex and the cooperation of its functions in the regulation of behavior and motorics. The latter circumstances find expression in two facts of capital importance: (1) in the development of higher nervous activity, that is, complex systems of conditional reflexes, and (2) in the intellectuallization and gradual acquisition of motions of an expedient character. In the newborn, myelination is only in the so-called primary areas of the cerebral cortex which are linked to organs of perception and themselves constitute their receptive spheres. Cortical development, according to the data of P. Flechsig,[17] consists in the fact that these primary areas are bound to the intermediate and final areas that are covered by a myelin sheath only gradually over the course of the first half year.

The most reliable indicator of cortical development is the development of conditional reflex activity. The basic laws of development of its development during the age of infancy are as follows. (1) In the newborn baby there are no conditional reflexes; in him we observe innate reactions of the dominant type.[18] (2) The development of conditional reflexes does not happen randomly, haphazardly, or without order, but is subject to the process of the emergence of a dominant reaction. There

[17] Paul Flechsig (1847–1929) was the German neuroanatomist who discovered the lateness of myelinzation in the infants. Flechsig first became famous because of Daniel Schreber, a respected judge, who woke up one day with the idea that it would be pleasant to have sex with a man. Since Judge Schreber was male, and a highly respected jurist, he decided this idea could not possibly have come from himself, and so he sued poor Flechsig, accusing him of implanting women's thoughts in him under hypnotism and trying to turn him psychologically into a woman using a secret "nerve language." Freud valiantly defended Flechsig, diagnosing Schreber as a repressed homosexual. This probably saved Flechsig's career, which is today most remembered for his work on myelination. Flechsig divided the cortex into (1) the "early" myelination zone (motor, visual, and auditory), (2) the "intermediate" myelination zone that borders it, and (3) "association," that is, working memory. These are the areas that Vygotsky refers to above.

[18] As we saw earlier with the scratching reflex, Vygotsky is using the vocabulary of Ukhtomsky on the "dominant," which underlies Vygotsky's own theory of development as a sequence of neoformations. Ukhtomsky had observed that a cat which was about to defecate could not be distracted with an electric shock; far from diverting it, the shock actually increased cat output. He generalized his observation into a theory in which each period of human life was governed by a particular "dominant" excitation—one that absorbed and even blocked all other forms of excitation, so, for example, the neonate period is governed by the unconditional (instinctive) reflex. Ukhtomsky, who was a Russian orthodox monk as well as a physician, believed that the purpose of life was for humans to develop to the point where the needs of others become their dominant. He died in besieged Leningrad in 1942, probably of starvation.

is a definite dependency on the dominant processes in the formation of a conditional reflex in the central nervous system. Only within the receptive areas can a conditional reflex be formed, under the influence of which there arise functional interactions with the character of the dominant. (3) The time and order of formation of the genetically earliest conditioned reflexes corresponds to the time and order of the emergence of dominants: since there exists in the newborn only a feeding dominant and a positioning dominant, the first conditional reflexes can only be formed in the sphere of these reactions, (4) much later there arise in the child visual and auditory dominants, and consequently the capacity for conditional reflexes linked to these areas. (5) As the dominant reaction is linked to instinctive localized activity in the subcortical region, the formation of primary conditional reflexes is not limited to cortical processes but points to the critical role of the subcortical centres in their formation, and consequently, the dependence of this process on instinctive activity.

The intellectualization of movements and their acquisition of a goal-oriented character appear much later in the development of the infant than the formation of the primary conditional reflexes. This intellectualization is manifested in the manipulation of objects by the child and in the primary acts of his instrumental thinking, that is, the simplest use of tools. The most primordial manifestations of this activity are observed in the beginning of the second half year. The formation of conditional reflexes is beginning to emerge from the sphere of direct influence of the subcortical dominant in this same period. Thus, the primary conditional reflexes are observed from the second month of life, and although they indicate, to all appearances, the role and involvement of the cortex, there is still, however, no systematic process of accumulating of personal experience nor any evidence of significant involvement of cortical functions in the behavior of the infant.

Consideration of the three epochs clearly confirms the basic laws of construction of the central nervous system presented above. Pallidal motorics do not vanish with the maturation of the corpus striatum, but are included in its function as a subordinate instance. In just this way, the movements which inhere in the striatal epoch are an important part of the activity of higher psychomotor mechanisms. This is confirmed by the fate of a number of reflexes which are observed in a mature age only with lesions of the brain. Such reflexes as the Babinsky reflex and others, pathological in adult humans, are at the same time completely normal physiological phenomena in the age of infancy. In the development of the child they cannot be elicited by themselves, as they are included as subordinate instances in the activity of higher centres and they act independently only in cases of pathological brain injuries (under the law of the emancipation of the lower centres).

Now we may proceed to consider those consequences that follow from the picture of the organic and nervous development in the age of infancy sketched out above. Above all, these consequences are detected most easily in the area of sensory and motor functions of the child, characterized mainly by his perception and behavior, that is, two basic aspects of relations with the external world.

The first thing that is shown to us by the study of the sensory and motor functions in the newborn and in the infant: the initially indivisible linking of perception and behavior. The link between sensory and motor functions is one of the fundamental properties of psychic activity and of the nervous apparatus. It was first imagined that the sensory and the motor functions were separate and isolated one from the other and only in the course of development was there established an associative link between sensory and motor processes. In fact, the relative independence of both arises only in a long process of development and characterizes the high level reached by the child. The initial moment of development is characterized by an inseparable link, forming a genuine unity, between the one process and the other.

In this way, the problem of the relation of perception and action is put in contemporary psychology in a completely inverse manner to the way in which it was put before. Previously, the problem was how we can explain the association of perception with action. Now the problem consists of explaining how the initially united sensorimotor processes in the course of development become relatively independent of each other and enable new, higher, and more flexible and complex integrations.

The initial answer to this question is given by the study of a simple reflexive movement. Every innate reflex represents in itself a sensorimotor unit, in which perception of stimuli and responsive movement represent a unity of dynamic processes; its motor part is simply a dynamic continuation of its perceptive part.

From the facts of the formation of conditional reflexes, we know that reflex arcs are mutable: the perceptive segment of one arc can be linked in a unitary apparatus with the motor part of another arc, and here it becomes clear that flexible, free, and to a high degree multivarious cointegrations between whatever perceptions and whatever movements are possible. Therefore, the aspiration arose on the part of many scholars to explain through the mechanism of conditional reflexes the whole development of sensorimotor processes. But this attempt proved fruitless for two reasons: (1) from this point of view may be clarified only the first part of the question, namely the unity of sensorimotor processes, but in no way can the second part of the question be clarified, that is, in what manner arises the relative independent and autonomy of each process from the other, already seen very clearly in action in the second half year of life. (2) This explanation would only be sufficient in cases if the whole of the behavior of the infant were exhausted by reflexes; in fact, separate reflex movements constitute only an insignificant and more or less incidental portion of the system of behavior in newborns and infants. Obviously, the explanation given does not exhaust the problem as a whole, but only covers a specific part of the sensorimotor processes, which is related to the group of unconditional and conditional reflexes.

For an explanation of the link between sensory and motor processes in the first year of life, it is necessary to take into account two other circumstances: (1) the holistic, structural character which distinguishes these two processes, and (2) the character of the central link between them, which is more complex than the one that takes place in a simple reflex arc.

Let us turn to the first circumstance. Even now we sometimes have to confront the claim that the movements of the infant present us with an aggregate of separate, disparate, isolated individual reflexes which are only slowly and gradually merged into a linked, whole dynamic process. Nothing could be more incorrect than this representation. The path of motoric development runs not from the addition of individual partial movements into holistic motor acts—not from the part to the whole—but from the mass, the group, the movements which cover the whole body, to the differentiation and individuation of separate acts of locomotion and then their recombination into a new unit of a higher order—from the whole to the parts. Such, in any case, are the instinctive movements which prevail in the infant. Therefore, the problem of the genetic relationship of instincts and reflexes remains a problem of prime importance for the whole of the study of the age of infancy.

There are two opposing solutions to this problem. According to one of them, the reflex is the primary phenomenon, and an instinct is nothing more than a simple mechanical chain of reflex actions in which the culminating moment of each reflex is at the same time the stimulus, or the starting point, for the subsequent one. According to another view, what is genetically primary is the instinct, and the reflex is a more recent phylogenetic formation which arose by way of differentiating the instinctive movements and isolating their individual components.

All the facts which are known from the study of instinctive activities of animals and infants compel us to admit the correctness of the second theory and to reject the first as not corresponding to reality. Let us illustrate this with two examples. We take the feeding with milk by the mother as a typical sample of instinctive activity. According to the first theory, the initial excitation (hunger or sensation of the maternal breast) only laid down an impulse for an initial reflex—movements of search for the nipple. Arising as a result of these movements, the contact between the nipple and the mouth causes the reflex of grasping the nipple with the lips, which as a new excitation results in sucking movements. The flow of milk into the baby's mouth with the help of these movements is the new stimulus for a swallowing reflex, and so on. The whole process of feeding seems a simple mechanical chain of separate reflex acts.

A genuine study of this typical instinct shows that what we have before us is a whole process endowed with a defined sense and direction, leading in a goal-oriented way to meeting the need that has arisen, rather than a mechanical aggregation of individual reflexes each of which, taken by itself, has neither meaning nor value but which acquires them only part of the whole. The instinctive action presents a complex, objectively goal oriented, and appropriate address of biological needs, and, because of this, the process is objectively meaningful as whole, each part of which, including each of the constituent reflex motions, is determined by the structure of the whole. The process of feeding never takes place in a mechanical, stereotypical repetitive sequence of each separate motion. Separate elements may be changed, but the entire process as a whole retains the sense of the structure. Watching the infant satisfy hunger, we can never predict that it is now a mechanical necessity that he will perform this or that motion which is the next link in a chain of reflexes. At every moment in the process, however, it is possible to predict with confidence that there will be one of the possible motions which must be carried out in the function for the next stage of the development of the whole process.[19]

In this way, we must acknowledge that instincts and not reflexes constitute the initial form of the child's activity and that development of motorics in the infant is above all characterized by the absence of isolated, separate, and specialized motions of one organ or another and the presence of massed movements activating the whole body *en masse*.

One and the same holistic character distinguishes the perception of the newborn and the infant. We have already given the proposition of K. Koffka,[20] which characterizes the perception of the newborn as a holistic perception of the situation, where against an amorphous background there appears an insufficiently defined and amorphous quality. All studies agree in showing that the initial moment of development in perception consists not of a chaos of separate impressions nor of a mechanical aggregation of impressions, or of a mosaic of different sensations, but of holistic complex situations, structures, brightly colored by affect. In this way, the perceptions of the infant, like his motorics, are characterized by an initial wholeness. And the path of their development lies likewise in the perception of the whole to perception of parts, from perception of situations to perception of separate moments.

This structural, holistic character, identically distinguishing sensory and motor processes, allows us to arrive at an explanation of the link which brings together the sensory and motor processes. The link between them is structural. This must be understood so that perception and action present an original, structurally indivisible, process, where the action constitutes a dynamic continuation of perception, with

---

[19] Note that "with sense" is used as an antonym of "mechanical": a machine has structure, but does not by itself alter the sequence or disposition of its parts, or understand the meaning of the whole. Vygotsky says that elements of the process may be changed and the whole will retain/maintain a "structure with sense," that is, the way the baby is held, the person feeding the baby, and even a bottle substituted for the breast can be changed and the baby will still understand the aim. Below, Vygotsky demonstrates this with the experiments of Volkelt.

[20] Kurt Koffka (1886–1941) was a student of Carl Stumpf and a central figure in Gestalt psychology, along with Max Wertheimer and Wolfgang Köhler (see Footnote 15 in Chap. 2). He wrote a monograph called *Growth of the Mind* (Koffka, 1925/1980) in which he argued that most early learning was simply sensorimotor learning. Unlike his Gestaltist colleagues, and rather like Vygotsky, Koffka believed that this sensorimotor learning was qualitatively different from later learning, which he called "ideational," and which he recognized was dependent on language. But unlike Vygotsky, Koffka considered the naming process all important; for Vygotsky, learning to name is only the beginning of learning concepts.

When Koffka came to the USSR to participate in Luria's Uzbekistan excursion, Vygotsky served as his translator (and Koffka remarked that Professor Vygotsky's Russian translations always took far longer than his German original). Koffka wrote a paper on the expedition that came to the very opposite conclusion from Luria's—Luria had found that uneducated Uzbek peasants scored differently on tests of lower skills such as perception as well as on higher skills such as syllogistic reasoning. Koffka reanalyzed Luria's data and showed that there was no big difference between Uzbeks and others on the perception tests, but there was a difference in syllogistic reasoning. Note that Koffka's interpretation is actually closer to what Vygotsky's theory would have predicted, as well as more consistent with the division of the brain into higher centres and lower centres (Harrower, 1983).

which it is integrated into an overall structure. In perception and action as two non-autonomous parts are found general laws for building a unified structure. Between them there is an internal, essential, sense-laden, structural link.

With this we come to the second important moment linked to the resolution of the given problem. We have found that both the sensory and the motor processes have essentially the same emergence of structures common to both of them. But the formation of structures is a function of the central apparatus. As shown by studies, such a central process that links sensory and motor functions and leads to the formation of a single central structure, consists in the age of infancy of drive, need, or, more broadly speaking, affect. Perception and action are linked through affect. This explains to us the most essential problem of the unity of sensorimotor processes and gives us the key to understanding their development.

We give two examples to illustrate this proposition.

In experimental studies on the discrimination of forms in the nursing child, a pattern directly related to the question has been found that is extremely interesting to us. The nursing child learns to recognize different forms: rectangles, triangles, ovals, and the form of a violin, identical when viewed in two-dimensional profile.[21] The child is presented with four milk bottles, different in form but absolutely identical in relation to other properties. In only one of the four teats covering the bottles was there a hole through which the child was able to get milk. As a result, nearly two-thirds of the 29 children between 5 and 12 months old who were studied learned to choose for themselves by its form a bottle with a teat that could give milk. The researcher, H. Volkelt,[22] was convinced again and again that the children without hesitation and with confidence chose a bottle from two or even a whole series of bottles. An especially strong impression was made by a number of supplementary critical experiments in which the bottle of the particular form perceived by the child as his own was never placed in the field of vision. In these cases, the behavior of the nursing child completely changed and gave the impression of an adult behavior: it appeared that he did not have his bottle; and he appeared to be looking for it (frustration and inhibition in all motions, a wandering gaze, and no reaching or grasping with the hands).

Analysis of these experiment, in Volkelt's words, shows: the success of the method rests, obviously, on the fact that the child seems to be drinking "triangular"

[21] This appears to mean that the bottles are the same when viewed from the side, that is, they have differently shaped cross sections but the same length, breadth, and presumably the same volume of milk.

[22] Hans Volkelt (1886–1964) was the son of the celebrated neo-Kantian philosopher Joachim Volkelt (see Footnote 15 of Chap. 2). Vygotsky cites his work on "pre-concepts" in spiders (e.g., when a spider will attack a fly in the web but run away from a dead fly on the ground). This was the basis of Volkelt's PhD work at Leipzig and his subsequent work demonstrating similar prelogical and nonintellectual "pre-concepts" in infants. Thanks to enthusiastic participation in the Nazi party and a popular article advocating "Aryanization" of preschools, he became head of the Froebel society and edited the journal *Kindergarten* under Hitler.

or "oval" milk. In other words, there is a holistic process of *perezhivanie,*[23] linked to feeding from a bottle of a particular form, a very strong link emerging in the nursing child between the quality of the attracting excitation with the *perezhivanie* of satisfaction (i.e., the quality most essential to life, in as much as the basic feeding product of the nursing child consists of milk) on the one hand, and the complex of qualities which correspond to a particular form of bottle, on the other. Thus, both are as yet still undivided, diffuse feelings, despite the separateness of their qualities from the point of view of the adult.

The experiment worked for Volkelt only in those cases where the researcher was able to create a kind of primitive whole. Only then would the *perezhivanie* caused by the experiment be adequate for primitive consciousness. It was in those cases that went in sufficient measure toward the propensity toward holistic perception which characterizes the primitive living being that success in the production of the experiment could be expected. Only in this way would the experiment of Volkelt, which created a primitive whole of milk and form, lead to an indubitable orientation toward the aspect of form. The same can be expressed otherwise, more to the point: only this mutual fusion of both sides of the *perezhivanie*, corresponding to the primitive consciousness of grasping form and taking in milk, makes it possible to demonstrate that the nursing child can distinguish forms, Volkelt concludes.

We see from these experiments that the emergence of a link between perception of a definite form and a definite action is possible only if the child has these processes included in same unified, undivided structure of affectively colored needs.

Another example relates to the area of the already mentioned processes of forming conditional reflexes. As we have seen, the basic pattern of the development of conditional reflexes in the nursing age consists of this: that the priority and the sequence of their development are subject to the order in which the basic dominants emerge. Furthermore, in the beginning stage such dominants are dominants of a subcortical, instinctive character that determine the sphere in which all new links between sensory and motor processes become possible. Consequently, the formation of conditional reflexes confirms the proposition that only the presence of a single dominant, which is nothing other than the physiological substrate of affect, provides the capacity for new conditional links between perception and action.

We may as a result of our review formulate a highly important and substantial proposition on the psychic life of the infant: it is characterized by the complete nondifferentiation of separate psychic functions, the exclusive reign of primitive

[23] Like the word "concept," the term *perezhivanie* can mean a perception or an experience in a very everyday sense, and that is how Vygotsky uses the term here and in the next paragraph. Also like "concept," the term can have a restricted, technical sense (e.g., in Chapter Four of *L.S. Vygotsky's Pedological Works Vol. 1: Foundations of Pedology* (2019)). Of course, the two senses are not completely unrelated: like Volkelt's preconcepts and true concepts, they are linked as well as distinct: in both cases, *perezhivanie* is a unitary moment of consciousness. Both meanings are given in the psychological dictionary published in 1931 by Varshava and Vygotsky: see Варшава Б. Е. и Выготский Л.С. (1931, p. 128).

holistic *perezhivanie,* and can generally be defined as a system of instinctive consciousness, developing under the ruling influence of affects and drives.

The latter proposition requires substantial reservation, as it has often led and leads to a completely incorrect interpretation of the entire course of psychic development in the child. Correctly noting the exclusive reign of the affects and drives linked primarily to the subcortical mechanisms of consciousness and behavior in the infant, many researchers conclude from this that affects characterize in general only a primitive, lower position on the ladder of psychic development and that with the progress of development the role of the child's affective tendencies retreats further and further into the background, so that the degree of affective behavior can be made into a criterion of the primitiveness or psychic development of the child. This is completely incorrect. The initial and primitive stages are not characterized by an enormous significance of affective tendencies, which extend throughout the whole of the development of the child in themselves, but rather by two other moments: (1) the reign of those affects that are most primitive in nature, immediately linked to instinctive drives and impulses, that is, the lower affects, and (2) the exclusive reign of primitive affects alongside the underdevelopment of the rest of the psychic apparatus, linked to sensory, intellectual, and motor functions.

The presence of affective impulses—an indispensable companion of each new stage in the development of the child from the lowest to the highest. We can say that affect opens up the psychic development of the child and the construction of his personality and closes the process, completing and crowning the development of the personality as a whole. In this sense, it is no accident that the affective functions show an immediate link to the most ancient subcortical centres which first develop and which lie at the base of the brain, as well as with the newest, specifically human, area of the brain (the frontal lobes) which develop the last. By this fact, we see an anatomical expression of the circumstance that affect is the alpha and the omega, the beginning and the final link, the prologue and epilogue of all psychic development.

Taking part in the process of psychic development from the very beginning to the very end as a qualitatively crucial moment, affect takes a complex path, changing with each new step in the construction of the personality, entering into the structure of the new consciousness which inheres in every age, and showing at each new stage profound changes in its psychic nature. In particular, affect carries out a complex development even during the course of the first year of life. If we compare the initial and final stages of this period, we cannot but marvel at the profound changes that occur in the affective life of the infant.

The beginning affect of the newborn constricts his psychic life within the narrow limits of sleep, feeding, and crying. Already, in this first stage of the age of infancy, affect takes on the basic form of receptive interest in the outside world, so that in the second stage of this age it gives place to an active interest in surroundings. And finally, the end of the infant age immediately confronts us with the crisis of age 1, which, like all the critical ages, is characterized by the rapid development of affective life and marked by the first appearance in the child's affects of his proper personality—this is the first step in the development of the child's will.

K. Bühler[24] proposed an extremely useful schema that allows the systematization according to genetic relations of the basic forms of behavior in animals and humans. Bühler gives his schema a universal significance, applying it to animals, children, and adult humans. He is trying to put this very scheme into the basis of an entire theory of infancy. Below, we shall critically consider the potential and the legitimacy of such a forcible extension of the interpretation of this scheme. But, as often happens, a construction which is extended unjustifiably beyond its limitations and, naturally, found to be ineffective, turns out to be quite adequate for the facts of a given, delimited, area of phenomena. So it is with the scheme of Bühler. It flawlessly reflects the development of behavior in infancy.

If we begin to consider, Bühler says, all meaning making, that is, objective, goal-directed modes of action in animals and people, we will see that, from the bottom to the top, there is a very simple and clearly distinct construction of three stages, which may be called instincts, entrainment,[25] and intellect. Instinct is the lowest level and at the same time the soil from which all that is higher springs. And in people there is not a single area, not one form of spiritual activity, which is not in some way reliant upon instinct.

These three stages, going from the bottom to the top, as we have already said, are true and consistent with reality and reflect development in the age of infancy. The first stage in infant behavior is governed by the instinctive form of activity. This differs from the same animal activity in the insufficient readiness of these hereditary forms of behavior. Indeed, the pathetic helplessness of the newborn human stems from a lack of ready instinctive mechanisms. In humans too, certain inborn elements of motivation and tensions sustain life, and in them all of higher spiritual organization stems from a blind pursuit of sustenance, of activities for welfare and for happiness. But everything is left quite undefined and sketchy, and all of it requires supplementation through entrainment and intellect. Compared with the strictly regular lives of insects, the instincts of humans seem vague, weak, diffusive, and rich with vast individual differences, so that we may wonder in one case or another whether it is the same natural apparatus or not.

In the incompleteness of instincts in the newborn, there clearly emerges a definite genetic sense. Human instincts, unlike the instincts of animals, do not include

[24] For a footnote on Karl Bühler, see Chap. 2, Footnote 19.

[25] Vygotsky uses the term дрессировка, *dressirovka*, literally "dressage." In English the term dressage refers to competitive horse training; but in Russian it has a much broader meaning and can include any kind of animal or even human training by conditional responses (i.e., by carrot, stick, and repetition). Bühler's categories, then, correspond to innate unconditional responses which are the product of phylogenetic adaptations, learned conditional ones which are the result of ontogenetic adaptations, and intellectual responses to novel situations. As Vygotsky points out, these do not exhaust the types of human behavior by any means—all of these behaviors are present in infancy and much of more mature behavior is neither innate, learned, or particularly intelligent, but it is free and voluntary behavior nonetheless (see Vygotsky, 1997, the *History of the Development of the Higher Mental Functions*, Chapters 3 and 4, for his immanent critique of this schema). We have translated дрессировка as "entrainment," but it should be understood as incorporating the rote learning of skills or habits through a system of rewards, punishments, and repetition.

almost finished and complete mechanisms of behavior. Instead, there are a given system of drives and certain premises and starting points for further development. This means that the specific weight of the instinctive form of behavior is much less in the child than it is in animals. Even such a process as walking, which the duck and the chicken master in a finished form immediately on hatching from the egg, arises in the child relatively late, as the result of a prolonged development. It is not a new idea that man's amazing plasticity and versatility in ability is achieved precisely by throwing off innate mechanisms. The chicken is well able to go on two legs immediately, but later it cannot learn to climb, to dance, or to skate. K. Bühler is right when he says that human instinct in its pure form can be seen only in severe idiots, those unfortunate beings who do not appear amenable to entrainment.

The second stage is characterized by the reign of acquired, personal experience, built on top of inheritance by means of learning, exercises, and entrainment. The first half year in the life of the child is essentially taken up with the acquisition of the art of ostension, sitting, crawling, and so on. All of this training, self-learning in play, takes place as a gradual exercise. The formation of conditional reflexes, habitual motions, and skills presents similar forms arising by way of learning and entrainment in relation to the second stage.

The third stage in the development of infant behavior is characterized by the beginnings of intellectual activity. Bühler was the first to demonstrate that by the end of the age of infancy there emerges in the child the simplest manifestations of practical intellect, visual-motor thinking, completely similar to the actions of chimpanzees in the famous experiments of W. Köhler. Therefore, Bühler proposed to call this phase of child life the "chimpanzee-like" age. At this age, the child makes his first inventions, of course very primitive but in a spiritual sense extremely important. The substance of the manifestation of intellect in the child consists of the first rational and expedient, noninnate, and not rote learned, but in the given situation newly emergent, actions of the hand which are associated with the simplest use of detours and the utilization of tools. The child shows the ability to use a rope to pull a distant object, to use one object as a tool with which to fetch another, etc. In his experiments, Bühler was able to show that a child without the beginnings of speech goes through stages of practical intellect or instrumental thinking, that is, grasping mechanical couplings and thinking through mechanical means to mechanical final ends. Even before speech, in the child develops subjectively meaningful, that is, consciously purposeful, activity.

In the experiments of Bühler, the first manifestations of practical intellect were located in the tenth or twelfth month of life. As we have already said, the actual development of the first utilization of tools goes beyond the age of infancy, but the beginning manifestations of this capacity undoubtedly occur in the second stage of infancy. A preliminary stage in the development of the use of objects in this direction may be observed already in a 6-month-old child. In a 9-month-old, these manifestations are observed in their deployed form. They can be taken as the first attempts to establish mechanical dependencies.

A preliminary stage in the development of this capacity is observed in a child of 6 months in the specific form of the manipulation of objects. The child is not satisfied with playing with only one object. He acts on one object, using it as an extension of his hand and, holding it, moves it to another immoveable object, hitting it, impacting it, just as a 4-month-old baby did previously only using the hands. This use of items is a preliminary stage of the use of tools. At 7 months we find the first traces of new activities with objects that are new in principle, namely changing the form of objects through compression, through crumpling, and through tearing. In these initially destructive activities are already the first methods of formation and transformation. Positive formation appears in the attempt of the 8-month-old child to insert one object into another. This manipulation of fixed objects with the help of moveable objects, this impact of one object upon another, the change of form of objects, and the first rudiments of positive formation can be correctly seen as the preliminary stage in the development of instrumental thinking. All this leads to the simplest use of tools. Using tools will create for the child a completely new period.[26]

In order to finish the consideration of the genesis of the basic neoformation, we must still speak of the development of social behavior in the infant.

We have already spoken regarding communication in the newborn. It is characterized by the lack of specific social reactions. The relationship of the child to the adult is so fused and inseparably interwoven in its basic life operations that differentiated reactions cannot be singled out. Specific social impressions and reactions occur in the second month of life. Thus, it has been established that a smile appears only as a social reaction at first. It is followed by other reactions which leave no doubt of this: we are dealing with differentiated specific social manifestations by the child. Between the first and second months the child will react by smiling to the sound of the human voice.

By the end of the first month, one child's cry, as we pointed out, causes a similar cry in another. At 2 months, the child's cries will almost always die down if anyone approaches. Finally, at 2–3 months, the child meets the gaze of an adult with smiling. At this same time, there appear a large quantity of forms of behavior from which it is already possible to judge that the child has joined into a social relationship with those adults who care for him. The child turns toward a speaker, listens for the human voice, and takes offense when one speaker ignores him. A month-old baby greets one who approaches with sounds or with smiling. He already shows a willingness to communicate. C. Bühler notes two exceptionally important factors which influence the development of beginning forms of sociability. First—this emanates from adult activeness. The child is essentially reactive at the very beginning. Adults care for the child and play around with him. From adults come all that the

---

[26] The word "tool" is perhaps slightly misleading: Vygotsky does not mean that there is a direct line between this instrumental thinking and child labor. The Russian word орудие is more general and less immediately work related than "tool"—it includes guns, kitchen utensils, and—here—children's toys. For example, many Soviet writers on infancy stressed how children learn to use a spoon (e.g., Zaporozhets et al., 1964/1971, p. 223; Leontiev, 1936/2005; 1981, p. 306). Using a spoon is linked to labor and life in an obvious way, and it also appears to be a good example of how tool use can be taught through collaboration (or, as Western writers like Bruner say, through scaffolding).

infant receives at this stage of his life: not only the satisfaction of his needs but also all of the amusement and excitation brought about by changes of position, by movement, by play, and by coaxing. The child is more and more reactive to the world of *perezhivanie* created by adults, but he is not yet brought into communication with other children staying in the same room in another crib.

The second condition for the *perezhivaniya* of communication consists in this: that the child must be in control of his own body. In certain positions and states, when the child has had its needs satisfied, the child masters enough surplus energy. In such a state his senses may be at least marginally active. At such moments he is capable of actively listening and looking around a little. If the comfortable and secure position in which the child found himself is changed to another which he has not yet mastered, then the whole energy is directed at overcoming the inconvenience. In the child there is no more energy to smile or to share a glance with a speaker. For example, children who cannot completely manage their bodies in a sitting position will be less active in sitting. The limits of activeness are reduced still more at the time when they are learning to sit, stand, and walk. In the supine position, the infant can communicate more easily than when sitting. The obstacle to communication in these cases is the deficiency in activeness on the side of the child.

At about 5 months, in this respect, there usually comes a turning point in the progress that children make in mastering their own bodies, their posture, and their movements, leading to this: 5- to 6-month-old infants are already seeking contact with peers. In the second half year, between two infants there have developed all of the basic social interrelationships that characterize this age. They smile at and babble the one to the other, they give and take back toys, and they flirt with one another and play together. In the second half year, the child develops a specific need for communication. We can very confidently assert that the positive interest in people is brought about by the fact that the needs of the child are being met by adults. The active pursuit of communication is expressed in the second half year in this: the child looks for other people, smiles at them, babbles, reaches for people, clasps them, and is displeased when he is disengaged from them.

In the works of C. Bühler and her coworkers, the inventory of these basic features of social behavior is specified for the first year of life. It is seen that the first phase of social displays by the child is characterized by passiveness, reactiveness, and a predominance of negative emotions (crying and dissatisfaction at the departure of the adult). The second phase is marked by an active seeking of contact not only with adults but also with peers and by the joint activity of children and the most primitive relations of domination and subordination, protest, despotism, obedience, etc.

What should interest us here is first of all two factors, closely related to each other and directly influencing the genesis of social displays at this age. The first is the common root from which the development of the social manifestations of the infant originates. Secondly, there is the unique character that social communication takes on in the age of infancy that separates the sociality of the infant from the sociality of an older child.

The common root of all manifestations of sociality in the age of infancy consists in a unique situation of development of which we have already spoken. The infant from the beginning is confronted with a situation where his behavior is intertwined and interwoven with the social. His path to things and to the satisfaction of his own needs must always pass through a relationship with other people. That is why the social relations of the newborn still cannot be differentiated or isolated from the general shared situation with which they are intertwined. Later, at the beginning of differentiation, they continue to maintain their primeval character in this sense: communication with adults remains the basic path through which the activeness of the child himself is displayed. Almost all of the personal activeness of the infant flows into the mainstream of his social relations. His relations to the external world are always relations through other people. For this reason, if we can say that in the individual behavior of the infant everything is intertwined and interwoven into the social, the reverse proposition is also true: all the displays of sociality of the infant are intertwined and interwoven with his concrete, actual situation, forming with it a shared and indivisible whole.

The effect of the specific, uniquely infant, sociality that results is primarily evident in this: that the social communication of the child has not yet stood out from the whole of the processes that connect him with the outside world, with the things and processes that meet their life needs. This communication is still without the most basic means: human speech. This wordless, pre-speech, visual-action communication brings to the first plane such relationships as are not readily found in later child development. It is not so much communication based on mutual understanding as emotional expressiveness, the transfer of affect, negative or positive reactions to a change of central moment in any infant situation—(e.g.—Trans.) the appearance of another person.

An adult person is the centre of every situation in the age of infancy. It is natural, therefore, that the mere proximity or distancing of a human immediately means for the child a sharp and radical change in the situation in which he finds himself. If we do not shrink from figurative expressions, we may say that the simple approach and distancing of the adult arms and disarms the child's activeness. In the absence of an adult, the infant falls into a situation of helplessness. His activeness in relation to the external world seems to be paralyzed or, in any case, to a high degree limited and constrained. It is as if his arms and legs were immediately taken away, along with the capacity of movement, of change of position, and of the grasping of objects that he needs. In the presence of an adult, for the activeness of the child, the most common and natural path through another human opens up. That is why another person is to the infant always the psychological centre of every situation. This is why the sense of every situation for the infant is defined in the first place by this centre, that is, its social content, or, speaking more broadly, the child's relationship to the world consists in, depends upon, and derives its value from his most direct and concrete relationship to an adult person.

The Basic Neoformation of the Age of Infancy

Now after considering separately the major lines of development in infancy, we can answer the main question related to the basic neoformation of the age of infancy and in this way approach the analysis of the most important theories of the beginning period of child development. So, what that is new arises as a result of the complex process of development in the age of infancy?

We have already seen that the major aspects of child development reveal an inner unity, as each one of them receives its sense, its meaning, only by being included in a single unitary process of development of the basic neoformation of the age. Infant helplessness is linked to the still incomplete skeletal formation, to undeveloped musculature, to the predominance of the more mature vegetative organic functions, to the reign of the more ancient parts of the brain, to the immaturity of all the centres which define the specifically human forms of activeness, and to an instinctive consciousness centered around the most important necessaries of life—this helplessness not only constitutes a starting moment for defining the social situation of development in the infant but also points to two factors which are directly related to the basic neoformation: (1) a gradual growth in the energy resources of the infant as a necessary prerequisite of all the higher situated lines of development and (2) a dynamic changing of the primary relationship to the world in the course of infant development.

P.P. Blonsky singles out three main stages in infant development from the point of view of the interrelationship between energy resources and communication with the environment.[27] The helplessness of the child determines his place in the surrounding environment. During the childhood stage of absolute toothlessness, the child is a feeble being, lying in bed and needing care. From the child's side, social stimuli are mainly in the form of cries in reaction to pain, hunger, and discomfort. The interrelationship between him and his environment is based primarily on food.

[27] Where Zaporozhets, Elkonin, and Leontiev located a crucial turning point in infant development in the use of the spoon (see Footnote 26), Blonsky took a less culturally bound and more biologically based view. The relationship between the child and the environment, he reasoned, depends in a direct way on the child's energy resources, and this in turn depends on the child's ability to take in food, which depends on the child's teeth. (There is some basis for this in the history of early man because the ability to eat meat seems directly related to the ability of humans to undertake long journeys.) Accordingly, Blonsky divides childhood into three periods: in toothless childhood, the child is entirely dependent on milk and has very little energy as a result: the child can only lie down and sit up. In the period of incisors, the child is starting to move around. And by the age of 1, the child is the equal of an adult, so long as they are not outside, but in a quiet room doing nothing. Vygotsky agrees that the child's attention and ability to communicate depends on having enough energy. He even agrees that as soon as man has built walls and no longer depends on hunting and gathering, child and adult can concentrate on social communication, and when we are talking about social communication, the child and the adult are indeed peers if not equals. But of course Vygotsky does not agree that teeth are the essential neoformation: when communication is the main activity, teeth cannot be the main means.

It is utterly clear that most of all he at this time is linked to the mother, in nursing and nurturing.

With the eruption of the incisors, when the child is already a being moving about in bed, the interrelationship between him and the environment becomes incomparably more complex. On the one hand, the child seeks to utilize the power of adults for his own movement and to attain desired objects. On the other hand, he begins to understand the behavior of adults and has established a psychological, connection with them, albeit an elementary one.

In the second year of life, the child proves, in a sedentary room environment, equal to an adult, and relations of collaboration have been established between them, however, elementary and simple their collaboration may be. Thus, according to the three energy stages, we may distinguish three stages of communication with the environment.

Describing the social development of the child above, we have already pointed out that, on the one hand, the moment of energy which determines the greater or lesser capacity of activeness of the child constitutes the basic prerequisite for the development of social displays and communication with adults. Thus, the genesis of the basic neoformation has its roots deep in the most intimate inner processes of organic growth and maturation.

On the other hand, the social situation of development created thanks to the helplessness of the infant determines the orientation in which is realized the activeness of the infant, an orientation through other people toward the objects of the surrounding world. But if the child were not a growing, maturing, and developing being, if he did not change during the age of infancy and remained in the beginning state in which we found the newborn, the social situation of development would define the day-to-day life of the infant as a rotation in the same circle, without any possibility of moving forward. Then the life of the infant would be reduced to countless reproductions of the one and the same situation, as is the case in pathological forms of development. In fact, the infant is still growing and developing, that is, modifying his being, and therefore his life from day to day resembles not so much revolving and returning to one and the same situation as it does a spiral upward movement linked to qualitative changes in the situation of development.

In the course of development, the activeness of the infant grows, his funds of energy increase, his motions are perfected, his arms and legs are strengthened, new, younger, and higher sectors of the brain mature, and new forms of behavior and new forms of communication with his surroundings emerge. Thanks to all of this, on the one hand, the sphere of his relationship to reality expands, expanding and diversifying his use of paths through adults, and on the other there is more and more of an increase in the basic contradiction between the increasing complexity and diversity of social relations of the child and his inability to communicate clearly with the help of speech. All of this cannot help but lead to the basic neoformation of the newborn period—instinctive psychic life—changing in the most emphatic and radical way. The easiest way to understand this change is if we take into account the two basic features which set apart the newborn psyche: first of all, the child still not only does not single out himself but also does not single out other people from the shared situation arising on the basis of instinctive needs; secondly, for the child in this period there does not yet exist anything or anybody; rather what he experiences is more of an internal state than a definite objective content. Both features disappear in the neoformation of infancy.

This neoformation can be defined if we take into account the basic direction in which the whole development of the infant is going. As we have seen this direction consists in this: that the activeness of the child opens only one way to the outside world—the path which runs through another person. Therefore, it is quite natural to expect that, first of all, his joint activity with another person in a concrete situation should differentiate, stand out, and take shape in the infant's *perezhivanies*. It is natural to expect that the infant does not distinguish in his consciousness between himself and his mother.[28]

If the child is physiologically separated from the mother at the moment of birth, then biologically he is not separated from her until the end of infancy, until he learns to walk; and his psychological emancipation from his mother, the detachment of the self from the primordial commonality with her, comes only past the end of the age of infancy, in early childhood. It is for this reason that the main neoformation of the age of infancy can best be denoted with the aid of a term which originally appeared in German literature for the psychological commonality of the infant and the mother, commonality which serves as the starting point for the further development of consciousness. The first thing that arises in the consciousness of the infant might best

[28] In this paragraph, Vygotsky foresees not only the "false belief" problem posed by Simon Baron-Cohen and other researchers in the 1980s but Vygotsky also foresees a solution that does not rely on "egocentrism" but instead on the infant "Ur Wir;" the idea that the world of consciousness is shared in much the same way as the world of perceptions can be. This "Ur Wir" is the true neoformation of infancy.

Baron-Cohen's "false belief" task was this: Anne has a covered basket. Sally has a covered box. Sally takes a chocolate and puts it in her covered box. She then goes to the toilet. While she is in the toilet, Anne takes Sally's chocolate out of Sally's covered box and puts it into her own covered basket. When Sally comes back from the toilet, where will Sally look for her chocolate? Children as old as 4 years will answer that Sally will look in Anne's basket, and not in her own box. When you ask why, they answer that she will look there because that is where the chocolate is. Of course, that is correct—but that is not where Sally thinks the chocolate is.

Vygotsky says that the newborn sees, hears, smells, and feels the world, but only as a general condition, an overall situation, a state of being rather than seeing or hearing people and smelling and feeling things. The newborn feels hunger or fear or warmth or cold, but only as a condition, and not as a desire for objects such as a bottle or a blanket or a mother's arms. The newborn has yet to discover the world of objects, the world of people, and the world where objects come to you through people.

But the infant is different. The infant understands that objects come through other people. Because the child's "path to the outside world" is always through others, the first phenomenon to be differentiated from the newborn consciousness of the world as a general condition is a shared activity. The infant understands that other people have minds or else shared activity like peekaboo and social smiling would be impossible. But to the infant, worlds are always shared worlds, shared activities, and so on, and shared minds as well. This "shared mind" is the main neoformation of infancy, and it distinguishes the infant both from the neonate and from the speaking child at 1.

be identified as an "Ur-wir," that is, a "proto-we."[29] This is the initial consciousness of the psychic commonality which precedes the emergence of conscious personality (i.e., consciousness which has differentiated and singled out an "I") that constitutes the consciousness of a "we," but not the shifting, complex "we" which already includes the later consciousness of an "I" occurring at a later age. This initial "we" is related to the later "we" as a distant ancestor to descendants.

That in the infant there emerges a "proto-we" consciousness ruling all throughout this age can be seen from two facts of fundamental importance. The first one was illuminated in the studies of H. Wallon[30] on the development in the child of ideas about his own body. As the study shows, the child does not at first single out his own body from the surrounding world of things. He arrives at an awareness of external objects earlier than he learns about his own body. In the beginning, the child regards the limbs of his own body as alien objects, and long before he is conscious of them as his own, he unconsciously learns to coordinate his hand motions with his eyes, or both little hands. In this way, the infant, who does not yet know his own body—relates to his own limbs as if to alien objects—cannot, of course, have any idea of his self.

G. Compayré[31] beautifully defines this feature of psychic life as lacking its own centre of consciousness or personality. Strictly speaking, this psychic life cannot yet be called conscious. Actually, Compayré says, we cannot speak in the first days of life of consciousness in the strict sense of the word, that is, of self-awareness, which allows us the capacity of appreciating our existence. Of the child it may be said: he lives and he is not conscious of his life. But if there is no self-consciousness, there exists, undoubtedly, from the very first days, vague feelings and therefore conscious impressions. Compayré is quite right when he characterizes the primordial consciousness of the infant as passive. If we understand this word in the signification that it was given by Spinoza in distinguishing between passive and active, receptive and effective, mental states. It can be rightly argued that the primordial consciousness of the infant is still deprived of all active psychic states, that is, states that are

---

[29] The "Ur-wir" is the German expression for Vygotsky's central neoformation of infant consciousness. Vygotsky, who like most psychologists of his day used German as the main language of science communication, glosses the "Ur-wir" in Russian as a пра-мы, and we have followed him by glossing it in English as a "proto-we." But, as he says at the end of this paragraph, Vygotsky also has in mind something grander, a grandparent of the "we" that existed long before the differentiation of a paternal "you" and a child "I."

Perhaps the best way to understand the "Ur-wir" is neither a primitive "proto-we" nor a grandiose "grand we," but a "we" that is the analogue in interpersonal life of Goethe's Ur-phänomen, the invisible archetype of the phenomenon to be uncovered by a holistic science, for example, the whole system of colors and the way that human consciousness responds to color that can lie hidden from the eye in apparently colorless light, a system which is only partially uncovered by the painter or by the prism.

[30] For a biographical footnote on Wallon, see Footnote 3.

[31] Jules-Gabriel Compayré (1843–1913) was an educator and a moderate politician in the French Third Republic, where he served as a deputy from southern France. He completed a doctorate in philosophy (on David Hume) but he is most famous for a series of books on Rousseau, Pestalozzi, Herbart, and other as well as other "grand educators."

internally defined by the personality. In this sense, we can say that a child passes in a specified period through an animal stage of development which is characterized by the absence of consciousness of his own activities, his own personality.

If the first fact characterized the inability of the infant to single out his body from the surroundings and be aware of his own body and its independent existence, the second one speaks above all about how directly for the child social relations and his relations to external objects are merged. An illustration of this fact is found in the studies of S. Fajans[32] on the influence of spatially distal objects and the affective attraction to them of the infant and the preschooler. Studies showed that optically distancing of objects signified as well a psychic distancing proportional to the distance between the object and the infant; first there was a weakening of the affective attraction of the object. Along with the spatial removal, the contact between the infant and the goal was also suspended. The world at a distance appears nonexistent to him. His goals in the physical sense lie in the immediate vicinity.

The data given by Fajans show that in 75% of cases the affect for the object turns out to be significantly stronger if the object is situated nearby. In only 25% of the cases does removing the object not cause noticeable changes in affect, and never was there any strengthening of affect alongside the removal of the object. In the toddler in early childhood, in 10% of the cases, there was an increase in affect with the removal of the object. In 85%, there was no change in affect depending on the proximity or removal of the object, and only in 5% was the affect for the proximal object more than for the removed one. This was, of course, due to the narrow life limits of the infant.

The observation of Fajans requires, however, two addenda. If we look at the development of ostension, it is easy to see that the child initially grasps at an object that touches his hand. At a later age, the child gropes for the object even when it is far away. Instead of the primordial, directly acting, excitation, we now have a specific reaction to the perception of the object itself. C. Bühler places this fact together with the fact that the child develops a new relation to the object at a distance thanks to which all of his needs are now met by adults, thanks to increased social communication.

In this way, we see that social development in the child impacts not only the direct and immediate increase in his social displays but also in changing and complicating his relationship to things, in the first place to the world at a distance. The remote object is now the object of an affective desire to obtain it (despite the fact that it now falls beyond the sphere of reach), the object is included in the social situation of grasping through others.

Confirmation of this we find in other factual observations with which we would like to supplement the data presented above. We saw that the infant sets himself

[32] Sara Fajans-Glück was a student of Kurt Lewin and published her dissertation on Lewin's idea of "force fields" acting on small children. She and Kurt Lewin published a paper on this subject based on her dissertation, in 1933 (*Die Bedeutung der Entfernung für die Stärke eines Aufforderungscharakters beim Säugling und Kleinkind*), and Vygotsky seems to be citing this paper. So, this part of the manuscript was probably written in the year before Vygotsky's death.

only physically proximal goals and for the child the optical removal of the object is equivalent to the psychic distancing and the disappearance of it and of the affective impulses which attach him to the object. This distinguishes the infant from the small child. The second, more important, difference is that with the removal of the object and the inability to obtain it, the situation is easily changed for the child of early age: the object-related situation between the child and his goal is transformed into a personal social situation between him and the experimenter. In the age of early childhood, the social and the object situation are already sufficiently differentiated. Therefore, we observe the following curious phenomenon: the nonsuccess and incapacity to obtain the goal transforms the object situation into a social one.

For the infant, this is still not possible. For infants, the social situation and the object situation are still not separated. When an object is moved away, as we have seen, in the majority of cases the affective attraction disappears for the infant. But when an infant has already ceased to reach for a distant object, it is very easy to refresh his efforts and once more arouse a lively affect and a lively address to the object, if an adult is located in the direct vicinity of the goal. It is remarkable that renewed attempts to get the object are directed not to an adult, but rather to the goal. This new address to the object appears in an identical degree whether the goal is proximal or distal. One might think, the experimenter says, that the approach of an adult to the object arouses in the child a new hope or that a simple spatial proximity of an adult significantly enhances the intensity of the field surrounding the goal.

The toddler has the same or an even stronger reaction to another person in the situation of his own helplessness, but his reaction is of a differentiated character. When incapable of obtaining the object by his own efforts, he does not turn to the goal, which remains unreachable, but rather to the director of the experiment. The infant reacts completely differently. He continues to seek the unreachable goal, even though the object situation has not changed at all.

It is difficult to imagine a clearer experimental demonstration, first of all, that the centre of any object-related situation for the infant is another person, changing its meaning and sense, and secondly, that the relation with the object and the relation with the person have not been separated by the infant. In itself, the object at a distance loses its powers of affective attraction, but this power comes back to life with the same intensity as soon as next to the object, in immediate proximity to it, in the same optical field with it, there is a person. From a number of experiments we know the influence of the structure of the optical field on perception of an object in animals and in infants. It is known that the object perceived changes its properties depending upon the structure into which the object enters, depending on what is near to it.

Here, we encounter a completely new phenomenon: in the object situation nothing has been changed. The child perceives the object as remote and as inaccessible as before. He is not even to the smallest measure aware that he must seek the help of an adult to get the goal which is unattainable for him. But the affective urge for the object located at a distance depends on whether this object lies in the same field in which the child perceives the person or not. An object near a person, even if it is unreachable and located at a distance, exerts the same affective motivating force as objects which are located in immediate proximity to the child and attainable by his own effort. This could not be clearer than in what the experiments of Fajans show: the relationship to the external world for a child is completely determined by relations through another person, and in the psychological situation of the infant, its object-related and social contents are still merged.

Both considerations—(1) the child not knowing his own body and (2) the dependence of his affective attractions to things on the possibility of sharing *perezhivanie* of the situation with other persons—wholly and thoroughly confirm the dominance of a "proto-we" in infant consciousness. The first shows clearly and immediately from the negative side that the child does not yet have any consciousness of his physical "I." The second shows from the positive side that the simple affective desire flares up in the child in no other way than in the contact between the object and another person, in no other way than as the condition of psychic contiguity, in no other way than as the condition of "proto-we" consciousness.

Usually, the course of social development in the child is sketched in the opposite way. The infant is presented as a purely biological being, not knowing anything other than the self, wholly absorbed in the world of his own inner *perezhivanie,* unable to contact surrounding people. Only slowly and gradually does the infant become a member of a community, socializing their desires, thoughts, and acts. This presentation is false. According to it, the undeveloped psyche of the child is maximally isolated and minimally capable of social relations and of the environment, reacting only to primitive excitations of the outside world.

Everything which is known to us about the psyche of the infant impels us to categorically reject such a presentation. The psyche of the infant from the first moment of life is included in a common existence with other persons. The child does not initially respond to separate sensations but to surrounding people. The child reacts variously to a loud sound just as to a thermal excitation or an injection. Even at this time, the child responds differently to the affective coloration of the human voice, to a change in facial expression. A loud sound, if we consider it as pure energy, is far more imposing than the human voice, and despite this the child is as if deaf in relation to the first, more severe excitation but responds sensibly and in a differentiated way to the much weaker and more difficult to perceive excitation coming from the people in his surroundings. The child is not responding to excitations as such but to the facial expressions of the living people he is exposed to. In the early stages of psychic development, children show a preference for those impressions that are related to their psychic links with living people. The child is in contact, not so much with the world of lifeless external excitations, as through and over them though a much more internal, although primitive, commonality, with other personalities surrounding him.

W. Peters[33] beautifully defines the uniqueness of the *perezhivanie* which is particular to this stage. He says that the child perceives the world not in its objective categories, as something separate from his "I" but from the beginning knows only his own kind of "we" within which "I" and the other form a unitary, coherent structure and are, as it were, mutually constitutive. And, thus, since the child does not know at first his own "I" he, as F. Schiller[34] puts it, lives in another rather than, objectively speaking, in himself. But, and this is the most important, in the other, the child lives in the way we live our "I." Even in later ages, there persists in the child a trace of this inadequate isolation of his own personality from the social whole and from the surrounding world. To this discussion we shall return when considering the theories of the infant age.

W. Peters, we think, completely correctly explains imitation in infancy and in early childhood as that primordial peculiarity of a consciousness of psychic commonality. The child is much earlier on capable of true imitation than of the repetition of motions which arises in a purely associative way. Commonality as a psychic fact is an inner motive, an imitative act on the part of the child. It merges his proper activity in an immediate way to those he imitates. The child never imitates the movements of inanimate objects, such as a swinging pendulum. Evidently, his imitative activity rises only when there is a personal commonality between the infant and those whom he imitates. That is why so little imitation develops in animals and why it is so closely linked to understanding and intellectual processes.

We may take, alongside Peters, the vivid comparison of the activeness of the child standing on this stage in the development of consciousness with a group of close playmates playing with a ball: in the ball game, we have a full fusion of "I" with "thou" in a unitary action of inner "we."

Indeed, imitation may, to all appearances, be attributed to a number of specifically human characteristics. Already the research of W. Köhler has shown that imitation in the ape is limited to the narrow confines of his proper intellectual capacities. Imitation of complex, rational, and expedient action is never possible without understanding of the structure of a situation. In this way, chimpanzees can only

[33] Wilhelm Peters (1880–1963) completed his doctorate under Wilhelm Wundt on color perception in 1904. He then joined the Würzburg School, where in 1915 he published the work on the correlation of school grades; Vygotsky is quite critical of this study, which concludes that intelligence is largely hereditary because there is a significant correlation in school grades between generations. Like many German intellectuals (including Marx and Mendelssohn) he was from a Jewish family that had converted to Christianity; this meant that he lost his job during the Nazi years. He went to London and then Istanbul, and returned to Wurzburg after the war, where he worked for learning disadvantaged school children.

[34] Friedrich Schiller (1759–1805), together with his friend Goethe, constituted the "Ur-wir" of modern German literature, and the "proto-we" of German nationhood. Today his plays are best known through operas (e.g., Verdi's "Don Carlo," Rossini's "William Tell," Puccini's "Turandot," and Donizetti's "Mary Stuart"), and his poetry is best known through Beethoven ("Ode to Joy"), but to his own generation he was well-known as a critic. Vygotsky is probably referring to his criticism of sentimental and naïve poetry, where he remarks not only nature but children who make us feel both ashamed and superior in their lack of self, for example, when a child offers his father's wallet to a needy stranger.

imitate such actions as those that lie within the zone of their own intellectual capacities. All studies of imitation in the ape show that apes "ape" poorly. In them, we not only do not observe the propensity for imitation without measure made famous in fables, but the best possible imitations even among the higher apes are still immeasurably narrower than those of a human. The imitation of an animal is different in principle, in the limited zone of its own capacities. For this reason, the animal can learn nothing that is new with the help of imitation. The child, in contrast, with the aid of imitation, gives rise to a new behavior, never previously experienced.

Having uncovered the basic neoformation of infancy, we may proceed to a concise and concentrated review of some basic theories of this age.

Basic Theories of Infancy

Reflexological Theory[35]

According to this theory, the initial moment of development in the infant presents us with a creature of unconditional reflexes. All the maintenance and the development of the personality in the age of infancy, including its psychic and its social sides, are exhausted by the process of forming conditional reflexes, in their differentiation, in their complex coupling, and combining with each other and in the construction of ever higher and still higher superreflexes from the primary conditional reflexes. With this explanation, reflexological theory attempts to exhaust all the actual complexity of the process.

The development of higher nervous activity, in particular the process of the formation of conditional reflexes, presents without a doubt one of the most important aspects of development in the age of infancy, which for the first time lays a basis for the personal experience of the child. But this process is in a sense intermediate, in that it is due to other, more complex processes of development which act in the role of prerequisites in relation to the development of conditional reflex activity. And this itself, in turn, acts as a prerequisite for more complex and higher forms of psychological and social development of the child. Therefore, reflexological theory may appear adequate for the explanation of the concept of one intermediate aspect of development, but it inevitably leads to the simplification of development as a whole and to ignoring the independent regularity of higher processes of

[35]The Russian *Collected Works* has a long footnote here on the history and membership of the reflexological school, but for contemporary readers it is not really long enough. Reflexology was cofounded by Pavlov and his now forgotten rival Bekhterev. From Vygotsky's point of view, Bekhterev had the advantage of recognizing consciousness and mental states as legitimate objects of study. Bekhterev himself died suddenly and mysteriously after a visit to the Kremlin in 1927, and Pavlovism eventually became the official psychological science of the USSR. The Russian footnote lists, among the prominent reflexologists, N.M. Shchelovanov, M.P. Denisova, N.L. Figurin, and also N.I. Kasatkin, who was earlier cited to disprove Vygotsky's claim that newborns are not capable of imitation.

psychological and social development. By its very essence it is not adequate for the explanation of these aspects of development insofar as, on the one hand, it ignores psychological development of the child and, on the other, it deals with the development of social relations in the child from the point of view of laws relating the body to its physical environment. It is, therefore, inevitable that it allows the reduction of higher laws to a lower and a mechanistic account of development. This mechanism is sharply manifest in the fact that the theory we are considering is not able to specify the difference between social development of the child and animal development.

The Theory of the Three Stages[36]

This theory, the content of which we set out above, is distinguished by the same shortcoming as the previous one: it too attempts in one law to encompass the development of both animals and humans. To speak of the essence, it is a modified and supplemented reflexological theory since, on the one hand, it is not limited to the purely objective consideration of behavior but introduces into the circle of analysis inner psychic activity linked to instincts and skills and, on the other, introduces above the stage of entrainment another, third, stage—intellect, qualitatively distinct from the stage of skill formation.

This theory is also only adequate in application to the narrow area of the development of reactions in the age of infancy. It of necessity places in one stage the intellectual actions of apes and all of the higher manifestations of human thinking that develop in the child in the course of childhood. Its tendency to equate human intellect with animal intellect finds a clear manifestation in the designation of the last stage of infancy as the age of chimpanzeehood. The root and source of this error consists in ignoring the social nature of man.

We have only just seen that what occurs with infants is impossible in the animal world and, in principle, impossible in the chimpanzee's relation to the situation. Even a simplest relation to the situation, as we attempted to show with the example of the experiments of S. Fajans, in the infant is determined and conditioned by the social content of the situation. Neglecting this, the theory of the three stages shuts off any possibility of finding for itself the extant profound and principled distinction between child intellect and chimpanzee intellect, in spite of their outward resemblance. The differences stem from the socially mediated relation of the infant to the situation.

---

[36] According to the Russian *Collected Works*, the theory of three stages is that of Bühler: the three stages are, as Vygotsky pointed out earlier, instincts (innate, unconditional adaptations to the environment), skills/habits (learned, conditional ones), and intelligence (unprecedented adaptations to novel problems). Like reflexology above (and Gestalism below), these three stages cannot account for qualitatively human development because the *social* situation of development is not the starting point, so all three stages are already present and accounted for in animals.

The Structural Theory[37]

The structural theory of the age of infancy, as we have seen, correctly marks the starting point and not a few of the major features of the development of the infant. But it neutralizes itself when it is confronted with the problems of development as such. The beginning and initial moments of development are structures already. In the further course of development, structures complexify, become more and more differentiated overall, and penetrate one another. However, from this point of view, it is impossible to explain how in development generally there can arise anything new. From the point of view of the structural theory, the starting and ending points of development, as with all the intermediate ones, are equally subject to the law of structure. As the French proverb says, the more it changes, the more it is the same thing.

The structural principle in itself is not yet capable of giving a key to understanding the course of development. It is not surprising, therefore, that the structural theory appears more productive and capable of delivering a scientific explanation when it is attached to the most elementary, primitive, and primordial moment. The structural theory, like the two previous ones, attempts to explain on the basis of a general principle the development of animals and humans which turns out to be equally structural in the light of this concept. Therefore, although the theory is most productive in its application to infancy, it reveals its insolvency as soon as it is applied to the development of higher, specifically human properties of the child. Indeed, inside the very age of infancy it is powerless to explain the central problem of anthropogenesis, which in general is unsolvable from the point of view of theories which encompass with a single principle the development of animals and humans.

[37] When Vygotsky talks of "structuralist" theories, he is referring to Gestaltism, the holistic psychology of his friends and co-thinkers in Germany, notably Kurt Lewin. As we have seen, Vygotsky thinks that the Gestalists are correct in the way they delimit the period of infancy and also in the way they note features like perception, imitation, and social smiling as developmental milestones; Gestaltism is the trend of contemporary psychology which is most closely related to Vygotsky's own.

But close relatives sometimes quarrel more than distant acquaintances. Vygotsky's main criticism is that in Gestaltism, the means of development does not itself develop. The child is born with a Gestalt (a structure of perception), and the infant has the same Gestalt (perception). When the child begins to use tools, the Gestaltists explain this as a matter of perceiving the tool and the goal in the same field. Even language is seen as being a "structure" made of sound and meaning, rather than a cultural-historical practice which the child learns by mastering the acts of thinking involved in word meanings. In Gestaltism, everything changes—but nothing develops: some of the Gestaltists were aware of these criticisms, and as we shall see, Lewin tried to address them by distinguishing between intrastage structure and interstage structure.

The Theory Comprehending the Age of Infancy as a Subjectivistic Stage of Development[38]

According to this theory, the newborn presents a completely insular being, fully absorbed in its own subjectivity, and only slowly and gradually establishing contact with the objective world. The content of development in the first year of life is reduced to the transition from a state of complete absorption in subjective experience to intensive focus on objects and to the first perception of objective links. The dynamics of this epoch present a movement from "I" to the external world. Naturally, from the point of view of this theory, objective relationships are perceived by the child initially as a relationship of duty, not a relationship of being. Therefore, in speaking of this epoch, we should speak not so much of the perception of dependencies, but of establishing relations between objects.

The basic thinking behind the theory of the complete subjectivity of the age of infancy, of the path of development of this epoch from the inner core of the personality, from "I" to the external world, as we shall see, is represented even more clearly in the following theory, which we will discuss next. Our critique of it will be relevant to this theory as well.

The Theory of Solipsism as Inherent in the Age of Infancy

This theory is linked, on the one hand, with the previous theory taken to an extreme position and, on the other, with the theories of the age of infancy which have been developed by the school of psychoanalysis (S. Bernfeld).[39] The theory under consideration presents something of a synthesis of these two conceptualizations. In its most complete and consistent view, it is developed by J. Piaget, who says that infant consciousness is for us a mystery. One of the pathways for penetrating his consciousness consists of the pathway of regression. We know, Piaget says, what is the most significant feature that marks off the behavior and thinking of the child from that of an adult person—that is, egocentrism. It increases in measure as we descend the rungs of the age ladder. In the person of 18 years, egocentrism is expressed differently than in a person of 10, and in a 6-year-old yet another way, and so on. At 4 years, egocentrism occupies nearly all of child thinking. If we consider that the

[38] The *Collected Works* attributes this theory to Kurt Koffka, but this seems unlikely on two counts. First of all, Koffka was a Gestaltist, that is, a structuralist, and would therefore belong in the previous category. So in fact many of the arguments summarized in the previous category can be found in Vygotsky's Проблема развития в структурной психологии ("The Problem of Development in Structural Psychology," in the Russian *Collected Works*, Vol. 1, 1982, p. 195–238), which is translated simply as "Preface to Koffka," 1997a, pp. 195–232). Secondly, Koffka's book, "Growth of the Mind," which Vygotsky is very familiar with, is by no means subjectivist and includes ample discussion of the child's social relations—always within the Gestaltist paradigm of figure-ground structures. It seems more likely that Vygotsky has Stern's personalism in mind, particularly since Vygotsky seems to be ordering the theories from objectivistic to subjectivistic.

[39] For a biographical footnote on Bernfeld, see Footnote 2 in Chap. 5.

limit of egocentrism, Piaget believes that absolute egocentrism inheres in infancy, which can be defined as the first year of solipsism.

Logical thinking, for Piaget, develops late in the child. It always comprises something of the social. It is linked to speech. Without words we would think oneirically: in images, combining with vague feelings and having totally individual and affective meanings. This thinking, as opposed to socialized, logically mature thinking, we observe in dreams and in some patients. It is called autistic thinking. Autism and logical thinking—two poles—: one, purely individual, and the other, purely socialized. Our normal mature thinking constantly oscillates between these two poles. In dreams and in a few mental illnesses, a person loses all interest in objective reality. He is immersed in a world of his own affects, which finds expression in figurative emotionally colored thinking.

The infant, according to this theory, also lives as if in a dream. S. Freud speaks of the narcissism of the infant as if he has no interest in anything other than his own self. The infant takes all of the surroundings as his own self, just as the solipsist does, identifying the world with his own ideas of it. Further development of the child consists in the gradual decline in solipsism and a gradual socialization of thinking and of consciousness in the child, who is accessing an external reality. The egocentrism which is peculiar to the child of later ages consists of a compromise between the original solipsism and the gradual socialization of thinking. The degree of egocentrism can, therefore, measure the progress of the child on the developmental path. From this point of view, Piaget interprets the series of child reactions which he observed in experiments as proximal to the type of behavioral forms often manifested in the age of infancy, for example, magical relations toward things.

Even from this simple exposition of the theory it is easy to see that it presents an attempt to depict development in the age of infancy from a viewpoint that is inside out. This theory is the direct polar opposite of the conceptualization of infant development we have presented. We saw that the very beginning moment is characterized by the fact that all the life manifestations of the infant are intertwined and interwoven into the social, that the elongated path of development unfolds in the child a "proto-we" consciousness, and that the consciousness of an inseparable psychological unity, the lack of the possibility of self-separation, constitute the most distinctive properties of the infant's consciousness. The theory of solipsism asserts that the child is a presocial being, completely immersed in the world of his own dreamlike thinking and subordinated to self-contained affective interests. The fault which lies at the foundation of this theory, as with the theory of Freud, consists in the incorrect counterposition of two tendencies: (1) that of satisfying needs versus (2) that of adaptation to reality, that is, the pleasure principle versus the reality principle, and autistic versus logical thinking. In actual fact, the one and the other do not present polar opposites but forms closely linked with one another. The tendency toward satisfying needs is in essence merely the other side of the tendency to adaptation. Pleasure also does not exclude reality. Not only do they not exclude each other but in the age of infancy they nearly coincide.

In just the same way, logical and autistic thinking, affect and intellect are not two mutually exclusive poles, but two inseparable psychological functions whose forms are closely linked to one another, acting in each age level in inseparable unity while embodying new and ever newer relations between the affective and intellectual functions. This question is genetically answered from the point of view of to what extent autistic thinking may be taken as primary and primitive. Freud, as we know, defended this point of view. Contrary to it, E. Bleuler demonstrated that autistic thinking is a late developing function. He countered the thinking of Freud that, in the course of development, the mechanisms of pleasure are primary, that the child is isolated by a shell from the external world, living an autistic life, and hallucinating the satisfaction of his own internal needs. Bleuler says that he sees no hallucinatory satisfaction in the infant; he sees satisfaction only with an actual meal of real food. Observing the older child, he also does not see that the child chooses an imaginary apple over a real one.

The newborn responds in all of his drives to reality and to the spirit of realism. Nowhere can there be found or even imagined a living entity, which does not respond in the first place to reality, which does not act on it, that is completely oblivious of it, no matter how low its stage of development is.

E. Bleuler has pointed out that the autistic function requires maturation of complex preconditions in the form of speech, concepts, and memory capability. The autistic function is not so primitive as simple forms of the realistic function.

In this way, the psychology of animals, as well as the psychology of the infant, knows only the reality function. The autistic thinking of the child makes major successes following the development of speech and the most important steps in the development of concepts. In this way, autistic thinking not only does not coincide with the unconscious and nonverbal, but is itself based on speech development. It turns out to be not the original, but the derivative, form. Autistic thinking is not a primitive form of thinking; it can develop only after that thinking which works with the aid of remembered imagery, takes precedence over the unmediated psychic reactions to actual external situations. Ordinary thinking—the reality function—is primary just as necessary to every viable psychic living being as actions that correspond to reality.

There have been efforts made to limit the use of the theory of solipsism to only the neonatal period. Supporters of this version have explained that the stage of solipsism does not last very long in the infant and already at 2 months has lost its absolute character. The first breach takes place at that moment when the child begins to answer the voice or smile of an adult with an overall animation or with an answering smile. In general, in the light of the known data on the sociability of the infant, it is difficult to accede to a conception relating to a child of more than 2 months. It is applicable, according to our definition, in full measure to children who are severely retarded and to idiots.

This second thesis of Piaget's[40] in relation to infant autism also applies more to oligophrenics than to normal children. This compromise point of view, strictly

---

[40] What exactly does Vygotsky mean when he says: "Piaget's second thesis on child autism?" The English translation of the *Collected Works* translates this vaguely as "Another of Piaget's statements", but this is simply wrong: the text clearly says that there is a second assertion. The first

speaking, does not contradict but confirms Piaget in his idea of the primacy of autistic thinking. Moreover, one cannot but agree with Bleuler, who demonstrated that precisely the primitive stages of development exclude any possibility of nonrealistic thinking. Beginning with a particular stage of development to the original realistic function is joined an autistic one and this develops alongside it. The imbecile, says Bleuler,[41] constitutes the true realistic politician. In him, autistic thinking is simplified along with realistic. In recent times, K. Lewin showed that imagination—one of the most striking manifestations of autistic thinking—is extremely underdeveloped in mentally retarded children. From the development of a normal child, it is known that this function only begins to develop noticeably in him from preschool age.

We think therefore that the theory of solipsism should not merely be limited but replaced by its opponent, as all of those facts which are presented in its favor have their true explanation from the opposing point of view.

So, W. Peters demonstrated that on the basis of egocentric speech and egocentric thinking in the child lies not in autism and not in willful isolation from contact, but is precisely opposite in psychic structure. Piaget who, according to Peters, stresses the egocentrism of children and makes of it the cornerstone that explains the originality of the child psyche, has yet to determine that when children talk to each other they do not listen to each other. Of course, outwardly it may seem as if they do not attend to each other, but this is precisely because they retain still to some extent traces of unmediated contact which is the dominant feature that characterized at one time their consciousness.

In conclusion, we wish to just show that the facts cited by Piaget find their true explanation in the light of the above teaching concerning the main neoformation of the age of infancy. Piaget, analyzing the logical operations of the infant, anticipates the objections that his theory may evoke. One might suppose, he writes, that the

assertion appears to be that autism and self-observation is primary. This is really not satisfactory to Vygotsky from a genetic point of view: where did this self-observing-a-self come from? Piaget derives it by going backwards from the egocentrism of older children. Vygotsky says this kind of "primacy of autism" may occur, but not in normal children: the primacy of the autistic function is a sign of a severe developmental pathology.

So the second assertion appears to be Piaget's assertion that the coefficient of egocentrism is an index of development. The more egocentric the child is, the less developed he is. Here, Vygotsky says this is ALSO not true of normal children. With normal children, egocentric or "autistic" thinking develops along with logical thinking (and after the child acquires speech, we see a zig-zag path from logical, epistemic thinking to autistic, deontic thinking). It is only with anomalous development (e.g., brain damage), when children cannot develop culturally, that we can say that the more egocentric the child is the less developed the child is.

[41] Paul Eugen Bleuler (1857–1939) was a Swiss psychiatrist, Freud's student and Piaget's teacher. He was, as a doctor, a biologically oriented psychologist, he was also an enthusiastic champion of psychoanalysis, responsible for the concepts of "schizophrenia," "autism," and the idea of "ambivalence" (e.g., loving and hating your parents at one and the same time). As Vygotsky notes in the second chapter of *Thinking and Speech*, Bleuler fell out with Freud over the concept of "hallucinatory satisfaction." Freud did not respond to criticism very well, and Bleuler left the International Psychoanalytic Association in 1910, complaining that it was more like a religious cult or a political party than a scientific institution.

infant employs an action to get a result simply because he believes that his parents will fulfill his wishes. According to this hypothesis, the method which is employed by the child for the purpose of operations on objects only amounts to a sort of language, employed by them to make contact with persons in proximity; this is not magic, but requesting. In this way we might suppose that a child of 1½ or 2 years resorts to his parents when he requires anything and simply says "Please!", unconcerned with specifying exactly what he wants, so convinced is he that his wishes are known by his parents. But, in Piaget's words, if this hypothesis might seem plausible for a child who is already beginning to speak, then until that moment it is absolutely unsound. As one of the basic arguments against this hypothesis, as the best proof that the primitive behavior is not social and the behavior of 1-year-old cannot be regarded as social, Piaget considers the following circumstance: the child does not yet distinguish between persons and things. Therefore, Piaget holds, at this age we may speak only of solipsistic, and not about social, behavior.[42]

However, as we have seen, in the child of 2 months, there is already all of the subsequently developing and increasingly complex specialized reactions of a social nature (to the human voice and to the expression on a human face), the active seeking out of contact with other person, and other symptoms which without a doubt demonstrate that even a child of the age of infancy distinguishes a person and a thing.

We have seen from the experiments of Fajans that the child's relation to the object is wholly determined by the social content of the situation in which the object is given. Is it possible to say of the child's behavior in these experiments that he does not distinguish people from things? What is true in Piaget's thinking is only that for the infant the social and object content of the situation is not yet differentiated. Unlike a child of 2 who has mastered speech, the infant is not able to differentiate between a request for aid to an adult and a direct action on an object. As we have seen in experiments with distant objects, the child who has already given up reaching for an unattainable goal will again, with the vivid enthusiasm, renew his attempts once in the vicinity of the goal there appears a person. True, the child does not turn to the experimenter for aid, but continues to reach directly for the object, and this gives the impression of magical behavior. But the experiment unmistakably shows that this appearance of magical action emerges in the child only under the influence of a situation with an unreachable goal which suddenly becomes reachable in way that is ordinary for the child, through another person. The child is not yet conscious of this path and does not know how to employ it deliberately, but only in the presence of this path are his quasi-magical actions actualized. A careful analysis of the

[42] Recent evidence shows that infants as young as 3 months old (and even cats, dogs, and magpies) do understand object permanence. So, as with Piaget's observations of self-directed speech we cannot explain Piaget's results with Piaget's explanations. But, as with Piaget's observations of self-directed speech, Vygotsky can explain them; he explains the child's propensity to look away from an object that cannot be seen and to talk to objects that are too far away to reach in the same way—it is not the "magic" of egocentrism, but rather the child's knowledge of, and even overgeneralization of, sociality.

experiments of Piaget would also have shown that the child reacts with magical actions not to the situation with the object that has disappeared, but to the situation the centre of which is the path to the object, which runs through a relationship to another person. In this way, the solipsistic behavior of the infant turns out, in fact, to be social behavior characteristic of the "proto-we" of infant consciousness.

References

Brodal, P. (2016). *The central nervous system*. Oxford University Press.
Bühler, C., Hetzer, H., & Tudor-Hart, B. (1927). *Soziologische und psychologische Studien über das erste Lebensjahr*. Fischer.
Bühler, Ch., Hetzer, H., & Tudor-Hart, B. (1927, published in Russian 1931). *Soziologische und psychologische Studien über das erste Lebensjahr*. Jena and Moscow.
Elkonin, D. B., & Zaporozhets, A. V. (Eds.). (1964/1971). *The psychology of preschool children*. MIT Press.
Harrower, M. (1983). *Kurt Koffka: An unwitting self-portrait*. University Presses of Florida.
Koffka, K. (1925/1980). *The growth of the mind*. Transaction Books.
Leontiev, A. N. (1936/2005). Study of the environment in the pedological works of L.S. Vygotsky. *Journal of Russian and East European Psychology, 43*(4), 8–28. https://doi.org/10.1080/10610405.2005.11059254
Leontiev, A. N. (1981). *Problems of the development of the mind*. Progress.
Lhermitte, J. (1925). *Les fondements biologiques de la psychologie*. Editions Gauthier-Villars. Science et civilisation.
Vygotsky, L. S. (1997). *Collected works Vol. 4*. Plenum.
Wallon, H. (1943). *De l'acte à la pensée*. Flammarion.
Wallon, H. (1949). *Les origines du charactère chez l'enfant*. Presse universitaires de France.
Zaporozhets, A. V., Zinchenko, V. P., & Elkonin, D. B. (1954/1971). Development of thinking. In D. B. Elkonin & A. V. Zaporozhets (Eds.), *The psychology of preschool children* (pp. 186–254). MIT Press.
Варшава Б. Е. и Выготский Л.С. (1931). *Психологический словарь*. Мособлполиграфа.

Chapter 7
The Crisis of the First Year of Life

Outline of Chapter 7: The Crisis of the First Year of Life

If we have done our translation sensitively and correctly, the attentive reader should discern a change in Vygotsky's voice. With this chapter, he is more tentative, more discursive, with more questions both to himself and to us, and with far fewer decisive answers. That is because with this chapter, we must leave Vygotsky's written manuscript. Fortunately, we still have transcriptions of the spoken lectures apparently given while he was thinking through the chapters which he intended to write.

This is one. It appears to be part of the same follow-up course that Vygotsky talked about in the *Foundations of Pedology* lectures (*L.S. Vygotsky's Pedological Works Vol. 1*, 2019). If so, the lecture was given at the A.I. Herzen Pedagogical Institute in Leningrad during the academic year 1933/34, that is, during the last year of Vygotsky's life. Like all the lectures after the first four chapters of this book, it appears in the Russian *Collected Works*, where a note says that it is based on a manuscript from the archives of the Vygotsky family. This chapter and the next three are, therefore, merely alternative translations of material which has already appeared in Volume 5 of Vygotsky's English *Collected Works* (1998). But placing this material in the context of this second volume of Vygotsky's pedological works, after the first four chapters that detail the basic concepts of age-related development and following the critical example of the chapter on birth and the stable example of the chapter on infancy enables, we think, a much better understanding of why it is organized the way it is.

Vygotsky begins, once again, by analyzing empirical content: the "being and non-being" of walking, talking, and self-control in the 1-year-old. He then announces that he will concentrate on only one of these: "autonomous" speech. For Vygotsky, the very name "autonomous speech" presents a theoretical problem. On the one hand, he must demonstrate that it is not truly autonomous and is in fact a form of communication with others and with the self (as he did with Piaget's "egocentric

The material in this chapter is from the 1984 Russian edition of Vygotsky's *Collected Works*.

L. S. Vygotsky, *L.S. Vygotsky's Pedological Works. Volume 2.*, Perspectives in Cultural-Historical Research 10, https://doi.org/10.1007/978-981-16-1907-6_7

speech"). On the other hand, he must show that it differs from speech proper, or else this period cannot be clearly distinguished from early childhood. Vygotsky solves this problem by, on the one hand, considering "autonomous speech" to be a kind of "Ur-Speech" or "Proto-speech" (by analogy with the "Ur Wir" which is prior to the child's sense of other), and, on the other, enumerating four ways in which this "Proto-speech" must differ from true speech: phonetically, semantically, as communication (that is, pragmatically), and in the combination of ideas (syntactically). Vygotsky concludes the lecture with reservations; Vygotsky himself worries that his point of view on this leading neoformation is "insufficiently developed" and even says this lecture has been too centered on one line of development (speech). But while he cautions against ignoring the secondary actors in the drama (non-speech lines of development such as teething, walking, etc.), he is confident of his preliminary results on theoretical grounds. Speech is the concrete form that the relationship of consciousness to the environment—and even the relationship of consciousness to itself—must take in future development.

I. **The social situation of development at one and some neoformations.** Vygotsky says that the observable content of the crisis is manifest in three ways, which we might call "Proto-walking," "Proto-talking," and "Proto-will." In each case, he points out a dialectical contradiction having to do with the unity of being and nonbeing in any act of becoming:

   A. The child is and is not walking: the neoformation of behavior is coming into being.
   B. The child is and is not talking: a neoformation of speech is coming into being.
   C. The child is and is not controlling himself: a neoformation of thinking is coming into being.

   But then Vygotsky says he will "put aside" the first and the last lines of development and concentrate almost entirely on the second, speech development. Why, the reader may ask, doesn't Vygotsky put speech development last in his list, since he intends to dwell upon it and put the others aside? If we take the child's social situation of development as the totality of relations between the child (the site of development) and the environment (the source of development), we find that Vygotsky in his discussion of the social situation of development, the lines of development, and the neoformations, will almost always proceed from the site of development to the source of development. As Vygotsky explains, speech development is most obviously linked on the one hand with the child's social relations (with others) and on the other hand with child consciousness (the social relation of the child to himself).

II. **Critical review of theories on the origins of speech.** Vygotsky begins his critical review of extant theories on the origins of speech by dismissing the associative theory, that is, the theory that the child simply "associates" a sound with an object after many moments of experiencing them together. Since the theory solves the problem of development by simply abolishing it and reducing the development of speech to the accumulation of vocabulary, there would be little point in disputing it, were it not for the fact that subsequent theories which tried to explain how speech does develop have unfortunately taken on the simple, "one and for all," associative model of how meanings are acquired.

A. The first post-associative theory was Stern's. Stern believed that the child not only accumulates vocabulary by learning the names of some objects, the child also understands that everything (including invisible objects, imaginary objects, abstract sets of objects, actions, etc.) can, in theory, be named.
B. Vygotsky then discusses very briefly—in a single paragraph—the Bühler theory, which is simply a negation of the instantaneous character of Stern's theory. Vygotsky, interestingly, seems to support Stern here: he suggests that Bühler's theory rests on data taken from cases of abnormal development (in Viennese deaf children).
C. Next, Vygotsky discusses Wallon's work. Wallon argues, contrary to Bühler, that the child really does make a discovery, but Wallon also argues, contrary to Stern, that the child doesn't discover the conventionality of language at all but only new ways of getting and playing with objects (by asking for and describing them).
D. Finally, Vygotsky considers the work of Kurt Koffka and the Gestaltists. Koffka sees the discovery of speech as essentially the discovery of a "structure," similar to the ape's discovery that a banana can be reached with a stick. In this way, Vygotsky says, the Koffka theory treats language as a way of getting and playing with objects, just as the Wallon theory did. What all these theories have in common is the Sternian idea that meaning comes to the child ready-made, once and for all. What they all lack is any attempt to describe or explain the transitional stage between no speech and speech, and it is to this task that Vygotsky now turns.

III. **Proto-speech to speech proper: Lines of development**

A. Early Descriptive Work on Proto-Speech: Darwin and Stumpf. Vygotsky reminds us of the infant's social situation of development—that is, the basic dialectical contradiction between being and nonbeing that must characterize any age period. According to Vygotsky, it is the contradiction between the child's maximal sociality and the child's lack of the means of social communication. This dialectical contradiction brings into being a wide variety of surrogates for speech.
B. Proto-speech as the Dialectical Unity of the Grammatical Environment and the Nongrammatical Child. Vygotsky now elaborates these early observations of proto-speech by revisiting Darwin's four distinctions as if they were lines of development connecting the child's own consciousness with proto-speech as an emergent critical neoformation.
C. Some Case Studies. Vygotsky now illustrates using some concrete examples. Once again, he follows the order established by Darwin: phonology

(sounding), semantics (meaning), pragmatics (communicative functions), and lexicogrammar (organizing).

D. Situational Meaning and Volitional Wording. Vygotsky, always interested in experiments which show how children think when relatively free of direct adult influence, now considers proto-speech as precisely such an experiment. He finds two features which he believes suggestive of child thinking.

IV. **The neoformation of the crisis at one**

A. Proto-speech or Pre-speech? Vygotsky suggests that the emergence, development, and disappearance of proto-speech delimit the crisis at 1, making it a unique period of development, distinguishing from infancy and early childhood, and giving it a critical character. He even suggests that proto-speech is itself the neoformation, and not simply a symptom of the new structure of consciousness that is the true neoformation. But as soon as he makes this surprising suggestion, he has some reservations. Recalling the two other manifestations of the crisis from the beginning of the lecture, namely, learning to walk and temper tantrums, he asks if the relationship between proto-speech and speech is really the same as between learning to walk and walking. In other words, does proto-speech really disappear, or is it, in essence, the same as speech proper?

B. Yes and No. Vygotsky replies by going through the categories of sounding, meaning, communicating, and organizing once again, but this time considering them in the light of the concept of transitional form.

C. The Development of Word Meaning. We already know about this development from the negative side: we know that children who cannot get beyond proto-speech will remain essentially speechless. But we also know that children can transcend proto-speech quite suddenly, after a long period of latency, and we can see that even in aphasics, words of proto-speech offer a wide number of meanings. Word meanings, contrary to what Stern believes, are never simple, and therefore cannot develop "once and for all"; there are at least three dialectical leaps (to indicative meaning, to nominative meaning, and to signifying meaning) in their development, and, contrary to what Stern believes, these are mostly taken quite without the child being aware.

D. The Criticality of Proto-speech. Vygotsky notes that a true understanding of the Crisis at One offers a whole approach to speech development (that is, an approach based on the multilayered, palimpsestic nature of word meaning). This approach will offer an alternative to "bourgeois" views on word meaning (i.e., views which either treat meaning as copyrightable individual productions or treat meanings as a kind of common currency, like money). However, Vygotsky concludes cautiously, with some reservations. As with the "unity of being and non-being," and as with the emergence of proto-speech in interaction rather than unilaterally from the child or from the environment, Vygotsky sees in the "sublation" of proto-speech the dialectical character of development, with those things which are "set aside" persisting in a dependent form in the more permanent accomplishments that last.

Chapter 7: The Crisis of the First Year of Life

The empirical content of the crisis of the first year of life is extremely simple and easy. Although its critical nature was not underlined, it was studied before that of the other critical ages. To speak of walking, of such a period when it cannot be said of the child that he is either walking or not walking, of when, to use a highly dialectical formulation, concerning the formation of walking—it may be said that there is a unity of being and nonbeing, that is, what is and what is not, everyone knows that it is a rare child who begins to walk all at once, although there are such children. A more meticulous study of a child who begins to walk all at once would show that in general we are dealing in this case with a latent period in its origin and formation and the relatively late emergence of walking itself. Yet, after the beginning of walking, there is often an abrupt cessation. This indicates that fully matured walking has not yet taken place.

The child in early childhood is already a walking child—doing so badly, with difficulty—but nevertheless this is a child for whom walking is the basic form of moving through space.

The coming-into-being[1] of this walking is the first moment in the content of this crisis.

The second moment pertains to speech. Here again, we have a process in development when speech both exists and does not yet exist, when it cannot be said whether the child is speaking or not. This process is also not accomplished within a day, although there exist cases where a child suddenly begins to speak. Here too we confront a period of latency in the establishment of speech, which lasts approximately 3 months.

The third moment—from the aspect of affects and will. E. Kretschmer called these hypobulic reactions. By this he had in view that, linked to the crisis in the child, there emerges the first acts of protest, opposition, counterposition, "insubordination," in the language of authoritarian family enculturation. These phenomena Kretschmer suggested should be called hypobulic, in the sense that they are referring to volitional reactions presenting a qualitatively completely different stage in the development of voluntary reactions and are not differentiated into will and affect.

---

[1]Vygotsky is referring to Chapter VII, sections 84–111 of Hegel's *Logic* (1830/1972: 128). When we think of pure being (as opposed to being something) the abstract, featureless thought always tends to disappear into its opposite, nonbeing or nothing. But the development—the emergent "truth"—of being (e.g., of walking, talking, and consciousness) is the unity of being with nonbeing. Hegel call this unity of being and the nonbeing that borders it "becoming," but Vygotsky uses становление, which we have translated as "coming-into-being."

Such reactions of a child in the age of crisis are sometimes shown with very great strength and sharpness, especially if enculturation has been incorrect, and they acquire the characteristic form of hypobulic seizures, the description of which is linked to the teaching on difficult childhood. Usually, the child to whom something has been denied or who has not been understood, displays a sharp increase in affects, often ending with the child lying on the ground, starting to frantically scream, refusing to walk, or if he walks, stomping his feet on the ground, but there is no loss of consciousness, no drooling, and no enuresis, and other symptoms characterizing epileptic seizures do not occur. This is merely a tendency (which makes the reaction hypobulic), sometimes directed against certain prohibitions, rebuffs, and so on, and it is expressed, as it is usually described, in a kind of regressive behavior, as if the child is thrown back to an earlier period (when he throws himself to the floor, flops, refuses to walk, etc.) but it is utilized, of course, completely differently.

It is these three basic moments that are usually portrayed as the content of the crisis of the first year of life.

We will first of all put to one side the two other moments and approach this crisis from the angle of speech. I have chosen speech because, to all appearances, it is most often linked to the emergence of child consciousness and to the child's social relations.

The first question has to do with the birth process of speech. How does the birth of speech come about? Here we have two or three counterposed points of view or theories, mutually exclusive of each other.

The first of these is the theory of the gradual emergence of speech on an associative basis. To some degree, this theory is already defunct, and fighting with it means fighting with the deceased, with something that is of historical interest only. One ought, nevertheless, to mention it because as always happens, theories die out but bequeath as a legacy some conclusions, which, like their children, outlive their parents. Some followers of the aforementioned theory still hamper the development of the study of the development of child speech, and without overcoming their errors, there cannot be a correct approach to this question.

The associative theory presents the matter in a way that is exceptionally straightforward and direct: the connection between a word and its meaning[2] is a simple associative link between two parts. The child sees an object, for example a clock, and hears a complex of sounds "ч-а-с-ы" [that is, ",часы" the Russian word for

[2]The Russian word Vygotsky uses is значение. We might translate this as "value," in which case we emphasize that it is a scientific concept and can be further subdivided into "meaning" or "sense," as Vygotsky does in the final chapter of *Thinking and Speech*. Marx used "value" (Wert) as a scientific concept, which he further differentiated into "exchange value" and "use value"; in some ways, Vygotsky's distinction in *Thinking and Speech* between "sense" and "meaning" is comparable, because "meanings" are generally exchanged word values, while "senses" are word values in use. Saussure (1972: 114) and Gestaltist psychologists like Wolfgang Köhler (1966: 52) used "value" to emphasize meanings that are defined not by immediate, contextual relationships to objects but by abstract, decontextualizable relationships to other meanings. Because Vygotsky is using the word for both every day and scientific concepts, we have chosen to translate it as "meaning," but it should be understood that this can refer to either exchange-meanings or use-senses.

clock, spelt out—Trans.], and between the one and the other a certain link is established so that it suffices for the child between one and the other, he establishes a certain connection, sufficient so that, upon hearing the word "часы" ("clock"—Trans.), the child recalls[3] an object that is associated with these sounds. In the picturesque expression of one of the students of H. Ebbinghaus, the word reminds us through this associative link of its value in much the same way as an overcoat reminds us of its owner. We see that hat, and we know that the hat belongs to somebody, and this hat reminds us of that person.[4]

From this point of view, therefore, all the problems are removed. Firstly, by itself the relationship between the meaning of the word and the word is sketched as something that is to the highest degree elementary and simple. Secondly, any possibility of the subsequent development of child speech is excluded: if associative dependencies are formed, they may then be refined, enriched, and in place of one dependency we may place twenty, (but—Trans.) the associative link itself does not develop in the proper sense of the word, if by development, we understand a process where at the next stage something new arises that did not exist before. From this point of view, the development of child speech is reduced exclusively to the development of vocabulary, that is, a quantitative increase, the enrichment and **refinement** of associative links, but development in the strict sense of the word is completely ruled out.

This proposition is very clearly formulated by the same student of Ebbinghaus when he says that the meanings of children's words are acquired all at once and for all time. This is a capital, not subject to change and not subject to development throughout life; that is, the child acquires knowledge and develops, but the word, throughout the child's development, remains unchanging. From this point of view, the question of the emergence of child speech is eradicated, because, on the one hand, everything comes down to the slow accumulation of articulation and

---

[3]The English word "remember" may be translated as either вспомнить (to recall) or запомнить (to memorize); English doesn't clearly mark this distinction. But in Russian, these two words are very different: one means to take something out of your memory and the other means to put something into it. They are different Russian words and their meanings exclude each other in Russian in a way they do not in English. In the same way, "meaning" and "sense" can mean the same thing in everyday English usage, but they too represent different words in Russian and German, words whose meanings repel each other. Both are good examples of the point made in Footnote 2 just above: Saussure's and Köhler's conviction that the precise value of a word is determined by other words and not by its relation to an object or even a concept.

[4]Hermann Ebbinghaus (1850–1909) was a German school psychologist who is best known today for creating the IMRAD (Introduction-Method-Result-And-Discussion) format still widely used in science papers. He was hired to study why child ability in school declines during the day, and instead performed experiments using randomly generated consonant-vowel-consonant nonsense syllables (e.g., "yag" or "tul") on his own forgetting. Note that the very design of his experiment precludes anything but associative principles for learning by excluding the meanings which make words memorable and relying only on experimentally produced associations. Nevertheless, his main discovery was that both learning and forgetting are exponential rather than linear in their mathematical description. This was rather hard to explain from the point of view of the associative theory, which would seem to predict a more linear curve. The student of Ebbinghaus included William Stern, and he may be alluding to Stern here.

phonation movements, and on the other—to the preservation of the link between objects and the word which designates this object.

The associative point of view has long been dead and buried, and it would be pointless to further criticize it now. Its inadmissibility has become so clear that we need not dwell upon it any more. But although as a whole, it is long since buried, in the succeeding theories its notion that the meaning of a word is acquired **once and for all**, that it is the sole asset of the child, has nevertheless persisted. It seems to me that it is in consideration of this that we must begin to build a correct theory of child speech. The research which followed the associative theory excluded the question of the development of word meanings from its field of view. The associative theory was accepted on faith, but it was nevertheless understood that associative psychology incorrectly explained the mechanism for the emergence of word reference; what was aimed for was an explanation of the origins of words in a way that would satisfy the requirement of **once and for all**. Then, historically, there arose a second group of theories, of which the typical representative is W. Stern.

According to Stern's theory, the first word constitutes a fundamental step in child development. This step too is all at once and for all time. However, it does not consist of a simple associative link between sound and object, because such associative links exist in animals as well (it is very easy to teach a dog to turn his eyes to look at an object that you name). In essence, says Stern, the child first makes the greatest discovery of his life: he comes to know that each thing has its name, or (as a second way of formulating one and the same law) the child discovers the link between sign[5] and meaning, that is, discovers the symbolizing function of the word, that all things can be referred to with signs, with symbols.

This point of view has been very productive for factual research; it discovered facts which could not be discovered by the associative theory. It suggested that a slow and gradual accumulation of associative links in the development of speech does not occur; rather, after the discovery, there is a sudden growth in child vocabulary.

The second symptom, which was indicated by Stern—the transition of the child from a passive to an active expansion of his vocabulary. No one has ever seen any animal attempting to understand human words or asking for the names of objects which had not been named. For the child, says Stern, it is characteristic that he knows as many words as he has been given but then begins to ask about the names of objects; that is, he acts as if he understood that every object should be named in some way. Stern believes that this child discovery should be considered the first general concept of the child.

Finally, the third symptom consists of the following: in the child, there arises the first questions about naming, that is, active extension of the vocabulary leading to

[5]Vygotsky uses the term знак, which is sometimes translated as "symbol" (e.g., in the title "Tool and Symbol in Child Development") but which we have translated as "sign," in order to show that it is not simply a vague word for any metaphor but a scientific genus with content that can be specified: it covers gestures and names as well as true symbols (that is, words that refer to concepts rather than simply present or nonpresent physical objects).

the child asking about new things: "What's this?" Indeed, all three symptoms belong to early childhood, but they stem from that discovery of which Stern speaks.

What can be said in favor of Stern's theory?[6]

First of all, what speaks for it are three symptoms of capital importance, which always indicate whether there has been a fundamental turning point in the development of the child's speech or not. Secondly, this theory more profoundly illuminates, in terms of the specific features of human thinking, the act of formation of the first child's sense-making word; that is, it rejects the associative character of the link between sign and meaning. Third, changes in speech development which occur do so catastrophically and have a near instantaneous character.

In this way, there is a good deal of data which tells us that Stern's theory has been groping toward something that is really going on in the life of the child. But what speaks against the theory is its completely incorrect interpretation of these moments. I have expressed my thinking to Stern himself. In response, I heard that a range of thoughts had troubled him ever since the creation of his theory, that is, since the writing of the book *Die Kindersprache* ("Children's Speech"—Trans.).[7] Part of these objections were voiced by other critics as well. As a result, Stern is working to change his own theory, although not in that direction which was previewed by my objections, but in a different way which I will discuss below. Traces of this revision can be found in recent studies by Stern.

What speaks against this theory? In my view, some facts of capital significance which must be mentioned in order to clear a way to the proper solution to the question.

Firstly, it is improbable that a child of a year or a year and 3 months should be so intellectually developed as to himself be able to make such a fundamental discovery as the link between sign and meaning, and form this first general concept; that he is such a theoretician as to be able to make this great generalization, that each thing has its own name. Such, as Stern argues, is the substance of speech. For we adults, the sense of speech lies in this: that each thing has its own name. It is hard to assume that a child of one and a half years has discovered this sense of speech. This does

---

[6]This rhetorical question is treated as a subheading in the English *Collected Works* but not in the Russian *Collected Works*. We follow the latter, for three reasons: there are no other such headings in the chapter, neither the title chapter nor the rest of the chapter seem to justify highlighting the advantages of Stern's theory in this way, and this lecture was given in spoken form long before PowerPoint slides.

[7]Vygotsky uses the German title of the Sterns' book and inserts a Russian gloss in parentheses himself. He might have met Stern on his trip through Germany to London in 1925 (see van der Veer & Zavershneva, 2011 for his precise itinerary, which took him through Berlin). If so, Vygotsky was unimpressed; he subsequently wrote a very critical review of *Die Kindersprache* (Clara & William Stern, 1907/1928), published as Chapter Three of *Thinking and Speech* (Vygotsky, 1934/1987). Stern philosophy assumes that the child has the rudiments of personality, and therefore language, at birth. From Vygotsky's point of view, Stern's alterations to his original theory (e.g., Stern, 1919) made it more innatist and metaphysical, not less. Stern's broad emphasis on personalism from birth runs through all of the theories Vygotsky criticizes in this chapter. With the repudiation of extreme forms of behaviorism, it has arguably become the dominant current in child psychology today.

not fit with the intellectual level of a child who has not even discovered the mechanism of a matchbox; it is so contrary to the syncretic thinking of the child!

Stern acknowledges this objection as very just.

Second, experimental research shows: not only does the child of a year and a half not discover the logical substance of speech, but even the school age child has not yet completely understood what a word is, does not tell himself what a link between an object and a word means, and even many adult persons, especially those retarded in their cultural development, do not realize this even to the ends of their lives.

As shown in the studies of J. Piaget, H. Wallon and others,[8] the child at school age sometimes still has a tendency not to understand the conventions of speech, but to consider the name of a thing as some attribute of it. For example, when you ask a child of 3 years why a cow is called a cow, he will answer you: "Because it has horns" or "Because it gives milk"; that is, to the question of the reason for a name the child never says that it is simply a name that people have invented as an arbitrary designation. He will always look for an explanation for the name in the properties of the thing itself: a herring (селедка) is called a herring because it is salty (соленая); or because it swims (плавает) in the sea; a cow is called "cow" because it gives milk, but a calf is called "calf" because it is still small and doesn't give milk.

Tests were produced for children of preschool age. A range of objects were named and it was asked why these objects were so called: as sound symptoms,[9] conditionally, and so on. Objects were so called because they suit their properties—such was the sense of the responses. In early childhood, the child always draws on

[8] Piaget (1929/1971: 81) and Wallon (1930/1943: 274) attempted to discover if children understood that language is a convention—an agreement by the speakers of a language to call a particular thing by a particular name. Both discovered that children appear to be quite sensitive to similarities in sound and similarities in meaning. Some of Vygotsky's examples require an understanding of Russian to follow: in each case, a similarity in sound offers the child a similarity in meaning. For example, the Russian word for herring (seledka) sounds a little like the Russian word for salty (solenaya), the Russian word for cow (korova) sounds a little like the Russian word horn (roga). The adult cow (korova) gives milk (moloko), and these words have the same number of syllables. A calf (telenok) is still small (malenki), because both words have "len" in the middle. In all of these cases, the child is trying to discover similarities in sound which are clues to similarity in meaning. The child does not understand that some word meaning is simply conventional, and the clues that the child is looking for in the sounds of speech may have existed once but are now lost in the history of language.

[9] A "sound-symptom" value is onomatopoiec—the value is derived from the sound, as in "bow-wow" for "dog," "moo-cow" (Joyce, 1916/1992) or "rao" for "lion" and "chuffa" for "train" (Halliday, 2004). It is easy to see how these values might be considered aural attributes of the objects they name. "Conditional" values, in contrast, are the result of a conditional reaction—for example, Pavlov ringing the bell before a dog's dinner. Unlike sound-symptoms, conditional values are much freer. This, and only this, makes Stern's principle that everything can be named possible. But even conditional values are not "arbitrary," since they require a shared convention, and shared conventions often do draw on sound-symptoms, similarities with other word-values, and other iconic and indexical resources. It is only from the point of view of some other shared convention that language conventions can seem "arbitrary" in the sense of unmotivated, as Vygotsky makes clear in the second paragraph where he compares the false "naturalness" of the mother tongue to the false "naturalness" of feelings for the fatherland that fed the fires of World War I.

the properties of things. This is what gave rise to Wallon first remarking that the child even later does not understand this conditionality but maintains the notion of a word as one of the attributes of the things, or one of the properties of things.

After him, this was likewise demonstrated by Piaget and other authors.

H. Wallon recollects Humboldt's well-known linguistic anecdote (and, by the way, analogous facts were published by linguists of different countries during the last imperialist war). In Humboldt's anecdote, a Russian soldier explains why water is called "Wasser" in German, but in French such-and-such, and in English so-and-so. "But after all, water is вода ("water"—T) and that's what it is—not 'Wasser'." According to the soldier, our language is correct, and everyone else refers to water incorrectly. This is for Von Humboldt (and it seems to me as well) a fundamental trait, a symptom of the following: the name of a thing is so tightly bound up with it that it is difficult to imagine that the name might be different.

Consequently, experimental work also shows that a child at this age does not make such a "discovery."

I will not set out all of the objections against the Sternian theory here; I only note that experimental analysis of the first questions of children show: the child never asks about the titles but only about the purpose and sense of the thing.

The most serious flaw in the Stern theory, in my view, is that it assumes a well-known logical fallacy, which has received the name *petitio principii* in logic. We might translate this coarsely as "ass backwards" or "putting the cart before the horse." The essence of the affair consists in the following: instead of saying how in the child, there is formed a general conception of speech, it is from the very beginning deduced by the child. This is the same fallacy as if one imagines that language originated from some mutual agreement, that people lived separately, could never come to agreement, and then got together and agreed, "This will be called such and such, and that will be so-and-so." What is the flaw in this theory? It assumes that the meaning of language exists before language; that the idea of language and the benefits it gives exists before the emergence of language.

Stern does the same thing. Instead of explaining how there emerges in the child the understanding of the link between the sign and its meaning, how this understanding at different stages of life varies, he assumes: from the beginning it is discovered, that is, the child, not having speech, already has the conception of what speech is. From this theory, speech follows from the concept of it, while the real course of development is that in the process of speech, the child develops a certain idea concerning it.

Finally, Stern's view completely eliminates the question of the development of child speech, its semantic side, since if at the age of one and a half years I made this discovery, the greatest in my life, then it only remains for me to draw the conclusions from it I might need.

K. Bühler, in a parodistic paper, put it very well when he said that Stern depicts the child and his speech development in the form of a rentier who acquires capital and then clips coupons.

Depending on this Stern comes to propositions which stand in flagrant contradiction with all the factual data of research. As is known, the basic idea of Stern's monograph “Die Kindersprache” consists in this: speech development at 5 years old is already completed, and afterwards only nonmajor changes take place; meanwhile as contemporary studies demonstrate: a range of new concepts become possible only at school age. It appears to me that the basic flaw in Stern’s conception consists in the attempt to transfer the most important development to the outset. Stern’s central idea lies in this: all development is like a leaf from a bud. By this path, Stern arrives at personalistics. Thus in him there is a tendency to push development to the very outset, that is, to place in the first position the beginning stages of development and to confirm their governing significance. Here there are other authors—K. Bühler, A. Gesell—who argue that in essence, the whole of child development turns on the axis of the first years of life.

All of this compels us to reject Stern’s point of view. It must be said that at this time, it is already being abandoned in psychology. Instead, we have a number of new points of view. These I will consider briefly.

The Bühlerian point of view. What Stern says is that an instantaneous discovery is the result of microscopic movements, growing from day-to-day and extending over many months, that is, there is an attempt to demonstrate that the discovery is molecular in formation. Bühler argues his theory on the basis of observations of deaf-mute children in Viennese schools.

The point of view of H. Wallon. The child really does make a discovery at this age. Whether by chance or not is another question. So Wallon is likewise inclined to accept a kind of “Eureka” in the child’s consciousness. Wallon holds that the child’s discovery is not accidental. However, what the child discovers is not the general concept or the rule that everything has its own name, but only a way of handling things. If a child discovers that some things may be opened (for example, you open or him the lid of a box), he will try to open all objects, even those which do not have a lid. The whole history of the development of speech is based on, Wallon believes, the child was given the opportunity to name things, that the thing can be named. This is like a new activity with objects, and, just as the child has discovered it in relation to one thing, so he can take it and transfer it to a whole series of other and apply it in relation to a whole series of other things. In this way, for Wallon, what the child discovers is not logical sense, not a link between sign and meaning, but a new way to play with things, a new means of handling them.

From the point of view of K. Koffka and all of structural psychology, this first discovery of the child is presented in the form of a structuring act. A child discovers a kind of structure “thing-name,” just as an ape discovers the function of a stick in that situation where the fruit lies far away and cannot be obtained other than by the aid of a stick. Now the theory of Koffka joins with the theory of Wallon.

The theories of Bühler, Koffka, and Wallon correspond better with the facts than the Stern theory, since they arose as critiques of this theory, but they all include in themselves the Sternian flaw, which derives from associative theory, that is, the assumption that everything happens here once and for all time: the child discovers a structure, a way of dealing with things, he discovers there that the meaning of these words is not subject to change and to development.

In this way, although these theories mitigate the intellectualism of the Sternian theory and go counter to his most gravely idealistic thesis—breeding speech from the concept of this speech— they are in relation to the origin of speech as flawed as the Sternian theory, because they allow immutability in the emergence and development of the child's words. Let us try in a few words to demonstrate the most essential in the contemporary studies on the moment of birth of speech so as thereby to map out the central point of the crisis of the first year.

I commence with facts. Whoever carefully observes the birth of child speech cannot overlook a very important period in its development which has become the object of intense scrutiny in the last decade and which is still very little dealt with in textbooks. At the same time, it is of the greatest significance for understanding the development of child speech.

Thus far, we have spoken of two periods in the development of child speech. We have tried to show that even in the age of infancy, when the child has no language in the strict sense of the word, the very social situation of development leads to the emergence in the child of very large, complex, and multiform needs in communication with adults. Because the child cannot come and go on his own, or move an object closer or further away, he must act through others. None of the child's other ages requires such a vast number of forms of cooperation, albeit elementary, as infancy does. Actions through others are the basic form of activity of the child. This age is characterized by the child's deprivation of the most basic means of communication: speech. In this lies a very particular contradiction in the development of the infant. The child cocreates a number of surrogates for speech. We have already lingered over the gestures that arise in the child and which lead to what, from the point of view of speech development, are important gestures, such as pointing. In this way, communication with those around is established.

We have pointed to a series of forms, substitutes for speech, that is, means of communication which, although they are not the means of speech, still constitute some kind of preparatory stage in the development of speech. We then spoke of speech development in early childhood, when the child learns the basics of adult language. Between the first period, which is called the language-less period in child development, and the second, when the child builds up the core knowledge of his native language, there exists a period of development that W. Eliasberg suggested we call "autonomous child speech" (W. Eliasberg, 1928). Eliasberg says that a child before beginning to speak our language makes us speak his own language. This period is precisely what helps us understand how the transition is resolved from the nonlingual period when the child is babbling to the period when the child masters the speech in the proper sense of the word. The transition from a period of languagelessness to language development is achieved by means of autonomous child speech.

What is this period? In order to better address this question, a few words, the history of this question and the history of **the introduction of this concept** into science are necessary.

The first to describe autonomous child speech and to understand and appreciate its great significance, was, as strange as it may seem, C. Darwin (1881), who did not directly engage in the questions of the development of the child, but being an observer of genius, was able to note, following the development of his grandson, that prior to passing into a linguistic period, the child speaks his own unique sort of language. Its uniqueness lies in, first of all, the sound make-up of words employed by the child being sharply different from the sound make-up of our words. The motorics of this speech, that is, its articulation and its phonetic aspect, do not coincide with our speech. There are usually such words as "pu-fu" or "bo-bo" and sometimes fragments of our words. These are words that differ according to the external or sound form from words of our language. Sometimes they resemble our words, sometimes they are sharply at variance with them, and sometimes they are reminiscent of our words, garbled.

The **second** difference, more substantial and more important, which drew the attention of Darwin was that the words of autonomous speech **differ from our words in their meaning**. A well-known example of Darwin's is often cited in textbooks. His grandson, upon seeing a duck swimming in a pond, began to call it "u-a," whether imitating the sounds or the name given to it by adults. These sounds were produced by the child whenever he saw a duck swimming on water. Then the boy began to call by the same sound milk spilled on a table, all liquids in a wine glass, milk in a bottle, apparently shifting the name to wherever there was water, a liquid. Once the child was playing with some old money with images of birds. He also called these "u-a." In the end, all small round shiny objects that resemble money (buttons, medals) were called "u-a."

In this way, if we trace the meaning of the word "u-a" in the child, we may find some primordial meaning, from which proceed all of the others (a duck on the water). This meaning is almost always very complex. It is not dissected up into separate qualities, like the meanings of individual words, such a meaning presents a whole picture.

From this primordial meaning, the child proceeds to a series of other meanings, which derive from the separate parts of the picture. From water it becomes a puddle, any liquid, and subsequently a bottle. From a duck it becomes a name for money with a picture of an eagle, and from them—buttons, medals, etc.

One may bring forth many examples of meanings for the autonomous word "pu-fu." It means a bottle of iodine, iodine itself, a bottle that one blows across to make a sound, a cigarette from which smoke rises, tobacco, the process of extinguishing a flame because there as well one requires blowing, and so on. The word, its meaning, embraces a whole complex which cannot in us be labeled with a single word. These words in the aspect of their meanings do not match our words, and not one of them can be completely translated into our language.

With autonomous speech, it never happens that the child can say **iodine**, **bottle**, **cigarette**, that he can not only speak about but also can distinguish between the various constant properties of objects (iodine, bottle and so on) but that he continues to say "pu-fu" out of capriciousness. In fact, what is inaccessible for the child is both our words and our concepts.

We will come back to the analysis of child meanings. Now we shall limit ourselves to establishing the facts. Everyone is now in agreement that the meaning of such words are constructed differently from those we have.

Thus, we have found two traits that distinguish children's autonomous speech from the general course of development of child language. The first difference—the **phonetic** construction of speech; the second—the **semantic aspect** of child speech.

From this follows the third feature of the child's autonomous speech whose merit was appreciated by Darwin; if this speech in its sounding and its meaning relations differs from our own, then the communication with the aid of this speech must sharply differ from communication with the aid of our speech. Communication is only possible between the child and those people who understand the meaning of his words. Is it not true that we, that you, not knowing the history of the word "u-a," would not understand what it meant to Darwin's grandson?

This is not communication which is in principle possible with all persons, as it is with the aid of our words. Communication is only possible with persons who are adepts of the code of child speech. For this reason German authors have for a long time contemptuously referred to this language as "Ammensprache" (nursemaid speech—Trans.) that is, language of wet nurses and nannies who were thought by researchers to have artificially created by adults for children this characterized that it is only understood by the persons who are raising the given child.

Adults, attempting to adapt to the child's language, actually allow the distortion of ordinary words which are taught to children. When the nurse says "bo-bo" to the child instead of "больно" ("bol'no," i.e., "It hurts"—Trans.) then, of course, we are dealing with a distortion of speech, one which adults accept in order to communicate with the child. In relation to children of later ages, we always make another mistaken assumption: since from our point of view the child is small, it seems to us that all things should to him appear small. For this reason, we say to the young child "housie" when pointing to a skyscraper, and "horsie," pointing out a big horse, losing from sight that a big house and a big horse must appear to a small child gigantic, and it would be more true to say "mega-house" or "maxi-horse." Such distortions do take place, but it would be untrue to say that autonomous child language is in the language of nurses and nannies. The fact is that before mastering our articulation and phonetics, the child masters some of the rudiments of words and rudimentary meanings which do not coincide with ours.

Even when we are adept at the meanings of child words, understanding the child can take place in no other way than in some concrete situation. If the child says "u-a," it might be a button, milk, a duck on a pond, or a coin. You do not know what he has in mind. If during a walk in the garden, a child cries "u-a" and reaches forward it means that he wants to be carried to the pond. If he is in his room and says "u-a," it means that he wants to play with buttons.

Communication with children in this period is only possible in concrete situations. The word can be used in communication only when the object is before the eyes. If the object is before the eyes, then the word becomes understandable.

We see that the difficulty of understanding is very great. According to my ideas, **one of the most relevant hypotheses is that which would show that all of the hypobulic displays of the child stem from the difficulties of mutual understanding.**

This means that we find a third feature of autonomous speech: it permits communication, but in other forms and of a different character than the communication that becomes possible to the child later.

Finally, the fourth and last of the major distinguishing features of autonomous language consists in this: the link possible between separate words is also completely unique. This language is usually agrammatical, and has no objective means of uniting separate words and meanings into coherent speech (in us this is done by the aid of syntax and etymology). Here govern very different laws for linking and joining words—laws joining interjections, passing through each other, resembling a series of unlinked exclamations which we sometimes issue in the grip of strong affects and excitation.

These are the four basic features which confront us in the study of autonomous child speech. I believe that they were all more or less clearly recognized by Darwin, who first described the speech of his own grandson. Despite the fact that this was done by Darwin, his observations have not been appreciated or understood. Many examples of his were quoted but no one was able to generalize from them and to understand that we are dealing with a unique period of child speech development. Therefore, although some researchers have carried out the precise recording of the first words of the child and accumulated a great deal of factual material that characterizes autonomous speech, the teaching on the autonomous speech of children after the appearance of Darwin's article has withered away somewhat. Nobody has understood that it is a question of a special period in the development of child speech.

The study of this question has been revived thanks to the observations of the well-known German scholar C. Stumpf. He carried out observations of his own child whose development was very peculiar. Stumpf's son first for several years (3 or 4 years) spoke with the aid of autonomous child speech, that is, not as the normal child does, by making himself understood with the aid of this speech only at the end of the first or the second year of life. The boy understood the language of people around him, but always answered in his own language. Since this was a developed language (the child had devised it for a number of years), he had complex rules for combining and structuring individual words. The child used his own language, refusing to speak in German until one fine day his parents returned home in the evening to learn from the nurse (or the governess) that the child suddenly made the transition to regular German language, abandoning autonomous speech. This story is exceptional, and not a rule. If at the stage of autonomous speech the child is delayed for several years, this is anomalous child development. But because of the delay of several years, the autonomous speech was splendidly developed and its rules could be studied with a completeness with which they would not have been explained had the period lasted just several months between the end of the first year and third quarter of the second year, as usually happens in normal development.

However, this information of Stumpf's was looked upon as merely a curious case. It required several decades of scientific work in order to observe two basic facts which today form the basis of the study of autonomous child speech.

The first fact is that autonomous child speech does not present a rare case, but a rule, a law, which is observed in the speech development of every child. The law may be formulated in the following way: before the child in a nonlinguistic period of development makes a transition to the mastery of adult language, he manifests the development of autonomous child speech. I have already indicated the features that distinguish it. It should now be made clear that the term **autonomous** is not entirely fortunate, but it is more or less entrenched in science and in the contemporary literature. The speech is called autonomous because as if it is constructed according to its own laws, different from the laws of the construction of speech proper, a different semantic system, a different form of communication and a different form of cohesion. For this reason, it has received the name autonomous.

In this way, the first proposition consists in this: that autonomous child speech is a necessary period in the development of any normal child.

The second proposition: in many forms of underdeveloped speech, in disorders of speech development, autonomous child speech very often acts a defining feature in the abnormal form of speech development. For example, a delay is often expressed primarily in the child being held back in the period of autonomous speech. Other speech disorders during the age of childhood similarly lead to autonomous speech sometimes lingering for a few years in children but still performing its basic genetic function, that is, that of a bridge by which the child crosses over from a nonlinguistic period to a linguistic one. In the development of normal and abnormal children, autonomous speech plays an essential role.

We cannot say that the child receives in its entirety this speech from nannies or from wetnurses, that is, that this is the language of wetnurses. This language is of the child himself, for all of the meanings are established not by the wetnurse, but by this very child; the child often creates his "bo-bo" from fragments of normally uttered words. For example, the mother says "стакан" ("stakan," or glass—Trans.)—a complete word—but the child transforms this into "кан" or into something else.

In every normal course of child development, we may observe autonomous speech which is characterized by three moments. **The first moment:** The speech motorically, that is, in its articulatory and phonetic aspects, does not coincide with our speech. It is usually such words as "pu-fu," "bo-bo," fragments of our words; sometimes it, as researchers now say, resembles a language of radicals, that is, language in which only (morphological—Trans.) roots exist but not fully formulated words. In meaning, they do not coincide with any one of our words, and not one of the meanings of "pu-fu" or "bo-bo" may be completely translated into our language. If we take the generally known example of Darwin's observations of his grandson, for whom "u-a" first designated a duck floating on the water, and then liquids, and then money with the image of an eagle, and then anything round, here we see the same thing. There are many examples of how the child's word, its semantic value, covers a complex of things which for us are not designated by a single word.

The **second** feature. The meaning of autonomous speech does not coincide with the meaning of our words.

The **third** feature. Along with their own words, there exists in the child an understanding of our words as well; that is, the child, even before starting to speak, understands a range of words. He understands our formulation of words like "stand up," "sit down," "bread," "milk," "hot," and so on, and this cannot interfere with the availability of their second speech. Therefore H. Idelberger and others are inclined to believe that autonomous child speech exists with a near or at least some sort of link with our speech.[10]

Finally, and **lastly.**

Autonomous child speech and its meanings are devised with the active participation of the child.

It is a fact that in the development of every child, there exists a period of autonomous child speech. The beginning and the end of it mark the beginning and the end of the crisis of the first year of life. Of the child in possession of autonomous speech, it is actually not possible to say whether there is speech in him or not, because there is no speech in our sense of the word, but it is not a mute period, as he is still speaking, that is, we are confronted with the requisite transitional form that signals the boundaries of a crisis.

Not a few writers have been so caught up by an extreme critique of this theory that they claim that this language is created exclusively by the child himself. W. Eliasberg, for example, believes that the child forces others to speak to him in his own language. But it would be incorrect to say that this is the language of the child himself. In isolated cases, it is true, for example, when the child of C. Stumpf at five does not wish to converse in the language of others, although perfectly understanding what they say. But this speech cannot be considered either as "Ammensprache" (i.e., the speech of wetnurses—Trans.) or as strictly autonomous language—it is always the result of the child's interaction with surrounding people.

Having familiarized ourselves with some of the basic features of autonomous child speech, we proceed to some facts which have been taken from the observation of normal and abnormal children and which will help us to picture more clearly some of the features of this period and make possible some conclusions concerning the development of child speech. Consider the following examples of children's words (from the nursery and from the home) in the second year of life, in the stage of autonomous child speech.

Nona, 1 year and 3 months. A girl in a group nursery group. In all, she has 17 separate words of autonomous speech. Among them "kh-h" which means a cat, fur, and all furry things, then hair, especially long hair. We are dealing with a word that is phonetically constructed differently and whose meaning, however, is not as rich as the meaning of "u-a" in Darwin's example, but which is not constructed as are the meanings of our words. At first, "kh-h" signifies by similarity to a cat's sound, but then the similarity of feeling of a furry cat is transferred to all fur, and then to hair.

We observe more interesting and complex formation of words in children when autonomous speech has been delayed or when we have a diary which is kept over a long time.

---

[10]Vygotsky is referring to the PhD thesis that Heinrich A. Idelberger completed in 1903–1904, for the University of Zurich in Switzerland, entitled *Hauptprobleme der kindlichen Sprachentwicklung nach eigener Beobachtung behandelt*. Vygotsky also refers to this material in Chapter Five of *Thinking and Speech*.

Angelina—1 year and 3 months. Her word "ka" has had eleven meanings throughout its development. At first (at 11 months), it was a yellow stone that the girl played with. Then it also denoted egg soap, then all stones of any color and any shape. Then by the time she was 1 year and 1 month, it indicated *kasha* (i.e., porridge—Trans.), and then big pieces of sugar, then all sweets, kissels, cutlets, bobbins, pencils, and soap dishes. So here, the meaning extended from a yellow stone to yellow soap. This much is understandable. Then it defines any stone at all: this is also understandable. Then everything that is sweet, such as kissels, can take on this meaning, just as sugar is so-called. But a pencil or a bobbin does not have any relationship or common traits with these objects. "Ka" in this case represents the beginning of the words "карандаш," "катушка" ("karandash"—that is, pencil—and "katushka," that is, a bobbin or a spool of thread—Trans.) in adult language. Here there may be a similarity of sounds. But the child takes up only the first "ka."[11]

Some objects are included in the meaning of this word because of one trait and others because of another. For example, the yellow soap comes in because of the trait of color, kissel—by the trait of sweetness; stone—by the trait of hardness, and "katushka" and "karandash"—by their sound similarity. All these meanings form a family of objects which are designated by the one sound "ka."

Can we understand this "ka?" The father of the girl—a physiologist who kept a diary—wrote that the word presented a riddle, because it was painfully difficult to guess what the child had in mind in saying "ka," and understanding was always solved with the aid of the **visual** situation. Here we see a clear illustration of situational understanding and the impossibility of understanding the meaning of words when they are separated from a concrete situation.

Our words can be substituted for the situation; however, the words of autonomous speech do not have this function but have only the mission of indicating this one or that in a situation. They have an indexical function, and a nominating function, but they do not have the signifying function, which can represent nonpresent objects and meanings.

This proposition relates to the basic properties of autonomous children's speech. The words of autonomous speech have indicating and nominating functions, but they do not have any signifying function. They do not yet have the capacity of

---

[11] We remember that earlier Vygotsky pointed out that it is difficult, in a very short period of time, to see how the child's proto-speech might be developing in the direction of speech proper. In the previous paragraph, Vygotsky said that it might be possible to see this in instances when speech proper development is delayed, or when a parent takes good notes.

Angelina is the former (Zhenya, below, is the latter). Angelina forms a chain complex, where each element of the chain has some element of meaning in common with the last element in the chain, but the beginning of the chain seems to have no direct connection with the end. A yellow stone looks like yellow soap because of its color, and "kasha," a staple of cracked wheat, reminds Angelina of stones because of its brown color. Sugar is like "kasha" because of its granular form, and kissel (a kind of fruit jelly) is like sugar because of its taste.

At this point, however, the proto-speech chain appears to fall under the influence of the Russian speech in the child's environment: "cutlet," "karandash" and "katushka" all begin with the sound "ka."

replacing nonpresent objects, but may only in the visual situation single out aspects and parts and give to these parts a name. For this reason, with the aid of autonomous speech, the child can only speak of what he sees, as opposed to using developed speech, when we may speak of objects that are not before our eyes.

One more distinction between autonomous child speech and our own—the relationship that exists between individual word meanings. For the development of child concepts and child words, the most essential consists in the development of a system of relations of generalization between the meanings of distinct words. In the speech clinic of the Experimental Defectological Insitute (EDI), there was at one time a child who knew the words *table, chair,* and *wardrobe,* but did not know the word *furniture.* At this time, for the development of the child's speech, the essential moment consisted of the emergence of relations between meanings. The word *furniture* was not simply another word for a series of words such as *table, wardrobe.* The word *furniture* was a higher concept, which included in itself all of the foregoing. This was precisely the essential moment that was not a property of autonomous child speech. A trait by which autonomous children's speech can always be distinguished from speech which has already made the transition to a higher level consists in the lack of relations of generality between different meanings of words.

What are these relations of generality? We will call relations of generality the relations of such words as, let us say, *furniture* and *chair.* One is the higher concept; the other is the lower one. The relationship between *table* and *chair* does not constitute a relationship of subordination.

In autonomous children's speech, the relations of generality do not exist. From the child's vocabulary, we can see that his speech is made up of words which, let us say, lie in the same rank next to each other, rather than relating to each other in a certain kind of hierarchy. In contrast, more particular meanings are given within a single word, for example, "ka"—a yellow stone and all stones of any color; soap dishes with soap in general and specifically yellow soap. Different degrees of generality exist within the meaning of one and the same word, and these words are not in any relation of generality with each other.

If you take any lexicon of autonomous speech, you will find no words that stand the one to the other in such a relationship as *furniture* and *table; flower* and *rose,* that is, the meanings of the words are different in generality and stand in a defining relationship the one to the other. One has the impression that in autonomous child speech, meanings of words still immediately reflect this or that object, this or that situation, but do not reflect the link that objects have between them, other than the situational link which is given in a visual picture, establishing the content of the original meaning of the word in autonomous speech. It follows that the meaning of a word of autonomous speech is not constant but situational. One and the same word now means one thing and in other situations—another. The word "ka" in the lexicon can mean, as we've seen, 11 distinct things, and in every new situation, the word can mean something new. The meaning of words is not constant but variable in dependency with the concrete situation. This meaning is, we repeat, not object-oriented, but situational. For us, every object has a name, no matter what situation it finds itself in, but in autonomous child speech, an object can have a different name depending upon the situation.

Let us take an example from anomalous development. One of the children in the clinic is studied. The child uses words зеленина (zelyenina, "greenery"—Trans.) for light colors and синина (sinina, "blackery"—Trans.) for dark ones. If you give the child two leaves—light yellow and dark yellow, the first will be called greenery and the second blackery. If you give the child the same dark yellow leaf and some brown ones, the same yellow leaf receives the name greenery and the brown one: blackery. One and the same color is called differently depending on what lies alongside it. The child designates things as light or dark-colored, but absolute color quality for him does not exist. There are relative degrees: lighter and darker. The word meaning is still devoid of object-oriented consistency.

There is an analogous example in the observation of the son of Stumpf, who called one and the same color differently. Green on a white background and green on a black background had different names, depending on the structure in which the color was perceived.

The boy Zhenya—5 years and 6 months—belonged to a group of children who hear but begin to speak late and who develop independence with difficulty. The parents appealed to the clinic complaining that the child was not developing speech properly and that he understood only poorly the speech of others. This complaint of poor understanding is usual with children who use autonomous speech. Pathological autonomous speech differs from usual speech in phonology and semantics and therefore presents major difficulties in communication between the child and other children or adults. Often a translator, who knows the meanings of the distorted words and can translate them into our language, is required. An example of Zhenya's lexicon were words that were explained in picture-naming conversations with him. Очки узки (*ochki uzki;* literally, "narrow glasses"—Trans.) meant eyes, кон ("kon," literally, knight, steed—Trans.): horse, and so on. In these words, we can see the first sentences.[12]

---

[12]Vygotsky believes that in ontogenesis there is always an interaction between the "final form" of adults in the environment and the proto-form that the child is constantly creating on his own. By studying this interaction, we may be able to design final forms that are more easily accessible to the child. Of course, it is easy to study the final form without the child (in adults). But it is not so easy to study the child's form without the final form.

For this reason, Vygotsky is always interested in what the child does without the final form. For example, in Chapter Five of *Thinking and Speech*, Vygotsky devises an experiment that allows us to see what the child does without adult concepts (the blocks experiment) and in Chapter Eight of *The History of the Development of the Higher Mental Functions* Vygotsky wonders if the child can achieve base 10 counting systems by using blocks and "numerical figures." Similarly, Vygotsky is always interested in cases of pathological "autonomous" development.

Here Vygotsky wonders if an abnormal child who does not accept adult speech will ever devise grammar. Zhenya does manage to put two word meanings together: in "ochki uzki" (narrow glasses) one word modifies another, and in "kon" we have two word meanings—both the knight and his horse. That is why Vygotsky says that they are the child's first phrases. But is it grammar? Grammar is an abstract system of rules. But Zhenya's constructions are more like imaginary situations or memories of stories. Imagine children on the playground, making fun of a child with

When a child who understands adult speech sufficiently well delays in autonomous speech, there arises the need for linked communications, and the child still in autonomous speech takes the path of forming sentences. But these **sentences**, because of the lack of syntactic linking, little resemble our own. They are more like a simple stringing together of words or distorted sentences in our language, for example, "You me hold," etc.

And here are two more cases which may serve as concrete illustrations.

The child uses the word "труа" (trua—Trans.)[13]: walk, go for a walk—and then uses this to refer to all accessories for walking: shoes, galoshes, caps. Then "*trua*" conveys that the milk has been drunk, that is, it went for a walk.

F. A. Rau discussed a girl in whom autonomous speech was highly developed and displayed a special type of word formation that exists in several languages. For example, "f-f" meant **fire** and "ding"—some object that moves, hence "fa-ding"—**train** but the cat was—"tpru-ding". This is complex word formation from distinct root words in autonomous child speech which does not transform itself on time into the usual speech. We are here dealing with an exaggerated form.

One boy discovered such general categories as **insects, birds.** "Петук" (петух) (that is, "petuk" instead of "petukh"—a mispronunciation of the usual Russian term for a rooster or a cock—Trans.) meant the general word **bird.** Such more robust designations constitute signs of a richly developed autonomous speech and present an excellent opportunity to consider the transition from autonomous speech to speech proper.

I still wish to demonstrate the significance of autonomous child speech for one or the other stage of development at which the child has arrived; to show how the development of children's speech is realized in features of the child's thinking, what features of his thinking must flow from the features of autonomous speech. It seems to me that there are a few such features which are very easy to establish, once we have clarified the nature of autonomous child speech.

---

small eyes: "Your eyes are like goggles—they are narrow as necks of bottles!". Imagine a play-story enacted with objects including chess pieces: "Once upon a time there was a king and a queen and a noble knight upon a steed…." Like the complexes of *Thinking and Speech* and the numerical figures of *The History of the Development of the Higher Mental Functions*, we have something which both is and is not grammar.

[13] In his work on imagination and creativity, Vygotsky makes the important point that children are busy using their imagination and their creativity for quite other purposes than making adult-style art. Here we see that one of those purposes is trying to recreate the huge leap that humans made when they created words of more than one morpheme (e.g., "fire-car" for train).

How does the child do it? "Fire-car" is very similar to the Chinese word for train. But "Trpu!" in Russian is an exclamation, like the English word "Whoa!" This is what you say to Russian horses when you want them to stop. We can imagine a child who says this to a cat who is trying to get away, So "trpru-ding" means something like "whoa-ding."

F.A. Rau (1868–1957) was a German teacher who became one of the founders of deaf education in the USSR. From 1925, he was a professor in the second Moscow State University. He worked with Vygotsky in the scientific research institute of defectology, and the child mentioned here is probably deaf.

First of all, as has been said, the meaning of words in autonomous child speech is always situational, that is, it derives its realization when the thing intended by the word is in front of our eyes. Consequently, at the stage of autonomous speech the possibility of verbal thinking does not yet exist separately from the visual situation. As soon as the word is divorced from the visual situation, it cannot realize its meaning. A child cannot think with the aid of words outside of a visual situation. Consequently, at the stage of autonomous child speech, the thinking of the child acquires some initial features of verbal speech thinking, but those which still cannot be detached from the visual. The link between verbal and visual thinking is most clearly manifest in words only such relations are possible that reflect the direct relations of things among themselves, whereas the meanings of the words of autonomous speech are not in relation of generality to each other, that is, a single meaning cannot be related to another meaning, such as, for example, *furniture* has a relation of generality to the word *chair*.

Secondly, how, thanks to this, can words be joined up with each other? In just such a way as objects are joined in the eyes of a child. For example, *train goes (steam goes)*. They can only be united in such a form which reflects the link between immediate impressions. The connection of things established through thinking are still inaccessible to thinking at this stage in the development of autonomous speech. For this reason, thinking is still highly dependent in character. It amounts to something like a subordinate part of the child's perception, his orientation to the surroundings, a series of affective- volitional thoughts and utterances of child in which the intellectual content recedes to the second plane.

What does this affective-volitional content of child words mean? It means that what the child expresses in speech corresponds not to our assertions but rather more to our exclamations, with the aid of which we make affective appraisals, affective attitudes, emotional reactions, and volitional tendencies.

If we analyze the content of autonomous child speech and the degree of thinking that corresponds to it, we find that to the extent that autonomous child speech conveys affective content, it is not yet separated from perception. It conveys impressions perceived, it registers, but it does not deduce or infer anything. It is saturated with the volitional and not the intellectual moments that are linked to thinking in the proper sense of the word.

In this way, we consider that autonomous child speech not only in itself presents an extremely peculiar stage in the development of child speech, but also that this stage corresponds to a peculiar stage in the development of thinking. Depending on which stage of development speech is going through, thinking reveals determinate features. Before a child's speech reaches a certain level of development, his thinking also cannot go beyond a certain limit. The stage that we encounter may be equally characterized as a specific period in the development of speech or as a specific period in the development of child thinking.

When does a normal child experiences a period of autonomous child speech? We said that it is in the critical period of first year, that is, in the transitional period, when the child paves the way from infancy to early childhood. It usually starts at the end of the first year and ends in the second year. With the crisis of the first year of life, the normal child makes use of autonomous child speech. Its ending and beginning mark the beginning and the ending of the crisis of the first year of life.

Does this mean that we may consider autonomous child speech as a central neoformation of the critical period? Yes, it seems to me. But this point of view is not sufficiently worked out, and therefore, it is necessary to be very cautious in making conclusion in relation to the nature of neoformations of any critical age. In any case, the emergence of autonomous child speech as form of transition between the nonverbal and the verbal presents us with one of the most important facts.

We have distinguished other moments in the crisis—the establishment of walking, hypobulic and affective outbursts in the child, and so on, but the problem always consists not of laying down neoformations, but of finding among them the one that is central. After all, what is important is to understand neoformations from the point of view of the whole, from what is transpiring across the age that marks a new stage in development, the structure of all of the new changes.

Can we consider that autonomous children's speech is simply the first phase in the development of speech, not different from it in principle, and that, as a consequence, there is no difference between the study of autonomous child speech and the discovery theory of Stern? I might put the question thus: is autonomous speech in its essence our own speech? Or perhaps: if it does not coincide in the construction of words or in values, might it be the same in its "core?"

I would reply thus. The "core"—the essence of autonomous child speech—is ours and is not ours, and that in this lies all of its originality as a transitional form between nonverbal and verbal communication. In what is it ours and what can it give rise to? In what it is our speech—this is so clear that it need not detain us. What is more important is to say in what it is not ours. It seems to me that it is not ours not only in the sense that the word does not sound that way and has a different meaning, it is not ours in a deeper sense: its principle of construction is completely different than our speech, because it in general does not have a stable meaning. Let us draw a parallel, analogous distinction. Consider the behavior of apes in the experiments of Köhler. The animal, as we know, in some cases, utilizes a box or a stick in the quality of a tool. In its external aspect, the essence of this operation is the same as that of a human when he utilizes a tool, and this gives Köhler grounds to claim that the utilization of sticks by chimpanzees is in fact and in type an action similar to human action.

Critics say: But what sort of tool use is it when sitting on a box which an ape uses as a stand causes the box to cease being a tool, turning into a thing for lying and sitting on and when the ape in this situation dashes about the site, tries to jump to the fruit, tires, and then sits down on the box upon which the other ape is sitting to dab away the perspiration? As a result, it sees the box, but cannot utilize it in this situation as a tool. What is this tool that outside of an active situation loses its tool properties? Köhler himself said that primitive man, requiring a stick for digging the earth, prepares it in advance. Whereas this situation, in the ape there is something of the new, it is nevertheless not at all that which is in primitive man; although he stands nearby something from which can be born the use of tools, but the use of tools is not here yet.

Something similar may be observed with autonomous children's speech. Imagine a speech in which words have no established meaning, but in each new situation mean something other than in the preceding one. In the example which I gave earlier, the word "pu-fu" meant a bottle of iodine, and in another it meant the iodine itself, etc. As a result, words like this naturally differ from words from the stage where they have stable meanings. Here symbolization does not yet exist at all. The words of autonomous children's speech also differ from the words of the stage when some generalized more or less stable and constant meanings are formed in the mind. Here the word means everything and therefore nothing at all.

What is at the beginning of each symbol? With all of the fantastic and all the controversy of the range of propositions in the theory of N. J. Marr,[14] one proposition seems to me undeniable: the first words of human language, as he puts it—the first word means everything or a great deal. And the first words of child speech mean almost everything. But what are these words? Words of the type "this" or "that"; they may be applied to any object. Can we say that this is a real word? No, this is only the indicative function of the word itself; from it, subsequently grows something symbolizing, but while a word that means everything is just a vocal pointing gesture, this is conserved in all words, because every human word indicates a certain object.

At last, the final distinction.

If we present the matter such as Stern does (word meaning, the link of the word meaning with the word is very a simple thing, organized in an elementary way), then, of course, "the core" is just like this or not like this. But the truth is that the study of autonomous child' speech has a greater value, in that it allows us to reveal the "core" of the word; the series of its functions, for example, the indicative. Further, we find that in childhood, the nominative function of the word likewise arises. This is an important transition (in "pu-fu" there is not yet a signifying function).

---

[14] Nikolai Jakovlevich Marr (Никола́й Яковлевич Марр, 1864–1934), half Scottish and half Georgian, grew up speaking many different languages (his father and mother, having no common mother tongue, communicated in French). Even before the revolution, he developed the theory that Caucasian languages, like his own Georgian, had a common root with Semitic languages (such as Arabic and Hebrew) and even Basque. After the revolution, he developed this into the extremely fanciful idea that all languages had a common origin in a single language that had exactly four words: sal, ber, yon, rosh, all of which were exclamations (like "Wow!" "Aha!" "Oh, no!" and "Yay!"). He also believed that "national languages" were simply a myth, and that working people's dialects all over the world have more in common with each other than they do with the dialects spoken by their rulers.

Although Marr's doctrines were official dogma on linguistics, Vygotsky is not afraid to dismiss them as fantastic (i.e., absurd). But both he and Volosinov were able to find important truths in the Marrist theories. Volosinov takes from Marr the idea that the sociogenetically original function of language (in cultural history) was not representational but expressive. Vygotsky, in turn, develops this into the idea that the ontogenetically original function of language (in child development) was indeed indicative but that the object indicated and the affect of the indicator are not yet differentiated.

When we speak of autonomous child speech, we have in mind not a single stratum but a mutlistratal construction of the "core." Autonomous child speech can be presented in itself only as a transitional stage of development, which in relation to speech proper is at one and the same time both our speech and not ours, that is, it contains something that is of our speech, but much in it—is not ours. We know that children who do not rise above their autonomous speech, that is, idiots and aphasics, remain as a matter of fact speechless, although their autonomous children's speech, from our point of view, seems to convey a symbol. For example, the aphasic instead of **bottle** says "pu-fu." He can, with this word "pu-fu" mean a range of concepts.

For a child, speech does not yet exist in his consciousness as a conscious principle of symbolization, and for this reason, the discrepancy with Stern's "discovery" is colossal. It is quite another thing to show how through the transitional formations arise such phenomena as the first stage of child speech. In this sense, we observe a series of leaps in the development of child speech not only on the border of the autonomous and nonautonomous, but also in its subsequent development.

Understanding the periods of emergence and establishment of child speech enables us to enter the depths of its course of development, which allows us to arrive at a correct theory of speech development and to uncover insufficiencies in the constructions of bourgeois science concerning this problem.

We should not lose from view the other neoformations—walking, hypobulic seizures, etc.

Since I am reminding myself to be cautious, I would not now embark on theoretical considerations and must necessarily restrict myself to demonstrating where, from my point of view, and in what direction to seek the general change with which we are dealing in the critical age to be described. It seems to me that the central age neoformation relates to speech.

I consider that the development of the child, considered from the point of view of stages of development in the personality, from the point of view of the relations of the child with the environment, from the point of view of the basic activities at each stage, is tightly linked to the history of development of child consciousness. If I wished to give a formal response to this question, I could indicate the well-known words of K. Marx on this: "Consciousness is relationship to the environment."[15] And it is true in essence that the relation of personality to the environment characterizes in the closest way the construction of consciousness, and consequently, it seems to me that the study of age levels and their neoformations from the point of view of consciousness constitutes the legitimate approach to the true resolution of this question. And the benefits here are not small, for contemporary science is still ignorant of how to study the facts that characterize consciousness. I do not want to make an error, and, pointing at the relationship to the environment to consciousness,

[15] Vygotsky appears to be referring to Marx, K. and Engels, F. (1845/2010). *The German Ideology*, Part I: Feuerbach: the Opposition of the Materialist and Idealist Outlook A. Idealism and Materialism, where Marx says that language is as old as consciousness and represents practical consciousness itself, as it is the human relationship to the human environment. Vygotsky also refers to this statement in the conclusion of *Thinking and Speech*.

to speech, I do not want to reduce everything to speech. I must go and look from above and from below, from symptoms such as teething, walking, and child speech; I must interest myself in both the primary and the secondary actors in this drama. It seems to me that the study of the changes of the child's consciousness and the changes in speech theoretically are central to the understanding of all of the other changes with which we have to do here.

To understand the ages theoretically means to find the changes in the personality as a whole, within which all of these moments have appeared clearly to us, some as necessary preconditions and others, as given moments and etc.

But it is difficult to understand immediately how the change in the structure of consciousness stands with respect to the acquisition of speech. Habitually, everyone has limited himself either to pointing out their kinship or the fact that one or the other distinguishes man from animals and appears as a specifically human heritage; or else with the aid of an analogy (which is what I used to do) we argued that speech in relation to the social space of the child plays the same role that walking does in relation to physical one. This analogy is not worth much. Not one of the works known to me can answer the simple question of where the relationship between these neoformations can be found.

From the genetic point of view, we have spoken of what distinguishes the basic accomplishments of the child in the critical age. Does the child accomplish new achievements in the critical age, or does development carry out only destructive work? To this question, we would give the positive answer. We have seen more than once that in the critical ages, as in all epochs of development, the child accomplishes new achievements, otherwise, development would not be development.

But where lies the difference with the accomplishments of the child in the critical period? They bear a transitory character. The accomplishment of the critical age will never persist in later life, while the accomplishments which the child makes in the stable age will persist. In a stable age, the child learns to walk, to speak, to write and so on. In the transitional age, the child achieves autonomous speech. If this persists for the whole of life, this is an abnormality.

In autonomous child speech, we find multifarious forms, typical of the crisis of the first year. The beginning of this form and the end of childly speech can be seen as symptoms of the beginning and the end of the critical age.

True speech emerges and autonomous speech disappears together with the end of the critical age; although the feature of the accomplishments of these critical ages consists of their transitional character, they still have a very great genetic significance: they constitute a transitional bridge. Without the formation of autonomous speech, the child would never pass from the nonlinguistic to the linguistic period of development. In truth, the accomplishments of the critical ages are not erased, but only transformed into a more complex formation. They perform a unique genetic function in the transition from one stage of development to another.

The transitions which arise during the critical ages and in particular autonomous child speech are endlessly interesting, for they present in themselves portions of child development in which we see the dialectical laws of development made bare.

References

Darwin, C. (1881). *Наблюдения за жизнью ребенка, Санкт-Петербург*. (Russian translation of Darwin's "Observations of the Life of a Child").

Eliasberg, W. (1928). *Über die Autonomische Kindersprache*. [On the autonomous speech of children] Berlin-Wien.

Halliday, M. A. K. (2004). *The language of early childhood*. Continuum.

Hegel, G. W. F. (1830/1972). *Hegel's logic*. Clarendon.

Joyce, J. (1916/1992). *The portrait of the artist as a young man*. Bantam.

Köhler, W. (1966). *The place of value in a world of facts*. Liveright.

Marx, K., & Engels, F. (1845/2010). The German ideology. In *Volume Five The collected works of Karl Marx and Frederick Engels*. Lawrence & Wishart.

Piaget, J. (1929/1971). *The child's conception of the world*. Routledge/Kegan Paul.

Saussure, F. (1916/1972). *Course in general linguistics*. Open Court.

Stern, W. (1919) *Die menschliche Persönlichkeit* [Human personality] (2nd ed.). Barth.

Stern, C., & Stern, W. (1907/1928). *Die Kindersprache* [The speech of children] (4th Edn). Oxford, England: Barth.

Stern, C., & Stern, W. (1928). *Die Kindersprache* [The speech of children] (4th ed.). Oxford, England: Barth.

van der Veer, R., & Zavershneva, E. (2011). To Moscow with love: Partial reconstruction of Vygotsky's trip to London. *Integrative Psychological & Behavioral Science, 45*(4), 458–474. https://doi.org/10.1007/s12124-011-9173-8

Vygotsky, L. S. (1934/1987). Thinking and speech. In L. S. Vygotsky (Ed.), *Collected works, volume one*. New York/London: Plenum.

Wallon, H. (1930/2015). *Les origines du caractère chez l'enfant*. Paris: Quadrige.

Wallon, H. (1945/2015). *Les origines de la pensée chez l'enfant*. Paris: Quadrige.

Wittgenstein, L. (1958). *Philosophical investigations*. New York: Macmillan.

Chapter 8
Early Childhood

Outline of Chapter 8: Early Childhood

At the beginning of this lecture, Vygotsky lays out three tasks: tracing the developmental path of the major neoformations of early childhood, describing them, and establishing the link between these neoformations and the next zone of development. So in the first third of the lecture, we follow the child's generalizations from sensuous perceptions to sensible or rather "sense-able," that is, semantic and systemic, ones; for example, we follow the child's behavior from nonplay and quasi-play to true play. The next third of the lecture describes those neoformations as semantic and systemic consciousness, made possible by the generalizations made available through speech. The final third relates these neoformations to the next zone of development at three, which parents in Europe and the USA sometimes refer to as the "terrible twos," or "threenage-hood," but which Russian parents associate with a whole constellation of negative symptoms which they call, after the Pleiades, "The Seven Stars."

I. **Tracing the developmental path of the neoformations**. Vygotsky focuses on the social situation of development at the commencement of early childhood: that is, the child's largely nonverbal relationship to the environment. To trace the developmental path of the neoformations around speech, Vygotsky discusses the nonspeech processes: physical processes like perception and play and their mental counterparts in child feeling and thinking in that order.

   1. Vygotsky invokes factual material from Lewin (Hannah trying to sit on a stone) and Slavina (repeating counterfactual sentences).
   2. He asks what brings out this abject dependence on the visual purview and dismisses the suggestion that it is brought about by a reflex art; these were inoperative even in infant feeding. Instead, he presents evidence from Leipzig that suggests to him that actions are linked through affect.

The material in this chapter is from the 1984 Russian edition of Vygotsky's *Collected Works*.

L. S. Vygotsky, *L.S. Vygotsky's Pedological Works. Volume 2.*, Perspectives in Cultural-Historical Research 10, https://doi.org/10.1007/978-981-16-1907-6_8

3. This raises the question of whether affect or perception can be said to be the dominant function. Vygotsky considers and rejects the idea that children are anti-realist or ego-centric and instead argues that the child believes in an "Ur Wir" or "grand-we" in which the inner world is shared just as the outer world is. Only in the second stage of early childhood does the child begin to speak of "I," to understand that sensations are not shared with others, and to "break away" from the sensory field.
4. Now Vygotsky returns to the toddler's physical activities, but this time in the context of play.
   (a) For Groos, everything is play; even rote actions concerned with exploring the properties of objects should be considered "experimental play."
   (b) For Blonsky, nothing is play, since the child is serious about everything.
   (c) For Elkonin, one may divide the toddler's activities into nonplay with rote actions; quasi-play with play objects but without an imaginary situation and without transferring object values; and true play, which can "break away" from the visual purview and transfer value from one object to another. True play, Vygotsky concludes, can only emerge with the simultaneous presence of a semantic and a visual field. The visual field was given at the beginning of early childhood, but the semantic field emerges at the end. This brings us to the emergence of the central neoformations of the age.

II. **Describing the neoformations**. Vygotsky describes two neoformations: speech pronunciation (i.e., articulation) and semantic-systemic perception (i.e., perceiving categories of meaning such as clocks instead of mere physical objects). In both cases, he rejects gradualistic, synthetic, and "bottom up" physicalist description and proposes a semantic, systemic, and "top down" functional description instead.

   1. Vygotsky considers communication a central line of development, so communication must play the same role that joint attention played in infancy. He begins with a critique of extant theories of communication in early years, especially the gradualistic, synthetic, and physicalist theory of the Sterns. Three aspects of the old theory seem dubious to Vygotsky:
      (a) The old theory is gradualistic.
      (b) The old theory is synthetic.
      (c) The old theory is "bottom up," that is, physicalist.
   2. Vygotsky now offers a semantic, systemic, and "top down" functional theory, probably based on the work of the Moscow/Prague School of Jakobson and Trubetskoy (though, perhaps for political reasons, he is somewhat coy about exactly where this new theory comes from).
      (a) The new theory is semantic. Vygotsky says that the new theory does not attempt to directly link functional values (i.e., meanings) to acoustic or to articulatory properties: The meanings of words have nothing to do

with what they sound like or how hard they are to pronounce. Instead, the acoustic and articulatory distinctions make up distinguishable structures, namely morpho-phonemes, and these structures have functional values. So the sound development of child speech is subordinate to sense development.

(b) The new theory is systemic. What the child must develop is not a collection of sounds but a system of morpho-phonemes to choose from. These systems appear even at the level of the whole language: The bilingual child who has two parents speaking different languages, learns to choose one language to speak to one parent and the other language to speak to the other.

(c) The new theory is "top down." The driving force of sound development lies in social communication by means of co-generalizations: the generalizations that the child shares in whenever the child uses a word from his or her speech community.

3. Vygotsky's next task is to show how this external, social process becomes internalized as an inner, psychological one. In order to do this, he turns to perception and argues that here too development is better understood in a way that is semantic, systemic, and "top down." He notes:

   (a) Humans have a good sense of the size of objects, and they do not think this size is changing when objects get nearer or farther way.
   (b) Humans have a good sense of the position of objects in space, and they do not think that objects in a room change their positions when they move their heads, or even when the whole room moves as in a moving train.
   (c) Humans have a good sense of color, and this does not depend on the surroundings.
   (d) Humans believe in stable forms, and despite what their eyes tell them, this does not depend on the angle of vision. A square table remains square, even when our angle of vision makes it look trapezoidal.

Vygotsky then boldly suggests that what the brain contributes to perception is precisely its meaningful structure—the very structure that humans derive from social communication and from co-generalization. This ability to treat objects as either visio-graphic images or as co-generalized meanings represents a new system in another sense: A psychological system in which functions such as attention, memory, and thinking can be related differently thanks to word values, and this new system of consciousness and its new potential for development brings us to the last section of Vygotsky's lecture.

III. **Relating the neoformation to the next zone of development.** Vygotsky promised to show us how the neoformations of early childhood might be linked to the next zone of development. In this last section, he does that and more: he argues that with semantic and systemic consciousness in the child we are in the presence of something specifically human for the first time.

1. The semantic/systemic structure of early childhood consciousness is directly linked to the child's ability to take part in true play, with imaginary situations and the "transfer of value" (e.g., the use of a chair as a horse)—Vygotsky illustrates this by comparing the child's attempts to draw visio-graphically with the child's ability to recognize purely logical geometrical figures—but because they are connected through word value, they now have the possibility of influencing each other.
2. Vygotsky says that these two aspects of child consciousness—its semantic nature and its systemic nature—are related. Vygotsky notes that the residual predominance of perception means that most of the child's semantics are concrete in nature: Objects are named by their properties, and it is not possible to rename objects as a result (one cannot call the sun "cow" because the sun is yellow, but a cow is horned).
3. This concreteness of semantic meaning, this inability to abstract even while generalizing, is what explains the phenomenon of Mondegreens—the words that children make up, inadvertently, when they are unable to correctly segment the sound stream into words. All of these made-up words, Vygotsky says, have a distinctively concrete character. Contrary to what the Sterns believed, the child cannot analyze words like "Moscow" into separate sounds and cannot combine them at will (i.e., the child can say "Moscow" but cannot isolate and say a combination like /sk/). Perception is maximally developed, and speech has offered the ability to name and thus stabilize the world of objects: at the end of early childhood, the child can turn his or her back on the stone and sit. But for that very reason, the child is unwilling to transfer names from one object to another.
4. Vygotsky reminds us that all this will change, and soon. As nonverbal perception is replaced by verbal perception, the child will learn new ways of ordering the "figure" of the visual-graphical world and the "ground" of meaning. In imaginative play, the roles of figure and ground can be reversed, with meaning foregrounded over visual perception. Before that happens, however, the child will try to turn the tables and become the source and not merely the site of co-generalizations. As Vygotsky remarks, by three, the child has learnt to control affect and can use it strategically: This separation of affect from will ushers in the crisis at three.

Chapter 8: Early Childhood

In approaching the study of each age, and early childhood is included in this, it seems to me that first of all we need to ask which neoformations emerge in a given age, that is, what in the process of development in a given stage, is newly constructed, not preexisting from previous stages. For it appears that the very process of development consists primarily in the emergence of new formations at each step of the process. Neoformations emerge at the end of each age, presenting as a result what has transpired in the period of development. The task of analysis consists, first of all, in tracing the path of the genesis of the neoformations; secondly, in describing the neoformations themselves, and thirdly, in establishing the link between the neoformations and the subsequent stages of development.

What constitutes the central neoformation of early childhood, that is, what is built up in development and what in this way is laid down as a foundation for subsequent development? This, here, is the central question. In order to approach an answer to this question, I would like to first of all gather up the known materials, that is, to look over a few of the important problems of this question in order to draw some conclusions from them. It will be necessary to consider them separately and then to move forward to a few generalizations.

Let us dwell, first of all, on the relationship of the child to external reality, to the external environment. Here at this stage of development, there are a number of moments which require us to characterize them in order for us to be able to conceive of the relationship of the child himself to an external reality. It seems to me that we may rely on good experimental demonstrations of the unique attitude of the child to the situation, in the sense of his behavior toward and his activity within it.

I imagine that no one has experimentally demonstrated this relationship better than the well-known German scientist, the structural psychologist K. Lewin.[1] To him we owe the best work clarifying this aspect. He has also attempted to build a theory of the unique behavior of the child of early age in an external situation.

What main features characterize the behavior of the child? I will point schematically to the principal ones. These are *Situationsgebundheit*[2] and *Feldmässigkeit*[3] (literally, "field-appropriacy"—Trans.), that is, the linked-ness to and of a given situation. The child comes into the situation and his behavior as whole is defined by the situation, entering into it as some sort of dynamic part of it. With *Feldmässigkeit*, Lewin has in view any situation which in structural psychology can be regarded as a field of human activity and in which that human activity can be considered linked to the structure of that field. The actions of the child, in Lewin's opinion, at this stage of development are entirely and absolutely "field" actions, that is, exclusively

[1] Kurt Lewin (1890–1947) was a Gestalt psychologist who was probably closest of all of the Gestaltists to Vygotsky's own ideas. Today he is probably best known for his creation of "action research," but in Vygotsky's time, he was best known for a theory of human behavior based on representing the environment as a field and human orientation to action as a kind of vector. He visited Vygotsky in Moscow, befriended him and wrote a very warm obituary when Vygotsky died. He left Germany when Hitler came to power (he was a Jew) and settled in the USA, where he founded action research.

[2] The German word Vygotsky wants here is not actually *Situationsgebundheit,* but rather *Situationsgebundenheit,* or "situation-bindedness," the binding between the child and the situation. It is not clear whether the mistake is Vygotsky's, that of his Soviet editors, or a word that Kurt Lewin made up (Ponomariov, 2013: 84f). When the child acts, it must be in response to the whole situation, rather than according to a memory or a wish.

[3] *Feldmässigkeit* (note that the umlaut, like the extra syllable in *Situationsgebundenheit* is missing from the Russian *Collected Works*) is a military term: It means something like "appropriateness in the battlefield," and actually refers to soldier's dress on maneuvers or in combat, as opposed to on parade: the soldier's use of his arms, his horse, and his choice of uniform must be conditioned by field conditions and not by foppery or flirting.

adapted to the structure of that field in which the actions are taking place in the perception of the child at present.

The experiment shows what this consists of: with each object comes a particular affect, attracting or repelling, instigating motives in the child. Each object "pulls" the child to it, in order to be handled, picked up, felt, or, contrariwise, left untouched; the object acquires what Lewin calls *Aufforderungscharakter*[4]—a certain compelling characteristic. In all things, there inheres a certain affect so compelling that in the child it takes on the character of a "compulsory" affect, and thus the child at this age is led through a world of things and objects, as if in a force field, where he must act at all times on things which attract and repel him. In him, there can be no indifferent or "disinterested" relationship with surrounding things. As Lewin so vividly puts it, the staircase beckons the child to be descended by him; the door, to be opened and shut by him; the bell, to be rung by him; the box, to be uncovered and covered by him; and the round ball, to be rolled by him. In a word, each thing is charged by the child in this situation with an attractive or repulsive affective force, an affective valence, and it will provoke him to act, that is, lead him on, accordingly.

To understand how the early age child acts in this or that situation, we can make a remote analogy with the way in which we ourselves would act, if we found ourselves in a situation where we too were in its power. For us, this is already rare. As an experiment, Lewin did this: The subject was invited to the laboratory; the experimenter then absented himself for a few minutes under the pretext that something had to be prepared for the experiment; and the subject was left in these new surroundings. He waited there for 10–15 min. In this situation, the subject often began to explore the room. If there was a clock, he checked what time it was; if there was an envelope, it was examined to see if it contained anything or if it was empty. There is, in the state of this person who finds that every action is determined by what he sees, a distant analog of the behavior of the child in early childhood.

From here comes a connectedness solely to the extant situation of the child. The child in early childhood, as opposed to later ages, cannot bring to the situation knowledge of other potential things; he in general is not preoccupied with anything which lies backstage of the situation, as Lewin expressed it, nothing which might

---

[4]*Afforderungscharakter* is glossed by Vygotsky as известный повелительный характер, that is, "a well-known" or "a certain" compulsory characteristic, and this is rendered as "a connectedness of the situation itself" in the English *Collected Works* (1997: 261). It's a little hard to see where such a mistranslation could have come from: perhaps the translator has one or both of the previous German terms in mind. *Afforderungscharakter* is indeed part of a system of concepts which includes *Situationsgebundenheit* and *Feldmässigkeit*. Because the child forms a whole structure with the environment, the child's wants and needs are not simply subjective phenomena: They can be modeled objectively as positive or negative vectors, or a tension between the child and the environment. For example, a child sees a step and is drawn to it; if the step is too high, there is no behavior appropriate to this field. So in this case, the step does not "afford" climbing for the child (although it may for the adult) and we can say it has no *Afforderungscharakter*. This concept, if not the word, is certainly well known and widely employed: It was developed by Lewin from von Uexküll's notion of functional "tone" and functionally tinged objects (1940), and it was later developed into J.J. Gibson's concept of "affordance" (1966). It is still widely used in design today.

alter the situation. And it is for this reason that such a big role is offered to the things themselves and to the concrete objects within the situation.

K Lewin described an experiment that showed how difficult it is for a child under 2 years old to sit down on an object that is outside of his field of view. This was an experiment with a large stone, which the child walked about, examined from all sides, etc. Then the child turned his back to sit, but as soon as he turned, he lost the stone from view. So the child held onto the stone when he turned to sit. Finally, one child recorded on film (this is given in Lewin's book [K. Lewin, 1926]) gets out of the difficulty in a unique way: He bends over, looks between his legs, so that standing with his back to the stone he still has it in his field of view.[5] And then he manages to sit. Not a few children aid themselves by placing a hand on the stone. In another case, the experimenter himself puts the child's hand on the stone and the child sits on his own hand, because he does not feel that, besides the bit of the stone which he touches with his hand, there exists the entire stone as a whole. In this situation, such linkedness of the child to the field of vision appears to demonstrate a unique activity of child consciousness.

To illustrate this, let me cite an example from our experiments. My co-worker L. S. Slavina[6] was given the task of seeing if a child in a free situation could verbally "break away" from the situation, if I may put it that way—(i.e.,—Trans.) could speak of what he did not see before him. In order to do this, we used the method of repeating propositions which has been widely developed in clinics. Two-year-old children repeat without any difficulty phrases like "The chicken is going," "Coco is going," "The dog is running." But saying "Tanya is going" when Tanya is sitting on a chair right in front of the child: This the child cannot do. The phrase elicits the reaction "Tanya is sitting." In all three trials, in all those cases where the attention of the child was drawn to the situation, all 40 children gave the incorrect response. The child finds it difficult, looking at Tanya sitting, to say "Tanya is going." That which he sees acts upon him much more strongly, and because of it, his words cannot break free of reality. This explains one of the facts that has long drawn the attention of researchers: In early childhood, the child is almost unable to lie. Only near the end of early childhood does there emerge in the child the most elementary capacity to say what is not in fact so. He is not yet even capable of fiction. A simple example also tells us this, one well studied in recent times. When the child is sick, at the moment of acute pain, the child affectively responds to it with crying and capriciousness. Yet he can be dangerously ill, and if he is not directly feeling pain, he is not bothered by any consciousness of illness. So at this age, a child cannot speak of

---

[5] In his lecture on play (2016), Vygotsky describes seeing the film of this experiment when Lewin visited him in Moscow.

[6] Leah Solomonovna Slavina (1906–1988) was born in the same small town as Vygotsky, Gomel, in Byeolorussia ("White Russia"). Like Vygotsky, she was from a Jewish family, and like Vygotsky middle class (her father was the town apothecary). She attended Moscow University in the 1920s, and became one of the "pyatorka," the five students who worked with Vygotsky. After the war, she finished a Ph.D. thesis on early childhood story-telling (another of the "Five," Bozhovich, was her supervisor).

anything else other than what is right in front of his eyes, or that which resounds in his ears.

What determines the behavior of such a character?

Firstly, what characterizes the consciousness of the child: the appearance of unity between sensory and motor functions. Whatever the child sees, he wishes to touch with his hands. Observing a 2-year-old child left to himself, we see that the toddler is endlessly active, endlessly bustling, but active exclusively in the concrete situation, that is, doing only what things in his surroundings impel him to do.

Previously it was believed that this sensorimotor unity emerges from a simple physiological reflex, but this is not so even in the age of infancy. The baby in swaddling clothes may sometimes spend hours calmly observing: Whereas in early years, it is a characteristic that every perception is surely followed by an action. This is not true in the age of infancy until the last phase, when there emerges a sensorimotor unity specific to this age.

The Leipzig School[7] drew attention to the fact that the primary perceptions of children are an affectively colored perception, that is, to the fact that the child sees each object with a different affective coloration. In other words, perception and feeling present themselves in an inseparable unity. We may have learnt to see things apart from the immediate emotions which they arouse, without showing keen interest in a range of things. But for the child in early childhood, this is not possible. Perception and affect are still undifferentiated; they are tightly linked the one to the other. The experiments of F. Krueger[8] and H. Volkelt[9] have shown that in us and in animals, perceptions always come with a tone of feeling. For example, blue and yellow colors produce in us feelings of cold and of warmth. A certain tone of feeling accompanies our notions, and this shows that genetically there are links between them.

This unity of affective-receptive moments yields a third moment of the characteristics of consciousness in early childhood—that of acting in a situation. We are dealing with a unique system of consciousness such that perception is directly linked to action. Consequently, if the system of consciousness is to be characterized from the point of view of the principal functions working together in the age of early (childhood—Trans.), we must say that it represents in itself a unity of affective

[7] This refers to the "Second Leipzig School" of Krueger, Volkelt and Sander, not the Original "First" Leipzig School of Wilhelm Wundt and Carl Stumpf. The Second Leipzig School, like the first one, was interested in perception and strongly holistic. However, they broke with Dilthey's humanism and Wundt's mechanism and became advocates of a romantic Nazi psychology which idolized the "German soul" and argued that even healthy adults had a kind of "unity of perception and action." This was the Nazi version of the "reflex arc."

[8] Felix Krueger (1874–1948) studied philosophy with Dilthey and psychology with Wundt. He was, as Vygotsky says, a member of the Second Leipzig School and a professor at the University of Leipzig. Later, he was rector of the University of Leipzig: like most of the Second Leipzig School, he was sympathetic to the Nazi party. But although Krueger signed the statement of German professors in support of Hitler, he also defended his Jewish students and was eventually removed as rector.

[9] For a biographical note on the Nazi psychologist Hans Volkelt, please see Footnote 22, Chapter 6.

perception, of affect and of action. This state of affairs is splendidly explained for us by the experiments of Lewin.

There is an attractive force in things, an affective charge in each thing that carries a source of attraction for the child in itself. In other words (and we may regard this as established by the experimental work of Lewin), the unique sensorimotor unity characteristic for this particular age consists in this: It is not in itself a primordial reflex link but rather a link through affect. That is, it is the affective character of perception that gives rise to such a unity. Therefore, we are dealing here with a completely original relationship to reality.

For the child at this early age, to be consciously aware does not in general mean to perceive or to treat a perception with the aid of attention, memory, or thinking. All of these functions are not yet differentiated; they act in consciousness holistically, subordinated to perception in so far as they participate in the process of perceiving.

Everyone knows, from simple observation, that memory in the child at early childhood manifests itself always through active perception—through recognition. Everyone knows that thinking at this age manifests itself exclusively in a visual-graphic way, as the capability of re-establishing a link, but a visual-illustrative one in a given situation. Everyone knows that the affect of the child at this age also manifests itself predominantly at the moment of visual-graphic perception of the object to which the affect is directed. Thinking for a child at this age, in so far as he already manifests intellectual activity, does not mean recalling. Only in the child of preschool age is there this thinking—that is, recalling, that is, depending on, his own prior experience.

There is one fact that has been called the fact of amnesia: we have all forgotten our age of infancy. Although individual persons of some genius, for example, L. Tolstoy, may claim that they remember the feeling of being constrained in swaddling clothes or the sensations of water and soap in bathing, here, it would seem, we are dealing with some complex reminiscence. So far as the consciousness of the rest of us is concerned, we have forgotten, and forgotten our early childhood as well. Hardly anyone remembers much that is clear from his childhood prior to 3 years of age (unless it is from the stories of those close to us), beyond some isolated and exceptional impressions, often fragmented and incomprehensible.

Linked recollections from the epoch of early childhood are usually not consciously held on to, and so unique is the organization of memory that it participates very little in the activity of consciousness. Memory moves to the first plane in succeeding ages. And it would be true to say of thinking in the child of early childhood that it means looking into certain affectively colored links and undertaking unique actions that correspond to externally perceived situations. At this age, what dominates is a visual affectively colored perception, which directly turns into action.

Perception itself is distinct in two peculiarities upon which we may dwell. The first peculiarity is its affective character. I.M. Sechenov considered passion to be the most important feature of perception of the child in early age.[10] Any perception at this early age is impassioned. He who sees a child looking at a new thing will see a perception that is substantially different from perception in us.

The second peculiarity (it amounts to a general law for all of subsequent development): When perception constitutes the dominant function of consciousness, then this means that perception is put into maximally favorable conditions for development. Since all of consciousness acts only on the basis of perception, perception develops earlier than other functions. This is linked to two basic laws of child development of which I wish to remind you. The first states that functions, like the parts of the body, do not develop proportionally or evenly, but that at each age there is a dominant function.

The second law states that the most fundamental functions, which are necessary at the beginning, which are the basis of others, develop earlier. For this reason, it is not surprising that the development of the psychic functions in the child begins with the development of perception. If all consciousness works to benefit perception, if perception is shaped anew for a given age, then, obviously, the very highest success that the child achieves is not in the area of memory but in the area of perception.

In this regard, there is the question of childhood autism. There are two points of view. (And it seems to me that the two of them constitute an inequality from the point of view of probability. The facts indicate that one of these points of view is closer to the truth.) According to one point of view, the logic of dreams constitutes the starting point of the development of child thinking. Thinking is autistic and wholly directed to the satisfaction of desires; it is not realistic thinking which, according to the point of view under consideration, emerges at relatively late stages of development. It is the "Lustprinzip"—the pleasure principle of S. Freud.

E. Bleuler, however, has shown that in fact this is entirely untrue. In the world of animals, we do not observe the autistic functions of thinking,[11] that is, thinking which is separate from action. The attribution to the infant of such states of consciousness, in which he has realized his desires, aspirations, and inclinations all exclusively through consciousness following the pleasure principle, is a purely logical construction. Pleasure for the infant in early age is linked to the real provision of food, with real stimulation, etc.

E. Bleuler drew attention to the following: If the point of view of Freud were correct, the autistic character of the child should decrease in measure to the child's development. It was Bleuler who first drew attention to the growth of autistic thinking after one and a half years, that is, after the first mastery of the word.

[10] Ivan Mikhailovich Sechenov (Ива́н Миха́йлович Се́ченов, 1829–1905) founded Russian physiology and discovered the electrochemical nature of brain signals. He was a student of Helmholtz, and his work formed the foundation for the "reflexology" of Bekhterev and the "conditioned reflex" of Pavlov.

[11] Neither Bleuler nor Vygotsky uses "autism" the way it is used today, as an asocial neuropsychological developmental disorder. Instead, both use it the way it is used in Freud and Piaget, as indicating the fantasy, wish-fulfillment life of young children.

We now have the work of Gabriel[12] which demonstrates that autistic thinking in the child increases as thinking is raised to a higher level—at age 3 and again at age 13, in connection with the formation of concepts. And this is understandable. After all, speech is one of the most powerful tools for the development of thinking not linked directly to the situation. Speech always enables the introduction of something not contained in a situation and always allows us to say in words something that is at variance with the given situation. For this reason, verbal thinking is linked to the emergence of autistic thinking in children.

Autistic thinking at an early stage of development as an important characterization of the child's relationship to reality is nearly nonexistent. It remains in an embryonic state for almost all of the first 3 years of life. As Gabriel has shown, here we are dealing with only the rudiments of autistic thinking.

In terms of the old psychology, it may be said that in the child of this age there is no imagination at all, that is, there is no capacity whatsoever to construct in thinking and in imagery a visible situation different from that which is given to him immediately. If we take the relationship of the child to external reality, we see that the child appears before us as a being who is realist to the very highest degree, whose difference from a child in later age lies in his situation-embeddedness, in that he is entirely in the power of those things that exist right now in front of him. Here we do not yet have that detachment from reality which lies at the base of autistic thinking.

Now let us consider the child's relationship to other people. The externals of the situation are at present very widely studied. A range of work has appeared that has, experimentally and through the path of systematic observations, demonstrated from the age of infancy onwards the presence of relatively developed forms in the child's attitudes to other people, relations that appear primitive only from the point of view of adults. These relations become increasingly complex during the age, to the point where not a few researchers openly speak of early childhood as that age where the central neoformation is the development of the basis of person-to-person relations, that is, the basis of social relations.

There have been some attempts to offer some theory in this regard, and it seems to me that one of these theories, which has also begun to be more and more elaborated on and experimented with, appears correct. According to this theory, the uniqueness of the social relations of the child lies in the following: The child at the moment of birth and in the age of infancy is separate from the mother physiologically (according to the old expression) but is not separate from her biologically—he does not displace himself or feed himself. A child who has begun to walk is already separate from the mother biologically but not yet psychologically separate—he still has no notion of himself as existing separately, outside of those concrete situations where he always has to deal with other people.

---

[12] The reference to "Gabriel" is a little puzzling, as his research interests (autism, the Crisis at Three, and adolescence) are quite central to Vygotsky's work. But we can find no other references to him, either in Vygotsky's work or in the work of his contemporaries. Jules-Gabriel Compayré, who is also referred to in Footnote 31 of Chapter Six, wrote on precisely these subjects. Is it possible that Vygotsky or Vygotsky's stenographer is using "Gabriel" as short-hand, to refer to him?

The first notion that the child has of himself as a being is a notion of his separateness, or particularity (not in the sense of setting himself apart from others but in the sense of separating himself from things upon which he operates and of opposing himself to things in a social situation, where he himself is intertwined with other people).

German researchers maintain that the two stages into which early childhood may be divided can be outlined in the following way: In the first, "Ur-wir," stage, there exists a kind of consciousness, the "grand-we," such that it precedes the understanding of "I" and from which the "I" only starts to stand out. In truth, there are a number of facts that show that the child is not aware of how much he himself understands nor how much is understood by others. As J. Piaget correctly notes, it appears to the child that adults know of everything he wishes. There is a study of the emergence in the child of two-word phrases: They emerge just when single words do not suffice for the child because so many of them are polysemic. The word for the child conveys such a variety of things, and in every situation, it is understood in a different way. Gabriel has well described these constant misunderstandings. According to him, researchers have been wrong to disregard the adult difficulty in understanding the child who has just begun to speak.

Permit me to quote an example from the experiments of Gabriel which I have already cited in another context. For a child in experimental conditions that included extensive clinical observations, a situation of misunderstanding of the child's words by adults was specially created. He requires something, adults do not understand him, he begins to get angry, and the situation leads to this: The adults ask him questions, to find out what it is he wants.

What is interesting here in relation to the theme that preoccupies us? It seems to me that the child does not know that what he thinks is understood only by himself and adults may not understand it. For a child, there is as yet no problem in being understood by adults. He says "pu-fu" and it seems to him that he will be given what is requested. This is so because adults unceasingly interpret the behavior of the child in order to guess his inclinations. For this reason, as Piaget correctly says, in the child, there is the feeling that adults must correctly understand his inclinations, in him there is no distinction between what is available to his consciousness and what is available to the consciousness of an adult. For this reason, the primary consciousness consists of a "proto-we," out of which only slowly is the representation of the child to himself distinguished.

The expression "I myself" itself emerges in the second stage of early childhood. The second stage is referred to by authors as the "stage of the external 'I' in the 'we'", and here, in this stage, is when the child opposes his own independent actions to shared actions with adults. For example, he seizes a spoon and wishes to eat by himself, protesting against being fed. But as far as speech comes into his consciousness, as far as his being understood by adults, as far as the inner side of the process, he remains entangled in the state of the "grand we."

Whether this is a true resolution of the question by the theory under discussion or whether it is not true, it appears to me at any rate that it correctly shows the uniqueness of the child's relationship to the surrounding people and the isolation from this child-adult unity of the child's own "I." The child's "I myself" appears relatively late. This stage is well described in one study as when the child understands far more than he can say. The child himself cannot intervene in the course of his own thoughts and ideas. I would say that wherever we are dealing with an external situation, then things control the child, but wherever the child actively relates to the situation, then this can be linked to the intervention of others, to an appeal to adults.

Let us now dwell on the basic types of activity of the child in the stage of early childhood. This is one of the most difficult, and, it seems to me, least theoretically worked out, of questions. The old definition of play as any child activity that does not pursue a result considers all of these kinds of child activity as equivalent to one another. Opening and closing a door by the child or playing horsie, from the point of view of the adult, are both given as entertainment, as play, not serious, not in order to obtain something or other. It is all called "play."

It must be said that many others have wanted to bring clarity to this question. The first was K. Groos,[13] who tried to classify child play and find a different approach to it. He showed that experimental games have a different relationship to the child's thinking and to his future goal-oriented nonplay actions than that of symbolic play, when the child imagines that he is a horse or a hunter and so on. One of Groos's students—A. Weiss—attempted to show that different types of play activity are very far from each other, or, as he put it, have little in common in their psychological relations. With this the question arises as to whether it is possible to designate all the different varieties of this kind of activity with the single word, "play."

P. P. Blonsky[14] believes that play is only a common term for the various activities of the child. As far as I understand him, Blonsky appears to take this assertion to extremes. He is inclined to think that "play in general" does not exist, that there exists no type of activity which would fall under this conception, because the very concept of "play" is an adult concept, whereas everything is serious for the child. And so this concept should be expunged from psychology. Blonsky recounts the following episode. When it was necessary to commission some psychologist to write an encyclopedia entry for play, he replied that "play" is a word which has nothing to back it up, that should be banished from psychology.

---

[13] Karl Groos (1861–1946) was a professor of philosophy at the University of Basel who wrote two monographs about play, *The Play of Animals* (1898) and *The Play of Man* (1919). As the titles imply, he took the point of view of evolutionary psychology, which says that play must have an evolutionary purpose. That is why he and his student Weiss insist that play is "future oriented," and has an adaptive function: It is a kind of training for hunting.

Groos refers to opening and closing doors or sitting on rocks, as a kind of "experimental play." He is drawing attention to something real and important: The child is experimenting with, and exploring, the properties of doors and of rocks. But for precisely that reason, Vygotsky does not consider this kind of play to be true play: It does not contain an imaginary situation, a "break with reality," and instead constitutes an adaptation: a form of work.

[14] For a biographical footnote on P.P. Blonsky, see Footnote 2, Chapter One.

I think that the most fruitful thinking was that which I heard in Leningrad from D.B. Elkonin[15] on breaking down the concept of play. Play must be approached as an utterly unique activity, and not as a ready-made concept that can amalgamate all kinds of child activity, and in particular those which Groos calls experimental play. For example, the child opens and closes a box, doing this many times over, takes things from one place to another. All of these are not play in the strict sense of the word. We may talk about whether these types of activity have the same relationship that babble has to speech, but in any case, they are not play.

What appears to me highly fruitful, responding to the facts of the matter and defining play positively, is that which this idea moves to the forefront, namely that play is a unique relationship to reality which is characterized by the creation of an imaginary situation or by the transfer of properties from one object to another.[16] This gives us the possibility of resolving correctly the problem of play in early childhood. From this point of view, there is none of the total lack of play which characterizes the age of infancy. In early childhood, we come face to face with play. Everyone will agree that a child at this age feeds and nurses a doll, and can drink from an empty cup, etc. But it appears to me that it would be dangerous not to see a substantial difference between this "play" and playing in the true sense of the word at preschool age—in the creation of imaginary situations. Studies show that play with the transfer of value, with imaginary situations, appears only in embryonic form near the end of the early age. Only during the third year of child's life[17], do

[15]D.B. Elkonin (1904–1984) worked at the Herzen Pedagogical Institute with Vygotsky, where these lectures were delivered; he was probably sitting in the audience. After Vygotsky's death, the Leningrad group pursued a different research direction from the group in Kharkov led by Leontiev; they were more interested in teaching and less interested in the theory of activity. However, they did adapt Vygotsky's original schema of ages of crises to a schedule of "leading activities" that did not include a clear role for Vygotsky's neoformations, his central and peripheral lines of development, or his crises. With V.V. Davydov, Elkonin worked out a theory of "germ cells" based on Vygotsky's ideas about analysis into units. For Elkonin, who studied preschool, play was a kind of germ cell (Davydov concentrated on concepts and school education). His most famous pedagogical innovation is the "Elkonin Box," a kind of cloze test used for teaching phonics. The idea is to match one phoneme to one box, for example, "cat."

Proto-speech at one (and also the proto-will at three, and the proto-self at seven, and what Halliday calls proto-conversation, proto-language, proto-narrative-and-dialogue, proto-turn-taking, and proto-variation (2004: 139) are all true prototypes: that is, they share the functional goal of the complete "ideal" version of speech, will, self, etc. For example, proto-speech is for interacting, proto-will for decision-making, the proto-self is for role-playing. Elkonin (and of course Vygotsky) rejects experimental play as play because it does not share the goal of "breaking away" from the context of situation and transferring value from one object to another, from one person to another, or from one situation to another. Experimental play is, therefore, not a proto-type for play at all, but only the negative starting point of play development: it is work rather than play, and the principle is that of rote, rather than role or rule.

[16]This refers to Vygotsky's lecture on play previously referred to in Footnote 5 above; Elkonin's research, referred to below, followed on from this lecture.

[17]Vygotsky says на третьем году, which is literally "upon the third year of life," but since the organism is living before the child is born, the meaning is that the child is 2 years old when play first begins to emerge.

there emerge games associated with the introduction of elements of imagination to the situation. In addition, these "playful" manifestations are rather scarce and are drowned out in a wide sea of those activities that Lewin described and which directly follow from the situation itself.

Already in Lewin, we find the idea that the definition given by him poorly resembles the creation of a play situation in the proper sense of the word. Creating an imaginary situation is very difficult for a child who is so tied to present objects that he must look between his legs in order to sit on a stone.

Finally, lastly, and most importantly, research has shown that in early childhood there is not yet the creation of an imaginary situation in the strict sense of the word. I would like to clarify this with a simple example. The child at two tends to her doll in a completely natural way, doing the same thing with it that a mother or a nanny does: She lays the doll down, feeds it, and even puts it on the potty. But it is interesting: in the child, there is no representation of the doll as a daughter, or of herself as the nurse or mama. She looks after the teddy bear as it were a (teddy—Trans.) bear, after the doll as if it were a doll, that is, this is play from the point of view of an adult, but it is in stark contrast to the play of a child of a more advanced age, when the child himself plays a role and things play roles too. There the doll is really a little girl, and the child is one of its parents; here, however, the doll is still, as before, affectively drawing the child to put it on the potty and to feed it just as much as, let us say, a round ball draws the child to it in order to be rolled. Here, there is no imaginary situation to expand upon—unlike when the child, himself distinctly playing a given role, distinctly changes the properties of a thing. For example, an experiment showed that for the child in the early age not everything can be a doll. The child at 2, who will easily dandle a doll or a bear, finds bottle-feeding very difficult and does it in a different way. Therefore, if, as it is said, play is characteristically that something can be anything, this does not yet characterize the play of the child in the early age. In this way, we have here something like play, but it is not yet conscious for the child.

This theory has always seemed to me extremely appealing, and now it has taken on a very special meaning. W. Stern has introduced into psychology the concept of *Ernstspiel* (serious play) and applied it to the age of adolescence, pointing out that such play bears a transitional character, between play and a serious relationship to reality, and that it constitutes a specific type of activity. As A. Homburger[18] and his students have pointed out, the concept of serious play is considerably more suitable for what is observed in early childhood: We are then dealing with play in which the play situation has not yet been differentiated in the child's consciousness from the real situation. When preschoolers play at father and mother, or at trains, they know distinctly how to conduct themselves on the plane of the play situation, that is, at all times to comport themselves in a manner that conforms with the logic of the situation that unfolds. By analogy with the way Lewin expresses it, in the preschooler, there emerges a certain closed field in which he is moving, but at the same time, he

[18] For a biographical footnote on Homburger, see Footnote 24, Chapter Two.

does not lose the notion of the real value of things. If a chair in play—a horse—must be moved from one place to another, the child is not prevented from moving the chair, even though a horse cannot be carried in one's arms. Play in the child of later age is characterized by the presence of both a semantic and of a visual field.

In early childhood, we confront quasi-play, or "play in itself." Objectively, this is already play, but it is not yet play for the child; inter alia, the experiment of Dohm[19] is extremely interesting because it shows how the child in the early age repeats a series of actions in relation to, let us say, the doll, but these are not yet linked to one situation, to where the doll has to go, where she has been called by the doctor, etc. There is no linking story to translate this into actions, no dramatization in the strict sense of the word, and no movement defined according to plan in this situation created by the child.

Let us consider the neoformations, which we mentioned, and speech in particular. We see that the very fact of the acquisition of speech is in stark contrast with all of which I have said thus far characterizing early childhood. In other words, it immediately begins to loosen the grip of sensorimotor unity, to split off the situated circumstances of the child. To the extent that the child develops, the attitude of the child changes, not only to the new but also to the old elements of the environment, for the character of their effects on the child too has changed. There is a change in the social situation of development which existed at the beginning of the age; since the child is quite different—the old social situation of development has dissolved, and a new age period commences.

Understanding what is new in the relation of the child to the environment in early childhood is possible in the light of the analysis of the development of child speech, for the development of child speech as a means of communication, as a means of understanding the speech of others, presents the central line of development of the child at this age and substantially changes the relation of the child to the surrounding environment.

The study of deaf-mute children has shown that this central neoformation—speech as a communicative function—does not emerge in them.

Speech serves the function of messaging; it serves as an activity related to other people, that is, it is external and collaborative—in the form of dialogue. Where speech manifests itself in this communicative function, it is linked to speaking and to saying; it manifests itself as sound.

The study of sound, that is, the external side of speech began a long time ago. The material here is very rich. Not a few theories have been forward. However, now that speech has begun to be studied in all its complexity from the semantic standpoint, there has been a shift in point of view concerning its external aspect. The development of the sound aspect of speech is usually presented in the following manner: Speech is made up of discrete sound elements most easily symbolized in

[19] It is possible that Vygotsky is referring to Hedwig Dohm (1831–1919), an early feminist and author who was one of the first to argue that children are socialized into gender roles (i.e., they are given by the environment and not by heredity). She wrote about the use of dolls for this purpose in an essay called "The Reform of Girls' Schools" in 1908.

writing. In a sense this thesis is irrefutable, because all vocalized speech is constructed of a finite quantity of elements. The child at first masters only a limited quantity of these elements; he does not possess all of the sound elements of speech, and there occurs some distortion, that is, the so-called physiological articulation distortions which we have in mind, that underdevelopment of the articulatory apparatus which is age related as opposed to that which is due to pathological articulatory distortions. Further development takes place in the differentiation of these elements and by two and a half years of age, by the end of early childhood, the child can handle all the baggage of sound. To the extent of mastery of the elements, the mastery of sound combinations increases. The situation appeared thus: being able to pronounce individual sounds, the child went on to master various sound combinations (the work of W. and C. Stern).

This glimpse of the development of speech has been put in doubt, as it leads to a number of inconsistent propositions. Let us present a few.

1. When the child has mastered all of the sounds, he should then master all of the combinations, that is, having mastered determinate sounds, the child should without difficulty be able to acquire new words—in this way, development should merely consist of a quantitative increase in the lexicon.

There has been some comparison between the path of development of the sound aspect of speech and the mastery of written speech. While this really is conditioned by the mastery of elements, it represents not the mastery of individual words but that of the principle proper to writing. With oral speech, the picture is different. In opposing this analogy between oral and written speech, the writers of old said that the comparison of oral speech ought to be with the mastery of elements and their combination when learning foreign languages; the child grasps words as complexes of sound, so that it is necessary each time to commit them to memory anew, just as we do when learning a foreign language.

But if I master the English alphabet, this does not yet mean I have mastered the English language. It appears that the way the child masters the words of a native language is not this path. The acquisition of the native language occupies an intermediate place between what goes on in the development of written speech and what goes on in the mastery of a foreign language. If mastery of the sound aspect of speech came from the elements of the ABC, only two paths of acquisition are possible: through a gradual learning of each new combination, as with a foreign language, or through the mastery of elements which provide the potential to produce any combination instantaneously, as with the development of written speech. In oral speech development, on the one hand, we find elements of that which is in written speech: instantaneous mastery of this or that set of words, that is, instantaneous mastery of structure, so that the child seems to have the capacity to master any word; on the other hand, as with the mastery of foreign words, each word must pass from the sensory plane to an active plane by memorization. In grasping the phonology of speech, the child does not have to memorize words, but each new word does have to be mastered separately.

2. With written speech, when the child has acquired the alphabet and learnt to write, it becomes easier to select an element. For him, it is easier to write the letter than the word: In audible speech, the isolation of the elements is the more complicated. The child articulates the whole phrase or word well, but is not able to name the syllables in it, let alone the individual sounds.

If the analogy between the development of speech in its audible aspect and written speech were true, this should not be the case.

3. If the path of development of speech lay from the sound to the complex, the difficulty of the analytical work done by the child would be very great. In real speech, the child never hears individual sounds but rather linked speech.

Consequently, from the point of view of these opinions, the child appears to be an analyst, he must seize the separate sounds—the letters of the alphabet: He must create his own alphabet, that is, he must carry out a mighty task of generalization which contradicts the facts of his real level of development. Presenting all this as coming from the child of a year and a half is unthinkable. Interpreting the question in this way, moreover, loses the link between the sound and sense aspects of speech, because in themselves sounds are senseless.

In this way, the old theories not only led to a complete break between the sound and the sense aspects of speech, but also to the absurd proposition that to study a word phonetically, a child must render it meaningless, and from the point of view of meaning, contrariwise, work on complexes that are without form from the point of view of sound, that is, in order to explain the development of the semantic aspect, we propose the disintegration of sounds and vice versa. The old theories ignored the real conditions which determined speech development, namely speech communication.

From around 1928,[20] thanks to the intersection of studies from different fields, new points of view appeared on this question. The ambition to revise the old

[20] Vygotsky is probably alluding to the Prague Linguistic Circle of Roman Jakobson and Nikolai Trubetskoy. The Prague Circle was founded, as Vygotsky indicates, in 1928. Trubetskoy and Jakobson demonstrated that sounds are designed for maximum distinctness, along contrastive principles, such as the voiced/unvoiced contrast Vygotsky discusses below. But these contrasts are not directly linked to functional values of words. So, for example, it is not true that all words that start with voiced sounds, like /b/, /v/, and /g/, refer to voices or vibrations or living things, while all words that start with unvoiced sounds like /p/ and /f/ and /k/ refer to things that are not living; it is not true that all words spoken loudly mean something big while all words spoken softly mean something small. Instead the relationship is indirect, conventional, and what Vygotsky would call "dialectical": The fact a thing is not some other thing allows us to see that a word is not some other word, and the fact that a word is not some other word allows us to hear that a sound is not some other sound: The fact that a cave is not a calf allows us to see that "cave" and "calf" are different words, and the fact that these are different words allows us to hear that the vowel is longer and the consonant voiced in one word and shorter and unvoiced in the other. But this means that phonemes are not concrete descriptions of the sounds we make—they are abstract contrasts in sounding which realize meaningful morphemes according to certain dialectical rules—rules of contradiction and contrast. This is why Vygotsky insists that morpho-phonemes are units of meaning and not simply units of sound.

teaching on the development of the sound aspect of speech swept through linguistics, pedagogy, speech psychology, the field of language pathology studies, and so on.

From the point of view of the old representation, the sound aspect of speech consists of a number of elements and their combinations. The old phonetics relied on the physiological nature of speech, on articulation, etc. Speech development was looked at through the prism of the fine motor movements of articulation: It transpired that fine movements were required for the mastery of this or that sound. Say, for example, that in order to master the sound /r/, we require a subtler motoric articulation than that required for the sound /b/. The development of motorics was considered the only source of development.

The new theory (phonology—as opposed to the old name, phonetics) began by noting that the real functional value of individual sounds of human speech is not directly linked to its physiological properties. There is also no proportionality between their physical (acoustic) properties and their functional value. From the end of the second half of development of the sound side of child speech, there is no parallelism with the physical properties of sounds but a dependency on the degree of functional value of sounds in human speech. The sounds /b/ and /p/, /v/ and /f/, /g/ and /k/ have the same physical (contrast—T), voicing/devoicing—a commonality across the whole of these series of sounds. Their functional value in speech does not coincide with their physical properties.

We have three orders of phenomena: (1) the development of the sound aspect of child speech, (2) physical and physiological difficulties, and (3) the development of functional values.

We can say the development of child speech finds a dependence not on the growth of complexity in physiological and physical difficulties, but a link to the development of functional meaning in speech. If it is still dependent upon physiological features, then this is because the physiological features themselves are linked to functional value.

How to determine the functional value of a sound in speech development? The question abuts a methodological problem, how analysis is to be applied in sciences that study whole formations. Analysis is needed here, but analysis disarticulates, while we must study them as wholes.

It is necessary to distinguish two types of analysis. The first—division into elements[21]—represents in itself an unsatisfactory type of analysis, destroying the properties of the whole; the second type is taking apart the whole into units which cannot

[21] Vygotsky uses the term разложение, and the English Collected Works has rendered this "decomposition," but this has the unfortunate connotation of "rot" or "decay" in English. What Vygotsky actually means could be conveyed by taking "decomposition" apart into "de-composition" or "uncomposing," but of course no such word exists in English. We have instead chosen the simple phrasal verb "take apart" for this word wherever possible. However, "take apart" is transitive and requires a noun object, and this is not always present in the Russian. Where no noun object is present, we have chosen "division" for taking apart the whole into elements that lack the property of the whole, and "separation" for taking apart the whole into base units which retain the property of the whole in some form.

be further separated and the study of cells which retain all of the properties of the whole. In the study of speech, we should conduct an analysis into units (in just the same way as we studied the problem of the impact of the environment on the child).[22] This type of analysis rejects the possibility of taking speech apart into separable sound elements. The sounds of human speech have defined values. This—first and most basically—is what characterizes them as human speech. When speech is taken apart into its elements, these lose their meaning, and thus the analysis of speech loses the properties in analysis; it is no longer separation into parts, but becomes an elevation to the general. In the new phonetics—phonology—the unit of analysis has changed, the phoneme is proposed as a unit of human speech and a unit of the development of child speech. From the point of view of the new phonetics, the development of child speech takes place by way of the development of a phonemic system and not by way of the accumulation of separate sounds.

The phoneme[23]—this is not just a sound, but a meaningful sound, a sound that has not lost its meaning, a certain unit, which possesses to a minimal degree of this primary property that belongs to speech as a whole. Sounds do not develop by themselves, but from the point of view of their value. Functional value depends on the development of semantic value. We may speak of the development of human speech only if and when the unity of sound and sense is preserved.

In language development, there do not exist phonemes in the absolute sense; there is only the relational consideration of one phoneme against the ground of other phones. Mastering the phoneme takes place on condition of the perception of other phonemes and in coordination with them. The basic law of perception of

[22] See Chapter 3, "The Study of Heredity and the Environment in Pedology" in *L.S. Vygotsky's Pedological Works Volume 1. Foundations of Pedology* (2019), pp. 45–63.

[23] Vygotsky is using the word "phoneme" is a slightly different sense than we use it today. Earlier, Vygotsky made the point that there is no proportionality between the acoustic or articulatory properties of phonemes and their function in adult language, for example, it is not the case that long sounds represent long things or even that loud sounds represent big ones. Of course, it is indeed possible to imagine child speech where children make long drawn-out sounds to show length and shout to indicate large size (and of course children do this even in mother tongue). One reason why it is possible to imagine this is that in adult language there are units which do have a systematic relationship to meaning. But these units are not simple sounds and the relationship they have to meaning is not at all direct or iconic (i.e., it is not mimetic, like drawing out sounds for length or shouting them for size).

For example, in English, whenever you mean more than one discrete object, you use /s/ or /z/ at the end of a noun ("cats" or "dogs"). Whenever you want to say that some event or act happened in the past, you use /d/ or /t/ at the end of the verb ("played" or "worked"). In both cases what you add on is not a specific concrete sound but a purely abstract unit of some kind; these abstract units, which do have functional value, are what Vygotsky means.

Today, we would not call Vygotsky's units phonemes, because linguists use "phoneme" to mean elements which do not by themselves mean anything and which must therefore be defined by their acoustic or articulatory properties (i.e., /s/ as opposed to /z/ or /d/ as opposed to /t/). For the analysis of meaning, these are elements and not units. Today, we would call Vygotsky's units of sound and functional meaning phono-morphemes, or morpho-phonemes, or simply morphemes (/s/ or /z/ as opposed to nothing, or /d/ or /t/ as opposed to nothing). That is, actually, what the Prague Linguistic Circle (Trubetskoy and Jakobson) called them.

phonemes—the law of perception of the sound aspect of speech, like all laws of perception—is the perception of something against the ground of something else (figure on ground). Every phoneme is perceived and produced as a phoneme against the phonemic background, that is, the perception of phonemes takes place only against the background of human speech.

In characterizing the development of oral speech in children, it is necessary to point out that it happens not by the type of written speech, not by the type of learning a foreign language, but as if along the middle line between these two types that is now being revealed. Thanks to his hearing of adult speech, the child can access a much more extensive background in speech than the "figures" which were at his disposal. As soon as a phoneme appears against this background, there appear analogous structures, that is, perception takes place structurally.

Having grasped the structure—the relationship of the phoneme and its background—in one particular case, the child masters the structure as a whole. For example, the conjugation of one verb leads to mastering the rules of conjugation. K. I. Chukovsky and Marchlewski[24] have strongly emphasized the influence of the speech background, the influence of the semantic aspect of speech on the development of sounds.

Let us sum up:

1. The sound aspect of child speech is developed in direct functional dependence upon the sense aspect of child speech, that is, subordinated to it.
2. The sound aspect of speech functions according to the laws of phonological relation; that is, a word can be recognized against the background of other words. For the child in early childhood, the background consists of sense-able[25] speech, that is, the speech of people in his surroundings.
3. The growth and development of speech is linked to the differentiation of sense.
4. The path of development in speech is not a path of developing the elements of speech. In every language, there are separate systems in which meaningful types of relations between sound units are built up. The child assimilates the system of their construction. Within it, he grasps various types of relationships and immediately begins to master the structure. This explains the saltatory development of child speech. The problem of multilingualism as well may be considered within this light. The old contention that in the child who simultaneously learns two languages the development of one language hinders the development of another

---

[24] Kornei Ivanovich Chukovsky (1882–1966) is probably the best-known children's writer in Russian; the humor magainze *Krokodil* is named after one of his early stories. The early Vygotsky (*Educational Psychology*, Vygotsky, 1997a: 270f) disliked his work because of its nonsense, its talking animals, and its focus on lower level psychological functions such as recognizing and repeating sounds. Here, however, he appears to take a more favorable view of his work!

Zofia Marchlewski (1898–1983) was, like Chukovsky, a journalist and a translator, later an important official in the Union of Soviet Writers.

[25] Vygotsky says сенсорная речь, which means something like "sensory speech" or "sensuous speech," but since this has an erotic *double-entendre* in English that Vygotsky does not intend, we have chosen to render it as "sense-able," even though this is not, strictly speaking, English.

takes on a new light and is disproven. It turns out that as long as the two languages are mastered by the child as closed structures and the courses of their development do not intersect. The experiments of Pavlovich and Ilyashevich,[26] in which one language was taught by the mother but the other by the father and neither parent spoke to the child in the language of the other showed that when they formed closed linguistic structures that were formed under the conditions of a certain type of cooperation, they did not mutually exert an influence delaying all development. This leads to the proposal of developing language under conditions of cooperation, which appears here in the role of a determining factor.

In this way, here once again the subordination of the appearance of speech sound to speech sense is emphasized.

What, then, is the path of emergence of this aspect of sense in speech? It was held that this path consisted of the link "thing-name" and the fact of communication itself was ignored. Thus, according to W. Stern, the child of one and a half years makes the discovery of the word, yet the 7-year-old still cannot. S. Bernfeld, criticizing this proposition, shows that according to Stern, the concept arises from itself, a vicious circle is obtained, and this is Stern's mistake.

In order to explain how the first syncretic generalization is constructed, we must not be distracted from the real situation of development, the situation of collaboration. K. Bühler and K. Koffka hold that the proposition that what the child discovers is the word is incorrect: The child discovers a structural relationship. And here is their error. It lies in the fact that social interaction is discounted; *for* in operating with a thing its naming is immaterial, naming is a function of communication.

Speech is a means of social communication. It springs from the need for a means of communication. Spontaneously babble is only peculiar to the child. The whole feature of communication is that it is impossible without generalization. The sole way of communicating without generalization is the indicative (the pointing) gesture, prior to speech. Each element of language which the child shares with an adult or receives from an adult is a generalization, albeit a very primitive and incomplete one, nevertheless, a generalization. In the first stages, it is only possible for the child with visio-graphic images. The child is not able to bring into generalization any absent object, not in a position to speak of absent objects.

The development of generalization is brought about by the act of communication. The prevalence of passive speech over active persists throughout childhood. The child learns to understand speech earlier than he construes generalizations. In this way, the assimilation of speech is not a question of the child inventing words, but rather of distorted, deformed words from the speech of adults, that is, of the

[26] Vygotsky reports in detail on the experiment of raising a child in two languages in "On the question of multilingualism in childhood," written in 1928 and published in 1935: This is available in Volume 4 of the English Collected Works (1997b: 253–259). However, Pavlovich and Ilyashevich are not mentioned. The experiment of speaking one language to one parent and another language to another is fairly close to Vygotsky's own upbringing, since his father spoke Russian and his mother preferred German and Yiddish (S. Dobkin, in K. Levitin, *One Is Not Born a Personality*, 1982, p. 24).

deformed understanding by the child of adult speech. This means that the child is developed as a whole socially, as a social being. But the meaning of the child's words at each age level varies, so that the degree of adequate communication of the child with adults is changing at every age level. The type of generalization, in its turn, defines the type of communication that is possible between the child and the adult. The social situation gives rise to different senses of words, senses which develop. There is the "Ur Wir" in early childhood. Undifferentiated communication is divided up, and there is a change in the type of generalization, so that the old contexts of communication turns out to be exhausted. A new type of generalization calls for a new type of communication. We offered earlier examples of generalization in autonomous speech ("pu fu") as examples of the indicative function of generalization showing the limited scope of communications made possible with such speech. When generalization reaches a definite level of development, the old situation of communication annihilates itself, and are faced with a critical age. The propositions cited above permit us to understand more profoundly the interrelationships between the environment and the child in the development of child speech. During stable ages, the social situation (communication) does not change; only small delicate, invisible, molecular changes occur in generalization, which, accumulating, yield shifts and crises. Going back to the former day-to-day situation of development becomes impossible. The need for a new type of communication arises and is realized.

The central neoformation of early childhood is linked to speech; thanks to this the child makes anew and varies the link with the social surroundings from that which obtained for the infant, that is, the relation to the social unit of which he himself is a part is changed.

In the last few years, a revision of the basic teaching on the development of child speech has been going on. The basic principle according to which the analysis of the development of child speech is being reconstructed: This is an analysis in connection with, against the background of and in the closest dependence upon, the ideal forms, that is, the developed speech of adults. The old theory of language considered word meaning while bypassing its function as a means of communication. Speech was considered outside of its social function, as an individual activity of the child. In the field of speech rich material accumulated that gave us the capacity to expand a diagnostics of speech, but we remained committed to a completely unknown principle for explaining development.

Children's speech is not a child's personal activity, and breaking it off from ideal forms—adult speech—is a grave mistake. Only the examination of individual speech as part of dialogue, collaboration, and communication gives the key to understanding its changes. Not one question (grammatization, two-word propositions, etc.) can be explained outside of this aspect. Every one of the child's words, even the most primitive, constitutes a part of a whole, within which it interacts with the ideal form. The ideal form is the source of the child's speech development.

Such is the genesis of child speech development. We see that the source of the neoformations is linked in a close way to the relationship between the child and adults—to collaboration with them. This is what impels the child on the new path of generalization, to the mastery of speech, etc. Mastering of speech leads to rebuilding the whole structure of consciousness.

In order to create yet another point of support for our conclusions, we now turn to the question of the relationship between perception and things.

Human perception is organized according to very complex principles. The first of these principles consists in constancy, that is, in the stability of perception. If you study the features of human perception, you will see that in the development of several of its aspects, there are one and the same characteristics If I look at a match at a certain distance from my eyes, and then remove it to a distance which is 10 times greater, it would appear that the match must be reduced 10 times in size, since the image on the retina changes strictly in proportion to the distance of the object from the eye. How do I distinguish between a tumbler and a decanter? Only by the different image cast upon my retina.

An object, for example, a match, that is removed to a distance that is ten times greater or more, seems to me the same as before. In this way, we say that the object keeps its value constant regardless of its distance, and in spite of its different character on the retinal field.[27] The biological value of this constancy is vast in the extreme. The mother who removes to 10 steps away must melt away in the eyes of her infant, and must expand by a factor of 10 when she comes back to its side. You understand what it would be like if we had that sort of perception. Walking around the room, we would see objects growing and shrinking.

The same thing pertains to the position of an object in space. How do I distinguish an object which moves from an object which is fixed and unmoving? The moving object leaves a series of tracks of its different moments on the retina of my eye. In this way, I know of the movement of any object. On the basis of this, we experience that illusion when at the window of a train it appears that everything is moving past us. From the point of view of elementary physical laws, the thing should have happened in this way. If I turn my head to the right, all objects that lie on my right side must shift their places on my retina. If I turn my head to the left, then the same thing happens with those objects lying on the left. This very process is, strictly speaking, what occurs. Yet we perceive it differently.

And we may say also in relation to color: E. Hering[28] estimated that a piece of coal in the afternoon radiates as much white light as a lump of chalk at night. This

---

[27] Vygotsky's idea is that the acquisition of the knowledge that objects are constant in size regardless of how they seem to change in perception is a precondition for being able to walk around, because without it infants would not be able to cope with the changes in retinal image that walking around brings about.

Note that this suggests that even here, in perception, there is the function of evaluation: The brain has to assign meaning to raw perceptions that are transmitted by sense organs. For Vygotsky, the main neoformation of early childhood is twofold: first, systematicity (the saltatory or "step-wise" creation of systems of choices in sound) and second, semanticizing (the imposition of meaning on visual and aural perceptions). Both of these take place through speech.

[28] Karl Ewald Konstantin Hering (1834–1918) was a physiologist who worked on a wide range of topics. He worked on binocular vision (such as the problem of how we know that objects are stationary and it is our head that is moving which Vygotsky just discussed), on color perception,

is a very interesting moment. But the perception of the color of coal or chalk does not depend on the conditions under which they are perceived—here we are dealing with a constancy of color.

Finally, stability of form. We always look at things from a certain angle. I now am not seeing the surface of this table as a rectangle. Each time I look at the table from different points of view, there will be completely different geometrical forms on my retina, and yet I will always perceive the thing from the point of view of constant form. I can cite still more examples, but in principle, these will be speaking of one and the same thing.

The perception of the size of the object, its color, form, position in space—all of this must in the course of development become constant, independent of the conditions of observation. Not a few researchers have tried to explain this constancy based on the properties of perception itself: The nerve bundles linking the retina to the cortex have both paths that are both toward and away, both centripetal and centrifugal paths, and these do not constitute motorics, but they do participate in the act of perception. that is, the retina is lit up (i.e., excited) from both within and without (O. Pötzl),[29] excitation goes to the brain, but from there it finds its once way again to the retina.

A number of perceptual disorders may be explained by the fact that although there are still "petal" paths (i.e., "towards" paths, or paths toward the brain, i.e., centripetal paths—Trans.), the fugal paths (i.e., the "away" paths, or paths away from the brain, i.e., centrifugal paths—Trans.) have been disturbed, and the regulation of the nervous system has been disrupted, so that the patient begins to perceive as if perception were exhausted by only the peripheral organs.[30]

---

where he demonstrated that the perception of color was based on color oppositions rather than simply on detecting the three major primary colors (which is today the basis of printing technology). He also created the "Hering illusion" (left), and co-discovered the "Hering-Breuer" reflex (the automatic tendency to breathe in after you breathe out and to breathe out after you breathe in).

Hering was a lifelong enemy of Helmholtz: Helmholtz, the empiricist, tended to locate his explanations in the environment, while Hering, the nativist, tended to locate his in the child. For Vygotsky, of course, all explanation has to take the relationship between child and (social) environment as an axis with two poles, and locate development along that axis.

[29]Vygotsky is reporting here on work by the Gestaltists, especially Otto Pötzl, who believed that the basic properties of perception were a "structure" of nerve bundles connecting the eye and the brain. As we know, the image on the retina of the eye is upside down. The idea is that just as the brain is able to turn the image right side up again, the brain is able to correct retinal images for size, color, form, etc.

Otto Pötzl (1877–1962) was a student of Krafft-Ebbing and a successful neurologist and a psychiatrist. He admired Freud, and was active in the Vienna Psychoanalytic Circle. Pötzl syndrome was named after him: In this syndrome, people experience "mind blindness," cannot read words, and sometimes even decide that their arms and legs belong to dead bodies. Vygotsky would explain this as a lack of two-way traffic between the brain and the limb: The brain is receiving sensations from the limb as if from the outside, as if from an alien being.

[30]Vygotsky appears to be referring to the kind of agnosia that Oliver Sacks (1998) writes about in *The Man Who Mistook His Wife for a Hat.* His interpretation of agnosia is that while the brain is receiving sensory information, it is not giving feedback to the senses, and so constancy of size, color, form and above meaning is lost. That is why he says that perception is "exhausted," that is,

This explains constancy: The retina is lit up from within—we experience this perception as an excitation of the center. The (centri-Trans.) fugal paths are myelinated later than the (centri-Trans.) petal paths, and as a result, the perfection of perception is to be accomplished in the process of development. However, it does not happen in such a way that we perceive separately the colored surfaces, the geometrical forms, and then to this we add our knowledge—and I see a person or an object. In the room, I see a lamp, a door, people. This, of course, is semantic perception (i.e., meaningful, literally "sensible," perception—Trans.). The presumption that semantic perception is given to us from the outset is erroneous. The infant does not see and does not perceive just as we do. Only after 3 years does the perception of the child maximally approach to the perception of an adult person. This approach is co-created by semantic, or objective, perception. This proposition has a number of implications. I will allow myself to dwell a moment on them separately, because we will need to confront them, particularly when we encounter the preschool age, play, and so on.

To give an example, there exist patients who suffer from a certain disorder of the brain: agnosia, that is, the loss of semantic perception. They see objects, but they do not recognize and cannot name them. The patient says: it's white, it's cold, it's slippery, it's circular, but he does not know that it is a watch. In contrast, our perception cannot see a part of the general but always sees the general purpose of the object.

For me, this room is can be reduced to the perception of separate objects. I see separate objects, but what do I see first? General features or individual ones? I say that this is a lamp, and that is a cabinet, and simultaneously I perceive that this is a lamp, etc. This means that perception has become generalized perception. When you see that this is a watch; this means that you perceive not just the color, the shade, the form, but you identify common features that characterize a given object. This is sense-making perception, generalized perception, this is the assignment of this given thing to a definite type of thing.

For a long time, until the work of structural psychology, this act was not entirely clear, but now it appears very simple and straightforward. The basic law of human perception asserts that our perception is not construed from various elements which are then summarized, but instead construes as wholes. From the point of view of this law, we may speak of generalized perception. The law of general perception asserts: No single objectively perceived property is isolated; it is always perceived as part of some whole. A perception is completely defined by the character of the whole in which it is included as a part.

What does it mean to see only a generality? It means that a thing is not perceived as a part of the structure given (i.e., the visual purview—Trans.) but only as a semantic structure. If we investigate the perception of the infant, when it is shown two things laid right next to each other, it turns out that their perception is completely defined by the structure into which they are placed. This is shown by the

---

entirely used up, by the activity of the organs of sensation (eyes, ears, nose, etc.), and the brain does not reciprocate in making sense of the sensations.

following experiment of H. Volkelt. When you place a small ring and a large ring together, the perception of the infant varies each time depending what thing lies next to the thing. Therefore, it is natural that the perception of each thing depends on the visible structure.[31]

Constancy of perception arises in connection with a number of activities of the child. Up to 3 years of age is, as experiments show, the age of the emergence of sustainable semantic perception which is not dependent on external positioning. It is in relation to this, for example, that we need to understand the child's first questions. The most striking thing is that the child suddenly starts asking. **Suddenly—** this means that we have actually come to a more or less decisive leap. The child begins to ask questions: "What is this? Who is that?"

A semantic perception is a generalized perception, that is, a perception which constitutes part of a more complex structure, and which is subject to all its basic laws of structure. And while constituting part of a directly visible structure, it is at one and the same time part of this other, semantic, structure, and thus it is very easy for this semantic perception to become paralyzed or hindered.

Let me give you an example. Before you there is a puzzling picture. You need to find a tiger or a lion, but you cannot see it because the parts of its body, those that make up the body of a tiger, constitute at the same time parts of other forms in the picture. This is why it is hard for you to see it. This law has in recent times been used successfully in military camouflage. One German scientist created a system of camouflage based on the fact that for military purposes it is important not only to paint some weapon or other the color of the ground but also to arrange it so that it is part of a different structure. This is the best of camouflage methods. I cite this as a kind of example to show how things may be perceptible in different structures and from different angles of view depending on how they are presented.

A generalized structure is a structure that goes into a structure of generalization. You have a semantic perception, because you recognize the visible structure (i.e., you perceive it as a semantic whole).

As new studies have pointed out, the first questions of the child appear to be immediately linked to the development of semantic perceptions of reality, with the development of the fact that the world has become for the child a world of things that have defined senses. How then with the aid of human speech do things acquire a semantics; how does semanticized perception emerge? It seems to me that this question is well answered by contemporary psychology with the link to the development of word meanings.

---

[31] Vygotsky refers to a set of experiments by the Leipzig school. For example, if you train an infant to take a larger ring, and then you place the large ring next to a much larger object and the small ring next a much smaller object, the infant will go for the small ring and not the large one.

On p. 289 of Bernfeld's *The Psychology of the Infant*, Bernfeld (1929) speaks of a similar demonstration by Stern—he made a miniature model of a baby bottle for his 8 months old and held it very close to the infant when the infant was hungry: The infant became excited and tried to take the bottle and drink from it, even though it was only one fifteenth the usual size. Stern concludes that "Grössenkonstanz" (size constancy) is lacking in infant perception. Note that more recent research suggests that size constancy is present at birth (Slater et al., 1990).

What is word meaning? We have already spoken of the assortment of answers given to this question by associative psychology, by structural psychology, and by the psychology of personalism. At present, psychology may have given various answers to this question, but two propositions may be stated as well established. First, that word meaning develops, that the semantic side of speech develops, and second, that there is no simple associative link, that word meaning comprises more complex psychic processes. What are these? We can refer to them by saying that all word meaning is a generalization, that within each word meaning lies generalization and abstraction; we name with one and the same word different thing. Why should this be? Already T. Hobbes[32] had said that *we use the same word for* different things, that if there were as many words in the world as there are things, then everything would have its own name. As there are more things than words, the child, whether he wills it or no, must designate with one and the same word different things. In other words, every word meaning must conceal within itself some generalization, some abstraction. To say this means that the question of the development of word meaning is already answered. After all, it is clear beforehand that generalization in a child of one and a half years and in an adult person cannot be one and the same, and so although the child's word has acquired a meaning and he names things with the same words as we do, nevertheless, his path of generalization of this thing, that is, the structure of the generalization—is different in him.

The emergence of generalizations in the mastery of speech leads to beginning to see things not simply in their situational relationship to each other but in the generalization that lies behind the word. Here, among other things, we have beautifully confirmed the correctness of the dialectical understanding of the process of abstraction. In itself, the process of abstraction and generalization is not the selection of features and an impoverishment of the object; instead, in the generalization, the connections of this object with a number of other objects are established. Thanks to this, the abstraction becomes ever richer, that is, through the word, it enters quantitatively more links and more representations of the object than in the case when we simply perceive the object.

Researchers say that in the history of the development of the child's perception, it can be seen that the process of abstraction is a process of enrichment rather than impoverishment of its features and properties. What, then, is this semantic perception? In sense-making perception, I see in the object more than is contained in a direct act of seeing; the perception of the object constitutes already a certain degree of abstraction and perception contains footsteps toward generalization.

---

[32] The writings of Thomas Hobbes (1588–1679) about linguistics are less well known than his writings about politics, but in many ways even far more far reaching. He was the first person to suppose that language was man-made (he argued that when Adam disputed with God they communicated by pure thinking). As Vygotsky says, he showed that there were fewer names than things in the world, so every name has to function as an abstraction. On the one hand, that abstraction is, of course, a kind of social agreement—a social contract—and in this way Hobbes' ideas prefigured the work of de Saussure. On the other, because names referred to actual objects, they were essentially universal signs: that is, their meanings were constant even if the signs themselves changed.

I have already raised the notion that any generalization is directly linked to a communication, that we can communicate only to the extent that we are able to generalize. Contemporary psychology has adopted the position expressed by K. Marx[33] when he said that for man the object exists as a social object. When I speak of this or that object, this means that I do not simply see the physical properties of the object but also generalize the object by its social purpose.

Finally, and last of all: to the extent the child's interest in the people around him develops, so too does his communication. A most interesting phenomenon emerges. If we return to the example which I gave concerning the incapacity of the child to orient himself in a given environment, we said the following. When the child needs to sit on the rock, he cannot do it by himself, because he cannot see the rock. This is linked to the child's being able to act only in relation to those things that he has immediately before him. In Hegel, there is an analogous proposition, the meaning of which can be boiled down to this: animals, unlike people, are slaves of the visual field: They can look only at what is striking to the eye. They cannot select some detail or some part if it is not striking. Children in the early childhood age may also sometimes appear to be slaves to their own visual field. If you place at one end of a room a very strong lamp, and at the other—a small one, so that both lamps are in the field of vision of the child, and you attempt to draw his attention to the small lamp, an infant will never have the capability of satisfying your request. Already, though, the child in early childhood can glance to the side which is less lit. In this way, the child in early childhood does perceive the visual structure, but already as a semantic structure.

It is interesting that it is only at this age that in the child, there is created a stable picture of the world, of orderly relations between objects that are first disarticulated with the help of speech. Before the child of early childhood age, there emerges for the first time not the blind man's buff of the given structural field which was there in infancy, but rather a world that is structured and formed with objects, things that take on a certain value. This period is when the child's object-structured world has just emerged, so the child asks questions about the value of what he sees, and for this reason, the child finds it difficult to transfer words. In early childhood, it is not

---

[33] The Russian language *Collected Works* of L.S. Vygotsky gives a long quotation from the Theses on Feuerbach. However, the source of this is probably not the *Theses on Feuerbach* but rather Marx's *Economic and Philosophical Manuscripts of 1844*, where Marx (1844/1969) says:

> In the same way, the senses and enjoyment of other men have become my own appropriation. Besides these direct organs, therefore, social organs develop in the form of society; thus, for instance, activity in direct association with others, etc., has become an organ for expressing my own life, and a mode of appropriating human life.
>
> It is obvious that the human eye enjoys things in a way different from the crude, nonhuman eye; the human ear different from the crude ear, etc.
>
> We have seen that man does not lose himself in his object only when the object becomes for him a human object or objective man. This is possible only when the object becomes for him a social object, he himself for himself a social being, just as society becomes a being for him in this object.

The Economic and Philosophical Manuscripts were published in German about a year before Vygotsky wrote this.

yet the case that a few individual words name certain designated objects and the child can call by different words one and the same thing, to call a chair a horse, etc.

I refer here to research by my colleague N.G. Morozova,[34] who showed that a child of less than 3 years cannot perform experiments which involve changing the names of objects. You give, let us say, a child up to 3 years of age a watch, a bottle, a pencil, and then you change the names and ask the subject to point to or to pick up the desired object, using for this the changed name. That which is a fascinating game for a preschooler, the child in early childhood cannot carry out at all; the experimenter is faced with a child's misunderstanding of the instructions, and even when the instructions are demonstrated by the experimenter, the test still cannot be carried out.

We studied the ability of the child to understand the symbolic game played out before him and the child's own ability to play and discuss such a game. We agreed with the child that the pencil was a patient, this was a house, this was a kindergarten, this was a cab driver, etc. (conditionally giving names to other objects) and we demonstrated a corresponding situation without saying anything further. For the child of less than 3, the test could not be carried out. Clear success with the most elementary series (of experiments—Trans.) began at 3 years and 8 months; naturally, it is possible with a still easier series that this might be available earlier, but not in early childhood.

As a rule, the active participation of the child in the experimental name transfer of objects (which constitutes an easy task for a preschooler) at this age cannot be done. Thus, this is the age of occurrence and consolidation of a meaningful, world shaped by objectives, but it is not an age such that the child in the early childhood age can play with values and transfer them as the preschooler can.

So from what I have said, it has been shown that in the age of early childhood, alongside the emergence of speech, there emerges for the first time what seems to me the most substantial and positive trait of human consciousness in subsequent stages of development, namely sense-making and systemic structuration of consciousness. Together with the speech for the child, first of all, the beginning of sense-making, of a conscious awareness of the surrounding reality. What I said of perception is a good illustration of this thought. The perception of geometrical figures, on the one hand, and of pictures representing known objects, on the other, have different roots. Perception of *Sinn* (sense)[35] emerges not from the further develop-

[34] Natalia Grigor'ievna Morozova (1906–1989) was an early member of Vygotsky's circle, interested in child studies and medical work. After she graduated from teacher's college in 1925, she worked with Vygotsky under the leadership of Krupskaya at the People's Commissariat for Education, doing child studies such as this one. Many of Vygotsky's letters to her concern her struggles with depression and firmly reassure her of the importance of her work and the significance of her contribution. In fact, she was a member of the "Pyatorka" (the five closest students of Vygotsky, which Vygotsky sometimes joked about). After Vygotsky's death, she became a professor at the Institute of Defectology.

[35] "Sinn" is a German word, left in German in the Russian text, meaning something like "sense." Note that Vygotsky distinguishes between being able to perceive geometrical shapes (e.g., knowing that a circle is a circle and not a polygon or an ellipse) and being able to draw pictures. The one

ment of purely structural properties, but is directly linked to speech and is not possible without speech.

By the systemic structuration of consciousness, we should understand, it seems to me, the specific relationship of different functions to each other, that is, that for each age level definite functions stand in a certain relation to each other, and form a definite system of consciousness.

Early childhood is characterized by a relationship of separate functions such that a perception that is affectively colored and therefore through the affect leads to action constitutes the dominant and is located at the center of the structure, and around this operate all of the other functions of consciousness. For a preschooler, it is memory, and for other ages—some other functions. Different cross-functional relationships emerge here.

The systemic structure of consciousness can be arbitrarily called the external structure of consciousness, while the sense-making structure, the character of generalization, is its internal structure. Generalization is a prism, refracting all of the functions of consciousness. By linking generalization with communication, we see that generalization is a function of consciousness as a whole, rather than simply that of thinking. All acts of consciousness are generalizations. Such is the microscopic structure of consciousness. In the form of a general thesis, I will say that changing the system of relations of functions to each other is in direct and very close connection with the meaning of words, with the fact that the meaning of words begins to mediate psychological processes. If we consider the child's word meanings in this age, it will be seen that the meanings of the words lie in generalized perceptions, that is, the structure of the group of objects to which the given object belongs (as opposed to a pointing gesture, which refers to any or almost any object). The child thinks chiefly in generalized perceptions, that is, general perceptions constitute the first extensive forms of structuration in child word meaning. Generalized perceptions of objects make up the first structure of child word meaning, which leads us to a very important conclusion: At this age, the child already speaks, and by the end of the third year, the child speaks well. At his disposal, there is material that is vast in content, and the child is now no longer merely at the mercy of the visual situation. However, this material is still concrete material. In the vocabulary of the child, there are very few words which do not have concrete meanings. This is how in two different situations the child's word refers to one and the same, to an identical, perceived thing or object.

I can present a simple example taken from the observations and experiments of Piaget.

What meaning does the word have for the child?

---

is linked to logic and to thinking, and the other to perception; hence in preschool, we teach about shapes, but drawing emerges already in early childhood. From this Vygotsky appears to suggest that the Gestaltists are wrong to assume that drawings are linked to the kinds of figure-ground perceptual discernment that formed their experiments. Instead, he suggests, the child's drawings are the fore-runners of written speech.

J. Piaget demonstrates that, for a child of this age, separate types of meaning for one and the same word are not yet differentiated enough, for example, the words "on ne peut pas" («нельзя», or "one can't do that"). One cannot light a match twice; one cannot talk at dinnertime; one cannot tell lies to Mommy; that is, all physical ethical and other "one cannots" merge into one and belong to the group of forbidden actions. This means that internally the meaning of these "one cannots" is not differentiated. The given example shows the extent to which the child is consciously aware of the perception of one object or another. The internal organization of thinking remains scanty. The child does not have a feeling for the individual word. The internal organization of verbal thinking is constrained by the things that are represented in words, because the words are not linked for the child to anything else besides the concrete objects which they refer to. When you ask a child this question, why a cow is called "cow," he answers, "Because it has horns" or "Because it gives milk." If you ask whether one might call a cow something else, he answers, one cannot. If he is asked whether the sun could be called "cow," he answers, this is not possible, because the sun is yellow, but a cow is horned.

In this way, the word for the child serves to designate the object itself, or the properties of the object which are hard to separate from it. That is why at this age, up to the third year, there appear children's formulations which constitute deformed words. This is not because the child finds it hard to say, to repeat, or to find another word but rather because of the way that words are comprehended. Children's words, such as "mazeline" (instead of Vaseline), "mokree" (instead of compress), have as their basis the above indicated feature of child speech. The word is understood together with some other leading word ("mokrie + compress" or "Vaseline + mazat'") because it relates to one and the same object.[36] Naturally, at this time for the child although he says it, the word itself is not known. For him, the word is a transparent glass through which the child sees that which lies beyond the glass, but he cannot see the glass itself. Thus, the organization of speech presents great difficulties. The whole speech of the child at this age is quite unconscious. The child speaks, but he is not aware of how he speaks, he cannot deliberately choose words or sounds that he requires. For example, such words as "Moscow and Leningrad," he will say easily but if you ask him to say the sound combination "sk" or "gr," then a child of less than three cannot perform the task, even though these sounds are not

---

[36] In Chapter Six of "The History of the Development of the Higher Psychological Functions" (Vygotsky, 1997b: 128), Vygotsky gives a number of examples of what we might call "mondegreens": that is, child distortions of adult words (as when a child mishears "They hae slain the Earl o' Moray and laid him on the green" as "And Lady Mondegreen," or "Glady the Cross I'd Bear" as "Gladly the Cross-eyed Bear").

The examples in Chapter Six include мокресс ("mokress) instead of "compress," which the child creates by amalgamating the Russian word for something wet with "compress," and Mazeline," which the child creates by amalgamating the Russian word for "smearing" with "Vaseline." In each case, Vygotsky points out, we have something that is the very opposite of grammatical metaphor: The wording is used to make something general or abstract into something more immediate and concrete.

difficult for him because they go into a general structure of words which he systematically produces.

If we attempt to define how much the child is aware of the word as such, we can observe that behind the word lies only the object referred to in speech that the differentiation of the word and the object has not yet been carried out in the manner that it takes place in later ages.

What results from this change in the structure of consciousness? In early childhood, primary generalizations emerge which lead to a definite type of generalization, making a defined correlation of the functions. How does the child perceive the external world and act upon it? Perception constitutes the basic function of this age, maturing early. Here the most important changes in perception take place, it is differentiated from internal *perezhivanies;* constancy of size, shape, etc. appears. The general law of psychic development states that the functions which dominate in a given age are those set in maximally favorable conditions. This explains all of the changes which exist in perception.

Most substantial of all is the interrelationship between the semantic and the systemic structure of consciousness. The dominance of perception implies a certain nonindependence, a certain dependency some dependence of all other functions on perception.

In the light of the foregoing the correlation of functions to which we have referred above is clear. Memory is realized in active perception (recognition). It acts as a moment defined in the act of perception itself, constituting its prolongation and its development. Attention likewise must pass through the prism of perception.

Thinking presents a visual-illustrative-practical restructuration of the situation, of the field of perception itself. Most of all, thinking is developed in generalization. Throughout this period, the child speaks and is spoken to by others about what he sees. Standing before things, he names them, and this is where there appears the link with object reference. Thus, all functions work within perception. What are the consequences which emerge from this for perception itself? We have shown that sense-making perception does not mean simply attaching the activity of thinking, the activity of generalization to perception. Perception, transformed in a new relationship with thinking, is no longer on the affective-motoric plane, as it was described by Lewin.

Over the course of subsequent development, it will change. Perception in later age periods will include recalling, generalizing, etc. Here emerges the correction of memory and perception (its orthoscopic quality),[37] the possibility of moving its structure and background thanks to the function of attention, categorical perception, that is, making sense of it. Perception as a function is transformed into a complex system with subsequent changes, but the basic features are acquired here. The systemic structuration of consciousness explains the emergence of a constant picture of

[37] Vygotsky appears to be considering the idea that speech may be a source of development for perception. One example of this is constancy—because objects are named, the brain assumes them to be the same, even though appear to change in size. That is the "orthoscopy" that Vygotsky is referring to. Unlike Bühler, Volkelt, and the Gestaltists, he does not believe it is inborn.

the world. Categorical perception, the perception of objects as representatives of a group of objects, constitutes the second feature, the feature of generalization.

Nonverbal perception is incrementally being replaced by verbal. Linked to the naming of objects, there emerges objective perception ("perception in objects," that is, in categories of objects—Tr). Objects in a room appear differently to the infant and the child of early childhood. The fact that the child is moving from mute to verbalized perception brings on substantial changes in perception itself. Previously it had been assumed that the function of speech consisted in its substitution for objects. Studies have shown that this is a late emerging function, and the advent of speech has a different meaning. The advent of speech leads to this the emergence of another way of seeing—of placing figures against a background. Speech alters the structure of perception thanks to generalization. It analyzes it and classifies it into categories, heralding a complex logical processing, that is, the singling out[38] of the object, the action, the quality, etc.

What does such a systemic consciousness signify for internal perception, for introspection? The generalizations made by the child are generalizations of perception. In the inner world what the child is most aware of is his own perception. In him there is fairly rich introspection on the plane of visual and auditory perception ("I see," "I hear poorly"). This characterizes his internal activity ("Let me have a look"). Active directedness and spontaneous excitation in the activity of perception—such is the volitional form that its internal activity takes. Spontaneous memory and thinking have not yet emerged.

In this way, the systemic structure of consciousness sheds light on the perception of reality, and on the activity in it, and on attitude to oneself. At three, the child is already in possession of his affect, the old social situation of development turns out to be unsatisfactory, and the child enters the Crisis of the Third Year, ushering in a new communicative situation.

I would be inclined to consider the emergence of this systemic consciousness of which I have spoken as the central, characteristic moment of consciousness, in so far as it is for the person essential that he does not simply perceive the world but understands the world, and in so far as his consciousness moves always on the plane of something semantic.

To say that humans act with consciousness and to say that they act with sense—these are not one and the same. This gives me grounds for proposing that the central neoformation of early childhood consists precisely in the emergence of consciousness in the proper sense of the word. I believe that here for the first time we encounter distinctly a consciousness in those characteristic moments which distinguish humans from the psychic life of animals and from the psychic states of humans which are insufficiently conscious and formed. I might remind you, not to validate this point of view but to introduce it into the context of a broader theoretical

[38] Vygotsky uses the term вычленение. It is hard to translate this with one English word and it would be misleading to use many, so we offer "singling out" as a rough equivalent. Unlike 'singling out', however, the Russian term means that the object is made to stand out against the background, as when you resolve an object through focusing a telescope.

understanding, of the words of K. Marx with respect to consciousness and its link with speech. That aspect of consciousness that Marx had in view, when he named language as practical consciousness, consciousness that exists for other people and therefore for myself—this very consciousness, which he calls a historical product—appears in actuality alongside speech, that is, in every case, when the child begins to semanticize through speech objects and his own activity which becomes possible in conscious communication with others, rather than the direct social communication which existed in the age of infancy.

To put it in other words, I believe that in early childhood, we find the stage where semantic and systemic construction of consciousness emerges, when historical human consciousness appears, existing for others and, therefore, for the child himself. It is on the basis of this center that we can understand all of the qualitative features relating the child to the external situation, and the relationships that link the child to other people, as well as the unique types of activity which we meet with here. In other words, it seems to me that this hypothesis, resting on the factual basis of the establishment of semantics and a system of consciousness, explains very well all of the problems which I have attempted to tackle.

Let me say in conclusion that, since there emerges for the first time a differentiated system of individual functions in a defined structure, at the center of which lies perception, and since the basis of perception is generalization, since objectively we are dealing with the emergence of the most basic features of human consciousness, this must be considered as one of the neoformations which first make their appearance in this age.

References

Bernfeld, S. (1929). *The psychology of the infant*. Routledge.

Gibson, J. J. (1966). *The senses considered as perceptual systems*. Allen and Unwin.

Groos, K. (1898). *The play of animals* (E. Baldwin, Trans.). Appleton and Co.

Groos, K. (1919). *The play of man* (E. Baldwin, Trans.). Appleton and Co.

Levitin, K. (1982). *One is not born a personality*. Progress.

Lewin, K. (1926/2019). *Vorsatz, Wille, und Bedürfnis*. Springer.

Marx, K. (1844/1969). *Economic and philosophical manuscripts of 1844*. Progress.

Ponomariov, I. V. (2013). Situational binding in cross-cultural studies, the works of L.S. Vygotsky and his school. *Dubna Psychological Journal, 3*, 77–94.

Sacks, O. (1998). *The man who mistook his wife for a hat*. Touchstone.

Slater, A., Mattock, A., & Brown, E. (1990). Size constancy at birth: newborn infants' responses to retinal and real size. *Journal of Experimental Child Psychology, 49*(2), 314–322.

von Uexküll, J. with von Uexküll, M. (1940). *A foray into the worlds of animals and humans: With a theory of meaning* (Joseph D. O'Neil, Trans.). University of Minnesota Press.

Vygotsky, L. S. (1997a). *Educational psychology*. St. Lucie Press.

Vygotsky, L. S. (1997b). *Collected works* (Vol. 4). Plenum.

Vygotsky, L. S. (1998). *Collected works* (Vol. 5). Plenum.

Vygotsky, L. S. (2016). Play and its role in the mental development of the child (N. Veresov & M. Barrs, Trans.). *International Research in Early Childhood Education, 7*(2), 3–25.

Chapter 9
The Crisis at Three Years of Age

Outline of Chapter 9: The Crisis at Three Years of Age

The Russian edition of the *Collected Works* (1984, p. 415) says that this chapter, like the last one, is a transcript of a lecture delivered at the Herzen Pedagogical Institute in Leningrad during the academic year of 1933–1934, that is, during the last year of Vygotsky's life. It is, however, only a fragment. In the first paragraph of this chapter, Vygotsky promises to look at the crisis from three points of view (neoformations, lines of development, and zone of proximal development), but he does not keep any of those promises here. Instead, he says that we must first look at the factual material, from which he will derive the social situation of development. The Soviet editors argue that this "factual material" is not cited, but they believe it to be the work of Elsa Köhler (1926). That is possible, but for Vygotsky "factual material" is not necessarily, or even primarily, published research. Vygotsky uses his own clinical experience, but he also has enormous respect for the practical experience of parents and teachers, and he considers folk concepts to be factual material too. Therefore, we can take his discussion and refinement of the "seven stars," which occupies almost the whole of this chapter, to be Vygotsky's preliminary discussion of factual material.

As he discusses this factual material, Vygotsky refines it, preparatory to reconstructing it in the concepts laid out in Chap. 2 of this book. First, he divides the seven stars into two groups: the three most important symptoms of negativism, stubbornness, and recalcitrance, and the less important ones of self-will, deprecation, protest-rebellion, and despotism/jealousy. Second, he notes the "say so" elements of the first three: the child says no because you say so, the child says insists because the child says so, and the child is obstinate because of a general "да ну" ("yeah, right!", spoken sarcastically) to everything social in the environment. Language, as practical consciousness, as the child's relation to his or her environment, is the pole star around which each of the seven stars revolves. Third, he notes that all of these

---

The material in this chapter is from the 1984 Russian edition of Vygotsky's *Collected Works*.

L. S. Vygotsky, *L.S. Vygotsky's Pedological Works. Volume 2.*, Perspectives in Cultural-Historical Research 10, https://doi.org/10.1007/978-981-16-1907-6_9

elements suggest a critical change in the social situation of development—that is, the relationship between the social environment and the child. The child has tried to self-emancipate, to "turn the tables" and become the master of his/her own development.

I. **Assumptions and approaches.** Vygotsky assumes that critical periods, like stable periods, have neoformations, but these are "of the transitional type," that is, nonpermanent. He then lays out his three tasks: defining the neoformation, identifying lines of development, and then considering the zone of proximal development, that is, how the neoformation is linked to the stable, permanent neoformations of the next age. Vygotsky warns that none of this can be simply derived from the assumptions and approaches—all of it must arise from an analysis of the social situation of development. Because the social situation of development is a relationship between personality and environment, it has both internal and external traits. These traits are recorded, as folk concepts, in two tiers—referred to as primary and secondary. It seems possible that the "internal" symptoms on the side of the child's personality are primary and the "external" ones having to do with interaction with the environment are secondary; that is, at any rate, the order in which Vygotsky presents them in the paragraph and in the lecture.

II. **The social situation of development: Seven stars.** Vygotsky now describes the social situation of development by enumerating the seven "first tier" symptoms:

1. Negativism: The child refuses to do something, even though in some cases it is something that the child actually wishes to do. Vygotsky points out that the only way to explain this apparent contradiction is that the motivation likes not in the immediate context of situation, but rather in a generalized social relation with others.
2. Stubbornness: The child insists on doing something, even though in some cases the child has no wish or no strong wish to do. This is not simply the inverse of negativism, because the generalized social relation is not with others, but rather with the self.
3. *Trotz Alter*, or Recalcitrance: Unlike negativism, defiance is directed to the norms of enculturation rather than to a specific interpersonal relation. Unlike stubbornness, recalcitrance is directed to negating the environment and not towards affirming the child's developing personality. Vygotsky notes the use of sarcasm in expressions like "да ну!" ("Yeah, right!"), suggesting that the child can now say one thing and mean another.
4. *Eigensinn* or "Self-will." The child insists on doing things alone even the child has neither the ability nor the confidence to perform an action. Where defiance is directed to the environment, self-will is directed toward the personality.
5. Protest-rebellion. Vygotsky calls this and the next two symptoms of "secondary importance." However, he apparently does not mean that they belong to the second tier, as he discusses the second tier in a later paragraph. Protest-

rebellion is quarreling and swearing directed toward other people—once again, a verbal form of conflict.

6. Deprecation. Like protest-rebellion, deprecation is a verbal form of conflict: the child rejects, neglects, and demeans things in words. Unlike protest-rebellion, deprecation is directed toward objects.
7. Despotism/jealousy. Despotism is the desire for absolute control over other people in the family, especially parents. Jealousy, on the other hand, is usually directed towards siblings Both suggest to Vygotsky an orientation towards power, and Vygotsky thinks the difference simply has to do with whether the child is an only child or has siblings.

III. **The central line of development: Self-emancipation.** Vygotsky generalizes and says that self-emancipation is the central line of development. All of the symptoms are directed against authority and towards autonomy. All of the symptoms are sudden and seem separate from changes in the environment. Nevertheless, all the symptoms are linked to the child's relation to the environment. Vygotsky deduces that the child's previously unmediated affective relations with the environment are changing. Just as birth and infancy represented a physiological but not a biological separation, the crisis at one and early childhood represented a social but not a psychological separation, so with the crisis at three the child takes the first steps toward true psychological autonomy. Vygotsky ends with a short description of secondary symptoms, which appear to be more external than internal changes, and a short case study, which also focuses on the child's external behavior. Note that "self-emancipation" is a general line of development for all crises and it is not specific to the crisis at three. The form of self-emancipation specific to the crisis at age three, the child's "turning the tables" on the environment through negation in speech, is elaborated in the next chapter.

IV. **The central neoformation: Missing?** Vygotsky apologizes for the preliminary nature of his conclusions. He notes two apparently new aspects of the child's behavior in the crisis at three. Firstly, there is an orientation of the child's behavior toward the social relationships in a situation rather than toward the situation as an undifferentiated whole. Secondly, there is an orientation of the child's behavior toward facts and acts rather than toward things and people. But Vygotsky concludes this lecture by simply confirming what other researchers have noted—that the Crisis is a crisis in social relations. What this means for the neoformations and for the next Zone of Development (ZPD) is elaborated in the next lecture.

Chapter 9: The Crisis at Three Years of Age

We have three points of view, with the aid of which we will guide our analysis of the crisis at three years.

Firstly, we must presume that all of the transformations, all the happenings, that take place during the period of the crisis group themselves around some sort of neoformation of the transitional type. Consequently, when we are to analyze the symptoms of the crisis, we are going to presume to answer the question of what newness emerges at this designated time and what is the fate of the neoformation which disappears afterward. Next, we should consider how the central and peripheral lines of development change place.[1] And finally, we ought to evaluate the critical age from the point of view of the zone of its proximal development, that is, its relationship to the subsequent age.

In considering the crisis at three years of age, we cannot approach it with a theoretical scheme alone. For us there can be no other path than the path of analyzing factual material, so as to understand, in the process of analysis, the basic theories which have been put forward to explain this material. In order to make sense of what goes on in the period of three years of age, it is necessary first of all to consider the situation of development—internal and external—in which the crisis happens. Consideration ought to commence with the symptoms of the age. Those symptoms of the crisis which have been advanced to the first plane in the literature have been referred to as the first belt of symptoms, or the seven stars of the crisis at the age of three. All of them have been written of as folk concepts and they need to be analyzed in order to acquire a precise scientific meaning.[2]

[1] Vygotsky says that the central line of development is the line of development which leads to the central "dominant" neoformation, while a peripheral line of development is a line of development which leads to a less central, "subordinated" one. For example, at birth the central line of subcortical development leads to the central neoformation of independent but largely instinctual mental life, while the line of shared, inter-cortical consciousness is a peripheral line of development. In infancy, this "inter-cortical," interpersonal and later social and cultural consciousness becomes the central line of development leading to the central neoformation—the Ur wir of shared consciousness we see in exchanging smiles, peekaboo, etc. It seems to be a property of crises that lines of development on the child's end of the child-environment axis move to the center stage while lines of development on the environment's end must wait in the wings.

The present chapter is another good example: in early childhood, meaningful (affective) perception is a central line of development and negation is peripheral, but during the crises these lines of development change places, and the result is a transient neoformation: the disjunction of affect and a kind of negative proto-will. This transient neoformation of proto-will only persists in a subordinated and hence more voluntary form in preschool (e.g., in certain negative roles the child takes in play activity, in the mastery of negative options in speech, and in volitional absent-mindedness in thinking).

[2] In many cultures, parents tell stories about the "Terrible Twos" or "Threenagers," the period of "difficult childhood" that Vygotsky calls more scientifically the Crisis at Three. This ubiquity in itself is powerful evidence for the internal and necessary nature of the crisis. Coincidentally, many cultures also have folk stories concerning some group of seven stars in the sky. In the East, these stars represent the disciples of the Buddha; in the West, they are the Big Dipper in Ursa Major that help indicate the pole star, and in Russia they are the "seven sisters," the Pleiades in the constellation of Taurus. As we remarked in the outline, Vygotsky uses the "seven stars" to indicate the factual material he is going to analyze. His analysis differentiates between the folk, negative meaning of the symptom and what for him is a scientific, and positive, meaning. In each case, Vygotsky shows that the positive content of the symptom has to do with a freeing of the symptom from an external goal or an immediate affect and a focus on the social axis.

The first symptom by which the onset of the crisis is characterized: the emergence of negativism. It is necessary to conceive clearly what we are talking about here. When people talk about child negativism, it must be distinguished from ordinary disobedience. In negativism, all the child's behavior goes contrary to that required of him by adults. If the child does not want to do what displeases him (if, for example, he is playing, and he is required to go and sleep but he does not want to sleep), this will not be negativism. The child wants to do what pleases him, that which he desires but which is forbidden to him; if he still does it, this will not be negativism. This will be a reaction in opposition to an adult demand, a reaction which is motivated by strong wishes in the child.

We will term negativism only those manifestations of behavior of the child when he does not wish to do something merely because it is the proposal of some adult, that is, this reaction is not to the content of the action, but to the proposition of the adult. Negativism includes in itself, as a trait that distinguishes it from normal disobedience, that the child **does not do something because it was proposed to him.** A child playing in the yard does not want to go into the house. He is sleepy but he does not obey and disregards his mother's request. And if he is asked for something different, he would do whatever was pleasant to him. The negativist reaction of the child is to not do something simply because it is requested. Here there is a specific shift in motivation.

Let me give you a typical example of behavior, selected from observations made in our clinic. A girl in her fourth year of life, with a prolonged crisis of three years and with clearly expressed negativism, wishes to be taken to the conference at which we evaluate the children. The girl has even gotten ready to go. I invite her. But since I have called her, she will not go. She keeps struggling. "Well, then go all by yourself." She will not go. "Well, then come with me"—she does not come. When we leave her alone, she begins to weep. She is sad that we did not take her. In this way, negativism forces the child to act contrary to her affective wish. The girl wanted to go, but because we proposed it, she would never agree.

In its most drastic form, negativism produces an opposite response to any proposal made in an authoritative tone. A number of authors beautifully describe similar experiments. For example, an adult approaches a child and says, in an authoritative tone, "This dress is black," and receives the answer "No, it is white," When one says, "It is white," the child answers "No, black." The will to contradict, the will to perform the opposite of whatever he is told, this is negativism in the true sense of the word.

Negative reactions differ from ordinary disobedience in two substantial moments. Firstly, they place the social relation, the relationship to other people, in the front of the stage. In a given case, the reaction of the child is not motivated by the content of the situation itself, whether or not the child wants to do what he is asked. Negativism is an act of a social character: it is first of all addressed to a person, not to the content that has been requested of the child. The second essential moment—a new relation of the child to his own affect. The child does not act directly under the influence of affect but proceeds contrary to his own inclinations. Concerning these relations with affect, let me remind you of early childhood just before the crisis at three. The most characteristic of early childhood, from the point of view of all of research, is the complete unity of affect and activity. The whole child is in the grip of affect; he is completely inside the situation. During preschool age, motives also appear in relation to other people, which follow immediately from those effects which are linked to other situations. If the motivation for the refusal of the child lies within the situation, if he does not do something because he does not wish to or because he wishes to act otherwise, this is not negativism. Negativism—such a reaction, such a tendency—is where the motive lies outside the given situation.

The second symptom of the crisis at three years is stubbornness. If negativism requires us to distinguish it from ordinary opposition then with stubbornness requires us to distinguish it from persistence. For example, the child wants something and tenaciously presses for it to be done. That is not stubbornness; that is found before the crisis at three. For instance, the child wants to have a thing but cannot freely obtain it. He insists that this thing be given to him. That is not stubbornness. Stubbornness is a sort of child reaction such that when he insists on something it is not because he wants it badly but because he has asked for it. He insists on his own demands. Let us say, the child is called in from the yard to the house. He refuses; he is argued with and convinced, but because he refused, he still does not go. The motive is that the stubbornness of the child is linked to the initial decision. Only this will be stubbornness.

Two things distinguish stubbornness from ordinary persistence. The first moment: like negativism, it is related to motivation. If the child is tenacious in something, this is not stubbornness. For example, he loves sledding and therefore will strive to stay out in the yard all day.

The second moment. If negativity is characteristic a social trend, that is, the child does something contrary, opposite to what he is told by adults, here, with stubbornness, it is characterized by a tendency of relating to himself. We cannot say that the child passes freely from one affect to another; no, he does so only because *he spoke thus:* he holds to that. So we have a different relationship to motivation in the personality of the child itself than we did before the onset of crisis.

The third moment is usually referred to by the German term "Trotz" (Trotz). This symptom is considered so central to the age that the whole of the critical period was called "trotzalter"—in Russian, the age of recalcitrance.

In what does this last symptom differ from the first? Recalcitrance distinguishes itself from negativism in its impersonality. Negativism is always directed against the adult who is now urging the child to one action or another. But recalcitrance is rather directed against the norms of enculturation established for the child, against the form of life; it expresses the child's own discontent, the cry of "да ну!" ("Yeah, right!"—Trans.)[3] with which the child answers to everything that is proposed, and everything done. Here the fixation of recalcitrance is not in relation to people but in

[3] The expression "да ну" literally means something like "Yeah, right" or "Yeah, well!" or "Yeah, yeah, yeah!", but of course literal meaning is not the point at all. Vygotsky's point is that the child is now able to say one thing and mean quite another. Note that a key to doing this is intonation—where the words say one thing but the music says something different; or, to put it more techni-

relation to the whole form of life which has been shaped at three years, in relation to the norms that are laid down, to the toys that previously interested him. Recalcitrance differs from stubbornness in that it is directed outward, related to the outside, and caused by the desire to insist on one's own desires.

It is quite clear why, in authoritarian bourgeois family enculturation, recalcitrance acts as the gravest symptom of the crisis at three. Before this, the child was docilely fussed over; he was taken by the hand; suddenly, he has become a recalcitrant who is unhappy with everything. In the place of a silky, smooth gentle child, there is some who-knows-what that at all times resists whatever they are doing with him.

From the usual lack of compliance, child recalcitrance differs in its tendentiousness. The child is defiant; his displeasure evoking "да ну!" is tendentious in the sense that it is in reality imbued with a latent rebellion against all that the child had previously been the case before.

There is still a fourth symptom, which Germans call "Eigensinn" (literally, "own will"—Trans.), willfulness. This consists of the child's tendency towards self-sufficiency. This did not exist before; now, the child wants to do everything by himself.

Among the symptoms of the crisis that we are analyzing there are still three more, but these are of secondary significance. First—protest and revolt. In a number of separate manifestations, everything in the behavior of the child begins to bear the character of protest, something which earlier it could not have done. All these child behaviors acquire the traits of protest, as if the child was carrying out an intractable war with those in his surroundings, a state of unceasing conflict with them. Frequent child quarrels with parents are commonplace. A linked symptom is deprecation. For example, a child of good family will begin to curse. C. Bühler vividly describes the horror of the family when the mother heard the child call her a "дура,"[4] something he previously neither could nor did say.

The child seeks to reject toys, neglects them, and in his lexicon there appear words and terms which signify all that is worst, negative, and yet related to things which in themselves do not cause any unpleasantness. And finally, we point out another symptom found in different ways in different families. In a family with only one child we encounter despotic wishes. The child has the desire to exercise a despotic control in relation to those in the surroundings. The mother must not leave the house; she must stay in the room as he demands. He must receive all that he demands, and only what he wants, not what he does not want. The child will seek thousands of ways in which to exercise power over those in the surroundings. Now

---

cally, the prosody contradicts the articulation. For this to happen, the child has to have a clear understanding of the multi-stratal organization of speech and therefore its productivity.

[4] Like English, Russian is full of curses that apply uniquely to women ("bitch," "whore," etc.). The term "дура" is relatively mild; it simply means a fool, but it is definitely feminine, and not simply in its grammatical gender: because English doesn't have grammatical gender (except a very few words such as pronouns) to render it in English we would need two words, for example, "silly cow," "stupid bitch," or "dumb broad."

the child is attempting to return to the state of affairs enjoyed in early childhood when in fact his desires were fulfilled and he was master of the situation. In a family with several children, this symptom appears as the symptom of jealousy towards younger or older siblings where these exist in the family. Here the same tendency to dominate, towards despotism, towards power, serves as the source of jealous attitudes towards the other children.

Such are the basic symptoms that fill the descriptions of the crisis at three years of age. It is not hard to see, considering these symptoms, that the main form that the crisis takes lies in such features that allow us to recognize in it a revolt, as it were, against authoritarian enculturation. It is as if the child were protesting, demanding autonomy, and outgrowing the norms and forms of care that developed during the age of early childhood. The crisis in its typical symptoms so evidently takes the character of a rebellion against the care-giver that it strikes the eye of every researcher.

With the symptoms indicated, the child appears hard to teach. The child, previously not given to trouble and difficulty now appears as a being who has become difficult for adults. Thanks to this, the impression is given that the child has changed abruptly in a short period of time. From the babe in arms, he has become an obstinate, stubborn, negative, nay-saying, jealous or despotic being, such that all at once the image he has in the family has wholly changed.

It is not hard to see that in all of the symptoms described there are also outlined certain changes in the social relations between the child and proximal persons. All of this was established chiefly according to the account of family enculturation since early childhood enculturation in bourgeois countries almost exclusively takes the form of individual family enculturation. True, we now have a variety of preschool institutions, and in different countries there are institutions of social assistance for those with defects and forms of charitable enculturation, but the path of mass experience in bourgeois enculturation in early childhood, as opposed to in school, age is that of individual, family enculturation. All of these symptoms say one and the same thing: in relation to the child's proximal family surroundings, to which he is linked by affective attachments, outside of which his very existence would be unthinkable, something has dramatically changed.

The child in early childhood is a human being who has always found himself in the power of unmediated affective relations with those in his surroundings, to which he is linked. In the crisis at three years of age, what he finds is what may be called a rupture: there may be conflicts, the child may blame the mother; games which are proposed at an inopportune moment may bring outbreaks of rage, and there may be a change in the affective-volitional sphere which indicates increase authoritativeness and activeness in the child. All of these symptoms turn around the axis between the "I" and the people in the surrounding it. These symptoms tell us of changes in the child's relationship to people surrounding and to his own personality.

In general, the symptoms taken together give an impression of child emancipation: it is as if before adults took him by the hand, but now there is in him a tendency to walk alone. It has been noted by not a few researchers as a characteristic part of this crisis. I have often called your attention to the thinking of Charles Darwin: A child at the moment of birth is physically separated from his mother, but is incapable of feeding or even displacement without his mother. Darwin held it an expression of the biological lack of independence in the child, his biological nonseparation (in the marsupials there exists a morphological adaptation—the pouch in which the young are placed after birth). Continuing this thinking of Darwin's, we must say that the child is early childhood is biologically separate but psychologically he is still not yet separated from the people in his surroundings. Beringer[5] gives us grounds for saying that the child under three years of age is not socially separated from his surroundings, and that with the crisis at three years of age we are dealing with a new stage of emancipation.

Now I should at least briefly speak of the so-called second order symptoms, that is, of those that follow from the basic symptoms, of their further development. The second order symptoms are in turn divided into two groups. One—these are the symptoms which arise as a consequence of the child's attunement towards independence. Thanks to the changes in the social relations of the child, his affective sphere, all that is most cherished, most valuable and which most affects him with strong and deep lived experience, the child enters into a whole range of internal and external conflicts, and we very often deal with neurotic reactions in children. These reactions are of a painful character. In neuropathic children in the crisis at three years we often see the emergence of neurotic reactions, for example enuresis, that is, nocturnal urinary incontinence. The child, who has grown used to cleanliness, in an unfavorable turn of the crisis often regresses in this respect to an earlier stage. There are night-time terrors, restless sleeping, and other neuropathic symptoms, sometimes extreme difficulties of speech, stuttering, and sharp intensification of negativism, stubbornness, so-called hypobulic seizures, that is, a specific type of attack which externally resembles a seizure but which is not in fact a pathological seizure in the proper sense of the word (the child shakes, throws himself on the floor, pounds hands and feet), but which can be extremely acute features of negativism, stubbornness, deprecation, and protest, about which we have already spoken.

Let me cite an example from our own observations of a perfectly normal child with a very difficult course of the crisis at three years of age. The child was in the fourth year, the son of a tram conductor. Despotism manifested itself in the child with exceeding rapidity. All that he demanded had to be fully carried out. For example, when he walked on the street with his mother, he required her to pick up a scrap of paper, even though it was a scrap of paper that had no use whatsoever. The child was brought to us with a complaint about seizures. When his desires were refused,

[5] This may refer to Kurt Beringer (1893–1949), neurologist, psychiatrist, and professor best known for self-experimentation and research on mescaline, morphine, and cocaine, as well as coffee and tea. He was the author of a book on heredity and schizophrenia, and joined a Soviet-German expedition to study syphilis among the Buryat-Mongols in 1928. During World War II, he was allowed to join the Nazi party by a special dispensation from Hitler (Beringer had been a Freemason, and Freemasons were excluded from the party) and he served on the T4 extermination program for mentally ill people. After the war he claimed to have hidden many of his patients and saved them from extermination, so he was not prosecuted.

he would throw himself to the floor and begin to shriek, pounding with hands and feet. However, this was not a pathological fit, but a form of behavior which not a few authors have considered as a regression to the reactions of the age of infancy, when the child shrieks and hammers with hands and feet. We observed in our child fits of impotent rage and when he was not able to otherwise protest, making a scandal. I give this as an example of a complication of the crisis at three years, which constitutes a second order symptoms: they are not among the basic traits of the crisis, but represent a continuum—from difficult enculturation within the family to a state which brings neurotic and even psychopathic symptoms.[6]

Let us draw some theoretical conclusions, that is, let us try to determine what kinds of events are taking place in the development of the child, what is the sense, what is the significance of the symptoms we have described. We shall attempt to present them theoretically, as an initial rough attempt, based on some knowledge of the factual material, on several of my own observations (because the crisis is linked to a difficult childhood which I was able to study) and on some attempts to critically rework the theories of this age that have been proposed. Our attempt—something highly preliminary and somewhat subjective in degree—does not pretend to become a theory of critical ages.

When considering the symptoms of the crisis at age three, we already noted that the internal reconstruction takes place along the axis of social relations. We pointed out that the negative reaction that appears in a child of three must be distinguished

[6]Vygotsky clearly says that there are two groups of secondary symptoms. He clearly announces the first group: symptoms that are a result of the child's drive for independence. He clearly says that this first group of secondary symptoms can range from mild problems with upbringing to symptoms which look like "neurosis" (that is, personality disorder) and even "psychopathology" (that is, insanity). That is the first group. But what is the second group? The second group appears to be missing!

There are several possibilities. The first possibility is that Vygotsky just means to say that the first group are the nonpathological symptoms—the ones which reflect a difficult upbringing but not the ones that reflect neurotic and pathological symptoms. This possibility seems unlikely, because Vygotsky then goes on to argue that there is an unbroken continuum. If there is an unbroken continuum, then there is only one group, and not two.

A second possibility is that Vygotsky forgot all about the second group. Vygotsky is a brilliant lecturer, but he sometimes does get carried away. We know that he often repeats things that he already said. (He knows this too; notice how often he says that he already said something!) We also know that he sometimes thinks of things to say while he was saying something else, and it may sometimes happen that he forgets to say them.

A third possibility is that Vygotsky did not forget the second group, but that the stenographer somehow missed it—there are, after all, obvious gaps in the stenographic record. For example, as we'll see, this chapter ends rather abruptly, right in the middle of an argument, and long before Vygotsky can keep the promise he made to consider the crisis at age three from the point of view of the neoformations, the lines of development, and the zone of proximal development. Of course, it is possible that Vygotsky did not have time for this in a single lecture. But if that was the case, there ought to be some note that these topics will be taken up the next lecture. So there must be at least a small gap in the stenographic record at the end of this chapter, and it would not be surprising if there were also some gaps in the middle.

from mere disobedience, and that stubbornness which appears as a feature of the crisis must also be delineated from simple persistence on the part of the child.

1. The negative reaction emerges from the minute that the child is indifferent to your request or even wants to do what he has been asked to do, but nevertheless refused it. The motive of the refusal lies not in the content of the activity to which he is invited, but in his relationship to you.
2. The negative reaction is shown not in the refusal of the child to the act which he has been requested to perform, but rather in the fact that you asked him. Therefore, the true essence of the negative stance of the child is to do the opposite, that is, to display an act of independent behavior in relation to what you have asked him to do.

So too with stubbornness. Mothers, complaining of difficult children, often say that they are stubborn, persistent. But persistence and stubbornness are different things! If the child wants something very much and persists until it is achieved, this has nothing to do with stubbornness. The stubborn child insists on what he may not want much, or not want at all, or long ago stopped wanting, in order to enforce his own requirements. The child insists not on the content of the desire, but because this was what he said, that is, there appears social motivation.

The seven symptoms known as the "seven stars" of the crisis have shown that the new features are always linked to this: the child is motivated in his acts not by the content of the situation itself but by his relationships with other persons.

If we generalize the factual picture of the symptoms of the crisis at three years, we cannot disagree with the researchers who claim that the crisis, strictly speaking, happens first of all as a crisis in the social relations of the child.

What, in essence, is reconstructed during the time of crisis? The social position of the child in relation to surrounding people, to the authority of the mother, the father. What is happening as well is a crisis of the personality—the "I"—that is, there emerge a range of acts, the motives of which are linked to the expression of the child's personality and not to any given momentary desires; the motive is differentiated from the situation. To put it simply, the crisis proceeds along the axis of restructuration of social interrelationships between the child's personality and the people surrounding him.

References

Köhler, E. (1926). *Die Personlichkeit des dreijährigen Kindes*. Hirzel.

Выготский, Л. С. (1984). *Собрание сочинений Т.4*. Педагогика.

Chapter 10
The Crisis at Age Three and the Crisis at Age Seven

Outline of Chapter 10: The Crisis at Age Three and the Crisis at Age Seven

Vygotsky begins by promising to complete his lecture on the crisis at age three and link it to the crisis at seven and even to the crisis at thirteen. He notes the very preliminary state of theories of the crisis in pedology and therefore suggests that we stay at a descriptive and empirical level before we attempt a theoretical explanation. Vygotsky then reviews the "Seven Stars" material that we viewed in the last chapter, the crisis at three, and in places he repeats it almost—but not exactly—word for word. He arrives at the conclusion with which he ended that lecture: that the crisis unfolds along the axis between the personality and the social environment.

But here he notes that this conclusion is highly general—that it would apply to nearly all the crises. So Vygotsky does not simply return to his data; he turns instead to matters of method. First, he asks what a holistic analysis is and how it works. Second, he notes that extant theorizations of the crises have tended to be one-sided, emphasizing either the environment or the child, but not linking them in a single unit. At the same time, extant theories have tended to see each crisis as linked instead of understanding their distinctness. Vygotsky ends by contrasting the crisis at three with the crisis at seven, and showing that they are both very similar—they both involve transitional neoformations—and very different—because the neoformations are very different.

Let us elaborate these four points into a fuller outline.

The material in this chapter is from the collection published by G.S. Korotaeva in 2001.
The first edition (1995) of Korotaeva's book did not have this lecture in it, but the later edition (2001) did. Korotaeva notes that the lecture was given at the Herzen Pedagogical Institute in Leningrad on 17 April in 1933.
On internal evidence (e.g., Vygotsky's references to the preceding lecture), it appears to be a follow-up lecture to Vygotsky's lecture on the "seven stars," which can be found as "The Crisis of Three" (1998: 283) in the *Collected Works*. (See Part II, Chap. 8 of the present book.)

L. S. Vygotsky, *L.S. Vygotsky's Pedological Works. Volume 2.*, Perspectives in Cultural-Historical Research 10, https://doi.org/10.1007/978-981-16-1907-6_10

I. **What is a holistic analysis, and how does it work?** In order to understand the specificity of each critical age, we need a unit of analysis that will allow us to make comparisons. This unit must include both the personality and the environment. But analysis into units cannot proceed by vivisection, as if we were cutting sense organs and motor tissue away from bones and internal organs and then trying to stitch them back together again. If we want to understand how personality and people in the environment form a unity, we cannot cut the personality off from the people in the environment and then trying to reattach them. Such an analysis requires two basic concepts.

II. **Previous theorizations of the crisis have been one-sided.** Vygotsky acknowledges "immense theoretical difficulties" of analyzing the crisis at three in such a way that we include both the environment and the child and in fact include the environment as "internalized" by the child. But we can understand its necessity if we simply contrast it with two other methods, which we can call "Russian Environmentalism" and "German Innatism":

   1. Russian Environmentalism. This is the "externalist" method of putting the social environment first and considering the internal changes in the child as mere reflections of that environment. Vygotsky associates this approach with the vulgar Marxist Aron Zalkind.
   2. German Innatism. This is the "internalist" method of putting the child organism first that Vygotsky associates with Busemann, Kretschmer, and other Nazi psychologists. Vygotsky criticizes Busemann for locating the whole of the crisis in the child and merely using environment to explain variation. He criticizes Kretschmer for confusing the crisis at one with the crisis at three.

III. **The crisis at three is unique, because it has a unique neoformation and a unique next zone of development.** Vygotsky now synthesizes. He agrees with the German innatists that the crisis is essentially internal in nature, but he rejects the biological conception of the "internal." He agrees with the Russian environmentalists that the environment is the ultimate source of development, but he rejects the purely sociological conception of the "external." The child's relationship with the environment must, therefore, be represented psychologically. To do this, Vygotsky borrows a concept from Kretschmer: hypobulia, or "weak will." For Kretschmer, who confuses the crisis at age three with the crisis at age one, this is simply a moment of strong affect, of impoverished motive, and the "weak will" will linger on after the crisis to be nourished into strong and vigorous German will. For Vygotsky, however, the crisis at age three is utterly unlike the crisis at age one. It is characterized precisely by the differentiation of affect from will. Because in the crisis at age three affect paralyzes will, this "protowill" must disappear with the end of the crisis. Thus hypobulia has two characteristics which allow Vygotsky to determine that it is a neoformation of the crisis at three (and therefore only the specific lines of self-emancipation that lead to this neoformation are the Central Lines of Development). The two characteristics which identify it as the neoformation are:

1. It is new, that is, unique, original, and without any precedent in early childhood. Vygotsky uses the work of Katz to demonstrate this: a child has a strong affective desire to go to the zoo with his mother and brother but has an even stronger will to refuse going. This is very different from the relatively immediate affective perception which formed the basis for speech development in early childhood.
2. It is transitional, that is, impermanent and temporary, and it persists only as a dependent part of the neoformation of the next zone of development. It does not mature into will proper but instead appears as its antipode, mastering the child instead of allowing the child to master it. It is only in the next age period, preschool, that the child will be able to master both will and affect through the experience of play. For the crisis at three, this ability to divorce affect and will is the actual zone of development, and the ability to reunite them in preschool play is therefore the zone of proximal development.

IV. **Although each crisis is unique, we can use the crisis at three to understand the crisis at seven.**

1. The Symptoms of the Crisis. As Vygotsky noted in the crisis at three, the divorce between will and affect makes a completely new kind of unity of will and affect possible in a later stage. Instead of analyzing the symptoms himself, Vygotsky asks the students to read the literature and think of their own experience. He does, however, give a general characterization of the seven-year-old: it is an age when the child's personality seems to be "pulled out," when children undertake apparently unmotivated clowning, and persist in it despite threats and even punishments. He says that prior to age seven, children seem relatively transparent: the inner and outer personality seems to coincide, and he argues that Chaplin's humor depends largely on reproducing this preschool behavior in an adult person.
2. Lines of Development: Vygotsky deduces that the seven-year-old has somehow managed to insert an intellectual layer between the external self and internal self. He then compares this with similar structural changes in other age periods, one from the child's past and one in the child's future.

First, he compares the insertion of intellect between the external and internal selves with what happens to perception in early childhood when generalizations are inserted between vision and understanding; that is, when we learn to see a clock as a time-teller and not simply as a mysteriously marked wood or metal object with hands on its face.

Second, he compares this insertion of intellect with what happens much later on, when a school child or even an adult learns the rules of chess: instead of objects to be sorted by color or shape, there are now threats and opportunities.

In both cases, there is a radical reconstrual of *perezhivanie* arising from changes that are essentially "internal," the same kind of reconstrual of sound we see when the child acquires speech.

1. Critical Neoformations. With the crisis at seven, Vygotsky sees two such radical reconstruals:

a. The child begins to understand that affect is his affect—that anger, fun, frustration are things that are happening to a self, and not simply a kind of weather that just seems to accompany certain activities.
b. The child begins to co-generalize *perezhivanies*, including affective ones.

2. The Next Zone of Development. As he often does, Vygotsky concludes the chapter by comparing and contrasting development with disease, ontogenesis and pathogenesis. In pathogenesis, a severely retarded child experiences rejection and derision at every step, but simply cannot generalize the experiences into any feelings of depression. In ontogenesis, what takes place is a proto-self, a self-absorption and self-love that is a basic precondition for the formation of self-esteem and confidence. These contradictory *perezhivanies*, from which the child cannot yet consistently and coherently select, are the foundation the child's next zone of development, the conscious awareness and mastery of school age.

Chapter 10: The Crisis at Age Three and the Crisis at Age Seven

I wish today to return to a theme which we commenced but did not complete, that is, the theme relating to the critical ages. I would like today to complete the presentation of the study of the crisis at 3 years which I began, and that of the crisis of seven, which separates school age from preschool.[1]

I would link this crisis at three to our subsequent account of the transitional age, which will be for the future.

If you remember, I was able to give you, at that time when I spoke to you of the symptoms of the crisis at three, a very detailed list of a whole series of symptoms that appear in this crisis at 3 years old. We spoke of the stubbornness, the obstinacy, the willfulness, the sulkiness, the protestation, in a word, of the whole range of symptoms which are manifestations of the crisis at three, as the material is

[1] In order to strengthen the position of women in the workforce, and also to weaken the influence of the traditional family in bringing up the new generation, the Russian revolution sought to establish a wide range of child preschool institutions. The Soviets used the term детский сад, literally "gardens for children," a translation from German, to cover the whole range of child preschool institutions, from two to 7 years old. So the term "kindergarten" really corresponds to "preschools," and not simply to the transitional year between preschool institutions and elementary school.

Within this general level of preschool "kindergartens," there were, of course, sublevels and subgroups. There was младший дошкольный, or junior preschool, for children of 3–4 years of age, and средний дошкольный middle preschool for four- to five-year-olds, and then старший дошкольный, or senior preschool, for kids who were 5–6 years old. Typical kindergarten usually had several groups of each sublevel of each type. The highest level was called подготовительная (к школе) группа (6–7 years) or simply подготовительная группа ("the preparatory group"). The crisis of seven separates school age from the senior preschool (старший дошкольный). However, "transitional age" (переходном возрасте) in the next paragraph probably refers to the crisis at thirteen and the subsequent stable period of adolescence, which taken together constitute the transition from childhood to adulthood.

presented in productions and descriptions, mainly in the work of bourgeois researchers observing the child in the developmental period of the 3-year-old crisis chiefly in the terms of an authoritarian family enculturation. And so it now remains for us to draw some theoretical conclusions, that is, to attempt to identify what events occur in the development of the child that condition the appearance of these symptoms. What is the sense, what is the meaning, that these symptoms have?

Today I should do the same in relation to the crisis at 7 years, and for this reason I wish, before leaping into it, to make a few prefatory remarks on the theory of the critical ages at three and seven.

The pedological problem, as you well know, still finds itself at a very early stage of development, and when we speak of the theory of the long since discovered and well-studied ages, we have no real theory of them to speak of. Yet we do have some budding rudiments of a theoretical approach to understanding this age. Matters are complicated when we speak of the problem of those ages[2] which are not discussed, which European literature began to elucidate not long ago, and which have been elucidated more scantily than the stable ages.

You remember that my attempts to present theoretically the crises at 3 and 7 years constituted in themselves initial, rough attempts, based on some knowledge of factual material, on some of my own observations, those that I have witnessed because the crisis is linked to the difficult child, and on some attempts to critically rework some of what has been proposed in the theory of these ages and to link them to a few general ideas that I have formed.

This is just something to a large degree preliminary, to some degree even subjective, and it cannot pretend to be anything like a theory of these ages. So I shall attempt to sharply limit the factual side of describing the elucidation that I shall attempt to give.

We have shown you that the 3-year-old crisis symptoms indicate that, when the inner restructuring of the child is accomplished, the crisis proceeds along the axis of social relations.

Recall to yourselves one or two of the symptoms that we analyzed together. If you remember, we said that the negative reaction that manifests itself in a child at 3 must be strictly distinguished from simple disobedience in the child; stubbornness, which appears here as a typical part of the crisis, must also be sharply distinguished from simple insistence of the child. If a child does not want to do what he is asked, or wishes to do the opposite, this does not by itself constitute a negativistic reaction in the child.

Say that you ask a child who is all played out to stop playing and go sleep. He refuses, and this is a disobedience. But it is not a negativistic reaction.

1. A negativist reaction arises from the minute that the child is indifferent to that which you ask, or even wants to do what you ask him to do, but will nevertheless

[2] Korotaeva adds the word критических or "critical" in brackets before the word "ages" in the very last sentence. We have preferred to leave the manuscript as it is, but Korotaeva's interpolation certainly makes sense.

refuse. The motive of refusal, the motive for the act, lies not in the activity itself to which you invite the child. It lies in his attitude toward you.
2. The negativistic reaction does not manifest itself in a refusal of the child in relation to that deed which he is requested to carry out; rather, it is found in relation to the fact that he is being requested, and therefore the true substance of the negative attitude of the child consists in this: to do the opposite, that is, to display acts of simple contrarian activity in relation to whomever has asked him to do things.

So too with stubbornness. Mothers very frequently say, complaining of difficult children, that they are stubborn or persistent. But being persistent and being stubborn—these are different things.

If a child wants very much to achieve something, and is persistent in achieving it, this has nothing in common with stubbornness. Stubbornness—this exists in the reaction of the child when the child insists on something whether he wants it or not, or when something has long since ceased to be wanted, or when it is wanted out of proportion to the power of persistence, or when the child insists not so much for the sake of the object but simply because he said so, that is, when there is a social motivation, a pure motivation originating from the very content of the effort itself, from the very challenge itself.

If you recall, we at one time took apart in great detail, step by step, the so-called "Seven Stars" of the crisis, and we have seen that these new features are always linked to the fact that the child begins to motivate their acts not from the content of a given situation but from their relationship with other people.

Therefore, there will always be a motive: either "I" or the motive of my attitude to others. This is what we saw in relation to negativism and in relation to stubbornness. I will not repeat what I said earlier.

Thus, it seems to me that if you just summarize the factual picture of the symptoms in the crisis of the 3-year-old, we cannot disagree with those researchers who say that the crisis at 3 years old, to speak of the essence, may be detached from the individual symptoms that express it and flows, firstly, from the crisis in the social relations of the child. What, in substance, is reconstructed during the time of this crisis? The social position of the child in relation to the people in the milieu, first of all in relation to the authority of the mother, to the authority of the father, and through the line of the crisis of his "I," that is, through the line of identifying acts, motives of which are laid down and linked to manifestations of the personality of the child <…>. To put it simply and shortly, the crisis revolves around the axis of the restructuring of the social relationships between the child 's personality and the people in the milieu.

This applies to nearly all of the crises, and to the crisis at seven as well. Therefore, it seems to me that since the aspect of the matter—the child's inner attitude to the people around him—has been relatively little illuminated for us compared with the history of other child ages, we must preface the theoretical analysis of the crisis with a few general remarks regarding the concepts from which we will consider these crises generally.

I will attempt to put the general content briefly. It seems to me that in order to anchor the question in firm ground, it is necessary to introduce a concept which entered science long ago and which pedology has employed relatively little in studying the social development of the child in the sense of his inner attitude toward the persons in his surroundings, in the sense of his active participation in the social situation.

We always recognize, at least in words, that it is necessary to study the personality and the environment of the child in their unity. It is in itself an indisputable proposition, which cannot in itself be presented in such a way that on one side there is the influence of the personality and on the other side the influence of the environment—both the one and the other acting in the manner of external forces which are then linked to each other and tug first this way and then that.

However, in practice we often do just that: wishing to study this unity, we first tear this unity into its constituent parts and then we nevertheless attempt to link them with one another like two mutually-interacting mechanical forces. And in this way the study of difficult childhood cannot proceed beyond the statement of the question: what plays the major role, the constitution (i.e., the child's personality—Trans.) or the environmental conditions; the psychopathic conditions of a genetic character or conditions of the external circumstances of development.

It seems to me that this rests on two basic problems, two basic concepts, which I now wish to make clear, because in relation to the internal attitude of the child to the environment we cannot discover the roots of the crises at 3 and 7 years. Here, then, is a theoretical attempt, which I take on my own head and undertake at my own risk, which must be discussed further when we try to explain the generally accepted material.

Firstly, what needs to be noted and what is a major drawback in our practical and theoretical study of the environment is that we study the environment in its absolute indices. Whoever works practically in pedology knows this well. We are producing society and family studies of the child[3] on the child in which what is reflected is the cubic area of housing, whether the child is sleeping alone, how many times the child is going to the public baths, when he changes his clothes, whether the newspaper is read in the family, what kind of education the mother has, and what kind the father has. This research—whether the child is 1-year-old, an infant, an adolescent, it is all one; it makes no difference to the research on the child himself. We study some absolute indices of the environment, we study the environment, believing that by knowing these absolute indices of the environment we will as well know at once what role these absolute indicators will play in the development of the child. Not a few Soviet pedologists in relation to this set this up as an absolute principle in their study of the environment, and it appears that in the textbook [by the pedologist

[3] In Soviet times, there was a practice of regularly and thoroughly examining the social and living conditions of children. Special commissions consisting of teachers, doctors, and social workers were engaged in this. They visited families and determined the conditions in which the child was growing up. Based on this comprehensive survey, a document was compiled. Vygotsky means that such a document was given to him as a researcher.

A.B. Zalkind—GSK) which has been issued, you will find this proposition: that the social environment of the child as the basis remains unchanged throughout the whole duration of development. If we keep in view only the absolute indices of the environment, in certain measure we must agree with this. In reality, though, this is a complete falsehood from both the theoretical and the practical point of view. The theoretical falsehood lies in the substantial difference of a social environment. The environment of the child differs from the environment of an animal in so far as the human environment holds a social environment; the child is a part of the living environment, that this environment never constitutes for the child an external environment. To say that the environment of the child is a social environment, to say that the child is a social being—this means to draw the conclusion that the child is himself a part of this environment, that is, we need a social situation that influences the development of the child, where the child himself cannot be part of the situation.[4] Consequently, the most substantial turn which should be taken in the study of the environment—a transition from absolute indices of the environment to relative indices of the environment, that is, a pedological study of the environment, but this means first and foremost to study what this environment signifies in relation to the child, how the child is related to the different indices of this environment. Roughly speaking, let us say that a child of 1 year doesn't speak, and the speech environment of surrounding parents and people remains unchanged. Whether the child spoke before 1 year of age or afterward, in absolute terms, the speech culture of those around him has not changed at all. I believe that everyone will agree that from the minute the child begins to understand his first words, from whenever he begins to say his first sensible words, his relationship to speech moments in the environment, his relationship to child speech roles, is very much changed. This simple example shows the great significance of this question in principle.

It turns out that each step forward that the child takes alters the influence of the environment upon him, alters not only the relation with the environment but also the influence of the environment upon him. The environment becomes, from the point of view of development, completely different from the moment when the child understands his first words; he has stepped across from one age to another.

In this way, we may say that it is precisely the pedological study of the environment that should have the most substantial change in form in comparison with what has usually been our practice up until now, and that it should change first of all toward an understanding that the pedologist is studying the environment not as such, not in its absolute indices, but in relation to the role of the child, and that the

[4] Leopoldoff-Martin and Schneuwly (Vygotskij, 2018) assume that this is a mistake, and what Vygotsky means to say is that the child cannot be part of the situation. It is also possible that Vygotsky simply shifts his point of view from that of Zalkind to his own view right at the point marked "i.e.". Vygotsky has been saying that the child is part of the environment, but in order to determine the "pure," absolute influence of the environment on the child as the textbook written by Zalkind claims to do we would really need a social situation where the child is not an active constituent of the situation but only a passive recipient of its influence. This is consistent with the critique Vygotsky makes in Chapter Four of *L.S. Vygotsky Pedological Works, Volume 1: Foundations of Pedology* (2019).

same environment in its absolute indicators is completely different for a child of 1 year, 3 years, and so on.

The dynamic changes of the environment in relation to the child are the main subject matter for pedological analysis of the environment, the relationship which comes to the foreground.

But there, wherever one speaks of a relationship, there is, of course, a second question: a relationship is never purely an external relationship, that is, a detailed inventory of the child, a detailed inventory of the social situation, from which, when the child is himself in fact a participant in this social situation, we can tear the child away and then re-establish the relation. This is impossible. It requires the introduction of several new concepts, and this brings us to the second concept of which I wished to speak.

It seems to me that one of the most important methodological questions consists of the question of how, actually, in theory and in study, we approach the study of unity. We often find it necessary to speak of the unity of the personality and the environment, of the unity of psychological and the physical development, of the unity of speech and thinking. What does it really mean, in theory and in research, to approach the study of this or that unity in which inhere the properties of some unity as a whole? It seems to me that what it means is, for research and for theory, to discover each time the leading unit, that is, to determine just those pieces which cannot be reduced to more simple moments of the unity, which one can handle and study, in which all the properties of this unity are combined.

For example, when one wishes to study the relation of thinking and speech, one detaches speech from thinking, thinking from speech, and then asks what speech does for thinking and thinking for speech. <…>.

If you wish to understand how a unity emerges, how it changes, how it influences the course of child development, it's important not to break the unity into its constituent parts—because in doing this we lose the essential properties which inhere precisely in this unity—but rather to take the unit of this unity of speech and thinking.

In recent times, we have attempted to argue that as a unit we need to take, let's say, meaning. It seems to me that the word meaning constitutes a part of the word, the speech formation, because a word without meaning is not a word, and, since every word meaning is a generalization, it constitutes a product of the intellectual activity of the child; it constitutes a unit of thinking and speech in irreducible portions. Whether this is right or wrong in a concrete instance does not interest us here.[5]

But I intend, if it is confirmed in the course of further studies and observations, to suggest a unit with which to study the unity of the personality and the environment. We find that this unit is called, in both psychopathology and in psychology,

[5] Obviously, there are some concrete instances (e.g., "Hey!" or "Hi!" or curse words) where the portion of thinking seems much reduced; similarly, there are some concrete instances (e.g., elllipsis) where the portion of speech seems to be minimal. But these are exceptions that prove the rule, because a study of speech development that only looked at such wordings would be much impoverished.

perezhivanie. It seems to me that the *perezhivanie* of the child is not a simplest unit with respect to which it can be said that it represents neither the environmental influence on the child or the peculiarity of the child itself, because *perezhivanie* is the unity of the person and the environment, as it is presented in development. So, in development, the unity of environmental and personal moments takes place in a number of *perezhivanies* of the child.

But for this we must agree on what such *perezhivanie* is.

It seems to me that *perezhivanie* needs to be understood correctly as it is established in contemporary psychology: *perezhivanie* must be understood as the internal attitude of a child or person to a particular moment of reality.

Every *perezhivanie* is a *perezhivanie* of something. There is no *perezhivanie* that is not a *perezhivanie* of something, just as there is no act of consciousness that is not an act of consciousness of something. But any *perezhivanie* is a *perezhivanie* of my own. In contemporary concrete theory, *perezhivanie* is introduced as a unit of consciousness in which all of the basic properties of consciousness are given as such, while in attention and in thinking the link to consciousness is not given.[6] Attention is not a unit of consciousness but some element of consciousness in which there is no series of other elements, and with it the unity of consciousness as such vanishes. Rather the actual dynamic unit of consciousness, from which consciousness is made up, is *perezhivanie*.

Perezhivanie, as has been said, has a bio-social orientation, that is, it is something that lies between the personality and the environment, meaning the relation of personality to environment and it indicates what a given moment of the environment signifies to the personality.

Perezhivanie constitutes the defining moment from the point of view of how this or that moment of environmental impact influences child development. This, in any case for the study of difficult children, receives positive conformation at each and every step. Each analysis of difficult children, of the changes in development which lead to difficult enculturation, indicates that the essential consists not in the situation itself taken in its absolute indicators, but rather in how the child experiences the situation.[7]

---

[6] Why does Vygotsky say that there is no link to consciousness with thinking? Vygotsky seems to be making the same point he made in *Thinking and Speech* about word meaning as a unit of analysis of the unity of speech and thinking. Word meaning is a minimal unit because it is not reducible any further and contains all properties of this unity. A sound without meaning is not really a word, but neither is a meaning without some potential realization in sounds. Similarly, attention without thinking (e.g., involuntary attention to a clap of thunder or a gunshot) is not consciousness, and thinking without attending to some object of thought in the environment (e.g., drug-induced fantasy or illness-induced hallucination) is not, in Vygotsky's view, conscious awareness.

[7] The word that Vygotsky uses for "experiences" is переживает, that is, the active voice of the verb form of *perezhivanie* and the word he uses for "is experienced" is переживается, that is, the passive voice of the verb. We have translated it as ordinary English verbs because, as we explained in Lecture 4 of Foundations of Pedology (see *L.S. Vygotsky Pedological Works Volume 1*), in the verb form it seems to be used as an everyday concept and an ordinary Russian word, and not as a scientific concept and a special unit of analysis. However, for Vygotsky, there is never any absolute

The literature has often described, and I myself have attempted to describe in several cases, where in one and the same family situation we encounter in different children different changes in development because one and the same situation is experienced in different ways: there are different *perezhivanies* in children.

I wish to stress, therefore, what is given in *perezhivanies* is, on the one hand, the environment in its relation to me, in how I experience this environment, and on the other hand, how all the features of the development of my personality manifest themselves in *perezhivanies*. One author has said that in *perezhivanie* is...the person in that person's present. He has in view a *perezhivanie* in which I am influenced by all of my qualities to the degree that they have developed throughout the course of my development, and to the degree that they can participate at this particular minute. Not all qualities participate in the determination of this present; it is important which ones take part. In *perezhivanie,* in its character, in the way of experiencing there are shares of a unity of the environment and the personal moment which cannot be further decomposed, in terms of how they are intertwined in this unity, in the development of the child. To give a somewhat general formal definition, it seems to me that it would be correct to say that the environment determines the development of the child through perezhivanie of the environment, and the most essential, therefore, consists in breaking away from absolute indicators from environment to personality and from personality to environment, because the child is part of the social situation, and (because—Trans.) the relationship of the child to the environment and the environment to the child is given through the perezhivanie and the activity of the child himself, if we may put it this way, the forces of environment acquire a guiding significance thanks to the perezhivanie of the child.[8]

If this is true, if this proposition has a certain theoretical weight, then this demands of pedology a profound analysis of the inner *perezhivanie* of the child. That is, the study of an environment transferred to a substantial degree to the inside

---

distinction between everyday concepts and scientific ones; each has the potential to become the other through research on the one hand or through everyday use on the other. Concepts are never really imaginary entities (e.g., "an experience"); they are always processes of linking a thought and some sphere of reality (e.g., "not simply passively undergo an experience but interpret, understand, and emotionally relate to the event situation"), so it should not surprise us when Vygotsky realizes a science concept by a verb rather than a noun.

[8] Korotaeva adds the word "reflected" to "there are (reflected—GSK) shares of the unity..." but this is not Vygotsky's original text, and we have removed it. We are also somewhat suspicious of the word "activity" in the last sentence in this paragraph, but we have left it in because there is no clear indication that it was not in the original text.

Korotaeva was a philosophy teacher, and doubtless had to teach Lenin's text "Materialism and Empirio-criticism." This stresses that consciousness is always a "reflection" of reality—this was intended to establish the prior existence of a material reality, because there is no reflection in a mirror without some object. But shares of the indecomposible unity of the environment and the personality are genuine acts of sharing—they are not just passive reflections in a mirror any more than they are just inert physical objects in the world. Similarly, *perezhivanie* includes the mental act of "over-living" an experience in order to understand, interpret, and make sense of it, so the addition of "activity" seems either unnecessary or a concession to behaviorism uncharacteristic of Vygotsky's thinking at this time.

(sic-GSK) of the child himself, and not merely the study of the external circumstances in which the child lives. This analysis becomes very intricate, and consequently we confront theoretical difficulties of vast scope. But despite all this, with respect to certain pedological problems, with respect to the critical ages, in respect to difficult childhood, various moments connected to the analysis of perezhivanies are becoming clearer and visible.

How are these *(perezhivanies*—Trans.) applied in the study of the critical ages?

The attentive study of critical ages demonstrates that in each one there occurs a basic change in the *perezhivanie* of the child, in the basic type of his *perezhivanie.* You go from one age to another. The crisis at three, to my eyes, presents an early moment of transition or turning, which is realized in this: from one type of *perezhivanie,* that is, one manner of experiencing the environment, the child proceeds to another. I would put it something like this: every crisis itself heralds, first and foremost, a change of *perezhivanie* which is analogous to the example which I gave earlier with respect to speech.

The environment as such does not change for the child at three. Parents continue to earn the same amount as before, for each mouth to feed there is the same budgeted minimum and maximum, the same newspapers are subscribed to, and underclothes are changed just as often, with the same amount of living space; the parents have not changed their attitude to the child. Because of this, observers who investigate the crisis will say that it is without any external reason at all that the child who was so good, so obedient, and so loving suddenly becomes moody, angry, and stubborn. This internal character of the crisis is underlined by all of the bourgeois investigators. The great majority of them explain the internal character of all crises by biological causes.

One of the most widespread theories for explaining the crisis draws a parallel between sexual maturation, and at the core of the crisis they see the inner biological maturation of the child, finding there the source of developmental change.

Other authors, such as Busemann,[9] who wish to stress the significance of the social environment in these moments, point out, correctly, that the crisis is completely different according to the environment in which it unfolds.

But the point of view of Busemann is not in principle different from the point of view which considers the crisis as a purely endogenous development. The crisis, he maintains, like all features, inheres in the child...but its...[10] expression changes according to different environments.

---

[9] Adolf Hermann Heinrich Busemann (1887–1967) was a teacher of religion and then a student of Narziss Ach. He wrote on many important psychological topics, including the crisis, the periodization problem, and the social views of adolescents. Vygotsky cites his work on the difference between "primary" (innate), "secondary" (environmental), and "tertiary" (consciousness, self-aware) links in psychological systems. Busemann's most important work was on the link between thinking and speech, kinds of adjectives and nouns and verbs that children used in their writing; Busemann tried to use these to make general statements about mental development.

[10] It is not clear where the ellipsis in this passage come from—Korotaeva does not explain. One possibility is the stenographer simply could not keep up with Vygotsky, as in previous examples

Here arises a fundamental idea which, very likely, will serve for us and for you as the object of debate and dispute; here arises the question which to me constitutes at all time a central one whenever I think about critical ages, that all of the bourgeois studies are either wholly untrue or untrue in many parts. First, we commence with the factual side of the matter. It appears to me that the bourgeois investigators are dealing with a very restricted circle of observations, that is, at all times they are observing the child under the conditions of the bourgeois family and an enculturation of a definite type. A few studies show how in other conditions of enculturation, this can happen otherwise.

The first work with children coming from nurseries to kindergartens[11] says that the crisis unfolds otherwise than does the crisis in children who are first undergoing preschool enculturation. But nevertheless the basic fact has been correctly noted; that is, the crisis, firstly, always takes place, in every case, during the normal flow of child development. The ages of three and seven will always in the pedological sense be turning points in development, there will always be a positioning of things such that when the inner course of child development has completed this or that cycle, the transition to the subsequent cycle will involve a definite revolving, and one age does not just flow on into another.

One age is somehow refracted and remade to give the beginning of a new stage in development. This is in the first place. Secondly, what constitutes the truth in these claims is the very general and very naive impression which observers have of the crisis at 3 years: the child is somehow changed beyond all recognition. For an interval of 3–5 months, he is not the child who he had been earlier, and I personally take as a true fact indication that the crisis is taking place (and this is the incomprehensibility in it) as some kind of process that has begun somewhere inside and is not well understood by others, since it is not connected with the changes taking place around the child. To put it simply, the crisis presents these essential features, that it presents a chain of inner changes in the child alongside relatively insignificant external changes. For example, when the child starts going to school, he changes from 1 year to another throughout the duration of the school age (and this is not surprising to us), for there are changes in the whole situation in which the child is growing, that is, the whole atmosphere of his development. When the child comes to kindergarten from the nursery, we are not surprised that the preschooler has been changed; here there is a transformation of the child linked to changes that have taken place in the conditions of his development. Essential to all crises is that internal changes are somehow disproportionately larger than the changes in the external environment, and for this reason always lend the impression of an internal crisis.

---

which were marked with parentheses. But another possibility is that Vygotsky is quoting Busemann, and he omitted some of Busemann's words here.

[11] As we noted above (see Footnote 2), "kindergartens" do not simply refer to a preparatory year prior to primary school around 6 or 7 years of age, as it does in the West. In the Soviet context, the term included a whole range of preschool institutions starting around age two, and nurseries can begin even earlier, so that women workers can return to production. For that reason, when Vygotsky speaks of crises, he is talking in general, for example, both the crisis at three and the crisis at seven.

This is something which constitutes the object of argument whenever it is necessary to talk of the critical ages, but my impression consists in this: that the crises actually have internal origins, which consist of changes of an internal character <... >.[12]

Here there is no precise correspondence between inner and outer changes in the destiny of the child observable in the transition from preschool to school. The child encounters a crisis. What has changed so drastically in the externals? Nothing. What has changed outwardly for the 3-year-old child? Nothing. Why does the child change so drastically in so little time? My thinking consists in this: we need to speak out not against the bourgeois theory of the critical age, nor against the fact that the crisis consists of a process very profoundly interwoven with the course of child development; rather, we need to speak out against their understanding of the innermost nature of the developmental process. If the whole of all that is internal in development is understood as biological—in the final count a change in the endocrine glands—I would not call the ages of crisis the ages of inner development. But I believe that inner development always takes place in such a way that we have in fact a unity of the moments of the personality and the environment, that is, each new step in development is immediately determined by the preceding step, that is, all that has already been formed and emerged in the development of previous stages. True, this means understanding development as a connected process, where all that is subsequent is connected with the previous and with the past, in which these previously established personality traits are now manifest and act. It seems to me that if only we correctly understand the nature of the inner process of development, then any theoretical objections to understanding the crisis in all cases as an internal crisis cannot stand. Personally, I imagine this as an internal process of development whose measure[13] is in units of *perezhivanie* such as those we attempted to explain previously. It seems to me that behind any *perezhivanie* the real influence of the environ-

---

[12] Both here and at the end of the previous paragraph, some crucial words seem to be missing, and we cannot speculate on what exactly Vygotsky said. But we do know that Vygotsky has said that the "bourgeois" investigators like Busemann are entirely or mostly wrong. First of all, the crisis is not identical in all children, varies a good deal according to conditions of upbringing, and therefore cannot be biological in origin, so that is entirely wrong. Secondly, their impression of an "internal" crisis is largely based on a mismatch between external changes and internal ones. But the crisis at three takes place before the changes brought on in preschool, the crisis at seven before those of primary school, and the crisis at thirteen before those of middle school. So, the impression of a crisis that is caused by a sudden change in the environment is mostly wrong.

But it is not entirely wrong. Vygotsky agrees that the crisis is essentially "internal" in origin—but for Vygotsky, that simply means it socio-psychological, not biological. This view is not consistent with the bourgeois views. But it is also not consistent with the mainstream Soviet belief that crises are caused by a mismatch between the needs of the child and the needs of capitalist society, and therefore unnecessary under socialism. It is consistent with Vygotsky's view that crises unfold along the axis between the child and the social environment, realized, after age one, in speech.

[13] Vygotsky says: измеряемый в этих единицах переживания, which literally means that the process is measured in units of *perezhivanie*. But in English this implies reducing the data to numbers, and Vygotsky is not speaking of quantification but analysis. Vygotsky uses "measure" here the way that Hegel uses it in the Logic (Hegel, 1830/1975, p. 157), that is, a "qualitative quantum"

ment stands, but only the real influence of the environment in a dynamic relation to the child. From this point of view, I might be allowed to say that the essence of any crisis lies in the restructuring of inner *perezhivanie* which, to all appearances, is rooted in changes in the basic moments which define the relationship of the child to the environment, in other words, in a change in the needs and in the impulses that drive the child's behavior. This growth and the change in needs and impulses represents in itself the less conscious, less volitional part of our personalities, and in the transition from one age to another there emerge in the child new impulses, new motives; in other words, the drivers of his activity undergo a re-evaluation of their driving forces. That which was to the child essentially important, the guide rail, has suddenly become only comparatively so or unimportant at the very next step. For this reason it seems to me that in this restructuring of needs and impulses, the change in the value system, is the basic moment in the transition from one age to another. Upon transition from age to age, the environment changes; that is, the child's attitude to the environment is changing, Other interests commence in the child, other activities emerge in the child, and the child's consciousness is restructured, if consciousness is understood as a relation to the environment.

I believe that everything that has been said thus far will become more clear and understandable when we now turn to a concrete attempt to theoretically explain the crises of three and 7 years of age. Here what we have said above should be recalled. For me, to explain any age period means to point out what it is that is new that arises in this age. The theory of ages is, for me, always an answer to the question of what arose in this period that was not at all present in the preceding ages of the child, and therefore the central question of the critical age is that of the nature of the neoformations which now emerge. Something emerges which is totally new in the critical age, but what exactly? I have tried to answer this question thus: it seems to me that the true, factual observation of many bourgeois investigators who hold that the critical period has a negative coloration, that these ages move to the foreground not so much the creative activity of development, as the destructive one. <...>. But at the same time it seems to me that they are not correct and that they go against their own facts when they do not pay attention to the specific neoformations which arise in the transitional periods.[14] These neoformations constitute neoformations in the full sense of the word, that is, there is actually within development emerging something new that was not present in the previous age and that constitutes an essential moment in the transition of the child to the subsequent age, without which the child cannot arrive at the subsequent age. But these neoformations are specific in character. Neoformations of the first year are different from neoformations of stable ages, in that in the stable ages when neoformations emerge, they constitute permanent

---

that functions as a complete characterization (as in "God is the measure of all things"). For this reason we have slightly altered the wording and used the word "measure."

[14] Leopoldoff-Martin and Schneuwly (2018, 149) say that it is not at all clear what "they go against their own facts" refers to. It is certainly true that some words seem to be missing from the stenogramme. But it seems likely that Vygotsky is continuing his argument against bourgeois investigators who hold that the critical period is entirely negative (e.g., Freud, Jung, Piaget, Spranger).

human accomplishments. For example, the child begins to walk, and so all his life long he will walk; he begins to speak—this is an accomplishment for a whole lifetime. He begins to be literate—all his life long he will be literate. But if the child utters his first word at 6 months, this is not a simple neoformation, but a neoformation that will be linked in time to a critical age, one without which there cannot emerge a new formation in the subsequent stable age. It is specific to the critical age.

I now turn to the theory, which in itself is more or less non-subjective, but which is only an attempt from a subjective point of view to imagine this.

I ask myself what specific neoformations of a transient nature arise in a crisis of 3 years, what stands in development for all the symptoms that have been studied so far. The neoformation which is set out can be designated and delineated very often on good grounds with a single word which already exists in psychology, the word "hypobulia." Kretschmer[15] by this concept wanted to explain the concept genetically and attempted to push the teaching that the will in the development of the child progresses through a number of stages such that each stage presents a qualitatively new formation than those it follows, and he suggested calling the early stage in the development of the child's will hypobulia.

Kretschmer did make one important mistake, which is now recognized by all as a mistake. It consists in this: that Kretschmer combined two ages: the crisis of age one and the crisis of age three.

Kretschmer's studies about hypobulia relate to the crisis of the first year of life. I have attempted to point out one of the disturbances of this first year of life. In childhood, we sometimes see in some of the propensities of the child who is experiencing the crisis of the first year of life some seizures of a hypobulic character; these are normally attacks that have a psychological explanation and an external manifestation in a turbulent discharge of motor energy, in the refusal of the child to do anything, in a whole plentiful series of turbulent motions. The child who is in the period of crisis of 1 year, if unhappy with something, will often sit on the floor, lie on his back, throw himself on the floor and pound it with his arms and legs. In the crisis of the first year of life, the most significant feature of hypobulia consists in the non-differentiation of affect and will; that is, the child's volitional motives stem from an instant of affect, which possesses the child at that moment. Undifferentiated affect and will leads to an important distinction which Kretschmer makes between will in the proper sense and hypobulia. When we observe hypobulic features and their psychological characteristics, we say that the most important difference between a hypobulic act and a volitional one is that the hypobulic act is governed by a release,

[15] Ernst Kretschmer (1888–1964) was a student of Robert Gaupp, the racial hygienist who laid the basis for the Nazi T4 project of murdering the mentally ill rather than treating them. Kretschmer is best known today for a rather naïve holistic psychology: the belief that physical constitutions reliably predict sychological temperaments (so for example the thin "asthenic type" correlated with schizophrenia, and the fat, jolly "pyknic" correlated with manic depression, etc. Vygotsky uses Kretschmer's holistic laws of transfer of brain functions as a framework for much of *Foundations of Pedology*, but he is much more critical of Kretschmer's work on the problem of age, precisely because of these biologizing tendencies. Kretschmer signed the vow of allegiance to Hitler and the SS, which Vygotsky bitterly denounces in "Fascism and Psychoneurology" (Vygotsky, 1934/1994, 327).

while the volitional act is governed by a motive. The characters of these incitations are completely different.

One may have influence on the volitional act, through a counter-motivation, by proving something. On the hypobulic act, drastic measures that are similarly hypobulic in character may have this effect: a warning, a sharp cry, that is, anything that immediately changes the affective state of that child. Indeed, I think that if you recall the analysis that I offered to you of the symptoms of the 3-year-old crisis, we have seen that at each time the most essential feature of the crisis at three is the differentiation of affect and volition; the most essential feature of all of these symptoms is that they are in a certain contradiction. Let me remind you today of the significance of negativistic persistence. The affect of the child attracts him to one side but does not motivate the negativistic reaction; the child negates, despite the fact that he does not want to. The child is persistent about something, as we often see; but in wanting to crush the will of the child you will also be persistent, and though the child knows that nothing will come of it, and he would be happy to find some way out of this position, he still continues to persist, as if in a state of (…).[16] Whoever knows difficult children will agree with me that negativistic reactions or stubborn reactions never coincide with an intense fit of affect. If someone says that a child is being negative, and you go and see that the child really finds himself in a fit of affect, then you will know that there is no negativistic reaction.

A trait of the negativistic reaction is that stubborn, persistent acts by the child are beyond the influence of affective motivation, and sometimes in sharp contradiction with that motivation.

There is a book by Katz[17] on conversations with children that were written down in the course of a whole series of years of conversations, with the idea that the unit of speech does not lie in the sentence but in the conversation, that is, a whole linked theme, which is formed, as he says, by a motive. One fragment from a living relationship between parents and children: some parents go to some suburban spot by boat with their six-year-old child, but the littlest one is not taken, since he is sleeping. When they return, they find him up on his feet; he knew that they had gone for a ride without him. He becomes angry and starts to describe how when he grows bigger he will go to America by motorboat towing another one hundred motorboats and he will go all by himself. His mother says that she will go down to meet him and

[16]Vygotsky probably means something like a "paralyzed state," a "rictus," or perhaps the psychological equivalent of a rictus, an "affective fit," that is, a temper tantrum.

[17]The name Katz is capitalized КАЦ in Korotaeva's book (Выготский, 2001: 221). She adds the note "Так в стенограмме," meaning that it is thus in the stenogramme. This suggests that neither the stenographer nor the editor understands the reference. However, it seems clear Vygotsky is referring to the work on child speech and child stories of David Katz (1884–1953), which Vygotsky cites in "The Problem of Consciousness" (Vygotsky, 1997a: 135), *The History of the Development of the Higher Mental Functions* (Vygotsky, 1997b: 231) and in other papers. Katz was the student of Georg Müller. His early work, to which Vygotsky refers here, was in child psychology. In philosophy, he was close to Hering and Husserl, that is, to phenomenology. Like many Gestaltists he was interested in perception—unlike most of them, he wrote on touch as well as on vision. When Hitler came to power, Katz, who was Jewish, fled to England and then Sweden, where he died.

wave her handkerchief at him from the shore. Then the child says that he will not go to America but names another suburban city that seems to him just as far away as America, and so on. The child does not calm down. Then the mother starts proposing something even more enchanting than this, proposing one of his favorite activities not often granted him—the zoological gardens. The child wants to go to the zoological garden, but he has become stubborn and must pursue this reaction to the end. The child wants to go to the garden, so he then starts to cry in his obstinacy because the older child leaves, the mother leaves, but he, in spite of what he wants, nevertheless, against his will, against what he wants, remains there and tries to cobble together his own boat. This is a typical example of the negativistic reaction, or a reaction of another type but close to it, which acts counter to the child's wish. The child forcefully wishes matters otherwise: if anyone could take him, shake him, bring him out of this state—that would be best—but it is as if he is in the thrall of some obsessional motivation which will not let him go. In this way, there is a differentiated affect and will that form a most distinctive feature of the symptoms of which we have been speaking. This is a hypobulia in the true sense of the word. Where the will is not differentiated from affect, there is in general no will, but there is nevertheless affect, a moment of commitment, a moment arising from desire, a feeling which now guides this or that act. Where the child may wish for one thing, but must do the other under the influence of this motive, that is where we are dealing with a will, a very primitive will, but a will in the strict sense of the word. To fully understand the common root from which grow the symptoms of the age of three, we need to focus on two moments. First of all, we need to ask ourselves in what consists this volitional will, what lies behind the word volitional. It seems to me that this analysis gives us a completely clear answer. This 3-year-old child who wants to go to the zoological garden but nevertheless stays home to cobble together a motorboat knows that he will not be able to make one. Why does he do this? Because the motive of his behavior in this given case lies in his attitude to his mother, which comes to the foreground and completely overcomes his attitude to his own desires.

The social attitude of the child to others and the assertion of the certain trend which has emerged in relation to himself, his "I," makes up the main motive for his behavior. Simply said, the relationship itself, the relationship with others, now becomes the motive of his activity, and it is completely independent of outward affects (…). In the end, the child understands that he will not travel to America, that he will not cobble together the boat; he also understands that his mother cannot take him for a walk when the walk has already taken place. Thus no real pleasure for the child can be expected from the situation in which he finds himself: he wishes to go to the zoological gardens, but he remains at home and persists in doing so. Why—what sense lies in this act? This sense: to do something in the sphere of the attitude to the mother, to show her that he will not go. In a word, the attitude itself becomes the motive.

What remains is to reply to the last question: What makes this child's behavior hypobulic and distinguishes from the volitional behavior of a preschool child? A contradictory position, which brings about the circumstance that the child makes these relations into another motive for his activity torn away from his own wishes so that child actually acts contrary to his own desires. In other words, there appears the paradoxical phenomenon that the essential content of the crisis at three consists in the differentiation of will from affect.

The crisis at three produces a strange impression. This is the age which first gives birth to will, to the activeness of a volitional type of behavior, but on the other hand, will possesses the child, that is, every volitional *perezhivanie* has the character of our *perezhivanie*, and whoever has seen a child who is being stubborn sees, in these remarkable cases, that the child is himself in a state of dissonance, in an affective discord with himself, and those researchers note correctly who in the 3-year-old note every manifestation of our own states, our own reactions.

I wonder if you have ever seen a child who negativizes, and who does the opposite of what you say, but does so in sly fun, that is, gets pleasure from doing it. Then before you is the play of the child, or any of a number of other psychological manifestations, but not negativism.

When we explicate the neoformations of this critical age, we must explain two things. Firstly, what appears that is new, that makes it a neoformation, and secondly, why this is not volitional, why it is transitional. It is because here we are dealing with a kind of will that constitutes the antipode of will. This is a will which masters the child himself. This is no mechanism of volition, with the aid of which the child acquires a certain freedom in his actions; this is a step in the development of this will, when this will possess him, when the child finds himself maximally incapable of volition.

For this reason, we have the right to disagree with the proposition that in the course of further development with the withering away of the crisis, hypobulia ceases to exist as a peculiarity equating every child with the difficult child type. Hypobulic behaviors give place to the development of volitional behaviors in the child and form part of the moment which arrives at the age of preschool.

In the preschool years, as we know very well, linked to the crisis, all is subject to the rule of play, which occurs regardless of moments of affect. The general course of development of the child in the preschool age is a new relationship which emerges here between the child and the parents even in conditions of authoritarian parenting—all of this is to a large degree due to the fact that, first of all, the child at 3 years of age went through the hypobulic stage. Development which lacks the crisis, this is development whose result is lacking will.

If I were to sum up in a single phrase that which I have attempted to say of the crisis at three, I would say that from the point of view of development the following is what occurs: **each crisis represents the emancipation of the child, the growth of his activity, his separation from his environment. However, such a separation, such a differentiation, and such activities do not necessarily imply the isolation of the child, but rather imply the emergence of more complex relationships of the child.**

The more emancipated the child is, the more complex and active his relationship with the environment becomes. I have many times cited the proposition that claims that the child at the moment of birth is physically separated from the mother but not separated from her biologically. This is true. The child who begins to speak and to walk is already to a considerable degree separated from the mother biologically, but not separated psychologically. Factually he constitutes an active participant in the situation, but the child is never, before the crisis at three, consciously aware of himself or that he exists in a particular relationship with (the people in—Trans.) his surroundings. The child under 3 years old may sometimes act to spite his mother, sometimes to please her, or anger her, or make her happy, but never does such things as to spite her consciously. And although this relationship exists, he is not consciously aware of this relationship with (the people in—Trans.) his surroundings. When a child in crisis at three in his behavior departs from the immediate influence of affect (which determines his behavior now), he is in such a stage of independence when his relations with surrounding people (although in a very primitive form) become a real relationship. I believe that it is not just a random fact that after the crisis at 3 years, role play appears in the child. No one has ever seen a child under the age of 3 years who plays at roles, that is, who now would be a mother, and after a minute a militiaman, etc.[18] This is understandable, because the child of under three is capable of imitating anything; he can see that his mother rocks the child, and he can feed a doll and so on, but this doll will not be a child, and he will not by himself change his role, but as soon as the child has passed through the crisis at three, play linked to roles commences, where the key to the play very often lies not in the external situation as such but in playing at certain relationships. Take a middle-class ambiance where a child is developing, one which is conducive to the child developing the game of "family," with a mother and children and all the rest of it. What is the object, the content of this play? The most important is that the child in play is actively recreating and discovering the relationships that he has seen earlier. Children in the play will listen to him just as he has listened to his own mother, and he speaks in the play with another child just as he has heard his parents speak of what is going on. What is new in his play is what makes the situation, the environment, the relationships that are now novel to him, the object of a new active voluntary awareness. He has discovered them.

In general, for the child who has been through the crisis at three, there emerge attitudes: he has discovered that others have a certain attitude to him, and that he has a certain attitude to the others.

I will not speak of this for long, but if the significance of the crisis at three is traced through future ages, we can see that it is analogous to the significance that the

[18] What does Vygotsky mean here? Surely many of us have seen children under three who can and do play lions or even human characters; some of us have done so ourselves. First of all, as Vygotsky makes clear in the next paragraph, Vygotsky is not referring to copying a visible action (as in the game of "Growl" or "Peekaboo") but rather performing an invisible character: a mother or a soldier. Secondly, Vygotsky has in mind role-play games with implicit rules as well as roles: there are guidelines as to what does and does not constitute the idealized model. Thirdly, Vygotsky's years, including designations like "crisis at one" and "crisis at three," are developmental years, not calendar years. Developmental years are defined by neoformations, and of course role play is one of the neoformations of early childhood. From that point of view, Vygotsky's statement that no one has seen a child of under "three" role play is not only true but tautological.

formation of child speech has for the development of future speech. Although externally (...)[19] it is absolutely not like this speech.

Allow me to speak briefly in the time remaining about the crisis at seven. I have no time and no need to dwell in the same way on the crisis at seven or on its symptoms. I will merely explain the basic features, in as much as this crisis at seven is much more familiar to our pedology. I will attempt to demonstrate some of the theoretical attempts to understand approximately what is happening to a child at age seven.

If for a child who went through a 3-year crisis, his attitude to the environment has radically changed, a number of moments of one *perezhivanie* have been replaced by *perezhivanie* of a different character, then for me it means that that the environment for the child has become different, that the unity of personal and environmental moments has become completely new; that the unity of the moments of the personality and the environment has become entirely new; that is to say that completely new *perezhivanies* have arrived, that old *perezhivanies* are replaced by the new ones of the critical age—this is to say that one type of the unity of the environment and the personality in the development has changed completely in another one.

This should be understood as the dawn of a new epoch of development.

The crisis at seven was discovered and described before any of the others. We all know that intrinsic to the period of 7 years of age is a structure of being in which the child's self begins to emerge, as if mechanically and hurriedly pulled out of him, pointing to a number of changes of an organic character. This is called the age of change itself, an age of up-stretching (i.e., of growth spurts—Trans.). Indeed, the child does go through drastic changes, but these changes are more profound and more intricate in character than those changes which can be observed in the crisis at three. It would require a long time to list all of the symptoms of the crisis at seven, for they are extremely varied. Let me convey the usual ones, the general impression of this crisis that is usually conveyed by researchers and observers.

What is most outwardly essential, and immediate in what strikes the eye of the simple observer when a child commences the crisis at seven? This: that the child's behavior toward the people around him suddenly loses its naiveté and immediacy; it is somehow not so immediate, not so naive as before, and not so understandable in all of its manifestations as it was previously. I will explain with two examples, which in a concentrated form comprise the rupture of this crisis, which we often come up against in nearly all 7-year-olds, in particular those with difficult childhoods. Sometimes they say that he has begun to act out, to make faces, to walk differently than he used to, something ostentatious, ridiculous, artificial has appeared in the behavior of the child. This is one type.[20] It is often said that, with some inap-

[19] There is at least one word missing here: "the same," "identical," "similar," "analogous?" Vygotsky's argument is that child proto-speech (or, as Eliasberg calls it, "autonomous speech," sounding with meaning but without wording) has the same relationship to speech proper that the child's "antipode of will" (will that is torn form affect) has to the child's future volition.

[20] What are the two examples of which Vygotsky speaks? One possibility is that Vygotsky is referring to two different types of "acting out" that appear in cases of difficult childhood. In one case,

propriate fidgetiness, clowning, or fooling around, the child is playing the joker. The child before 7 years of age may make faces, but no one can say of that child what we now say of this one. Why does this unmotivated clowning strike the eye? When a child looks at himself in a samovar, where his image is distorted, or he grimaces into a mirror, he is merely amusing himself, but when the child walks into the room with a mannered gait, or when he speaks in a squeaky voice, this is unmotivated, and it catches our eye. No one is astonished if a child in early childhood talks nonsensically, and fools around playfully, but if the child who fools around encounters criticism rather than laughter, it must give the impression of being unmotivated. In this way, in these terms, the loss of immediacy and naiveté that inheres in the child of an earlier age is manifest. I think that externally it appears correct that there is really an essential, externally different trait in the 7-year-old child, consisting of the loss of the child's immediacy, the appearance of strangeness, ambiguity, sometimes fanciful, artificial, mannered, and even strained traits of behavior.

We might continue down this path so as to uncover the factual content behind this impression, to analyze the symptoms, as we did in relation to 3-year-olds, but for the sake of brevity, we will proceed otherwise, and attempt to come immediately to an explanation, assuming this behavior of the 7-year-old child as well known and easily recalled.

Do your best to keep track of what is said and to check it against those experiences which are available with respect to these children.

The most essential features of this crisis at seven consist in what might be called the differentiation of inner and outer faces of the child's personality. What underlies the impression of naiveté and spontaneity in the child's behavior before the crisis? Naivety and spontaneity mean that the child outside is the same as inside; that what is inside and what is shared [what appears outside—GSK][21] are little differentiated from each other. One unfolds smoothly and crosses over into the other, and we read it as an immediate expression of the other. What acts can be called spontaneous ones? In us, adult persons, childish spontaneity and naiveté are very rare, and they produce a comic impression. For example, the comic actor Charlie Chaplin uses as one of the conditions of his comedy that in playing a serious person he suddenly starts to act with unusual spontaneity and naiveté.

---

something that is artificial, pretentious and absurd appears in the child (e.g., a child who begins to write his memoirs at the age of seven!). In other words, the child acts a role which is far above his age. In another case, something that is puerile, clownish, and silly appears in the child (e.g., a child who uses baby-talk or even proto-speech). In other words, the child acts a role which is far beneath his age. The second possibility is that there originally was a "second type" of behavior manifest in the crisis at seven in difficult children, but either Vygotsky or the stenographer left it out.

[21] Korotaeva points out that manuscript has "делает вообще" or "shared," "made general" or "communicated to others" instead of "manifested externally." Of course, "made general" or "communicated to others" is also possible here; in either case, the meaning is clear: prior to the crisis, there is a direct correspondence between the outer self that behaves and the inner self that thinks. But after the crisis the child will never be so simple and direct again—like Chaplin after the rise of Hitler and the invention of talkies (when he made "The Great Dictator" and "Monsieur Verdoux," films which are not at all based on the directness and naivete that Vygotsky discusses here).

What does this loss of immediacy imply? It implies a very simple moment, namely the introduction of a moment of intellect into our acts. Between *perezhivanie* and the immediate act this intellectual moment becomes wedged, and we will now see in what this consists of. What makes up the precise opposite of the naive and immediate action, such as is proper to the child? The deliberate and conscious act. This does not mean that the crisis at seven is a transition from the immediate, naive, undifferentiated *perezhivanie* to this extreme pole, but there does really appear in each of his *perezhivanies* some manifestation of this intellectual moment which can now be found. In what does it consist of? This is one of the most complex problems of contemporary psychology of the personality and contemporary psychopathology which in all probability cannot be perfectly elucidated, but which we may try to explain with an example—a problem which could be called that sense of *perezhivanie.* We will use an analogy with external perception which will be clearer. For a moment we will set aside what we are saying and consider instead external perception. You know that the essential difference of human perception lies in the fact that our perception is made up of a meaningful perception of objects, a perception of complex impressions of which we become consciously aware alongside their external impressions. I see it directly: it's a watch. To understand the features of human perception, it is necessary to compare this with that of patients with neurological or brain diseases in which this capacity has been lost. With such a patient if we show this object, he will be astonished; he sees it, but he does not know what it is, but when you start to wind the watch or put it to your ear to listen, or look at it to see what time it is, he will then say that this must be a watch. He then realizes that which he saw—it is a watch. In you and in me, one act of consciousness contains both that we see something and that what we see is a watch. An analysis of what this means is very complex, it shows that it always means the fact that our perception is not an independent part of the process of visual thinking.

Our perception is, as it were, legalized.[22] The process of visual thinking is realized in us in unity with its semantic designation of things. When I say that this thing is a clock, or when I see that this is a clock, and then I see on the tower something which is absolutely dissimilar, this means that I perceive each given thing as a representative of a class of things, that is, I generalize it. Speaking briefly, in every perception we carry out generalization. To say that our perception is semantic perception is to say that in every perception, our perception is a generalized perception.

What does this mean? It seems to me we may understand it thus if I looked at this room without generalizing, that is, the way an agnostic[23] looks or how an animal

[22] Vygotsky says that adult perceptions are легализировано, which means "legalized," "legitimated," or "made statutory," in much the same way that legal definitions stipulate how the terms of laws can and cannot be interpreted. Perhaps there is a parallel with the way "sense-value" is stabilized as "meaning-value" by definitions in dictionaries.

[23] The transcript says агностик and not "agnosic," but it seems clear that Vygotsky is speaking of agnosia and not agnosticism. Agnosia is the inability to make sense of the visual field; it is described in detail by Oliver Sacks in his book (later made into an opera) *The Man Who Mistook His Wife for a Hat* (Sacks, 1985).

looks, for me the impression of things would come into such a relation with each other as in my visual field. But since I generalize them, this means that I perceive a part not only in the structure of those things that lie next to the clock, but also in the structure of what is the clock, in the structure of the generalization in which I see it.

We can compare the development of semantic perception in humans to ways of looking at a chessboard: the way of a child who does not know how to play chess and that of a child who has begun to learn. A child who cannot play may play with the chess figures, he would determine the chess moves structurally, he would collect black colors, etc.[24]

The child who has learned to play will act otherwise. For the first child a black horse and a white pawn are not linked to each other, but the child who knows the knight's moves knows that the enemy is threatening the advance of his pawn. For him there is a unity. We can say that the child playing at chess sees the board differently from a child who cannot play.

In the same way, a good player differs from a poor one in that he sees differently. If an essential feature of perception consists in structural perception, that is, in the circumstance that perception is not the aggregation of individual atoms but presents in itself a different way of construing that defines different parts, then you understand that depending on the co-relations that I see in a chess board, I see it differently. Something similar to what we have here goes on in development of the perception of the child.

All perceptible reality for us is precisely a reality which we perceive just as the chess player perceives the chessboard. Not only do we perceive the proximity of objects or their mean distribution, but we also perceive their sense-making links and their inter-relationships. This is all I have to say so far about the semantic side of perception.

I think you will agree if I say that what I name in speech is not simply the meanings of objects. A child very often in his speech has to name not only the meaning of the objects, but his actions, other people's actions, his internal state. I want to eat; I want to sleep; I am cold. Speech as a means of communication leads to what we have to name, connecting with words, our internal state, but to connect with words never means to form a simple associative connection, but always means to generalize. Each word, after all, does not mean one unique thing. If I now say that I am now cold, and then 1 day I say that it is cold, this means a singular generalized cold sensation, alongside each singular impression. In this way there appears the *perezhivanie* of an internal process absorbing all of the sense of things.

---

[24]Vygotsky says движение фигурок будет определять структурно, which means "the movement of the figures would be determined structurally." But since the child doesn't know how to play chess, it is clear that "structurally" doesn't refer to relationships between friendly and enemy pieces on the board structured spatially or to moves such as openings, gambits and countergambits that are structured in time. So what does Vygotsky mean here? One possibility is a figure-ground structure: Vygotsky means the child moves the black pieces on black squares and the white pieces on white ones. Another possibility is that the shape of the piece suggests to the child a way of moving them, for example, a horse will gallop, a king will walk, and a castle cannot move at all. In any case, the child is not "playing chess" but rather "playing with chess figures."

In the infant there is no sense-making perception. He perceives the room not as separable chairs, a separable table; he perceives everything as a non-separable whole [in contrast to the adult—GSK], who examines figures which stand out against this background. So how does a child in early childhood perceive his own *perezhivanie*? The toddler is happy, angry, sad, but does not know of being happy, that is, at the moment when he is happy he does not know, just as the infant when he is hungry does not know he is hungry. There is a great difference between being hungry and knowing that it is me who hungers. The child in the age of early childhood is not consciously aware of his own *perezhivanies*. And at the age of seven, we begin to confront the emergence of a sense-structured *perezhivanie*, when the child begins to understand what it means to say that I am happy, that I am sad, that I am good, that I am bad, that is, in him there is a sense-making orientation toward his own *perezhivanie*. Just as a child of three discovered his own relationship with other people, so too the 7-year-old discovers the fact itself of his *perezhivanies*. Thanks to these three features that characterize the crisis at seven move to the forefront. First: thanks to the fact that *perezhivanies* obtain a sense, the sulking child understands that he is angry, thanks to this there arise in him those *perezhivanies*, those new relationships that were not possible prior to the emergence of semantic *perezhivanies*. As on the chessboard, where, with each chess move, there arises in me completely different links between figures, so too when they acquire a certain sense there arise in me there completely different links between *perezhivanies*. Consequently, the whole character of the *perezhivanie* of the child at this age is reconstructed just as the game is reconstructed when the child sees a chessboard when he has learned to play chess.

Second, and more importantly, for the first time with this crisis there arises the generalization of *perezhivanie*, or affective generalization, the logic of emotions. There are children who are severely retarded who live experience failure at every step. Children play and the child attempts to join in, but he is rejected; he walks down the street and people make fun of him; in a word, at every step he is a failure. Is there in him a reaction to his rejection? Yes, but in each individual instance but in a minute you see him being completely satisfied with himself.

Thousands of individual failures—yes. But a general feeling of inferiority—no. He does not generalize from what has happened to him so many times. In the child of a mature age there arises a generalization of feelings, that is, it has happened to me such a situation, a second time, and a third time; in me there arises an affective formation, a generalization, the character of which also relates to each individual *perezhivanie*, but affect, as we know, relates to singular perceptions or recollections. For example, I ask you, has the child of the age of early childhood or preschool detected that he talks differently? He has detected this, but in him there is as yet no actual self-respect, no self-love. The degrees of our demands on ourselves and our success in our position arise precisely in connection with this crisis. What is pride? The child in the age of early childhood loves himself, but pride as a generalized attitude to his own self which remains securely the same in different situations, self-esteem as such, as a certain generalized attitude to others and as an understanding of their value does not yet exist in a child of this age, Consequently, there arises a series of very complex formations which lead to this: starting from school age, the harsh difficulty of rapid and radical forms of change, different in principle from the other difficulties which are encountered in the years of preschool.

It remains for me to show what makes all this a crisis—the neoformations. I tried to explain what the neoformations that remain are: self-respect and self-esteem will stay, while the neoformations of the crisis will prove transient.[25] All that I have said, all of this which emerges on the basis of this and in the crisis at seven, is thanks to these: there emerges a differentiation between the inner and outer facets of the personality, there arises the first sense-making *perezhivanie*, and that, thanks to this, there emerges an acute struggle of *perezhivanies*. Inner struggles first become possible at this age. A child who does not know which candy to take, bigger ones or sweeter ones, is a child in a state of internal struggle, he hesitates. Inner struggles—contradictions of *perezhivanie* and choices between *perezhivanies*—are now made possible here. These are typical forms of difficult enculturation which we can encounter in the preschool age.

Conflicts or insoluble contradictions, contradictory *perezhivanies*, when the child develops, when two *perezhivanies* exist at the same time but the contradictions are understood as contradictions—here we are faced precisely with the birth of some new moment of the child's development, which is in itself a transitional moment, which for this reason gives the impression that every 7-year-old child (…).

But in fact where there exists the possibility of this inner bifurcation of *perezhivanie,* there exists the possibility of internal struggle of *perezhivanie*; there for the first time the child understands his own *perezhivanie*; there emerges an inner relationship in the child. There a transformation of these *perezhivanies* takes place. Without this transformation, school age would be impossible because, we repeat again, to say that the crisis at seven changes preschool *perezhivanie* into school age *perezhivanies* means that the environmental and personality moments which developed in preschool years have been destroyed, and have been changed into a new unity of environmental and personality moments, which makes possible the

[25] On the one hand, Vygotsky clearly says that self-esteem and self-respect are neoformations of the crisis at seven. On the other hand, Vygotsky says just as clearly that critical neoformations are transient and only persist as a dependent part of stable neoformation in the subsequent age period (i.e., in school age). This is clearly a contradiction.

But analogy with other crises may show that it is a real, dialectical contradiction and not a logical one. At birth, the neoformation is independent mental life, chiefly in the midbrain. This does not disappear in infancy, but it does hand most of its functions "upward" to the myelinating cerebral cortex. Similarly, at one, the neoformation is autonomous speech; that is, baby babble. This too does not disappear, but it does hand on its independent functioning to speech proper, persisting only dependently, as prosody (intonation and stress which are dependent on articulation in adult speech). At three, the neoformation is an opposition of will to affect. This persists, but only in a stable form dependent on imaginary play, not in the inherently unstable form of opposing "want" to "like." So when Vygotsky says that the "wedge" between inner and outer personalities that is the neoformation of the seven-year crisis (that is, the child's "acting out" and "acting up") persists, he means that it persists as a dependent part of the school child's self-love and self-esteem, not as narcissism and semi-autistic self-absorption.

developmental stage of the age of schooling, that the child's relationship to the environment has changed. This means that the environment has changed, which means that the course of development of the child has entered a new epoch.

References

Выготский Л.С. (2001). *Лекции по педологии*. Ижевск: Издательский дом "Удмуртский университет"

Hegel, G.W.F. (1830/1975). *Hegel's logic*. (W. Wallace Trans.) Oxford: Clarendon.

Sacks, O. (1985). *The man who mistook his wife for a hat*. Duckworth.

Vygotskij, L.S. (2018). *La science du développement de l'enfant: Text pédologiques (1930–1934)*. Traduits par I. Léopoldoff-Martin. Collection Exploration: Peter Lang.

Vygotsky, L. S. (1934/1994). Fascism in psychoneurology. In R. van der Veer & J. Valsiner (Eds.), *The Vygotsky reader* (pp. 327–338). Blackwell.

Vygotsky, L. S. (1997a). *The collected works of L. S. Vygotsky* (Vol. 3). Plenum Press.

Vygotsky, L. S. (1997b). *The collected works of L.S. Vygotsky* (Vol. 4). Plenum Press.

Vygotsky, L. S. (1998). *The collected works of L. S. Vygotsky* (Vol. 5). Plenum Press.

Vygotsky, L. S. (2020). *L.S. Vygotsky pedological works, volume 1: Foundations of pedology*. Springer.

Chapter 11
The Crisis at Seven Years

Outline of Chapter 11: The Crisis at Seven Years

This is material from the Russian *Collected Works*, Volume 4. It is fragmentary, as the reader will see in (at least) three ways. First, it contains a fragment (about a third) of Chap. 10 and so appears redundant in many places. Second, it omits any clear statement of the social situation of development and the lines of development laid out in Chap. 2 of the book. Third, we seem to have skipped an entire period: preschool.

Preschool was a stable period, and not a crisis, so the neoformations, which include make-believe and rule-based games, do not disappear. The child masters the ideal through imagination, obtains the unobtainable through creativity, and subordinates action to intention through meaningful play. But the social situation of development that obtained in preschool is now gone. Vygotsky says that the central neoformation of the crisis at seven is the insertion of a certain wedge, an intellectualistic and self-conscious moment, into the relationship of the child to his or her social environment—or rather, into the inner representation of that relationship.

This intellectualistic moment is not long-lasting; it doesn't represent a stable sense of self, but rather, like the "antipode of will" Vygotsky gave as the central neoformation of the crisis at three, it is a kind of antipode of the self, one which allows the child to internalize experiences alongside a representation of the experiencer, but which doesn't allow the child to experience that experiencer as a coherent and credible part of the experience. Woolley and Ghosseiny (2013) speak of both naïve belief and naïve skepticism at this age; a child may believe, on the one hand, that talking animals actually exist although we cannot quite understand what they say, and on the other, that nature documentaries are just another example of "fake news" (Song & Kellogg, 2020).

The material in this chapter is translated from the 1984 Russian edition of Vygotsky's *Collected Works*.

L. S. Vygotsky, *L.S. Vygotsky's Pedological Works. Volume 2.*, Perspectives in Cultural-Historical Research 10, https://doi.org/10.1007/978-981-16-1907-6_11

In a short first section, Vygotsky describes the features of the crisis as a general syndrome. Vygotsky then offers a comparison between semanticized *perezhivanie* and semanticized perception. In the third section, Vygotsky outlines a methodological argument against elementalism in pedology and in favor of the holistic approach. First, he argues against studying the environment only, criticizing the use of "absolute indicators" based in the unchanging family environment. Then, Vygotsky makes the case against bourgeois researchers who study biological "inner changes" of the child only. Vygotsky argues that the environment must somehow be seen as represented on the inside of the child. But how? Perhaps it is no accident that each time he comes to this question, he tells the story of how the child learning speech utterly transforms the relationship with the environment even though neither his socioeconomic status nor his endocrine system has changed.

I. **General Features of the Crisis.** Vygotsky identifies age seven as a crisis, and notes physical changes, such as "stretching out" or "shooting up" in stature, and the eruption of incisors and canine teeth (which Blonsky and other pedologists considered so important). But Vygotsky is mainly concerned with changes in doing, saying, and thinking, and he notes two types of features. It is not clear exactly what the two features are. Perhaps Vygotsky means:

   1. Behavioral features, for example, a shifty walk or a squeaky voice—like playing a role without any actual play going on, and without any encouragement from those around.
   2. Psychological features, that is, a loss of child-like directness and immediacy.
      But perhaps Vygotsky means:
   3. Acting OLDER than his age (mannered, ostentatious, pretentious behavior).
   4. Acting YOUNGER than his age (silly, buffoonish, clown-like behavior).
      Where in preschool, we can tie the child's "fooling around" to affordances in the environment (e.g., making faces in the mirror), and the child's "fooling around" at seven seems to occur independently of the environment and even when the child is criticized for it. Vygotsky says that just as the crisis at three was characterized by a differentiation of will and affect in attitude toward the environment, the crisis at seven is characterized by a differentiation in attitude toward the personality, between an outer persona and an inner self. Vygotsky is not speaking of a "pendulum swing," from innocence to calculation: what he says is that each moment of perezhivanie now includes an intellectualized moment. This idea of using moments of *perezhivanie* to analyze the age instead of trying to characterize it as a general syndrome is one he will return to.

II. **Semanticized *Perezhivanie* and Semanticized Perception: An Analogy**. We can think of semanticized *perezhivanie* as a kind of "ingrowing" or "introvolution" of semanticized perception—thanks to the development of memory in preschool, the value of the feeling of what happens to you as it happens to you can now become the value of the thought about what happened to you after it happened. Vygotsky compares the shift from nonsemantic to semantic *perezhivanie* with the shift that occurs when a child learns to play chess. *Perezhivanies* become related through a self. For example, the child's experiences of anger are recognized and remembered as the child's own anger rather than simply a feature of this or that annoying situation. The self becomes generalized through *perezhivanies*. For example, a child who experiences repeated frustration begins to develop feelings of inferiority. On the one hand, Vygotsky contrasts this proto-self with selfhood of the preschooler, which is always situational and cannot be carried from one situation to another. On the other, he contrasts the proto-self with the more durable forms of self-love and self-respect that come with school age. The child's proto-self is something like role play without a role to play, but it is also something like reactive teaching without a teacher to teach.

III. **Against Environmentalism and Innatism: For Analysis into *Perezhivanies*.** Vygotsky now demands a mode of analysis which includes both the child and the environment in every unit. He says that this is already recognized in principle, but it isn't carried out in practice. In practice what happens is that child and environment are taken apart and then "grafted" together. There are two ways of doing this:

1. The Russian way of projecting the environment onto the child: Vygotsky argues that this is the result of "absolute indicators" of social economic status—a vulgar "Marxism" applied to the child. He points out that socioeconomic setting of childhood may be stable throughout the crisis, but the child's relationship with it radically changes nevertheless (as when the child learns speech in the crisis at age one). Vygotsky proposes instead that we consider "relational" indicators, such as *perezhivanie*.
2. The Western way of projecting biological changes onto the child. For example, some bourgeois investigators (Vygotsky appears to have the Freudians in mind) project sexual maturation onto the crisis at thirteen. Others take a "middle" position locating the actual changes internally but arguing that they are expressed differently according to the environment.

Vygotsky synthesizes: The crisis at seven is indeed internal, and crises in general are internal phenomena because they do not appear to have any direct relation to changes in the environment. But our conception of the internal must be expanded to include both an internal representation of the environment and a co-generalized representation of inner life. At age seven, perezhivanie is not simply experienced, and it is experienced as life, the life of a proto-self.

Chapter 11: The Crisis at Seven Years

School age, like all the ages, opens with a turning point, or a critical period, described in the literature even before others were described as the crisis at seven years of age. For a long time, it was noticed that a child in the transition from preschool to school age changes very drastically and becomes more difficult than before with respect to enculturation. This is a kind of transitional stage: already not a preschooler but not yet a school child.

In recent times, a number of studies have dealt with this age. The results of the studies may be schematically expressed thus: the child of seven is above all distinguished by the loss of childish immediacy. The proximal reason for childish immediacy was an inadequate differentiation between inner and outer life. The *perezhivanies* of the child, his wishes and desires, behavior, and activity, usually present in the preschooler are still an inadequately differentiated whole. In us all this is highly differentiated, and for this reason, the behavior of an adult human does not appear so immediate and naïve as the behavior of a child.

When a preschooler enters the crisis, what catches the eye of even the most inexperienced observer is that the child suddenly loses naiveté and immediacy; in behavior, in relations with the surroundings, he becomes not as intelligible as he was previously.

Everybody knows that a seven-year-old child suddenly stretches upward in stature, and this indicates a series of changes in the organism. This age is known as the age of changing teeth and the age of upstretching. The child really does change dramatically, with deeper and more complex changes than those observed during the crisis of age three. It would take a long time to enumerate all of the symptoms reported in this crisis, so diverse are they in form. It should suffice merely to point out the general impression that researchers and observers usually have of them. Let me explain two features which are often encountered in nearly all seven-year-olds, especially those with difficult childhoods who are experiencing the crisis in a severe form. The child may begin to act pretentiously, to behave capriciously, and prance with a caper where he merely walked before. In his behavior, there may appear something ostentatious, awkward, or artificial; something silly, buffoonish, or clown-like: the child makes a fool of himself. Of course, the child under seven can also fool around, but nobody can say of him that which I have just said. Why is such unmotivated tomfoolery so striking to the eye? When a child looks into the samovar where a distorted form is reflected, or when he grimaces before the mirror, he is simply having fun. But when the child walks into a room with a jaunty strut, or talks like a duck—this is not motivated, and it strikes the eye. No one will be surprised if a child of preschool age talks nonsense, jokes, and plays around, but if the child makes a fool of himself where this earns condemnation rather than laughter, then it gives the impression of unmotivated behavior.

These features speak to a loss of the immediacy and naiveté that were inherent in the preschooler. I think that this impression is correct, that the external feature of the seven-year-old child consists in the loss of child immediacy, the appearance of quirks that are not entirely clear, and some fanciful, artificial, mannered, and exaggerated behavior.

The most substantial feature of the crisis at seven might be called the differentiation of the inner and the outer aspects of the child's personality.

What lies hiding behind this impression of naiveté and of immediacy in the behavior of the child before the crisis? Naiveté and immediacy imply that the child appears externally just as he is internally. The one smoothly flows into the other; we may read one as a revelation of the second. What actions may be called immediate ones? In adults, there is little child naiveté and immediacy, and their presence in adults produces a comical impression. For example, the comic actor C. Chaplin is different in that, playing serious people, he begins to behave with an unusually childish naivete and spontaneity. In this lies the main premise of his comedy.

The loss of immediacy implies the introduction into our actions of an intellectual moment, which becomes wedged in between the *perezhivanie* and the unmediated act, which constitutes a complete antithesis to the naïve and immediate action proper to the child. This does not mean that the crisis at seven leads from direct, naïve undifferentiated *perezhivanie* to the opposite extreme, but rather that in each *perezhivanie*, and in every manifestation of it, there appears some intellectual moment.

One of the most complex problems of the contemporary psychology of and psychopathology of the personality, which I shall try to explain with an example—this is the problem which could be called that of sense-making *perezhivanie*.

We shall try to approach this problem by analogy with the problem of external perception. Then it will be clear. The essential distinction of human perception is its sense-making and its object-related character. We are aware of whole complexes of perceptual impressions at one and the same time, alongside external impressions. Right away, for example, I see that this is a watch. To understand the features of human perception, we need to compare it with the perception of a patient who as the result of a neurological or cerebral disorder loses this capacity. If we show such a patient a watch, he does not recognize it. He sees the watch, but he doesn't know what it is. When you wind up the watch for the patient or you hold it to your ear and listen to whether it is running or not, or take a look at it in order to know what time it is, he says that it might be a watch; he guesses that what he sees is a watch. But with us, with you, and with me, what I see and the fact that it is a watch makes up one unitary act of consciousness.

In this way, perception does not occur apart from visual thinking. The process of visual illustrative thinking is done in unity with a sense-making recognition of things. When I say that this thing is a clock,[1] and then when I see on a tower something that is at first glance nothing like it and call that a clock as well—this means that I perceive each thing as representative of a definite class of things, that is, I generalize.

To put it succinctly, with every perception, we carry out a generalization. Saying that our perception is sense-making perception—this means saying that all our perceptions are generalized perceptions.[2] We might explain it thus: if I look at the room

[1] The Russian word часы used by Vygotsky means both a watch and a clock—so the example of semantic generalization used in this paragraph is an extension of the pathological example of inability to name an object which was used in the previous paragraph.

[2] Why does Vygotsky say that all our perceptions are generalized perceptions? If that were true, how could people recognize individual voices? The answer is that we recognize individual voices by generalizing the voice we hear to all the other occasions we have heard that voice. As Vygotsky makes clear, this ability is not universal—there are agnosics, for example, who are unable to recognize the voices of their spouses or their children precisely because they cannot generalize in this

without generalizing, that is, precisely as an agnosic or an animal sees it, the impressions are of things that enter into relationships with one another just as they are located in the optical field. But as I generalize them, I perceive the clock not only in the structure of those objects that are lying nearby it but also in the structure of its being a clock, in the structure of that generalization in which I see it.

The development of human sense-making perception may be compared to the ways in which a child who cannot play and a child who can play look at a chessboard. The child who cannot play may pick out the chess pieces, by color and so on, but the movement of the pieces cannot be structurally determined. The child who has begun to play chess will proceed otherwise. For the first child, the black horse and the white pawn are not linked together, but the second, who knows the moves of the horse, knows that the enemy knight threatens his pawn. For him, the horse and pawn are a unity. In just this way, a good player differs from a poor one—in the way they see the chessboard.

The essential feature of perception is its structuredness; that is, perception is not simply made up of individual atoms but presents an image within which there are different parts. Depending on the disposition of pieces on a chessboard, I will see them differently.

We perceive the reality around us as a chess player perceives a chess board; we perceive not only the adjacencies of objects and their continuities, but the whole reality of their links and relations. In speech, there exists not only the naming but also the meaning of objects. The child very early on happens to express not only the meaning of objects but also of the actions of themselves and of others, and of their internal states ("I want to sleep"; "I want to eat"; "I am cold"). Speech as a means of communication accounts for the naming of our internal states and their linking by means of words. Linking with words never means formation of a simple associative link but always implies a generalization. Each word does not denote a single thing. If you say that now you are cold and the next day you say the same thing, this implies that each singular sensation of cold is already generalized. In this way, there arises the generalization of internal processes.

In the infant, there is no sense-making perception: he perceives a room and does not perceive distinct chairs, tables, etc.; he will perceive it as an indiscriminate whole, differently from the adult who discerns figures set out against a field. How does a young child perceive his own experiences? He is joyful or displeased, but he doesn't know that he is happy, even as an infant who is hungry doesn't know that he is hungry. There is a big difference between the sensation of hunger and knowing that it is I who hungers. The child in early childhood does not know his own *perezhivanie*.

At seven years of age, we find such structures of *perezhivanie* beginning to emerge as when a child begins to understand "I am happy," "I am displeased," "I am good," "I am bad," that is, there emerges in him a sense-making orientation to his

---

way. However, it is true enough to say that all of our perceptions are generalized perceptions to one degree or another.

own *perezhivanie*. Just as a three-year-old discovers his own relationship with other people, so too the seven-year-old discovers the fact of his own *perezhivanie*. Thanks to this, a number of the features that characterize the crisis at seven appear.

1. *Perezhivanies* acquire sense (an angry child understands that he is angry), and thanks to this, in the child, a new relation to the self emerges that was impossible before the generalization of *perezhivanies*. As on a chessboard where with every move, there emerge completely new links between pieces, so here as well there emerge completely new links between *perezhivanies* where they acquire certain meanings. Consequently, the whole character of *perezhivanie* in the child of seven is reconstructed, as the chessboard is reconstructed when the child has learned to play chess.
2. By the crisis at age seven, for the first time, there is the generalization of *perezhivanies* or affective generalization and the logic of feelings. There are severely retarded children who at each step experience failure; normal children are playing, and the nonnormal child attempts to join in, but they reject him, he goes down the street and people laugh at him. In a word, at each step, he is defeated. In each case, there is in him a reaction to his own inadequacy, but if you look a minute later—he is quite pleased with himself. Thousands of individual failures, but no generalized sense of inferiority, he does not generalize that which has happened so many times before. In the child of school age, there emerge generalizations of sensations, that is, if with him there has happened such a situation, in him there arises an affective formation, the character of which refers to a single experience or affect, as a concept refers to a single perception or recollection. For example, the child of preschool age has no genuine self-esteem or self-love. The level of our requests for ourselves, for our success, for our position arises precisely in connection with the crisis of seven years.

The child of preschool age loves himself, but self-love as a generalized relationship to one's self, which remains the same in different situations, self-respect as such, a generalized those around, understanding one's own value in a child of this age does not exist. Consequently, around seven years old, there emerges a number of complex formations which lead to this: difficulties in behavior change dramatically and radically, and they are fundamentally different from the difficulties of preschool age.

Such neoformations as self-love, self-respect remain, but symptoms of the crisis (mannerisms, making faces) are transient. In the crisis of seven years, due to the fact that a differentiation of the internal and the external emerges, that for the first time a sense-making *perezhivanie* emerges, an acute struggle of experiences emerges as well. The child who did not know which candies to choose—the more plentiful or the sweeter ones—did not find himself in a state of internal struggle, even though he may have hesitated. Inner struggles (contradictions between *perezhivanies* and selections from his own *perezhivanies)* become possible only now.

There are typical forms of difficult behavior which in preschool are not yet encountered. Among these are conflicts, contradictory *perezhivanies*, and unresolvable contradictions. In truth, where this inner bifurcation of *perezhivanies* becomes possible, where there is for the first time the child's understanding of his own *perezhivanies*, and where there arises an internal attitude, there happens such a change in *perezhivanie* without which school age would be impossible. To say that in the crisis at seven, preschool *perezhivanie* is changed into that of school age—this means to say that there emerges a new unity of the environment and personality moments which yields the possibility of a new stage of development—school age. For the child, the relationship with the environment has been transformed, which means that the environment itself has changed, and therefore the course of the child's development has changed, and a new epoch of development has arrived.

It is necessary to introduce into science a concept which is little used in the study of the social development of the child: we do not study the inner attitude of the child to the people in his surroundings, and we do not consider him as an active participant in the social situation. In words, we recognize that it is necessary to study personality and environment in the child as a unity. But we cannot imagine the business so that on one side there is the influence of the personality and on the other—the environmental influences, so that they act upon one another in the manner of external forces. Yet in practice very often we do just that: wishing to study a unity, we first break it up, and then try to link one thing with another.

And in the study of difficult childhood, we cannot get past such this way of stating the question: Which plays the major role, the constitution or the environmental conditions, general psychopathological conditions of a genetic character or conditions of the external environment of development? This rests on two basic problems which require explication in terms of the inner attitude of the child to the environment during the crisis period.

The first major error in the practical and theoretical study of the environment is this: we are studying the environment with absolute indicators. Whoever practically undertakes the study of difficult cases knows this very well. You bring up the social-facilities inspection[3] of the child's environment, where the cubic housing capacity appears, whether or not the child has his own bed, how many times he goes to the baths, when he changes his clothes, whether the family reads the newspapers, and what kind of education the mother and father had. The survey is always the same, regardless of the child and of the child's age. We study certain absolute indicators of the environment as fixed settings, believing that with these indicators we may know their role in the development of the child. Many Soviet researchers have set up the absolute study of the environment as a principle. In the book edited by A. B. Zalkind, you will find the proposition that the social environment of the child in its basics remains largely unchanged throughout the course of his development. If we keep in view the absolute indicators of the environment, then to a certain degree this could be acceptable. But in fact, it is completely false from the point of view of both theory and practice. After all, the substantial distinction between the environment of the child and the environment of an animal consists in this: that a human environment is a social environment and the child is part of the living environment; the

[3] For a note on the source of these data, see Footnote 4 of Chap. 10.

environment is never external to the child. If the child is a social being and if his environment is a social environment, we may then draw the conclusion that the child himself is part of this social environment.

Consequently, the most substantial shift, which must be carried out in the study of the environment—a transition from absolute indicators to relative ones—is to study the environment of the child: first, it is necessary to study what it means for the child and what is the child's attitude to certain aspects of this environment. For example, the child of less than one does not speak. Once he speaks, the speech environment of those in the immediate environment remains unchanged. And the year before and the year after the absolute indicators of the culture of speech surrounding him is practically unchanged. But, I think, everyone will agree that from the minute when the child begins to understand the first words, when he begins to utter his first meaningful words, his attitudes to the moments of speech in the environment and the role of speech in relationship to the child are very much changed.

Each step in the progress of the child changes the influence of the environment upon him. From the minute a child steps from one age into another, the environment becomes completely different from the point of view of development. Consequently, we can say that our feelings about the environment should change in the most significant way in comparison to our usual practice hitherto. We need to study the environment not as such, not in its absolute indicators, but in relation to the child. The same environment in absolute indicators is completely different for the child at one year and three, seven, and twelve years. In the dynamic change of the environment, attitude comes into the foreground. But naturally, whenever we speak of this relationship, there emerges a second moment: this relation is never purely an external relationship between the child and the environment, each taken separately. One of the important methodological questions consists of the question of how in theory and in research to carry out actually the study of a unity.

We often go on speaking of the unity of the personality and the environment, of the unity of psychic and physiological development, and of the unity of speech and thinking. What does it really imply in theory and in research to approach the study of a unity and all of the properties which inhere in this unity as such? It means finding each time a guiding unit, that is, finding segments in which the properties of unity as such are combined. For example, when one wishes to study the relations of speech and thinking, artificially separating speech from thinking and thinking from speech, and then asking what does speech do for thinking and thinking do for speech—what is the point of treating them as if they are two different liquids which can be mixed together? If you want to know how a unity emerges, how it changes itself, how it influences the course of child development, it is important not to break up the unity into its constituent parts, because in so doing the essential properties which inhere in exactly this unity will be lost, for example, the unity in relation to speech and thinking. In recent times, an attempt has been made to elucidate such a unity—take, for example, meaning. Word meaning—this is part of a word, a speech formation, because a word without meaning is not a word. Since every word meaning is a generalization, it is a product of the intellectual activity of the child. In this way, the word meaning—the unit of speech and of thinking—proves irreducible.

We may identify a unit for the study of the personality and the environment. This unit in pathology and in psychology is known as *perezhivanie*. *Perezhivanie* is thus a simplest unit in relation to which we cannot say whether it presents in itself the influence of the environment upon the child or the features of the child himself; *perezhivanie* is a unit of the personality and the environment as it is presented in development. So in development the unity of environmental and personality moments is accomplished in a series of *perezhivanies* of the child. The *perezhivanie* must be understood as an inner attitude of the child as a person to this or to that moment of reality. Every *perezhivanie* is always a *perezhivanie* of something. There is no *perezhivanie* which is not a *perezhivanie* of something, just as there is no act of consciousness which is not an act of cognizing something or other. But every *perezhivanie* is also my *perezhivanie*. In the contemporary theory of *perezhivanie*, it is introduced as a unit of consciousness, that is, as such a unit where the basic properties of consciousness are given as such, whereas in attention and in thinking, there is no given connection of consciousness.[4] Attention does not constitute a unit of consciousness, but constitutes an element of consciousness, in which there is no series of other elements, and what is more, the unity of consciousness as such is lost, while the real dynamic unit of consciousness, that is, the completion from which consciousness is formed, would be a *perezhivanie*.

Perezhivanie has a biosocial orientation; it is that which lies between the personality and the environment, which means the attitude of the person to the environment showing what the given moment of the environment means for the person. From this point of view, *perezhivanie* defines how this or that moment of the environment influences the development of the child. This, at least in the study of difficult childhood, is confirmed at every step. Each analysis of difficult childhood shows that the essence does not lie in the situation itself, taken in its absolute indicators, but in how the child experiences this situation. In one and the same family, in the same family situation, we encounter in different children different changes in development, because one and the same situation is not experienced by different children in the same way.

In *perezhivanie*, consequently, there is given, on the one hand, the environment in its relationship to me, that is, how I experience this environment; on the other, it is affected by the properties of development of my personality. In my *perezhivanie*,

[4]Why does Vygotsky say that attention and thinking do not involve a given connection to consciousness? Surely my attention is, just like a *perezhivanie*, my own act of attending and also attending something in my environment; my thought is, just like a *perezhivanie*, my own act of thinking and also an intension—a thought of something in the environment. Yet it is possible, when we hear an explosion, to attend to something in an entirely involuntary way, and it is also possible, when we tie our shoes, to exercise practical thinking without any conscious act of will. *Perezhivanie*, on the other hand, requires not only the moment of experience but also the moment in which that experience comes home to consciousness and is deliberately and purposefully made meaning. It is this sense in which *perezhivanie*, but not attention or thinking, is an irreducible unit of consciousness: it is a small moment of consciousness in which the activities of consciousness such as attention and thinking are necessarily connected to consciousness as a whole.

there are effects of my own properties to the degree in which they have developed in the course of my development, participating at any definite minute here.

If some general formulaic proposition were to be given, it would be true to say that the environment defines the development of the child through the *perezhivanie* of the environment. The most essential, consequently, consists of the rejection of absolute indicators of the environment; the child is part of the social situation, and the relation of the child to the environment and the environment to the child is given through the *perezhivanie* and the activity of the child himself; the forces of the environment acquire a guiding power due to the perezhivanie of the child. This requires a profound inner analysis of the *perezhivanie* of the child, that is, the study of the environment which is transferred to a large degree inside the child himself, and not confined to the study of the fixed external settings of his life.

The analysis becomes very intricate, and we encounter great theoretical difficulty here. But nevertheless, in relation to different problems of the development of character, critical ages, difficult childhood, and some separate moments linked to the analysis of *perezhivanie* become somewhat clarified and salient.

A meticulous study of the critical age demonstrates that in them there occurs a basic alteration in the *perezhivanie* of the child. The crisis seems, above all, to be a turning point, which is expressed in the fact that the child passes from one way of *perezhivanie* of the environment to another. The environment as such does not change for the child of three. The parents continue to earn as much as before, for each mouth to feed there is the same budgeted minimum and maximum as before, the same number of newspapers subscribed to, the same living space, and the parents have not changed in their relationship to the child. The observers who are investigating the crisis will say that without any clear reasons the child who has behaved so well, who was obedient and affectionate, has suddenly become capricious, angry, and stubborn.

The internal character of the crises has been underlined by all bourgeois investigators. The great majority explain the internal character of the crisis by biological causes. One of the most prevalent theories to explain the crisis of 13 years is that a parallel is drawn between sexual maturation and the crisis and the child's internally embedded biological maturation is seen as being at the basis of latter.

Other authors, such as A. Busemann,[5] who wish to underline the significance of the social environment, correctly point out that the crisis has a completely different course depending on the environment in which it unfolds. But the point of view of Busemann is not in principle different from the point of view of that considers the crisis as a phenomenon brought about by purely exogenous causes. The crisis, as well as all features inherent to the child, Busemann takes to be not biological features but manifestations of changes in different environments. From this arises the thought that the bourgeois studies are wholly wrong, or at least wrong in some parts. Let us begin with the factual side. It seems to me that bourgeois researchers have taken a very restricted circle of observations, that is, the child is always observed by

[5] For a biographical footnote on Adolf Busemann, see Footnote 10 in Chap. 10.

them in conditions of a bourgeois family with a definite type of enculturation. The facts show that in other conditions of enculturation, the crisis unfolds otherwise. In children moving from a nursery[6] to kindergarten, the crisis flows differently than in children entering kindergarten from families. However, the crisis always takes place in the normal course of child development; three years and seven year ages are always turning points in development; there will always be such a state of things when the inner course of child development has completed a certain cycle, and the progression to the subsequent cycle will be a definite turning point. One age must somehow be reconstructed for a new stage of development to begin.

It is true that the most general, naïve impression which observers carry away is that the child, rather suddenly, has somehow changed beyond all recognition. For 3–6 months, he is no longer what he was before; the crisis unfolds as a process little understood by those around since it is not linked to changes which are taking place around the child. To speak plainly, the crisis appears as a chain of inner changes in the child alongside relatively insignificant external changes. For example, when the child goes to school, there are changes throughout the age of schooling from year to year, and this does not surprise, because the whole situation in which the child is growing has changed, the whole setting of his development. When a child moves from the nursery to the kindergarten, we are not surprised that the preschooler has changed, here are changes in the child linked to changes which occurred in the conditions of his development. But the essence of every crisis is that internal changes take place in a much larger measure than the changes in the external setting, and therefore this always gives the impression of an inner crisis.

It is my impression that the crises really are internal in their source; they do consist in changes of an internal character. Here, there is no exact correspondence between internal and external changes. The child enters a crisis. What, on the outside, has changed so drastically? Nothing at all. So why has the child so drastically changed in such a short time?

Our thought is that what we need to object to is not the bourgeois theories of the critical age, not the fact that the crisis consists of a process that is very profoundly woven into the course of the child's development; rather we need to oppose their understanding of the internal nature of this developmental process. If all internal development is understood as biological, then in the end this is change in the glands

---

[6]Vygotsky is referring to the state-run nurseries. These were multifunctional. On one hand, they were set up for orphans and abandoned children in the wake of the Russian civil war: But there were also state-run nurseries for children of 1–2 years for children from families. Some families had to bring children there because they had jobs and nobody could take care about children during the day, but in other families, they did not bring children to the nurseries because there were someone who can take care about children (e.g., a grandparent). Here, Vygotsky compares children from families who did and did not attend nursery schools before the kindergarten.

Note that kindergartens in Russia and the Soviet Union were for older children from 3 to 6 years. There were some levels of groups: младшая группа—junior group (3-year-old children), средняя группа—middle group (4 years), старшая группа—senior group (5 years), and подготовительная (к школе) группа—preparatory to the school group (6 years). Only the last is equivalent to kindergarten in a Western European or American setting.

of internal secretion. I would not call the critical ages the ages of inner development in this sense. However, I do think that inner development always occurs in such a way that we have a unity of personality and environmental moments, that is, each new step in the development of the child is immediately determined by the preceding step and by all that has occurred and emerged in development during the preceding stages. True, this means understanding development as a process where every subsequent change is linked to the preceding and to the extant ones, in which the former features of personality traits are now manifest and now active. If we correctly understand the nature of the inner process of development, there will be no theoretical objection to the understanding of the crisis as an inner crisis.

I imagine that for every *perezhivanie*, there exists a real, dynamic effect of the environment in relation to the child. From this point of view, the essence of each crisis is the reconstruction of inner *perezhivanie*, the restructuring of which is rooted in the change of the main moment that determine the child's relationship to the environment, precisely the changes in the child's needs, drives, and motives of child behavior. The growth and change in needs and drives presents the least conscious and least volitional portion of the personality, and in the transition from age to age in the child, there appear new drives and new motives; in other words, the engines of his activity are undergoing a reassessment of values. That which for the child was essential important now becomes relatively unimportant in the following stage.

The reconstruction of needs and drives and the reevaluation of values are the basic moment in the transition from age to age. This changes the environment, that is, the attitude of the child to the environment. Other interests commence in the child, other activities emerge in him, and the consciousness of the child is reconstructed, if by consciousness we understand the attitude of the child to the environment.

References

Song, S.-M., & Kellogg, D. (2020). The problem of articulate animals in Korean child conversation: A Hallidayan analysis, a Vygotskyan interpretation, and a Hasanian critique. *WORD, Journal of the International Linguistic Association, 66*(3), 149–165.

Woolley, J., & Ghossainy, M. E. (2013). Revisiting the fantasy–reality distinction: Children as naïve skeptics. *Child Development, 84*(5), 1496–1510.

Выготский, Л. С. (1984). *Собрание сочинений Т.4*. Педагогика.

Chapter 12
School Age

Outline of Chapter 12: School Age

This is the stenogram of a lecture given at the Leningrad Herzen Pedagogical Institute on the February 23, 1934, that is, less than four months before Vygotsky's death. At the time it was given, Vygotsky was also at work on the section of *Thinking and Speech* concerning school age, Chapter Six. The two texts are not simply contemporaneous; they have an inner link. Chapter Six of *Thinking and Speech* provides much of the empirical material that Vygotsky is reworking here: Piaget's sentence completion tasks, and the graduation memoranda (that is, the theses) on the school age learning of Russian grammar, literacy, arithmetic, social studies, and other classroom subjects written by his students at the institute. Here Vygotsky shows how this material and how the whole problem of thinking and speech fit in the overall pedological scheme he introduced in Chap. 2 of this book.

In the preceding three chapters (the crisis at three; the crisis at three and the crisis at seven; and the crisis at seven), students got a clear picture of how hard it is to fit Vygotsky's method into a class timetable. The next two chapters are an even more obvious example: Vygotsky does not, in this chapter, finish working through the factual material before the end of class. But it is nevertheless possible to read this chapter as a question: "What is the central line of development of school age and what is its culminating neoformation?" to which we may read Chap. 13 "Thinking in School Age" as the answer: "A central neoformation in school age is thinking; that is, the intellectualization of functions, but not the intellectualization of thinking itself, since this can only happen with concept formation in adolescence." Since the two lectures at the institute were presented close together, in that order—and since, as Jerome Bruner remarks (1987, p. 8), Vygotsky the lecturer is a master of suspense—this may well be how Vygotsky himself presented them in the lecture hall.

The material in this chapter is taken from the collection edited and published in 2001 by G.S. Korotaeva, who notes that it is the stenogram of a lecture given on 23 February 1934.

L. S. Vygotsky, *L.S. Vygotsky's Pedological Works. Volume 2.*, Perspectives in Cultural-Historical Research 10, https://doi.org/10.1007/978-981-16-1907-6_12

And this is how we will present these two chapters in these outlines. To pose the problem of the central line of development and its neoformation, Vygotsky once again offers us factual material to work through. In this chapter, that factual material comes from Piaget. In contrast to Piaget, Vygotsky paints a very positive picture of what the child brings to the social situation of development: which functions have become clearly differentiated, matured, and subject to the child's conscious awareness and free will, laying them out in the order they have developed: perception first, then attention, then memory. But when he introduces a study showing how development itself takes place—whether children remember perceptual images, or whether they attend better to structural relations, or whether they remember thinking—he arrives at the chief paradox: although thoughts are remembered better than any other material, thinking itself is neither consciously aware nor free willed.

I. **Factual Material: All of the Major Functions Can Be Thought About—Except Thinking.** Vygotsky tells the students that before working on practical but piecemeal problems of teaching (such as arithmetic, language teaching, science or social studies), they must replace the elemental introduction (e.g., Zalkind's pedology textbook, which has largely focused on environmental elements and on class consciousness) with a more holistic understanding of development. To demonstrate the central paradox of the school age, Vygotsky gives examples from Claparède and from Piaget: all of the major functions of childhood—perception, attention, memory—have become intellectualized and can be thought about. But the child still cannot think about thinking itself.
II. **An Unsuccessful Explanation: The Child Lacks Conscious Awareness and Thus Free Will**. Vygotsky now considers but firmly rejects the explanation that Claparède and Piaget give. Vygotsky notes that they begin by concentrating only on what is lacking in the child—lack of awareness and lack of self-control. The cause of awareness and free will is then an external one: awareness and free will arise as a result of many unsuccessful adaptations to the environment followed by a successful one (e.g., when you try to eat something that is too hot many times and eventually succeed by blowing on it). Vygotsky points out that Claparède and Piaget cannot explain:

   1. WHY awareness and free will arise: functions cannot simply appear just because they are required.
   2. HOW conscious awareness and free will are related: if they both arise from unsuccessful adaptation, they have only that external relationship, rather than mutually influencing and shaping each other.
   3. WHEN conscious awareness and free will arise: unsuccessful adaptations also occur in early childhood and even in infancy, and with the mentally retarded, but there is no resulting awareness or free will.
   4. WHAT emerges when conscious awareness and free will arise: Vygotsky says that the child is not "unconscious" (i.e., asleep) or "subconscious" (repressed); what really happens is that the child cannot make the act of thinking the object of thought, the same way that when you tie your shoes you don't usually make the act of tying itself into the object of thought

because you are just thinking of the outcome (i.e., the knot). So what emerges when conscious awareness and free will arise is that an act becomes the object of thought, and what fails to emerge in the school child is that the act of thinking becomes the object of thought. For conceptual thinking to emerge, thinking itself must be thought about.

Chapter 12: School Age

Today I would like to illuminate in broad terms the problem of intellectual, or, more broadly, psychological, development in the school age.

You have become familiar with the basics of different sectors of learning at school age, elucidated social-class development[1] at this age, and clarified the main type of learning and of development.

Before turning to the concrete study of separate segments of learning in children, say, how a child learns arithmetic or language or a system of knowledge in the area of natural sciences and how this mastery in the process has its own effect on the development of the child, it is necessary to explain to you in the most general terms the basic lines of intellectual and of psychological development of the child at school age.

For this, I imagine it is necessary to begin with some general moments that might characterize development at this age. How is it to be characterized? It seems to me that it first of all is to be characterized by its external, formal side: school age is preceded by several earlier ages. If the moment of departure of psychological development is some state of the child's psychological life which is distinguished by the nondifferentiation of different functions, of different types of psychological activity, or by complete nondifferentiation in the age of infancy, then school age has already left these other ages behind.

What has occurred in these ages, in regard to the psychological development of the child? What has occurred is precisely this: in each age, say, in early childhood, consciousness was developed in a definite way; in this age perception was placed in an exceptionally favorable condition: it is very well developed. At preschool age we have the same proposition with regard to memory.[2]

---

[1] In Chaps. 10 and 11, Vygotsky criticized the approach to the environment taken by Aaron Zalkind, who wrote the textbook being used on this course. In the textbook, the child's environment is defined by how big the child's house is, whether the child has his or her own bed, whether the parents are educated, and what newspapers they read. This is probably what Vygotsky means when he says that the students on the course have already studied "the development of social classes" at this age. It is probably true, however, that it is sometime in school age that preschoolers who are oblivious to the difference between the "popular students" and the poor ones, become more conscious of the big differences in socio-economic status between and even within families.

[2] See also *L.S. Vygotsky's Pedological Works Volume 1: Foundations of Pedology*, especially Lecture Five. But today we are well accustomed to the idea that children respond very differently to certain challenges—including biological ones, like Covid 19—than adults do. German research-

As a consequence, by school age the child has already done this, roughly speaking, at least twice, but as a matter of fact many more times if a delicate gradation of the restructuring of consciousness is made. In each age, one or another of the functions attains its maturity, and it is precisely at this age at the age when a certain function stands at the center that it proceeds in more favorable conditions for development and matures with maximal intensity. And you know that the most basic or elementary functions, serving as a prerequisite for the subsequent functions, mature earlier. To speak briefly, school age is characterized by this: we already have relatively mature perception and elementary memory in the child.

We may say without any fear of exaggeration that the development of basic, elementary forms of memory and the development of perception has completed three quarters of its work before school age. With a school child we get, in general, extremely close to the complex forms of perception and elementary memory in the school child.

There are grounds for believing that almost the whole of the path has been covered by these functions, or in any case, a significant part of their path has been covered. I think this is clear to you. For example, we might say that by school age, walking has covered three quarters of its path; in other words, the distance which remains for the walking of the child to reach its full maturation constitutes a ratio of one part to four, and three parts out of four have already been left behind. In any case, at school age we have before us a whole series of mature functions. In the psychological field, this relates to perception and to memory, which have been the center of development in the preceding age. This constitutes the basic prerequisite without which intellectual development is not possible at all. This is on the one hand.

On the other hand, since these functions have already carried out their transformation, they are highly differentiated. This is a very important moment to which I would draw your attention.

If in the beginning we have undifferentiated whole consciousness, that is, the nondifferentiation of separate functions, if in early childhood, in the age before schooling,[3] we have to deal with the fact that there emerges a certain system of relationships between the functions of consciousness, from which perception moves to

---

ers such as Jaensch had already noted, in the twenties, that young children have a tendency to "eidetic imagery," that is, the ability to recall an image so clearly that a listener who is looking at the object being described cannot tell if the speaker is looking at the object or not. Sometimes this is called "photographic" memory, but there is an important difference. "Photographic" memory, such as the memory that Vygotsky and Luria studied in Solomon Veniaminovich Shereshevsky (Luria, 1989/2000), includes words and in fact works by means of verbal images: Shereshevsky was a trained mnemonist, and an important part of his training was memorizing word lists. Today, eidetic imagery is believed to exist only about two to ten percent of children between six to twelve years old (Haber, 1979), and to gradually die out as children develop adult concepts But perhaps eidetism never entirely dies out, as most of us have had the feeling of memories that are so vivid they are almost like afterimages. Vygotsky interprets this as a living fossil—a lingering form of undifferentiated perception and memory.

[3] Vygotsky says предшкольном возрасте, which is normally translatable as "preschool" years, but it is clear from context that he means all of the years before school (i.e., from early childhood, through the crisis at three, and preschool years), and not simply the preschool years three to seven here.

the center, can we then say, that in preschool age the whole matter consists only in this: that in the place of perception at the center of the system there is memory? We may sometimes carelessly take this position, but in fact, this is not at all the case. Imagine the following scenario. First: we have a nondifferentiated holistic consciousness (because all of the separate functions are not yet differentiated), and consciousness acts in two or three basic modes, in which all the basic functions—consciousness, perception, memory, attention and thinking—are taking part. Imagine that we have, in the subsequent age, in early childhood, the differentiation of a consciousness in which clearly distinguished at the center is—let us say—perception. Can we then say that in the subsequent stage, that is to say in preschool age, it will in fact be the case that this Centre A has now been displaced and that there is now some other Centre B? To say this is not possible, because, as a result of this development, these centers are now powerfully developed themselves. Now they are already functions existing as forces in consciousness.

Moreover, all functions were related differently, the whole circle of consciousness was differently related to A than it now relates to B. All functions are differentiated. Due to the fact that the centers have moved, the relationship of all the parts has been transposed. At preschool age, there are functions available which are immeasurably more mature than the very center, arranging themselves in the form of a circle. All other functions have gone through the path of differentiation in relation to the previous center and are now being rebuilt in the sense of a new relation to B. Therefore, we are dealing with a more differentiated consciousness.

Now imagine to yourself at school age, when we have a powerful development of A and we complete the development of, let us say, B, we are dealing with functions which have twice reconstructed a center, so we have to deal with a much more differentiated consciousness than ever before.

To sum up, we may put it this way: The first moment of departure, which characterizes intellectual development at school age, consists of the circumstance that we are now dealing with relative maturity of the basic prerequisites of intellect or thinking in the strict sense of the word, that is, perception and memory.

The second point is that we have to do with functions of consciousness that are highly differentiated with regard to their functional relations.

This differentiation is so great that our usual list of names—memory, attention, thinking—does not cover even a tenth of what has now been objectively established in the analysis of individual functions in the school child, because memory includes a variety of functions, and thinking does too: visual, practical, concrete, abstract, etc. In a word, we have more differentiation within each function.

The prerequisite of maturity is that, first of all, we have more differentiated functions and more differentiation within functions, and secondly, that these moments taken together characterize the moment of departure of the psychological development of the schoolchild.[4]

[4] For example, in early childhood, the single function of 'affective perception' is differentiated into affect on the one hand and perception on the other (e.g., when the toddler wants something that is not present), and at three the child differentiates affect from will (e.g., when the child wants some-

We now move on to development itself. It seems to me that if you would attempt to say immediately that which is of essential importance, that which constitutes the basis for the duration of the school age, that which is on-going within consciousness, it would be necessary to say the following. As you probably know, school age is the age of intensive intellectual development of the child, precisely the age when if we continue to speak figuratively, intellectual functions, child thinking, are becoming the center of his conscious activity.

This must, of course, be understood very conditionally. First of all, it is necessary to stress that the word "becoming" rather than "have become." This does not mean that at the moment of school age, the child is a thinking being; it means that the child comes upon school age with very weak intellectual functions. We could say that the school child has miniscule [capacities in—Trans.] intellect but grandiose capacities in memory and even more grandiose capacities of perception.

Consequently, intellect does not constitute, at the very beginning, the most powerful or the most predominant moment in the activity of consciousness; on the contrary, it is initially still weak relative to the other functions that matured in previous ages. But at school age, it is undergoing its maximal development, while this is no longer the case with either memory or perception.

If we compare the initial and final moments of intellect in school age and the initial and final moments of memory or perception, it turns out that the initial and final moments of intellect will be greatly divergent, but the initial and final moments of memory or perception will diverge little; that is, intellect will become the center of development. But you know this in relation to all the other functions of the child. Let us say that for the age between 1;5 and three or four years of age, speech is developing in an intensive fashion—but then speech will develop significantly less; in this way the optimal period for the development of intellectual function for mastering the basic functions of human thinking as such is the school age. This requires consideration from two sides. Firstly, how does this development proceed? And secondly, what does this signify for the other functions?

Let us begin, first and foremost, with the second question—what does it mean for changes in the development of all the other functions? Take, for example, such a peripheral function as imagination or attention. It does not stand at the center in either this age or that age (gesturing--GSK).[5] I ask you, what changes in the development of attention come from the fact that at the center of consciousness stands neither perception nor memory, but intellect? What does the circumstance that it [consciousness—Trans.] is now acting in the period of greatest development for the intellect signify for it and for the other functions of consciousness? For any periph-

---

thing but nevertheless rejects it to spite his or her parents). Vygotsky discusses the former example in Lecture Five of the *Foundations of Pedology* and the latter example in this book, Chap. 9.

[5]G.S. Korotaeva adds К сожалению, схемы, приведенные Л.С. Выготским на доске, в стенограмме отсутствуют" ("Unfortunately, the scheme given L.S. Vygotsky on the board is missing from the transcript"). But precisely because no formal diagram is included in the lecture, it seems likely that that Vygotsky was just sketching a rough drawing on the blackboard for illustrative purposes rather than presenting a data-based graph or table (Выготский, 2001).

eral function it signifies two things (to speak approximately). First of all, it serves intellectual development itself, that is, this function thereby lives and acts in the epoch of the governance, the pre-eminent predominance, of intellectual processes, and all functions are, as it were, its servants—this is the central line of development. For example, imagine the development of speech in the child in the period of the maximal development of speech. Clearly, at this time all of the functions of the child must go along with the development of speech: the development of his motility, his attention, his memory, and the development of his thinking, his imagination, etc. In short, if you wish to trace how all other functions develop in the era of the maximal development of speech, then you will see them best in the work of speech itself.

In the second place, it means that signifies that each of these functions, in its turn, if we speak approximately, become intellectualized, that is, it changes itself by absorbing elements of intellectual activity. Or, if we may switch to a more figurative language to be more precise, we might put it this way: what does it signify to be the servant of the intellect? It signifies that each function works more and more in collaboration in a single system with the operation of intellect, that it has favorable conditions for its own development and moves and develops in so far as it is linked to this basic operation, it develops itself in this age and has autonomous movement in its development as such. Consequently, it acquires specific features linked to this: it is collaborating with intellect; it is becoming intellectualized.

How is this expressed in practice? What does it signify? It signifies that the first distinguishing feature that characterizes all the intellectual functions of school age is the conscious awareness of these functions. The child becomes consciously aware. That is first.

The second change which follows, thanks to the fact that intellectual development is advanced to the center and other functions develop in so far as they participate in intellectual development, means first and foremost, the following: the basic functions become intellectualized, or, to put it another way, they become conscious and aware; the child begins to approach them deliberately and intelligently; he understands the activity that he is undertaking.

If we wished to say in a general form what occurs with memory, attention, and imagination at school age, we would have to say that the most important consists in this: that they all become intellectualized; they become conscious: they become conscious attention, conscious memory, etc.

This leads to another moment, immediately linked to the first and extremely important, that all functions are becoming volitional. To the extent that they are conscientized, to the extent that they become intellectualized, to that extent they acquire a special property—that is, they are volitional.[6]

What does this mean? It seems to me that this implies something very simple. First of all, we empirically know full well that the child can not only learn that

[6]Vygotsky means a line of development that leads to volition, or free will, including the recognition by the child of necessity. We have chosen to translate this as "volitional" rather than "voluntary" because the word "voluntary" suggests something the child volunteers to do, or something that is optional or discretionary or not coerced or forced on the child.

which is memorable in itself but memorize that which he wishes to memorize, that is, there is a simple basic criterion for any volitional function—that is its intentionality; that is, there is the capability of activating a given function in a way that coincides with basic intentions; it becomes possible to intentionally relate some memorization, to memory, and to all other inner activity of the child.

Just as the child of preschool age develops intentionality in relation to activity—the child takes something in order to be able to make something else—so too in the school child there emerges volition, that is, mastery of internal activity; he creates an intention with respect to inner operations—attention, memory—and their volitional functioning becomes possible.

In this way, awareness and mastery of functions constitutes the central feature that characterizes the changes in all of these functions. That is why I wished to draw your attention to this: to put it in the usual psychological terminology, before our eyes unfolds a highly noteworthy displacement.

You, of course, know that psychology has for a very long time spoken of voluntary attention and logical memory; you have often seen these concepts in the pages of psychological books devoted to the age of schooling. But because in these old terms only one moment is covered—the volitional act of attention—what is essential in volitional attention and logical memory is not said: that logical memory becomes sense-making through this act.

In point of fact, these two moments are closely linked in form to one another. They become conscious in the sense of awareness; in so far as they are conscious, they become volitional. Therefore if one wishes to express in a concrete form the basic shape of psychological development at school age, then with the same right that we can say that volitional attention and volitional memory develop at school age—with the same right we can say that logical memory develops and logical attention develops.

Vronsky[7] has said that volitional attention—this is something which is maximally dependent on thought, which is maximally intellectualized, and which can maximally move in a dependency with thought.

If we pay attention to the fact that we are dealing with consciously aware and volitional functions, and that they do not constitute such at the outset of school age but become such over the duration of school age, we need to go back a minute earlier, to note that this is linked with the prerequisite which we spoke of at the outset.

I believe that we have already made it clear, (by—Trans.) the very fact of the greater differentiation in functions which we encountered at school age, (by—Trans.) the very fact that those functions such as memory and attention stand out sharply and come to the aid of consciousness. Is it easier to grasp (something—Trans.) differentiated, highly developed, and nearly matured, or (is it easier—Trans.) to grasp vague rudiments which are not differentiated and merged with other things?

Of course, it is easier to become consciously aware of that which is differentiated, that which is separated and that which clearly serves distinct and well-formed activities.

---

[7] Léopoldoff-Martin (Léopoldoff-Martin, 2018) assumes that this is a misprint for "Blonsky."

This means that differentiation and maturity, which we spoke of earlier, determine what may become consciously construed.[8] It was no accident that we spoke of these in relation to the following fact. Before anything else, all of what became consciously construed were two functions in the schoolchild: volitional attention and volitional memory. I believe that you will agree that, for example, what is linked to the prerequisites of development, at the end of the development of the previous age, those which constitute the most mature in the school age are perception and memory. Consequently, memory is the first which becomes consciously construed and before all the others becomes differentiated and matured and acts as the means for attentiveness. This is easy to understand. But when we speak of voluntary attention, it is important to note that attention as such is linked to different types of attentiveness. In particular, in the school child what advantageously develops is volitional attention linked to perception. For this reason, volitional attention is a fact, and in it is expressed in attention itself becoming volitional. I can now attend to any act; I can be attentive to that which I see and that which I hear. I can be attentive to what I am recalling. Now, when I recall something, I direct all my attention to the act of recalling itself Attention may be focused on clarifying errors in reasoning, etc. Attention can also be directed to separate acts. Volitional attention also has its own sphere of applications, specific to itself.

In relation to perception, external perception[9]: first of all, what matures in the first stage of the school age is volitional attention. Precisely because of this, it is always in

---

[8] In what follows, Vygotsky uses various forms of осознанность a good deal. There is no problem with the Russian—it's an ordinary word that means "consciousness," "awareness," or "knowledge" in the sense of knowing what you know and also knowing that you know it. But in English we need at least two words to render this idea, since "conscious" can just mean that you are not asleep and "awareness" has a slightly metaphysical meaning or spiritualistic savor. There is a further complication: in English we tend to reserve consciousness for persons and personifications. So, people can be consciously aware of their psychological functions, but if you say that a particular function (for example, attention or memory) becomes consciously aware, it has a slightly uncanny sound to it, as if the function had become disembodied and developed a ghostly consciousness of its own. We also hesitate to have Vygotsky saying in English that a function like attention or memory has been consciously realized at school age, because it sounds as if it was not real before school age. So, where Vygotsky speaks of the schoolchild developing a deliberate and "directable" grasp of functions like memory and attention, we will translate осознавать as 'consciously construed'. This should be understood in the sense of a function becoming intentionally meant but also in the archaic English sense of "Construe my meaning!"—a function becoming the clear object of consciousness, awareness, comprehension, and knowledge. As Spinoza would say, the function is not simply an idea, but an idea of an idea.

[9] Vygotsky's sudden mention of "perception, external perception" seems a little surprising. But there are three good reasons for discussing it here.

First of all, Vygotsky is historical. This means that, like Darwin, and like any good historian, he will often think backwards--he will take a developed function like volitional attention and think backwards to the moment when it first came into being, or rather when it changed from something that was functionally quite different into what it is now (this *genetic* method is discussed in detail in Chapter Three of *The History of the Development of the Higher Mental Functions*—see Vygotsky, 1997). He has just been discussing developed attention, that is, the child's classroom attention, the ability to attend to things that are not very interesting in themselves (like print), things that are not present (like Antarctica or the French Revolution) and things that do not even exist yet (like paying attention to potential errors in solving a math problem). From what does this

a close way linked to perceptions themselves, so that some researchers, and even one of the famous researchers Rubin[10] (a Danish researcher), as well as almost all of the psychologists who belong to the Gestalt school, are inclined to deny attention as a separate function. To Rubin belongs a work with the rather flamboyant title of "The Nonexistence of Attention." The notion that attention has no independent existence as such, that it is so until the end of life, persists. We cannot be attentive without collaboration with some other function. This is considered the basis of the fact that attention exists as a certain facet of the activity of some other function.

And so perception is the first function which takes part in the activity of attention. What does volitional attention mean? We have already said to you several times that volitional attention is characterized first of all by the ability to demarcate at will a figure and a background. If I am able to see something only in a way which is dictated by the structure of this thing, my attention is maximally nonvolitional.

But if I am able to see something so that each element of this thing may become the center of the figure, and everything else the background, then my attention has become maximally volitional.

---

developed attention develop? Not, it turns out, from undeveloped attention, as you might think. Instead, it is functionally differentiated from a well-developed function--namely external perception.

Second, Vygotsky wants to show us how a higher, sociocultural, specifically human form can be differentiated structurally from a lower, natural, biomechanical function. The distinction between external perception and volitional attention is a good example. It is not the case that volitional attention is simply a higher form of animal perception. It is not even true that it is a higher form of preschool perception. It is something new. It is a qualitatively different form of cultural behaviour; Vygotsky's sudden mention makes the "sudden displacement" or "rupture" concrete that he noted in 29 (when he discussed how logical memory is structurally differentiated from an experiential form). Some writers have claimed that Vygotsky rejected the distinction between lower and higher functions near the end of his life, but we can see here that if anything the distinction has become even sharper.

Finally, Vygotsky, in addition to having a great deal to contribute to present day debates (e.g., special education, "gifted" education, intelligence assessment, etc.), was also an active participant in intellectual debates of his own time. Some psychologists had argued that attention was essentially like perception: just as you cannot perceive without perceiving something, you cannot pay attention without paying attention to something, and that object determines the nature of the psychological act. But Vygotsky shows that even with external perception, it is possible for humans to change the way we see things volitionally, at will. Not even perception is completely determined by the object, and so attention too can be brought under the child's developing awareness and mastery. Although Vygotsky has made the lower and higher functions even clearly distinct, by emphasizing the role of awareness and mastery, he has also shown, in this way, how they might be developmentally linked.

[10] Edgar Rubin (1886–1951), was a Danish psychologist. He was a cousin and close friend of the great physicist Nils Bohr, and then a student of Harald Høffding and later Georg Elias Müller. At first Rubin was interested in the "nonsense syllables" of Meumann and Ebbinghaus, but he came to the conclusion that they were meaningless and taught us nothing about how the mind searches for and finds meaning.

He then developed the meaningful "figure-ground" tests that we now use (see the "Rubin vase" picture attached). This led to important discoveries of the basic laws about the relationship of figure and ground (e.g., that an enclosed space is more likely to be seen as figure than the enclosing space).The Gestalt psychologists (Wertheimer, Koffka, Köhler) were extremely interested in his discoveries, but he was too empirically oriented to join their group.

Concerning the first case, when our attention is entirely mastered by the structure of the field: it was about this case that Köhler remarked that the school child is a slave to his own sensory field, that is, that he can see only in the manner that things are given.

Allow me to offer some commentary on this question.

We know from the zoo psychology of G....[11] and from the words of Thorndike, the famous researcher in animal intelligence who created a post-Köhler era, that they both concluded that the most difficult thing in animal intelligence is attention. If attention may be brought to bear, then most experiments can be carried out, but sometimes you cannot carry this or that operation out because you cannot attract the animal's attention.

You surely know about the work of K.... dedicated to the methodology of these experiments, where he discusses this. Everybody knows, of course, of the "To you all is grey" experiments by Köhler.[12] He discusses how it is necessary to set up this experiment with animals in practice. It turns out that perception is in itself very easy to ascertain in animals but eliciting the attention of the animal to color is problematic: color differences are of no importance to the animals. It was necessary to employ an enormous signboard so as to catch their eyes. It was attempted in this way: utilizing a box in which fruits may be found the whole cover was made gray, and the same with the box. This did not help. It was necessary to take a small box, and to make the gray label huge; for any visual field, the gray label had to be huge when the experiment was carried out in relation to a number of animals, who proved to be completely incapable of distinguishing colors.

---

[11] There is a note from Korotaeva indicating that the ellipsis Г... "G...." was "Так в стенограмме." (thus in the stenogram). It is possible that Vygotsky is referring to the animal experiments of Gesell, who did comparisons between monkeys and young children. What seems more likely, from what follows in the next paragraph, is that the missing word is either "Гроос" (that is, Groos, who did experiments on chickens) or else "Гештальт", that is, "Gestalt." In that case, Köhler's experiments are what are meant. Since the next paragraph is about K... and not G..., it seems most likely that "Gestalt" is meant here (Выготский, 2001).

[12] Korotaeva notes: Так в стенограмме is, "thus in the stenogramme." This means that the stenographer did not write out the name in full. This was apparently unnecessary because the students were aware of who was meant. The experiments are described in considerable detail in The *History of the Development of the Higher Psychological Functions*, Chapter Nine (Vygotsky, 1997). Various animals are trained to find food beneath a darker grey rather than a lighter one, and what was the darker grey in one experiment becomes the lighter grey in the next, so that the animal is forced to judge and not simply perceive. The name Vygotsky gives to the experiments, "To you, all is grey," is a little joke, referring deftly to two things at once. First of all, there is the Russo-French proverb that all cats look grey (or yellow) in the twilight (see *The History of the Development of the Higher Psychological Functions*, Chapter One). Secondly, there is Goethe's couplet from Faust, where Mephistopheles encourages the good doctor to leave off theory and take up a life of pleasure:

Grau, theurer Freund, ist alle Theorie,
Und grün des Lebens goldner Baum.
(Grey, dear friend, is all of theory
And green is the golden tree of life!)

One might do it thus: you place the box, with the side which faces to the animal and is gray in color in a bright spotlight to highlight it, or you let fall on it the rays of the sun; briefly put, it is necessary that all parts of the visual field which should constitute the center of attention, should attract the attention of the animal.

Köhler succeeded in demonstrating that one may draw the attention of animals with the aid of an indicative gesture. If you take the ape by the head and direct its eyes in the right direction and then point, then this can play a role, even if the animal itself did not make use of a pointing gesture.

This means that the main difficulty in volitional perception is this: to cease being the slave of one's own sensory field, seeing the situation itself differently from that which confronts the animal and from that which the infant sees. The basis consists in being able to direct attention to one aspect and not to the other, or to put it another way, to make the gray color the center; the figure, and not the box to which the ape rushes. This is firstly what, it seems to me, is worth our attention: the complete lack of all volitional attention in animals.

Secondly, what merits attention is that a number of researchers have pointed out that volitional attention is very weak at the beginning of school age.

I used to read manuals for a number of secondary schools which proceeded from this fact of the learning established at school age. Indeed, one might say, in a certain sense, that the failure of learning-and-teaching during the preschool years is attributable primarily to the incapacity of volitional attention in the preschooler, that the beginning of school learning is immediately linked to this: it must become possible to attend deliberately to that which at a given moment does not rivet the child's attention, to focus attention on the lesson as such.

On the one hand, the attention of the school child is very weak at the outset, but over the duration of school age it is maximally set out from all of the other functions, correlating with the mental development of the child. This correlation is equivalent to 0,95. In fact, a correlation of 100 always confuses us, because a correlation of 100 is that of a thing with itself. If we obtain a correlation of 100 or 1, it always means that we are considering under different names one and the same thing. A correlation of 0,95 means that we confront one of maximal correlation; it shows to what degree volitional attention is linked to intellectual development, it shows to what degree it is linked with consciousness, with the intellectualization of the process of consciousness itself.

This means that conscious awareness and volitional attention— these will characterize the most important content of development in the activity of the school age.

If we turn to memory, it is natural that memory which is mechanical, or elementary or direct image memory, is starting to give place at school age to another form of memory which is characterized, firstly, by the fact that this memory is a verbal memory, in words, and the child is remembering not only the experience itself, as an impression, but a record of this impression, a record of this experience in words. At the same time it is more and more linked to logical memory, memory which is chiefly formed by the establishment of dependencies and links that exist between different parts of memorized or assimilated materials.

Very early, already in 1919, Bühler was able to demonstrate, with the aid of experiments, the following law which has remained inviolable in psychology: that thought is memorized more easily than any other material.[13] You know the main results of these experiments; it is reproduced differently, both quantitative and qualitatively. At the time, Bühler made use of this fact to refute associative theory. He showed that thoughts were not linked to one another by means of association but combined with each other through other laws. However, there has persisted one problem which has eluded a number of researchers until now: why thoughts are memorized better than other material. We are told that it is because thoughts have their own laws of combination and connection: when we consciously memorize the thought, it is through a logical link to thinking, and not to a memory that engenders another thought. Very well, but this only implies that in place of memory, the work of thinking begins; this does not mean that thoughts are memorized.

Now I say this to you. Let us assume one simple thing: thoughts are memorized differently from words[14] and from other material. And so I ask you now: why are thoughts memorized differently?

There are two possible cases: thoughts have their proper laws of motion. When we are given the beginning of their movement, then a thought is developed as a thought. Affects have their own laws: we set up an experiment which causes irritation or indignation. If for the second time the same conditions are created, is it possible to induce indignation once again? It is, but this does not imply that the experimental subject has remembered it. Speaking briefly, if I come to the same thought for a second time, this does not imply that I have remembered. I solved a problem, and in a year I was given the same problem, and I solved it once again. Does this imply that I remembered how it was solved? No.

Bühler says that thinking has its own proper laws of combination, proper to its own deployment, but this does not explain why thoughts are memorized differently; it only explains that in addition to the laws of deployment of memory there exist laws for the deployment of thinking. But we are interested in this question: it is possible to memorize thoughts better than other material <....>.[15]

---

[13] Bühler, in 1919, was part of the Würzburg School. The Würzburgers sought to show that thinking is not merely associative: we don't just associate images with other images that resemble, abut, or oppose them. Many laws of thinking not only do not involve the Aristotelian rules of association, they sometimes do not involve images at all. The Würzburg experiments demonstrated that thoughts are remembered very well without images. In fact, they are remembered better than images, and even better than "structures" (patterns). For example, we remember the meanings of a conversation or a written text rather better than we remember the actual sounds and spellings of the words, or the grammatical patterns of the wordings.

[14] Presumably Vygotsky is not referring to meaningful words, because these would involve thinking. Vygotsky may be referring to the kinds of artificial "words" that were used by Ebbinghaus in his memory experiments. These were sometimes random sequences of letters and sometimes nonsense words which were phonologically possible in a given language, but which had no meaning (e.g., 'plog' 'worple' or "sneverate" in English).

[15] We do not know why there are so many gaps in the manuscript; it is possible that the stenographer simply has rather undeveloped volitional attention! Fortunately, it is fairly easy to guess what

One of our contemporary authors has very humorously said that what I have sketched about overteaching constitutes from the psychological side a law of underlearning. What does it mean that even though ten times (i.e., nine, repetitions of a particular educational experience or pedagogical exercise—Trans.) would be sufficient, fifteen times will give better results? This implies that if memory was not realized through thinking, then with ten (repetitions—Trans.) I would not remember anything at all and I would only remember with fifteen.[16]

If such are the facts: ten times suffice, but fifteen times give better results, what does this imply? Why does fifteen times give better results than ten times? Because these ten times do not provide the whole of memorization but create the illusion of complete memorization thanks to the fact that memory is supported here by intellect. If memory did not enjoy the support of intellect, then at ten I would not remember at all.

In actual fact, what takes place is the following state of affairs: preschoolers need fifteen repetitions for this or that text while schoolchildren only need ten. And why is this? Because in the schoolchild, the primary symptom of development is that thinking comes to the aid of memory.

As a matter of fact, what is usually called overteaching constitutes an instance of under-learning. It implies that the child previously needed fifteen repetitions to remember something, but if he now requires only ten repetitions, this means that thinking has arrived to help out the memory.

Consequently, we can draw the following conclusion in relation to memory. Why are thoughts memorized better than any other material? We saw that in part it is memorized thanks to intellectualization. This is correct. But what is most important, most basic, what maintains its force afterwards—this is another matter. If this (i.e., intellectualization—Trans.) explained everything, then the law of overteaching and the law of underlearning would persist for the whole of school age, the transitional age(i.e., adolescence—Trans.), and into adulthood—but they lose their significance. Clearly, this explains the matter only at a certain beginning stage and this is

---

is missing from the paragraphs that follow. Vygotsky will argue that because memory is now differentiated, it can be subordinated to thinking (instead of the other way around, which is what happened in preschool).

[16] Some research into vocabulary teaching (Nation, 2012) shows that it takes somewhere between eight and forty repetitions of a foreign language word in order to be able to remember it. But which is it? Eight or forty? The answer, of course, depends on the word (and also on the learner and the circumstances and many other things besides). Here Vygotsky makes the independent variable both broader and narrower than these—he considers that the answer depends on thinking. This variable, thinking, includes the word meaning, and the learner, and the circumstance, but it makes these quite specific to the situation of a school child, a child for whom thinking in this way about the task of memorizing is a new experience. In order to demonstrate this, Vygotsky imagines a child (e.g., a child in early childhood or a child in preschool) who repeats a word without thinking about its meaning (a similar thing happens when people who are learning English repeat the word "a" or "the" or "of"). One way to look at this is that such repetition is an instance of "overteaching" that is, teaching more than would be necessary if the child were thinking about meaning. But, of course, Vygotsky wants to consider it as an instance of "underlearning" because Vygotsky is interested in the difference between the underlearning preschooler and the learning school child.

demonstrated by the fact that such memorization with the aid of thinking is not perfect because it disappears within fifteen days. Clearly, we need to look for other reasons why thoughts are memorized better than other material.

Research demonstrates that they are memorized better than other materials simply for one basic reason: because they are more consciously aware or, as is said, better structured. Thinking is more conscious than all other structures, that is, thoughts are more consciously aware than memories, and for that reason they are more volitional. That is, memory, to the extent that it is consciously aware, becomes maximally volitional, deliberate. Thoughts are remembered better, because they are more voluntary: it is more conscious and, as a consequence, volitional.

What is this volitional quality? Greater capacity for the operation of a given function, greater freedom in its deployment, greater independence of it from other moments. Let us take up the last of these. How does the logical development of memory proceed in school age? Studies have demonstrated many interesting things. Matters always begin with the superior memorization of thought; that is, initially memory becomes in one way or another logicalized in the area of thinking, and in particular, what is obtained is a stage which might be more suitable called the memory of the logical than the logical memory, for it is not the memory as such in a process of development that becomes logical, but rather what remains (of a memory—Trans.) which is logical, the best of it. But precisely because we do not have the magnitude of the memory itself, each of the functions presents a complex system of lesser functions, and precisely because it (thought—Trans.) constitutes the center of the rest of the system of memory, there emerges a tendency to rework all the material in such a way that it is retained in the image and likeness of a thought.[17]

How do we memorize, let us say, nonsense? We attempt to find sensible links, we attempt in some way to transform this material into the image and likeness of thought. One might imagine that our memory is a very rational being, to which we can attribute intentions like this. But in point of fact, this is attributable to the law of structuration. In any case, memorization methods are assimilated once and then

---

[17] Vygotsky distinguished earlier two moments in the differentiation of functions—an external differentiation (e.g., between affective perception and attention, as when school children attend to things they dislike) and an internal differentiation (e.g., within affective perception itself between affect and perception, as when toddlers like things that are not actually present). Now Vygotsky explains why school age children memorize thoughts better than other material by using an internal differentiation between memorizing and thinking to do this. In preschoolers, we have undifferentiated remembering and thinking: a preschooler who is asked to explain a concept is very likely to tell you a memory instead. In contrast, a school-age child who is asked to remember an important conversation or an anecdote is very likely to have retained only the logical links and not the exact sights, sounds and words. Adult mnemonists asked to memorize meaningless lists try to turn them into logically organized spaces by imagining each entry as a room in a castle or a setting at a table, and professional actors when they are asked to memorize a concrete tone of voice or facial expression will try turn them all into a coherent story or argument. Instead of a logical memory, they use memories of the logical. Similarly, when we are confronted by a nonsense text like Chomsky's "Colorless green ideas sleep furiously," we tend to render it incorrectly as a logical statement (e.g., "Even the most boring ecologist arguments can smolder and eventually burst into flame…")

passed on to all of the others. By virtue of this law, logical memory is conditioned as the memory of the logical, the memory of the logic, and thus are established the well-known structure of memorizing, the well-known techniques of memory, which gradually spread to other areas, leading to the logicalization of the memory itself.

I would like to show you that volitional attention is in equal measure logical attention, just as logical memory is in equal measure volitional memory.

Last, the results of recent studies. I have already spoken about this to one group of students, so I will simply repeat it in two words. This was a very large psychological study of a whole school, led by Brunovich[18], an Austrian psychologist, who attempted to clear up the psychological question of whether memory develops in childhood or does not develop. The material is divided into three types: visual material, structural material, and semantic material. The basic results of this capital work led to the conclusion that there is no single line of development in memory and that, while the development of memory in visual material, in sensory material, terminates at the boundary of school age and then goes into a near plateau, that of structure achieves a great advance here <... > (gesturing)[19] and logical, semantic memorization makes a further leap; at the same time the structural in the middle of school age reaches its plateau.

In this way, the development of memory is such that from one form of memory which has literally almost ceased to develop, development moves on to another and a third form. This has been experimentally proven in vast material.

The third moment consists in this: that semantic memorization does not repeat the structural line. This, it seems to me, is a moment of great importance in order to understand that of which we shall speak next.

In structural psychology and in other areas of modern holistic psychology there is the following tendency: structural principles explain all forms of psychological activity in animals and in humans. An attempt is made to explain everything with the aid of the principle of structuration: the features of the whole of the psyche, memory, including the semantic memory—logical memory too is to be considered a special case of structural memory.

Clearly, on the question of memorizing thought, we must deal with some more complex laws, of which I shall attempt to speak briefly, after the break.

I was asked to repeat what was said just before the break.

This study was most exceptional, in that it was undertaken experimentally, as a study into the broadest range of age material and qualitative material in order to resolve the question: whether or not memory develops in childhood and how it is developed.

---

[18] Léopoldoff-Martin says this author is unidentifiable, but it seems possible that Vygotsky is referring to Bühler's Hungarian student Egon Brunswik who did school psychology. He was working in Austria.

[19] Korotaeva marks the ellipsis '<...>' and also the word in brackets ('gesturing') as Так в стенограмме, "thus in the stenogramme," so this is not her insertion, but the insertion of the stenographer. Vygotsky is presumably pointing to something like the "parallelogramme of development" to show the differences between the developmental curves.

You know there are a number of controversial theories in this regard. The basic idea of this study lies in this: three types of material are given: firstly, visual sensory material, sensory memory; then structural material, that is, that where memorization took place under the direct influence of structures of different types and with different degrees of complexity and differentiation, some clear and some less clearly separated, and finally, material linked to the memorization of semantic content. The study shows that the development of all of these forms and types of memorization do not repeat one another but are located very definitely in certain ages. Thus, sensory memory nearly attains its maximum, nearly halting on a plateau, nearly at an even level, approaching its summit at the beginning of school age, the memorization of structural material is given during school age, particularly the first stage, where there is a well-known gradual increase. After this, memorization in the purely structural memory develops extremely little. But all of the functions are intellectualized, all of the functions become consciously aware, all of the functions gradually become volitional functions; there emerges the capacity for volitional inner psychological activity.

But what is interesting here are two circumstances. First, what does this imply—these basic laws of this awareness and this mastery? I state as a fact that they have become consciously construed, that they have become volitional. But a researcher cannot simply leave it at that, one must inquire, what happens from the psychological side, when functions become consciously construed, when functions become intentional? This is the first question to which we must give a response. Secondly, what has become of intellect itself? We have taken intellect in relation to other functions. What happens to intellect itself? Let me answer this question.

It is a noteworthy fact that in the development of school age children nearly all psychological functions become intellectualized, that is, become consciously construed and volitional, except for intellect itself. Intellectual operations are not consciously construed and are not volitional in this age.

Let me remind you of data which will confirm this fact, which you will encounter again many times.

We shall take that which we come across most often in the literature: the study of Piaget. Piaget demonstrated that the child of school age thinks and is capable of complex operations of thinking but is not consciously aware of thought. As Piaget says, in the child there is no act of awareness of his own thoughts; the child thinks and is capable of complex operations of thought in the school age, but he is not consciously aware of his thoughts, that he does not have, as Piaget puts it (using terms from someone else), the act of awareness of his own thoughts. His thought works just as memory works in the preschooler, that is, it works, and is capable of complex operations, but without any conscious awareness of this operation and consequently without the capacity to voluntarily make use of these operations.

Take this example which Piaget puts to us; it will remind you, in the rough, what this law consists of. He speaks thus: The child is given some task to resolve. For example, on foot a person covers a certain distance in fifty minutes, but on a bicycle the same distance only takes him five minutes, so how many times faster does the man move on a bicycle than on foot? The child answers, 45. You can see clearly how he got the answer.[20]

Instead of taking fifty and dividing by five, he subtracted; that is completely clear. But if you ask him how he got the answer, as the studies of Piaget have repeatedly shown, the child at the beginning of the school age is often unable to say how he resolved the task. He makes up the way that he solved the problem, and we know this based on simple observations of school practices. And we know what has to be done if a pupil is confused in solving a problem in calculation. The teacher suggests "Think aloud." Then the error can be untangled, because the child alone, in the course of solving it, cannot say what he is doing in resolving the problem, and gets confused.

The child, of course, thinks and even achieves the answer in some way, but he does not know how he did it, how he thought of it. That such phenomena take place constitutes a generally known fact. For example, we know that the motives of actions constitute a later area which becomes consciously aware in the transitional age. Even in adults, a significant part of our true motives is not always consciously construed. Only those that are most proximal to the personality, most deliberate, most intentional actions are consciously aware more or less completely in the sense of their motivation, and even then not completely so, with a number of intentions and true motives remaining poorly construed by consciousness.

There is a whole array of simple things; just take one simple example. In his experiments Claparède was able to demonstrate a whole series of things we are completely unaware of. For example, every one of us, let us say, knows what he is doing, but does not know how it is done <... > More or less, not in such a rough form, goes the thinking of the child who thinks automatically but is not consciously aware <...>[21] that is, in the era of the governance of logical memory and volitional attention in the thinking of this child, thanks to which only the memory becomes

[20] This is from Chap. 4, p. 116 of Piaget's 1924 book, *Jugement et raisonnement chez l'enfant.*

"Bel (9/ 2) It takes fifty minutes to go to Carouge on foot. On a bicycle you go five times faster. How much time does it take by bicycle? *45 minutes*. How did you count that? *I said fifty minus five, and then I got down to forty and then I saw that it was 45*. Spie (9; 3) gives 25 in response to the same problem but doesn't know how he did it. *I cannot explain to you, but I know how to count; it's easy, but I can't tell you*. In fact, he, like many of his friends, simply took half of fifty. (Mey (9;5) answers and pretends that he got 35 because he says 5 x7 = 35. Tiec (9 1/2 years) gives ten as an answer (dividing 50 by 5). How did you find 10? *One fifth of five is one and I added the zero*."

[21] Once again, some of the manuscript is missing. But what Vygotsky is saying is quite clear. During preschool and early school age, the child's thinking is dominated by memory and by conscious attention. We can actually see this when children count in English—they find it easy to remember 1 to 13, but when they get to fourteen they often confuse it with forty. This is because they are remembering sounds and attending to the order of words, and not thinking about whether fourteen is four added to ten or multiplied by ten.

Because in this period memory and attention are dominant and thinking is subordinate to them, it is memory and attention which develop fastest and which become deliberate, volitional, and active first. Thinking itself must lag behind, because it is not yet independent of memory and attention; it is only a dependent part of them (i.e., in order to think, the child tries to remember school practices, or pay attention to the teacher).

logical and only attention becomes voluntary; thinking itself remains unaware and involuntary. This is evident from simple experiments by Piaget. To take a simple example which Piaget gives and which clarifies from the practical side. There is such a sentence: "The boy did not go to school because he was sick." Does the schoolboy understand this sentence? He understands it well, but he is not consciously aware that he understands, so children often answer either that he was ill or that he did not go to school, when in reality it means that he did not go to school because he was sick. A child in life knows this, but when it is necessary to be consciously aware of it, he cannot.

Children are given tests in which they have to finish sentences after the conjunction "because…" or "although…" The child uses these conjunctions in the right place, but the child spontaneously, nonvolitionally uses "because" and "although" correctly, so how is it that in these experiments, he still cannot answer correctly? Because he cannot volitionally do the same thing that he can do non-volitionally.

In precisely this way, in the example the child understands the phrase "the boy did not go to school because he was sick" but he is not consciously aware of his understanding. He is able to construe the causal relationship, but he cannot volitionally reconstruct it. It is one thing to raise my hand when I need to get something, but it is another to raise my hand volitionally. It is known that a child in the age of infancy can reach for a particular object and raise his hand spontaneously, but he cannot deliberately do so.

Functions become consciously aware and volitional thanks to the central activity of the intellect, but intellectual operations remain unaware and nonvolitional. This is the node for resolving all sorts of puzzles in the psychological development of the school child, as a result of which the plusses and minuses and weaknesses of his thinking can be investigated.

But the full picture of intellectual development in the schoolchild is lacking in the work of Piaget, in part because he shows only the second side—the nonvolitional nature of the intellectual functions. Now, however, we face a very important question. The main feature of the development of the schoolchild consists in this: he has become consciously aware and become volitional in all of his functions except for intellect itself. But why are conscious awareness and mastery linked? Why does conscious awareness imply mastery, and why does mastery presuppose awareness?

If we answer this question, we will see why memory and attention become consciously aware thanks to the intellect, while this same intellect remains unconscious and involuntary. Research shows that conscious awareness never constitutes, as a

---

Édouard Claparède (1873–1940) was a Swiss psychologist. He was Piaget's teacher and also his first boss at the Jean-Jacques Rousseau Institute in Geneva. He wrote a book on sleep that anticipated many of Freud's views about the unconscious, and he was invited to join Carl Jung's group. However, he later disagreed with Jung and Freud about the nature of the unconscious mind and joined Janet's group. He was most famous for an experiment with a woman who had lost her memory and could not remember him. Claparède put a pin in his hand and stabbed her when they shook hands. The next day, although she still did not remember Claparède, she avoided shaking hands!

rule, a spontaneous development of the child, never constitutes a starting moment of the development of any psychological activity; in other words, psychological activity at the very beginning includes elements of a conscious attitude in a number of moments, but at the very beginning it is not in itself consciously construed.

You probably know that the first to introduce the concept of conscious awareness into science was Janet.... He was informed chiefly by research into mental illness. Following Janet, Claparède experimentally reworked this question. You know the results of his study, in which he was able to establish that a child reacts earlier to similarities than to differences, but is consciously aware of the differences earlier than the similarities, that is, that the process of conscious awareness often has the opposite path of development from the process of the development of a particular activity taken in its unconscious form.

From this Piaget draws the basic conclusion that conscious awareness is achieved by way of unsuccessful adaptation. If any function is working well, I need not be consciously aware of it. It is ready to become the center of my consciousness; if it acts unconsciously, if it leads to unsuccessful adaptations, then I begin to become consciously aware. An example from Claparède: I come home and try to insert the key in the lock of the door. I do this completely automatically, thinking of something else while I have the key in my pocket and while I am putting the key in the lock. But as soon as I see that the key does not fit, I begin to become consciously aware—of whether this is my door, of whether this is the right key. To put it another way, from wherever the difficulty comes, thence comes the need to think and to reason.

Indeed, this law, which Claparède maintained in psychology for a long time and which without verification was taken over by Piaget, contains a partial truth; to put it another way, consciousness of things, as Claparède put it, does not consist in the consciousness of contemplative luxury. It arises whenever there is need for it. But far more does the law of Claparède contain in itself a falsehood, and furthermore it implicitly contains in itself the following. Let me ask you this. So successful adaptation does not lead to conscious awareness, but unsuccessful adaptation leads to conscious awareness. Very well. We must ask--is consciousness in the child at all ages ready to be consciously aware of anything, so long as it leads to successful adaptation? Not so. Obviously, in order for awareness to arise at all, there must be some difficulty as a reason. But this difficulty does not explain to us why consciousness arises and how it can arise any more than, let us say, my need to arrive in Leningrad explains in what way I find myself here in one night. The need by itself cannot make me move here.

In general, any explanation for development by a need always leaves open the question of how such a need arose. I ask you, does the infant often have unsuccessful adaptations? Often. Why is he not consciously aware of everything? Of course, for thinking to emerge, some need is required. For example, there is a need for me to make sense of some complex situation. But does this explain why I am thinking of it? It does not. Or, for example, why two people think about one and the same thing and one understands, but the other does not.

Therefore, when we say that conscious awareness arises in cases of poor adaptation because a need arises—we are saying nothing, we are leaving the question unanswered. Or worse: we are pretending that as soon as there is some poor adaptation, all of the forces rush to that front, and then consciousness resolves this task. Both are wrong.[22]

<…> Thus, Claparède understands attention and memory, and what are the defects of this explanation? "Mastery," Claparède says, "must of course act after conscious awareness, not because it has an inner link with conscious awareness, nor because conscious awareness is the reason for mastery, but because both are derived from the same root, i.e. unsuccessful adaptation."[23]

Claparède says, when I fit the key into the lock, an automatic action will suffice, but when it ceases to fit, we require the application of some voluntary action, which must be volitional.

For Claparède conscious awareness follows on from unsuccessful adaptation. Mastery too follows from unsuccessful adaptation, with the aid of automatic and nonvolitional adaptations. Although they follow, the one and the other, from the same cause, they appear linked together, but they have no inner link the one to the other, one does not constitute a cause for the other.

The defect in relation to conscious awareness about which we are speaking applies to the explanation of mastery. Once his explanation is insufficient to explain conscious awareness, this implies that mastery cannot be regarded as a cause of conscious awareness, and consequently the reason for mastery and conscious awareness remains unclear: there is no such common cause.

---

[22] Why is the second explanation (which is that of Claparède and Piaget) even worse than the first (which is that of James and functionalism)? Vygotsky rejects the functionalist explanation of consciousness because a need itself must have an origin, the need is necessary but insufficient, and needs are shared but consciousness is not. Consciousness does not arise simply from a need, any more than birds evolve wings because they need them.

Vygotsky then offers a kind of immunological one! Consciousness is already dispersed in the body, like white blood cells. Just as when the body is infected, white blood cells rush to the site of infection. Similarly, when the mind encounters difficulty, the cells of consciousness rush to the trouble spot. The immunological explanation has all of the problems of the purely functionalist one, and it cannot tell us where these mysterious 'consciousness cells' come from.

[23] There is material missing from the beginning of the paragraph. But if we re-read the previous paragraphs carefully, we can easily imagine what fits. Claparède has introduced a new concept—mastery. For example, at school age, in order to study, children must control their attention, and use their memory. We have already seen how thinking helps them "underlearn" both tasks: by thinking, the child can figure out what to attend to and what to ignore, and by thinking the child can eke out memory using logic. In both of these examples, what we see is mastery of functions—but mastery that comes after conscious awareness.

Now, you might think that suggests that conscious awareness causes mastery. For example, when a child learns to play the violin, the child has to consciously pay attention to the music and consciously memorize it, and only then can the child practice and master it. But Claparède argues that there is no such "causal" link. In fact, there is no inner link between awareness and mastery at all. Instead, the link is an "outer" link: both of them have the same cause, which is unsuccessful adaptation. Learning is merely trial and error.

To say that volitional motions, that is, motions of the higher type, emerge when motion of the lower type encounters an obstacle is true if there is volition in my motion, but if it is not volitional then it is not produced when it is needed. This is a teleological answer; conscious awareness remains unexplained; there is no such common cause.

Volitional motion appears because it is necessary, because it serves adaptation, but in the mentally retarded child there also emerge adaptations. However, does conscious awareness arise? No, it does not. So, in this answer we have found an error of *petitio principii*,[24] that is, the explanation of the phenomenon refers to that which we have yet to prove. I ask, why does mastery emerge? Because it is needed. It arises because it is necessary, once it exists. But I ask myself, why is it so now, when it was not so before? There is no answer. Unsuccessful adaption can only explain why it is employed once it has originated. A third fault in the theory of Claparède is that in relation to school age this theory has given rise to a great deal of theoretical damage and confusion. Firstly, the explanation of conscious awareness by inadequate adaptation is inadequate and wrong; secondly the explanation of mastery from inadequate adaptation is inadequate and wrong, and thirdly the explanation of the link that is always observed between these two moments, as a linking up of two independent consequences of one common cause, is wrong.

Consider the fallaciousness of this proposition in the theory of Piaget, where it is it is now being tested most of all. Let me illustrate this idea. Piaget, as I told you, loses sight of the first side of the matter, that all the functions are becoming volitional and consciously construed. But he establishes the facts, which cannot be ignored and of which we have just been reminded, that the child of school age is not adequately aware of his own thinking operations and not adequately able to deploy them freely and volitionally. The question arises—why? Piaget answers. If awareness and mastery follow from bad, unsuccessful adaptations, then after all the child of school age must at each step encounter unsuccessful adaptations in thinking more often than in early childhood. Piaget says: development just takes time. All development calls for its own biologically appropriate tempo. He says that just because the child at school age cannot at every step link his thought to the thought of adult persons, therefore at every step he encounters unsuccessful adaptation, and this is precisely why, at the school age, learning-and-teaching of scientific knowledge, precisely why all school learning and teaching, there exists a solid chain of unsuccessful adaptations from the point of view of the preparation for thought. How does the child get out of this situation? He associates part of his own thought with part of the thought of the adult person, and what he obtains is a complex of his own representations and the representations of the adult person. Precisely because this is done forcefully, in the child there will develop, at eleven or twelve years, both conscious awareness and mastery.

What about this explanation? First, let us give him credit. To a certain degree, he is right. If school learning were not at every step making on him demands which he

[24] See Chap. 7 for Vygotsky's somewhat less elegant translation of Aristotle's Latin.

can satisfy in no other way than by bringing to bear his own thought, if the child at school age had not strongly developed his intellectual activity regardless of whether there emerged or did not emerge a demand for thinking, then thinking would have developed at a different tempo and we would not have had such a rapid motion over these years. But as a whole, can we think of the matter thus? In the child of preschool age thought operations are unaware of themselves and nonvolitional <...>.

By the age of 4, he has mastered this operation, and as a result awareness and mastery has been hammered into him, that is, through failures, through noncompliance with the thinking of adult persons, through the fact that child thought at every step, as Piaget has it, leads to a consciousness of his bankruptcy, his own inadequacy, through a sense of the superiority of adult thought that occurs under the auspices of the more successful adaptations which the child gradually links to his own insolvency—from this development there follows in the child a higher form of conscious awareness and mastery of his own internal processes, which characterize the beginning of the subsequent age. The insolvency of this point of view, properly speaking, has already been revealed by the analyses which we attempt to give the theory of Claparède, which Piaget presents in his own research.

Let me briefly explain in what area lie those psychological processes which will allow us in this case to offer a more or less true answer to this question and which will confirm all of that we know in this area.

I will now attempt to show that which this very experiment by Piaget demonstrates very well. We specify the first and basic question: What does "conscious awareness" mean? Conscious awareness has two meanings. <...> Piaget and Claparède, mixing up the terminology of Freud and general psychology, say: nonconscious thought, not fully consciously aware. We must present the matter like this: Piaget does not think that the child is not aware of his own proper consciousness, rather it means that consciousness is involved but not fully so. Initially there is unconscious thought—infant solipsism; then—conscious, socialized thought, but in the middle there are a series of stages, which Piaget designates as the gradual decrease of egocentrism, from egocentrism to a logical, socialized form of thinking.

What does this imply, that thought is not consciously aware? Piaget says that it is not fully consciously aware; it includes elements of the conscious and the unconscious, and it is not fully consciously aware.

Piaget and Claparède consider consciousness as a gradual transition from unconsciousness to complete consciousness. The fact is that there is a big difference between unconscious thought and conscious (we can say that I unconsciously tie a knot), between the consciousness of what I am doing and conscious awareness. I tie a knot, as in the experiments of Claparède; do I do it consciously? Of course, but I am not consciously aware of it, that is, my attention was entirely directed toward the act of trying itself and not to the way in which I did it.

Consciousness always represents some bit of reality.[25] The object of my consciousness in tying a knot may include the knot itself and what happens with it but not the study of the act itself - how I do it. This act itself may become the object—then it will be conscious awareness. Conscious awareness consists of an act of consciousness the object of which consists in the very activity of consciousness.

Here let us take a very simple thing which experiments have confirmed very well. A child in the preschool age is asked, 'You know what you are called?' The child answers "Kolya."[26] He cannot be consciously aware that the central question is not what he is called but whether he knows or does not know how he is called, that is, the object of his consciousness includes one part of the question. A child at this age knows his name, but he does not understand that he might be asked whether he knows this or does not know what he is called, that is, he knows his name, but he is not consciously aware of the knowledge of his name.

We now turn to concrete experimental study. It turns out to be the following very simple thing. The general setting or context for what I said—of conscious awareness and of mastery—lies in the fact of the development of a new kind of introspection or self-observation in the school age. We not only observe that which goes on around us, but we can also observe what is going on in ourselves. A child of school age, as studies have shown, resorts to what is known as verbalized, or spoken, introspection; that is, to put it otherwise, at school age what occurs in relation to introspection is the same as what occurs in early childhood in the transition from wordless perception to verbalized perception. Take a child at eight months and the child at

---

[25] Korotaeva has replaced the word "представляет" (that is, "is," or "presents," or "represents") with the word "отражает" (that is, "reflects", as in a mirror or as in thinking something over). Unlike the Soviet editors of Vygotsky's *Collected Works*, however, she is careful to tell us where she has changed the text and to tell us what the original stenogram had. But she doesn't tell us why she changed it. Korotaeva was a philosophy teacher, and taught philosophy texts by Lenin. In *Materialism and Empiriocriticism*, Lenin insists on a "reflection" model of consciousness: consciousness is a kind of mirror, reflecting reality. But Lenin wrote *Materialism and Empiriocriticism* before he had really studied Hegel Vygotsky, on the other hand, has studied Hegel and even, when he is writing this, studied Lenin's "philosophical notebooks" on the study of Hegel. So, this mirroring view is not the view of consciousness that Vygotsky takes. Instead, Vygotsky is building a semantic or semiological model of the human mind—based on verbal meaning. So 'represents' is really a lot better for Vygotsky and that's the word that Vygotsky probably used. That is certainly the word that Korotaeva found in the stenogram.

[26] This evidence may seem rather weak. After all, even very young children are able to respond to indirect questions ("Do you know your name?" "Can you clean up your room?" etc.) But these indirect questions could be simply interpreted by the child as direct questions ("Do you know what your name is?" = "What's your name?", "Can you clean up your room?" = "Go do it"). Is there no stronger evidence that three-year-olds, but not seven-year-olds, lack a conscious distinction between asking a name and asking who you are? Yes. Because the Korean language tends to drop subject pronouns and does not use plurals to indicate generality, the question "What is your name?" and "What are names?" are identically phrased in Korean. Song and Kellogg (2020) found that at least one three-year-old interpreted the second question as the first and refused to exchange names with her seven-year-old brother. But her brother had no difficulty at all interpreting questions about the nature of naming, gladly accepted the game of switching names with his sister, and could even switch "Mom" and "Dad" in play.

two years and eight months. At eight months, the child has wordless perception, that is, he sees this or that object but does not have a verbalized perception linked to speech. In the child at two years and eight months, there is inner perception.

This means during the transition from the age of infancy to the end of early childhood in the area of external perception of the child, what occurs? He begins to perceive internally. We say, to perceive internally means to perceive with conscious awareness, to communicate what has been perceived.

The same thing occurs in school age. If we compare the transition from preschool age to school, it turns out that here we find repeated in relation to introspection the shift which previously characterized wordless introspection.[27] Is it not possible to say, in other words, that the preschooler perceives his own inner processes in the same way as the infant perceives the external world? That is to say, he perceives distinctly, clearly, but he does not generalize.

What does this mean—to perceive in a wordless way? For example, the infant sees the shelves, the lamp, the table, the window, the light and perceives sounds, but he does not know that this is a "table," a "lamp," etc. What does internal perception mean? This means that the wardrobe is (an example of a—Trans.) wardrobe, and the window is (an instance of—Trans.) a window. These are generalized perceptions. The preschooler has introspections but does not generalize them, while at school age children are dealing with the transition to interior, or semantic, introspection. They start to make generalizations in the area of their own inner processes.

You remember that in one of the first lectures we talked about this comparison. I tried to briefly convey to you how the child's perception of the external world is recognized and tried to compare it with the perception of a chessboard. I attempted to show you that with each new potential the chessboard is linked to a new activity. The same goes for external perception as goes for internal, in this sense: you can perceive both the internal process and the external one in different ways, and to see different structures in it. As soon as the child makes the transition to a new stage of internal introspection, and better sees that what is going on within him (in connection with differentiation, maturation, etc., linked to the fact that intellect constitutes the basic function) it is clear that linked to this new form of introspection, a new form of inner activity will arise. As with a chessboard: If I see otherwise, I play otherwise. In external perception, the infant sees differently than a child at two years and eight months. But the child at two years and eight months, thanks to being able to see things differently, can he not handle things differently as well? Of course, in him there is a different form of activity. At school age, a new form of inner activity arises, characterized by a very simple thing.

Psychological operations that are not linked immediately to external action (so says Piaget, who I cite) are known as inner activities. After all, our psychological

---

[27] Vygotsky probably intended to say wordless perception, which is transformed into semantic perception at three. It's not clear if this was Vygotsky's mistake or that of the stenographer. Korotaeva does not note it, nor does Léopoldoff-Martin. See, however, Chap. 10 of this book, where Vygotsky uses the crisis at 3. and the formation of internalized perception, as an analogy for explaining the crisis at 7, the formation of inner *perezhivanie*.

operations are linked to external actions in this sense: when I speak, when I act, a whole psychological apparatus operates in me. But suppose I just sit in a chair and recollect things? This too can happen.

When I think, recollect, etc. I am carrying out an inner activeness; this inner activity of psychological processes is not directly linked to external activity. This new form of inner activeness in the school age consists of this: while during the preschool years these inner activities demonstrate an immediate link with action, with external activeness, in the school years we have a relative autonomy which emerges, inner activeness which is relatively independent of external activities. Here is already a child who can think, at the same time when he is doing or seeing something, one in whom has emerged a differentiation of inner and outer activities.

Now, we may ask, if we turn to these premises: in what relation does this fact stand to the problem of mastery and conscious awareness that interests us? What ensues in the area of intellectualization with school children? We said that what ensues is this very simple thing: they begin to generalize their proper psychological phenomena. This does not imply complete conscious awareness. Construing them—this means knowing not only the object that is represented in a given phenomenon of consciousness but knowing that very phenomenon of consciousness. If I begin to generalize that which I recall now, this implies that this operation which I now perform belongs to a class of recollections: I generalize it.

What does it imply to generalize a recollection? It implies that I consciously construe not only that which I recall but also the process of recollection itself.

One can say this: research shows that conscious awareness develops to the degree that concepts are developed, to the degree that word meanings are developed, linked to the psychological phenomena of the person himself.

This is the mechanism that explains to us why repetitions alone are not enough to develop conscious awareness; this mechanism shows that it is necessary to have a certain system of generalizations in order that I may become consciously aware.

Conscious awareness develops to the degree of generalization, and this is precisely what explains to us why and how conscious awareness is immediately linked to mastery, why it is precisely conscious awareness that constitutes the cause of mastery, and how the two processes, linked together, exchange the roles of cause and effect.

What does it mean to become consciously aware? It means to generalize one's own psychological processes.

Now I ask: thanks to the fact that in me there has emerged the concept of the object, has the capacity to act in relation to the object been changed? Yes. In the same way, to construe something means precisely to generalize it; and if I generalize my own process of activity, this implies that I obtain the opportunity of a different relationship to it. To put it crudely, it is as if there occurs its separation from the overall activity of consciousness. I am consciously aware that I recall, that is, I make my own recollection the subject of my own consciousness. A separation emerges. Any generalization distinguishes objects in a certain way.

For the infant, perception of a circle depends on whatever circle lies in front of him, but for the older child who can already generalize, the object may not depend on that structure to which it belongs.

So, the very fact of generalization indicates that the perception of an object is included in a different structure. And what of volition? In contemporary psychology, there is no other answer, besides: volition characterizes a peculiar attitude to the situation, not strictly dependent on the given situation, more freely acting <…>.

That is why conscious awareness, understood as generalization, leads immediately to mastery.

Now I would like to point out the following moment. I ask you whether this law explains to me why awareness appears later at all (as Claparède contends). Why does there first arise some action and only then do we become consciously aware of it? Why does a schoolchild first have an intellectual operation, and later he becomes aware of it? I ask, is it possible for me to first generalize something and only then perceive it. No. Consequently, in consciousness the operation must first appear, and only then can I become consciously aware of it. It is clear that whatever operation appears in an autonomous form, it would be senseless to think that it will be the object of my consciousness.

Consciousness is only capable of conscious awareness of its own proper operations. And it is thanks to this establishment of such relationships that we need to link them to their own proper activities. Is it clear why consciousness appears later, why the child is consciously aware of memory, or perception, but not consciously aware of intellect? In order to be consciously aware of something, it is necessary for there first to be that thing. Is there memory at preschool age? There is. Is there perception? There is. But intellect is itself is in the process of being born. It would be a miracle if intellect began with consciousness itself. It turns out that the intellectual function, with the help of which all the other different activities become consciously aware, is consciously construed later, because it emerges after them, and it must become consciously aware of others, and only then of itself.[28]

That is just why in the area of defining consciousness we must proceed along the same path that materialist philosophy and materialist psychology proceeded along

[28] In this paragraph, Vygotsky explains why conscious awareness tends to appear late. The child makes a mistake. The child corrects the mistake. The child is even capable of doing a problem correctly. But the child is not capable of explaining why he made the mistake, nor how he did it correctly. Why is this? Clearly, Claparède's explanation will not do. After all, if conscious awareness comes from making mistakes, the child should be able to explain why he made the mistake, even before he can do it correctly, and certainly after he can do it correctly.

Vygotsky's explanation is that intellect (thinking) is a function, like perception and like memory. In order to be consciously aware of a function, you need to have it, to grasp it, to master it. It's impossible for a young child to first be aware of perceptions--and only then start seeing and hearing. The child has to see and hear first, and only then will she or he be aware of seeing and hearing. It's impossible for a preschooler to be aware of memory first, and only then start remembering. And in the same way, it's impossible for a child to think about thinking until the child has mastered and become familiar with thinking. As Spinoza says, it is possible to have an idea without having the idea of the idea—but you cannot have the idea of the idea unless you first have the idea.

in their time. Back when it was the idea of autonomous self-consciousness that consciousness arose from self-consciousness and 'I' itself defined everything. No. We know that self-consciousness arises later than everything else, and when consciousness has developed, self-consciousness, a certain awareness of one's own conscious activity, can arise.

So it seems to me that there is a paradox, consisting in this: with other functions, consciously construing them and making them volitional comes thanks to intellectual activity, but intellectual activity itself develops at school age; conscious awareness receives its own proper development, but that consciousness is linked to the development of introspection that is semanticized, that is, the development of generalization, in school; this is linked to the emergence of new capacities for activity, volitional activity in relation to these functions, these determinations.

Let us give a few minutes to one more topic. Today I have outlined to you the general laws of psychological development at school age, mainly in the context of the relationship between intellectual and other functions and clarified the paradox which we and you spoke of. But I did not illuminate for you the very process of thinking as such in the area of the development of concepts at school age. This problem, it appears, in the proximal future will be affected by the analyses of learning and teaching the different types of study work, for example the analysis of algebraic thinking and social science thinking, and you will see that an essential step that the schoolchild takes in the development of his concepts is that his main links, which dominated during the preschool level, develop into the so-called preconcepts. This is a unique and interesting form of generalization, which governs the school age. I wish to explain it in two words, in order to point out how it is both the content of that I have spoken of thus far and its locus. Let me do this in order to complete the structure of today's lecture.

The schoolchild is already forming concepts. In what sense is he forming concepts? It is a simple empirical fact that he has begun the study of science, our arithmetic, our natural science, that is, he can explain arithmetic and he has science concepts. However, upon closer investigation it turns out that these concepts are not mature, that they stand in an early step of their development and that they merit the name of preconcept as a stage toward the development of concepts in the true sense.

How do these preconcepts differ from true concepts? They differ, it seems to me, as arithmetical concepts differ from algebraic ones. For those of us who know algebra, every arithmetical concept is a special case of an algebraic one. What does this imply? It implies that we in algebra have generalized the known arithmetical concepts.

For example, when the child has arrived a such a degree of abstraction that he is diverted from calling out the numbers and can write 5 + 7—he is diverted from the objects—in him there is a concept of a numeral not dependent upon the objects to which this numeral relates. But he still does not understand what a + b implies, because this is a generalization of all arithmetical concepts. In this way, any concept must comprise some element of conscious awareness of one's own generalization.

The child is mastering the decimal system at a very early stage of his formation, but for we and for you, the decimal system is a special case of all number systems.

We understand that the decimal system is a special case of all number systems. For the child, the decimal system constitutes the only existing system.

Now, I ask: is it the same, when for me the decimal system exists as a special case of all systems or when for me there exists only the decimal system? You yourselves understand that it is not all the same. In the first case it exists in relation to other systems, it exists as a more general concept to which it is related, and there are much more complex and delicate relations established when this concept can be included in a system of other concepts.

Generalization signifies the growth of generalization linked with relations with other concepts. My operations in the field of arithmetic are much freer to the extent that I form a generalization of my own arithmetical operations. The child is freed from dependency: five apples and five pears, but he then depends upon the rules of arithmetic. As Thorndike's experiments have shown, he understands the conventions of arithmetic as an absolute law, and he is bound by this law. But to the extent that he understands that our system of signs is only an uncomplicated system, he begins to use them all the more voluntarily.

So what characterizes the preconcept of the child? It has a high level of abstraction from real objects, that is, it has a high degree of generalization of some aspect of reality. This we can say. But does it contain other generalizations of its own operations? No. Preconcepts are characterized by this: they do not contain the slightest generalization in the transition to other, higher-standing areas. And this means that they cannot be consciously aware. Here we have preconcepts which are not generalized. And just as arithmetical operations are included in algebra and become consciously aware in algebra, and as a consequence become volitional in algebra, in the same way each preconcept of the child becomes consciously aware in later school age in his algebra, in his school concepts, and there emerges a free, volitional action in this or that area. For example, you ask the child to write the number 393. He will write 393 for you. Can he write 393 otherwise? He can only write it in one form. We can write 393 for you in countless ways, we can write 393 as 400–7, but the child cannot do this. Thus, Remes[29] made a special study into how a child may express this or that number, and it became clear that he can write it in only one manner.

Consequently, volition does not grow from generalization. If I understand that the number 393 can be divided, then I may say that I know what this number means. It means three hundreds, nine tens, and three units, if I understand that this is a case of division. Then I can expand it to 400–7 and so on. But if I do not know a single case of decomposition and do not understand that this is a decomposition of a number, then I do not understand the arbitrariness of the operation in relation to this action.

In this way, the same essence, from the positive side. The character of the thinking of the school child shows there are generalizations that make it possible to make

[29] This probably refers to Yevgeny Yakovlevich Remes (Евгений Яковлевич Ремез, 1896–1975) a Soviet math teacher in the Institute of Education at the University of Kiev, who later worked on approximation theory. He later worked at many pedagogical institutes.

all the child's actions conscious and voluntary, but which are of themselves necessarily unaware and nonvolitional.

That is why, from the positive side the thinking gives us the answer to the question of what the central features of the psychology of the school child are: volitional attention, logical memory, or consciously aware memory, nonconscious thinking or nonvolitional thinking. That is all that I wished to say.

References

Bruner, J. (1987). Prologue. In *Collected works of L.S. Vygotsky, Vol. 1* (pp. 1–16). Plenum.

Выготский, Л. С. (2001). *Лекции по педологии*. Ижевск: Издательский дом "Удмуртский Университет".

Haber, R. N. (1979). Twenty years of haunting eidetic imagery: where's the ghost? *Behavioral and Brain Sciences, 2*(4), 583–594.

Luria, A. R. (1989/2000). *The mind of a mnemonist*. Harvard.

Nation, I. S. P. (2012). *Learning vocabulary in another language*. Cambridge University Press.

Piaget, J. (1924/1956). *Le jugement et le raisonnement chez l'enfant*. Delachaux et Niestlé.

Song, S.-M., & Kellogg, D. (2020). The problem of articulate animals in Korean child conversation: A Hallidayan analysis, a Vygotskyan interpretation, and a Hasanian critique WORD. *Journal of the International Linguistic Association, 66*(3), 149–165.

Vygotskij, L. S. (2018). *La science du développement de l'enfant: Text pédologiques (1930–1934)*. Traduits par I. Léopoldoff-Martin. Berne.

Vygotsky, L. S. (1997). *Collected works* (Vol. 4). Plenum.

Vygotsky, L. S. (2019). *L.S. Vygotsky's pedological works, Vol. 1: The foundations of pedology*. Springer.

Chapter 13
Thinking in School Age

Outline of Chapter 13: Thinking in School Age

This chapter summarizes the lecture Vygotsky gave on 3 May 1934, that is, just a week after the lecture in Chapter 12 and just a little over a month before his death. The last chapter presented factual materials and noted the contradiction between the intellectualization of other functions and the nonintellectualization of thinking. The explanation given by Piaget appeared circular—the child is not aware of thinking because the child lacks conscious awareness. The explanation given by Claparède could not explain the specificity of school age—the child is not aware of thinking because the child lacks sufficient maladaptive experience.

Vygotsky's own explanation, in this chapter, is a more Spinozian one, although Spinoza is not invoked by name. Thinking about thinking is forming an idea of an idea, which Spinoza explicates as the form of an idea in so far as the idea is considered as a mode of thinking without relation to its object (Spinoza, 1677/1995, p. 81). It is possible for a child to form first ideas without forming any idea of the idea, just as it is possible for adults to experience an event without transforming it into meaning, that is, changing it from raw, relatively unmediated experience into a *perezhivanie.* But it is not possible to have the idea of the idea without first having the idea, just as it is not really possible to know the meaning of the experience you have until you have had the experience itself. So the child thinks, but cannot think about thinking without relation to its object.

I. **Review and Considerations:** Vygotsky begins his lecture by summarizing the homework and reviewing what he covered in the last class. He reminds the students of the paradox of intellect: being able to make other functions consciously aware and freely willed without being consciously aware or freely willed itself. Vygotsky also reminds them that neoformations in any age emerge

---

This chapter is taken from material published by G.S. Korotaeva in 2001 (Выготский, 2001). Korotaeva notes that it is the stenogramme of a lecture delivered on May 3, 1934 (On May 9th, Vygotsky suffered a throat hemorrhage and was brought home. He died four weeks later).

L. S. Vygotsky, *L.S. Vygotsky's Pedological Works. Volume 2.*, Perspectives in Cultural-Historical Research 10, https://doi.org/10.1007/978-981-16-1907-6_13

at the end of the age rather than at the beginning. Vygotsky notes that consciousness can reflect reality in very different ways: for example, as feeling or as thinking. He proposes that feelings—that is, sensations—are phylogenetically and even ontogenetically "primordial," that is, shared with animals and early to develop in humans. In contrast, thinking is a specifically human and late-developing function created through a process of generalizations. He says that he will give three considerations that support this proposal (but he gets a little carried away and gives four instead).

II. **The Central Line of Development: Generalization and Interrelation of Concepts:** Vygotsky now asks what it is that produces a specific mode of thinking for every age, and the intellectual mode of thinking that is conducive to classification, proof, and the kinds of arguments supported by considerations for school age. He suggests that this has to do with the way in which concepts can be related, and he once again proposes two considerations that allow generalization to enable the specific form of interrelation between concepts that we see in school age.

III. **The Central Neoformation: Conscious Awareness and Mastery in Thinking:** Vygotsky draws two conclusions. The first conclusion is that together, the system and the relations of generality constitute a defining moment for school age and indeed for every other age as well. But they also constitute a contradiction. On one hand, the system does not appear all at once. At each age, there is a specific circle of concepts specific to each age, and this does not actually correspond to the words used but rather to the act of generalization that underlies word use. For example, a child of two places "animal," "bear," and "bat" at the same level of generality, while a child of eight understands that all bears and bats are animals but not all animals are bears or bats. On the other hand, the relationships of generality require that one concept be useless without all the others. So for example, children do not learn numbers one by one but as part of a whole system, where one number can be re-expressed in infinitely many ways. So the second conclusion is that the ability of the child to communicate her or his understanding can lag behind his or her ability to generalize. Vygotsky warns that, for example, the new social science curriculum, which requires teachers to communicate concepts like "exploitation" and "class struggle" to second graders, overestimates the potential for communication in the child. The child can generalize, but this does not necessarily mean that the child is capable of higher level theoretical generalizations, something that lies in the next, or proximal, zone of development. The school age break with generalized visual representations is nevertheless a revolutionary one: the outer visual field, which was master, has now become servant, and the inner field of meaning, which was once dominated, can now dominate.

Chapter 13: Thinking in School Age

Last time we spoke to you in regard to some general moments which characterize the psychological development of the child at school age. Together we found that the outer aspect of the picture of psychological development at school age is paradoxical in the sense that (this is not denied by anyone) it is at this age that the development of higher psychological functions, that the general basis of higher psychological functions, consists in their intellectualization <...> awareness and subordination of them to voluntary control constitutes the basic feature which characterizes these higher psychological functions.

But alongside of this, as research shows, intellect itself, the thinking of the school child itself, remains unconscious and nonvolitional at this age.

This is, as I said to you, the paradoxical-looking picture that for the past few years now has become the center of all the theoretical discussions and debates, constituting the point around which all of the different theories of the school age bend. We attempted to explain to you this paradoxical proposition on the strength of a more correct understanding of what consciousness is in general; we then sought to show that awareness of one's own psychological functions constitutes, in general, a volitional act. For this reason, it is natural that, say, attention, memory, and perception can become consciously aware and become volitional at school age, but that at this age, thinking itself alone is in the first basic cycle of its main development, because thinking is not the thing from which development commences. Thinking itself begins as a precondition of the development of relatively complex perception, memory, attention, and other, simpler, elementary functions. So it is natural that, when elementary thinking starts to break through to this basic cycle, it must first complete the cycle and only then can it constitute the object of conscious awareness, passing into a higher stage of development, where the activity of a function is consciously aware and becomes volitional.

Now then, as I know, in my absence[1] you worked on very important and valuable material—the intellectual development of the schoolchild linked to his teaching-and-learning—linking the tempo of changes which teaching-and-learning brings about in the process of intellectual development of the child to the concrete course of teaching-and-learning in different subjects, and summarizing a lot of concrete material on how the course of development itself is carried out.

If we summarize what you have done up to the present time, it adds up, in my view, in such a way that you have now fixed the point of departure and the problems of psychological development; you have made up, you have worked out, the path of intellectual development, the basic concrete forms through which this intellectual

[1] This suggests that this lecture might be the follow-on lecture to the last one, on school age. That lecture was dated late February. This one is already in early May. So Vygotsky would have been absent for more than a month.

Vygotsky seems to be referring to the material in *Thinking and Speech* Chapter 6, Section 4, which is based on the work by Herzen Pedagogical Institute students.

development takes place, and all that remains for us now is to consider the fruits of this development, to see what this intellectual development leads to, from which starting points it goes forth and down which channels it flows, which central neoformations are created at school age, how the school child's consciousness and attitude to reality is reconstructed, and how school age ends and is exhausted as a period of development, thereby necessitating the restructuration of the whole situation of development and opening the door to the crisis, to the transitional age, and to the subsequent age, the epoch of sexual maturation.

Today, let me dwell on these results and on the development of the main neoformations. As I have said a few times, it seems to me that the main neoformations in each age are laid down by the end of the age. The content of the age lies in the emergence of these neoformations. It is difficult to expect that these will be given in advance; on the contrary, they are laid down at the end. It is always more correct to consider these central new formations as a whole in relation to the child and the personality, in his relation to the environment, to reality. Therefore, it seems to me that the central neoformation is always linked to some new architecture of the child's consciousness, if we understand consciousness not simply as an aggregate of subjective *perezhivanies* but instead understand consciousness in the strict sense of the word, going far beyond the merely psychological understanding of consciousness, and treating it as a relation to reality in the broadest sense of the word, as a relation to reality that is typical of humans, as a conscious relationship to reality. This is a general neoformation that consists of a new architecture of consciousness, one that emerges in the school child at the end of school age.

In order to have some vague idea concerning this new architecture of consciousness, we need to begin with analysis, and we need to pose a whole series of smaller, more particular questions, which would permit us to give a definitive answer to this (larger-Trans.) question. This question we shall save for the end, but now we will assemble the known data which will subsequently enable us to answer it.

I will start with that which appears to me to constitute the basis, the center. I will, in a few words, permit myself to repeat that which I have said intermittently many times but which each time has to be brought to memory in order that further propositions should be clear. I imagine it thus: consciousness is always a reflection of reality. This is the proposition outside of which a general account of consciousness in any science is not possible. But it seems to me that nobody, except for cowards who would oversimplify every problem, has said that consciousness must always reflect reality in the same way. It always reflects reality, but not in the same way. If consciousness were to reflect reality in one specifically defined way, then there could be no development of consciousness. Consciousness reflects reality not like a mirror, but in multifarious modes. At each stage in the development, both in the area of phylogenesis and in the area of ontogenesis, consciousness reflects reality differently. We all know the often-quoted remark by Lenin that the dialectical leap does not merely consist in the transition from nonliving material to sensate; there is also a dialectical leap that consists in the transition from sensation to thinking. This remark does not leave any doubt about the theoretical correctness of those who wish to consider the multifarious modes of reflecting reality in consciousness.

Is sensation the primordial form of consciousness reflecting reality? Without any doubt, yes.

And is thinking, as one of the highest forms of conscious activity, specific to humans? Yes, undoubtedly, it does reflect it, but if we recognize that the transition from sensation to thinking is a dialectical leap, the emergence of something new, then it follows that thinking reflects reality in a way that is different in principle from sensation.

You, who have been working a lot on the problems of gnosiology[2] and logic, know to what extent a reflection of reality worked over by thinking stands even higher than a higher empirical one based only on one's own experience of reflecting reality, and it seems to me that in psychology it is not only legitimate but simply necessary to admit that consciousness reflects reality differently at different stages. This is the first proposition.

Now, what is, roughly speaking, this difference in the reflection of reality? It seems to me that the most essential in the mode in which reality is reflected in consciousness that emerges in humans, as a new, human mode of reflection of reality in consciousness consists in the generalized reflection of reality in consciousness, which is the key culmination of the development of consciousness in the age of childhood and which each time is linked to the dialectical transition from sensation to thinking as the highest form of reflection of reality. From the psychological point of view, the transition from sensation to thinking signifies in the first place a transition from a nongeneralized to a generalized reflection of reality in consciousness.

Which considerations speak in favor of this, and which considerations might lead us to be able to apply them to the school child? I would point to three main considerations[3] which would lead us to believe so and which will be justified throughout the research, and in any case I do not know of any theoretical or practical consideration which might cause us to abandon this idea.

---

[2] Vygotsky uses the Russian term гносеология, which is the Greek term gnosiology transliterated into the Russian alphabet, and that is how we have translated it. Today, this would probably be called "epistemology" (as in the "genetic epistemology" of Piaget). But in Aristotle, epistemology is really just one branch of gnosiology, the branch concerned with scientific concepts. Vygotsky's concern is really broader—explaining how all concepts and even preconcepts are known.

[3] The "three considerations" are actually four: the link between generalization and communication, the zig-zag nature of the development of word meaning, the growth of introspection in the child, and the big difference between child consciousness and animal consciousness. However, as Vygotsky points out, these three points are really closely related to each other, so whether we say there are four or three is not very important. What is more confusing is the next six paragraphs, where Vygotsky talks about the relation between generalization and communication and then makes more general remarks about the social nature of consciousness.

Like Vygotsky's students, his readers will just have to get used to this apparent inconsistency. Fortunately, the inconsistency is really only apparent. You see, Vygotsky believes that development is a process of differentiation, and he develops his lectures accordingly. He gives you a big, complex idea with several interrelated parts, and then he differentiates it. Usually, he says he is going to differentiate it into three parts (the rule of three, the magic number three, from fairy tales, from Hegel). But because the ideas really are unitary and really are complex, we sometimes get less than three and even more often more than three.

The first consideration: This consists in that which I have spoken of several times already: the link between generalization and communication.

What constitutes, what is most typical, most basic, and most important for human consciousness and for its specific mode of reflecting reality?

The social and historical nature of this consciousness.

But I once spoke, and I now remind you, of the fact that human consciousness is not the product of individual development but is the product of the historical development of human society and that, as a consequence, human consciousness emerges, grows, and changes in the communication between people, that is, the fact that the matter does not occur in such a way that everyone in their heads grows a consciousness and these finished products are then exchanged. Instead, consciousness grows and creates its own basic functions through the process of communication. This fact requires elucidation, and to it must be given an appropriate position when we speak of the reflection of reality in human consciousness.

I said that experimental and theoretical analysis both have demonstrated that generalization and communication are two aspects of one and the same whole. Communication in the general sense of the word is enabled only when linked to generalization.

For a long time, we have known and we have often cited the fact that communication is impossible without signs, without speech, that is, unconscious communication is not possible, and only relatively recently have we begun to attend to the fact that communication without generalization, that is, not only without signs but also without the meaning of signs, is possible.[4] Let me cite an example. Imagine that I tie a knot in order to remember something that I must not forget. Does it constitute a sign? Yes, it seems to me. Can you say what it is that I wish to memorize by looking at the knot? No, you cannot. This sign is of a lone thought, a lone record, and a sign which you cannot interpret. We have surely encountered these in the study of a number of knot records used by ancient peoples and knot records now utilized by some peoples standing on lower steps of historical development.[5]

---

[4] Vygotsky sudden statement that generalization does not require communication is a little incongruous, given the preceding paragraph which says the opposite. It might be explained somehow in the gap in the record immediately before (e.g., "For a long time it was correctly thought that generalization without communication was not possible, and only relatively recently…."). It may be that it is simply a lapse by the stenographer, or perhaps even by Vygotsky himself.

But the rest of the paragraph suggests that Vygotsky has something else in mind—an exception that proves the rule previously stated that generalization is enabled by communication. Vygotsky says that the meaning of the knot in the handkerchief is known only to the person who made it; since it is a private code, there is self-communication but no possibility of generalization.

[5] Quipus were found in the Inca Empire in South America but also in Hawaii and China. The ones in South America do not have any known relationship with the spoken language; the ones that have been decoded are either numerical or refer to place names (rather as a postal code would). It is true that there are no known narrative quipus. But it is not true that they cannot be understood by others. They can be understood by the "quipucamayoc," the quipu specialist that Inca kings used—they were used as specialist book keepers.

You have heard that in Mexico,[6] there existed the so-called <…>, the main governmental chronicle books were done with the help of knots which were tied in ropes. But who could read them? Only those who tied them. So long as the sign is in such a state of development that it indicates only one lone thing and does not contain any generalization, then it still does not constitute a human word and it excludes any possibility of communication between people in the essential, human sense of the word. When we speak of adolescents, and even today, when we speak of the school child, I will try to show you this stage of generalization which leads the school child to new forms of communication between the schoolchild and other children on the one hand and adults on the other.

The first consideration, which allows generalization as a mode of reflecting reality in consciousness to be taken as the most important content of the development of consciousness in the child consists in this: when I study communication, I seem to see an expanding, growing, building, deepening of the activity of consciousness that is linked specifically to communication with humans, a historical feature without which man as a historical being could not have arisen.

The second consideration is very close to this and linked to speech. Each word, as Lenin formulates it, constitutes a generalization. Generalization also constitutes, as Lenin points out, a way of reflecting reality different in principle, not a dead mirror-like copy, but a zigzagging act which imposes a flight from reality and a return to it, which includes within itself a bit of fantasy, and speech is, on the one hand linked to communication, but on the other hand linked to a new mode of reflecting reality. He also said that the generalized way of reflection can be put at the forefront in the study of the evolution of children's consciousness.

The third consideration is based on the increase of specifically human properties in the sense of the child's relation to reality with each age, the extension of the perception of the world, the activity in the world and the child's relation[7] to his own self, his perception of his own inner reality, and the inner activeness of the child; and

[6]The quipu was widely used in South America, but not in Mexico, where Mayans developed a true writing system by 300 BC. Vygotsky is probably thinking of the Zuni in present-day New Mexico, who did use the quipu. Note, however, that the quipu is a true symbolic system and not a private code like a notched stick, as Vygotsky says here and also in Chapter 2 of Luria and Vygotsky 1930/1993. Vygotsky is taking this claim uncritically from Levy-Bruhl, who never did any field work and instead relied on the accounts of missionaries who were well-known to oversell the advantages of printed Bibles over local traditions.

[7]In general, we have striven to translate each Russian word by a single, unchanging English word, in order to allow the reader to see the comparisons that the Russian language itself evokes in the author's mind. But this is not always possible without doing some violence to English. So, for example, Vygotsky says отношения (ребенка к действительности), which means an objective relationship (of the child to reality) such as speech. But then, Vygotsky speaks of отношения ребенка к самому себе, which means the subjective attitude of the child toward the inner self. We don't want to set up a barrier to Vygotsky's generalization by translating it first as "relationship" and second as "attitude". So we have chosen the most general word "relation" in order to draw attention to the fact that Russian word is the same, and the affinity it suggests belongs to the Russian language itself: Note that later, when Vygotsky speaks of "relations of generality," he is once again using this Russian word.

if we look at the stages of how the relation to reality that is specific to humans develops, how a specifically human form of activity develops, (how) awareness of one's own inner psychological processes, introspection, the potential for inner activeness, then we will see that it is always closely linked to generalization.

Finally, **last of all**, it is also without doubt an established fact that in the area of animal consciousness, we are not dealing with even the rudiments of generalization. All attempts to inculcate animals with human speech, both in their success and in their failure end up the same—with the incapacity to develop in animals generalizations or communications in the social sense of the word. True, there have been some scholars in America who decided to begin not with generalization in ape offspring but with social enculturation. This is the third year of a heroic experiment in enculturating a chimpanzee offspring alongside a human offspring in exactly the same environmental conditions, with the belief that once they have created the necessity for communication, as a result, link by link, all of the rest will emerge. But already there is a report written in very pessimistic tones, that because of the differences between the child and chimpanzee, the inner hopelessness of this sort of attempts is becoming clear in advance, even if some important progress in terms of dressage has been made.[8]

All of this together gives to us the right, when we proceed to the study of consciousness and those transformations which arise in the course of further development, first of all to raise the question of what it is that in each age proceeds to the achievement of its own syncretic ways of thinking but in the school child emerges as a readiness to respond with knowledge, with the classification of concepts, with conclusions, and with consideration <…>.

But the nature of concepts lies precisely in this: separate concepts exist in a known relationship with each other. Roughly speaking, in the history of the development of thinking, matters never proceed in such a way that there is a separate working out of separate concepts and then they are somehow grouped together and enter into links with each other. Each concept emerges in a circle of other concepts and already has in its inner structure the origins (lit. the "preconvergence"—Trans.) of a certain relationship to other concepts. I once told you that this aspect is perhaps the most important for the whole history of child thinking, linked to the problem of the relationship between concepts. The relationship between concepts has been called in contemporary psychology the relationship of generality. Let me remind you of this in a few words.

[8]This is probably a reference to scientists Luella and Winthrop Kellogg. The Kelloggs raised a chimp called Gua with their son Donald. They were raised as brother and sister. At about age one, Gua outperformed Donald in certain tasks (e.g., using a spoon, obeying commands, drinking from a cup). But there were already important differences: Gua recognized clothes and smells, but Donald recognized faces. Donald began speaking at sixteen months, but Gua did not speak. In 1932, the Kelloggs ended the experiment because Donald was starting to use Gua's "food bark" instead of human words at mealtimes. Gua was sent back to the primate center in Florida, and died of fever shortly thereafter.

Every child word meaning has a generalization, and one generalization, that is, one concept, always stands to another concept in a definite relation of generality; either one concept is more general and includes in itself a whole range of concepts and is then a subordinate one[9] <…> or these concepts relate to each other as concepts of the same (order of—Trans.) generality, subordinate to some higher concepts—then it is said about these concepts that they are co-subordinated, a particular case, which along with a series of other special concepts along with other particular …. that is, that they are concepts of the same (level of—Trans.) generality. Analysis of thinking shows that in different forms of thinking the proximal elements will always be precisely those relations of generality which are possible between concepts at a given step of development. In order that this might be clearer and more concrete, and to give you the opportunity to transition directly to the school age, I should present two considerations which I briefly mentioned in discussions with you.

One of these has a direct relationship to the school age.

We may imagine matters as if at one pole, the smallest in its subordination will be the concept which is the most concrete, the most visual, the most closely related to reality in the sense of a single fact—a fact which is reflected in this concept, and as if at the other pole we place the concept, maximally abstract, maximally general, including the broadest sphere of this activeness, with all the other concepts somehow located along this axis (draws). The position occupied by the concept on this axis might be figuratively called using a geographical comparison the concept's (position on the line of—Trans.) longitude. Consequently, the longitude (position—Trans.) of a given concept can be denoted by the unique combination or unity of concrete and abstract moments, which are contained in the given concept. In any concept, there are contained both concrete and abstract moments, but no concept is ever an abstraction with a complete departure from reality; there is always some return to it, but different concepts make this zigzag to different degrees, and if you take such concepts as "rose" "flower," "plant," and "organism" (if we just take some at random) it becomes clear that I have constructed here concepts in a series of ascending position in longitude. On my imaginary longitude, these concepts are arranged on an ascending line of longitude.[10]

[9] This appears to be an error. If a concept includes a whole range of other concepts, it is superordinate and not subordinate, which is how Léopoldoff-Martin (Vygotskij, 2018) has translated this. But the Russian clearly says that subordinate and not superordinate, and Korotaeva has not marked or tried to correct the error, if there is one. Perhaps, Vygotsky means to say that the included concepts are subordinate?

[10] Vygotsky introduces the "measure of generality" that he places at the center of Chapter 6 in *Thinking and Speech* (Выготский, 1934). This is his explanation of how the child's word meanings develop into true concepts. Unlike Chapter 5 of *Thinking and Speech*, it is not based on complexes (teaching complexes forbidden in the USSR with the shutdown of the labor schools). Unlike complexes, it shows a clear path of generalization and abstraction to true concepts.

Note that Vygotsky uses "longitude" to mean what we would call "latitude." This is because he is thinking of the value on the line of longitude—that is, how far from the pole or how far from the equator.

Flowers: rose, violet, lily-of-the-valley. The question arises: are these concepts in the same longitudinal position? The same. They are all particular cases of the more general concept. They reflect different spheres of reality. The concepts will always be determined by the position on latitude in relation to a concrete sector of reality which is presented in them, which they reflect. Each concept, from this point of view, may be characterized in a developed system of concepts of known latitude and longitude that always determine their position in the system of concepts.

This latitude and longitude of the concept received its name in an experimental study of the measure of generality of concepts. Each concept has its own measure of generality, that is, its own combination of concrete and abstract moments, its own degree of abstraction, and its own segment of reality which it presents. This place characterizes the degree of generality of the concept. This relation between concepts is their relation of generality; for example, flower to rose is a relation of generality. If we pay attention to this, we may go on to a second moment that will make still clearer, it seems to me, the question of how these relations between concepts develop. Studies have shown that these relations of generality possess two basic properties. The first consists in this: in the development of adult persons, there are already in existence relations of generality between concepts, that is, the fact that each concept is not reflecting by itself some slice of reality, but each concept with its latitude and longitude always constitutes a point in a system of concepts and, consequently, contains the possibility of transition from this concept to any other concept, that this fact is the center to which the explanation of all forms of thinking accessible to human being is reduced.

For any given person, whatever the system of relations between concepts may be, such is the range of mental operations available to him in each given area.

We have spoken of how different arithmetic concepts in the schoolchild are from the general representations of quantity which exist in the preschooler.

A preschooler, and even a child in the early age, knows that he has five fingers, distinguishes two from three, and can collect four cubes and recognize groups of objects. What is it that distinguishes the concept of 4 or 5 that exists in a child of 3, 4, or 5 years old from the concept of 5 which exists in a school child at the end of the first year of teaching-and-learning?

The first difference consists in this: the arithmetic concept "five" contains in itself a relationship to all of the other arithmetic concepts. Take "five"—this means that you locate it as a certain point in a system of concepts and give all of the meanings of this concept to all of the others. Five—this is for us four plus one, and one less than six. How many ways can you express five? You can re-express it in an infinite number of ways, that is, the concept possesses the capability of movement through the measurement of the rest of the concepts. Consequently, there emerges a law which is called that of the equivalence of concepts. For us five is the square root of 25 and the cube root of 125, and the ratio of 5,000 to one thousand, and so on. All of this for us is five. Five is decisively related to all of this, but why is the concept of five in school age even richer than the concept of five in preschool age? How is this generalization formally explained? The concept has become more general, more abstract, it has become wider in scope, but clearer in content. Wertheimer[11] devoted a special study which attempted to show the superiority of primitive arithmetic to our own, to point out that it is more vivid and richer in content.

For us, 5—this is a discrete concept, but for the person who does not possess a developed arithmetical concept, this is five fingers or five members in my family or something of that kind. He (Wertheimer—Trans.) conducted experiments showing how much a preschool child's emotions are warmer, more colored, more full than a school child. A preschooler asked what five is may be less liable to answer than a schoolchild, but the schoolchild answers mechanically, while the preschooler thinks and says, "five is sometimes petals on a lilac blossom," or else something equally colorful, saturated with a certain content.

So why do we feel that "5" as an arithmetical concept is richer, and not more impoverished in content, than five as a generalized perception? This is because the arithmetical concept "5" includes the relation of five to all that remains; a thing does not exist in itself but in its links with the rest. Five is a generalization; "5" is not only a generalization but also a relation among other generalizations.

From this emerges the law of equivalence. I can make any kind of assessment with "5." The preschooler knows that there are five fingers and that on a lilac blossom there may be five petals but there are usually four, but he does not know more than this: four or five. The schoolchild knows (more—Trans.), because in him there is the relationship of 5–4. In him there arises the possibility of those operations of thinking that are not possible when the relations of generality are not there. As studies have shown, thanks to this there emerges the possibility of defining concepts. For example, we ask the child to define the following concepts: What is a dog? What is justice? etc. What does it mean to define a concept? If you possess the relationship between a given concept and the other concepts, you may give the equivalent of this concept. But if you do not have this relationship of generality or it is not well developed, then the definition is impoverished in possibilities. What goes on in your mind, according to what the research has shown, when we and you speak of some concept, let us say a mammal as Bühler did in his work? What goes on in your mind is not that which occurs when you perceive some mammal or other, but rather

[11] Max Wertheimer (1880–1943) was, with Koffka and Köhler, the founder of Gestalt (structural) psychology. He was the student of Stumpf in Berlin and Külpe in Wurzburg. His first major experiment, in 1910, tried to explain why we see a two lights flashing on and off in sequence as a single light moving from one position to another. This led to the idea that we tend to perceive whole structures rather than single objects. As you can see, this holistic idea does tend to favor the child's primitive arithmetic, as it is based on holistic perception (seeing quantities as more or less) rather than analyzing by counting.

Vygotsky critically appropriated the Gestaltists: the measure of generality is certainly a Gestaltist idea, which Wertheimer later developed into a book on "productive thinking." According to this book, productive thinking takes place by relocating concepts from one place on the measure of generality. Vygotsky's method is certainly, like that of the Gestaltists, holistic. But we can also see that he does not accept the Gestaltist emphasis on lower psychological functions and their disregard for language. Moreover, Vygotsky explains structure with function—and function with history.

something similar to what goes on when 325 is said; when "mammal" is said, I experience that structural place where you have placed me.

I can go upwards or downwards; I can go here and say what a mammal is, and so on. In this way, first of all, what emerges in the definition of concepts—this is its place in a system, in relation to other concepts, the point at which I obtain the opportunity to link a given concept to others, that is, to move in the system of my concepts.

This will become still clearer if we take a second property, which lies in this: the relations of generality constitute the basis for thinking in a developed human consciousness. Just as every age level has its own generalization of reality, so too every age level has its own way of reflecting reality in consciousness as a generalized picture of the world.

One example will clarify what we are dealing with here. We have already spoken to you about autonomous child speech, the initial stage in the development of child speech when the child makes a transition from babbling to speaking in words. In autonomous children's speech, in words there are no relations of generality at all; the words lie in the same rank, the one next to each other.

I cited the example which we observed—but as a rule only for a short period of time—in children in the early years during the period of dominance of autonomous speech. I not long ago looked over all of the material from Comrade Konnikova[12] and saw that the whole of it supported this rule. I did not find two words that could be related the one to the other as "flower" and "rose," so that one was above the other, in the speech of children who persist in their autonomous speech.

Let me give you one such example.

We have a child to deal with. This child knew words like "table," "chair," "wardrobe," "couch," and "bookcase," but he could not formulate in any way the word "furniture." But to obtain the new word "furniture" doesn't just mean to purchase one word by the expenditure of similar words but rather to subordinate all of the words to something new. When we told him that furniture was this or that, he told us: no, that's not furniture; that is a table, a chair, and so on. By the way, this child had a rich selection of clothing words, in which there were items by way of wardrobe details that even I, for one, did not know. There were many names for gloves, for mittens, for hats, for coats, etc. but he did not extend this to the word "clothing." When he saw for the first time a sleeveless vest on a comrade who had come from Germany to work with us and he asked what that was, he was told "clothing" and then this vest became "clothing." But the fact that everything is clothing was beyond him.

When we have such a case to deal with, you can see that the mere transition to relations of generality constitutes a giant step in the development of the child. We attach significance in the history of the development of child speech not so much to

[12] Comrade Konnikova refers to Tatyana Efimovna Konnikova (Татяна Ефимовна Конникова,1909–1975) who was a student and then a collaborator of Vygotsky's at the Herzen Pedagogical Institute from 1931 to 1934. Her Ph.D was on the transitional stage in autonomous speech, and the co-supervisors were Vygotsky and Levina. Vygotsky appears to be talking about the material from her Ph.D. work.

the moment when there is the first word that makes sense, but rather to when there is the first word which stands in a certain relation of generality.

Stern has said that the destiny of each child as a human resides with the first word that makes sense. This is untrue. The first word that makes sense may belong to many idiots or to deaf…or imbeciles, but the destiny of the child resides with the first relationship of generality which appears near the end of the period of autonomous speech.

If we were to summarize, we could say thus: the availability of a system and the relationship of generality between concepts constitutes the defining moment for the whole character of thinking that is specific to a given age, but this relation of generality emerges gradually, not developing all at once, and with each age level, we are dealing with a specific relationship of generality.

For example, as studies have demonstrated, in the child of early childhood age, leaving aside autonomous speech, it is not always the case that words arise from below, for example, let us say, rose, violet, lily-of-the-valley. The child says the word flower earlier than rose. But the relation of generality "flower: rose" are constituted differently in a 2-year-old than the relation "flower: rose" in a 5-year-old. Experiments have shown that the child of 2 years and seven months who has his own words will relate these words, not as [general to particular—GSK][13] but rather as if they were standing single file next to each other, instead of one including the other in itself, while in the preschool age, we always have relationships of generality that have relations with a concrete area of reality worked out. Nevertheless, for all of that we may say that it is typical of all of the child's concepts which are spontaneously developed, that is, without direct, systematic influence of teaching-and-learning on the proper grassroots experience of the child, or those concepts which emerge as everyday concepts, that they are typically lacking the system and the relations of generality between concepts that are proper to our concepts and more impoverished and constructed differently than those in us. There exist completely different relations of generality and sometimes they do not exist at all, and only with the transition to academic concepts which we observe in school age in connection with the course of teaching-and-learning does there emerge the first and most basic thing which Piaget was attempting to obscure.

What characterizes an arithmetical concept in the first place? It is the system. Do students learn first "one," then "two," then "three?" The most essential in the nature of the academic concept as a true concept, as a generalization, which historically occurs, consists in this: each concept is necessarily a part of a defined system of concepts and the most essential and general outcome of the teaching-and-learning of the child in school and the formation of academic concepts consists in this: as a result of teaching him a variety of concepts, there arises in him a system corresponding in basic and most primitive ways to the system of concepts, to the relations of generality between concepts. In the thinking of the child, it does not happen in such a way that the concepts which he has acquired earlier are separated by a wall

[13] Korotaeva has inserted these words, which she says are missing from the transcript.

from those concepts that he acquires later. This system constitutes the basic form of functioning for his concepts and in the area where they are first acquired, in the area of everyday concepts, but of course this is not completed at once, but throughout the course of the school age, undertaking this transition <…> that is, at the end of (primary—Trans.) school age phenomenon of unconscious thinking (according to Piaget).[14]

Now for the second conclusion.

I have already said in what areas we discover rudiments of (developmentally) earlier forms of thinking, in areas of purely verbal forms of thinking. So long as the child has not construed, as in school age, a system of relations of generalization between concepts, the thinking of the child cannot be emancipated, cannot break from visual-sensory basis of thinking—from perception and from memory and the law persists that the child finds it easier to think when he sees or when he directly relies on his own experience than when thought is left to its own devices.

I will allow myself, not in as much detail as I did in relation to the system, to dwell on some conclusions which emerge from this and which should be kept in mind when we speak of the central neoformations of school age.

If a child moves to new, higher, forms of generalizations and of relations of generality, does not this mean that the child is ascending to a new level of communication, and does not this find expression in the fact that for the first time at school age the child can be given the basis of scientific knowledge? With him you can communicate basic scientific information about reality. This is a mistake that arises in our teaching—it always rests psychologically on this question.

Let me offer an example.

This was the story in social studies, which before our eyes has now disappeared, leading to a radical restructuring of this question. What was overestimated? Everything was overestimated. First, the child's ability to generalize <…>.[15]

Second—we overestimated the potential for communication with the child.

As we know, every movement as well as every presentation of knowledge is a form of communication with the child, knowledge presented to the child. How is it that child studied but did not understand in the real sense of the word? Here there was a typical disruption of communication, which is expressed in the fact that the teacher conveyed a deep thought, but in the student's head, it became flat, the teacher transmitted a rich thought—in the student's head, it became poor. The profundity, the range, and the adequacy of communication were broken. And the main root,

[14]Vygotsky uses "school age" to refer to a developmental age period between the crisis at seven and the crisis at thirteen. The reference to Piaget is probably to Piaget's notion of See the end of Chapter 2. Vygotsky is probably referring to Piaget's *Le jugement et le raisonnement chez l'enfant*, p. 95, where Piaget notes that definitions are done unconsciously at this age (Piaget, 1924/1947).

[15]Vygotsky is offering a bold critique of the new Stalinist social studies curriculum, in which school age children are taught concepts like "revolution," "class struggle" and that the common ownership of factories, mines, and farmland enables the construction of socialism (see Chapter 6 of Thinking and Speech, also written at this time). For a description of how Vygotsky resisted this sudden Stakhanovite turn in school education, see Kellogg, 2019.

according to contemporary research, which most closely determines the course of learning, rests on this question of cultivating a system of communication and generalization at school age. What becomes possible here—the acquisition of scientific knowledge—shows that the child has risen to a new level of not only generalization, but communication; but he has not grown to the stage where communication with the highest theoretical generalization becomes possible.

I would like to say with respect to the new construction which the child has carried out in generalization and in communication, there is a new system of relations between functions. I have already said thinking for the first time separates the perception of concepts from its visual-sensory basis, becomes autonomous, and begins a cycle of independent development, opening up the possibility of movement in pure thought, pure, of course, not in the sense of spiritually complete detachment from reality but depending in every step on the proximal sensory and visual basis. About the meaning of the reflection of reality at its base, we can say that school age is the age of transition from a visual-sensory mode of reflecting reality to one of generalization.

Indeed, before school there was a generalized mode of reflecting reality, and in the school child, there was a sensory, visual mode of reflecting reality, but that which was the dominator is now become the servant and that which was the servant—here it has become dominant.

Here we have to deal with a different construction of the child's consciousness. If we consider the character of the perception of reality as a whole, what picture of the world emerges in the school child, how in him there is developed inner activeness, etc., then we would see that not only does what we have considered thus far change, that is, the inner structuration of consciousness, but the child's relation to external reality and to internal reality also changes; the character of the child's activity outside and the character of the child's internal activity changes.

That is everything that I wished to say to you today.

References

Kellogg, D. (2019). The story-teller's tale: Vygotsky's 'vraschivaniya', the zone of proximal development, and 'ingrowing' in the weekend stories of Korean children. *British Journal of Educational Studies*. https://doi.org/10.1080/00071005.2019.1569200

Luria, A. R., & Vygotsky, L. S. (1930/1993). *Ape, primitive man and child* (p. 1992). Harvester Wheatsheaf.

Piaget, J. (1924/1947). *Le jugement et le raisonnement chez l'enfant*. Delachaux et Niestlé.

Spinoza, B. (1677/1995). *The ethics* (Samuel Shirley, Trans.). Hackett.

Vygotskij, L. S. (2018). *La science du développement de l'enfant: Text pédologiques (1930–1934). Traduits par I. Léopoldoff-Martin*. Collection Exploration: Peter Lang.

Выготский, Л. С. (1934). *Мышление и речь*. Соцэкгиз.

Выготский, Л. С. (2001). *Лекции по педологии*. Удмуртский университет.

Chapter 14
The Negative Phase of the Transitional Age

Outline of Chapter 14: The Negative Phase of the Transitional Age

Marx, Andy Blunden argues (2017), wrote *Capita*l twice: first he worked through the factual material to work out his basic concepts in the *Grundrisse*, and then he returned and re-established all the factual material by working it through his basic concept to produce his *magnum opus*. Vygotsky does this too, as we saw in Chapter 5 on the newborn and elsewhere. But he inverts the usual procedure for this lecture, the last in our book.

Previous lectures almost always began with factual material of one kind or another, worked through them with an eye to establishing the social situation of development and the main line of development, and ended with a clear description of the central neoformation of the age, how it resolved the social situation, and what it implied for the upcoming stage. This was even true of critical ages like one, three, and seven.

Unlike the previous lectures, where the time limits of the period were more or less as laid out at the end of Chapter Two, Vygotsky needs to define his object of study. Are we speaking of one age period with phases or two different age periods with different neoformations? Is this period really negative? Is it only a phase? And in what sense is it transitional?

As a result, there is no mention at all of the social situation of development, and the only mention of the line of development—a "schizoid" thread in the line of development of the adolescent personality—is not very auspicious. Instead, Vygotsky focuses on establishing the neoformation and discovers that it is a transitional one. The "negative phase of the transitional age" is neither negative nor a phase, nor really a part of the stable transition age: it is instead the crisis at age thirteen, which ends childhood proper and begins adolescence. The *magnum opus* that Vygotsky has in mind for

This chapter is taken from material published by G.S. Korotaeva in 2001. Korotaeva notes that it is taken from the stenogramme of a lecture delivered on 26 June 1933.

L. S. Vygotsky, *L.S. Vygotsky's Pedological Works. Volume 2.*, Perspectives in Cultural-Historical Research 10, https://doi.org/10.1007/978-981-16-1907-6_14

adolescence is actually already written—it is the single longest work Vygotsky published in his lifetime, his *Pedology of the Adolescent*, which we will translate and bring to you in Volumes Three and Four of this series.

I. **One Age or Two?** Vygotsky points out that the transition from school age to adulthood is far too long and gradual to be a crisis or even a single period. Theoretically, some writers, especially the Germans, see it as one long stable period with a "negative phase" connected to puberty only at the outset (rather the way "the terrible twos" are blamed on teething). Other writers, especially the Americans, see the transitional age as a single long crisis period, which is a period of "storm and stress" from beginning to end, rather the way we sometimes think of the wars and plagues of the European middle ages. Vygotsky argues that both points of view are wrong. The Germans are wrong to see the "negative phase" as merely a loss or a lack of something and the Americans are wrong to consider the whole long period as one of undifferentiated crisis and not to see the stable period that follows the "negative phase." Vygotsky proposes to take a positive approach to both the crisis at thirteen and the stable period of adolescence that must follow it. Vygotsky notes that development is process and neoformations are products, just as tree growth is a process and the tree's rings are products. Some neoformations, however, are more like the spaces between rings—they do not exist independently, but only in relation to stable neoformations. Such neoformations (e.g., proto-speech, the disjunction of will and affect, the seven-year-old's "acting out") are neoformations nonetheless and their role in development is no less positive for being hidden behind more stable neoformations (speech, will, a layered ego). Vygotsky proposes to find the hidden neoformation at age 13 and thus understand the positive destiny of this critical period wrongly called a "negative phase."

II. **Method and Mistakes.** Vygotsky lays out three theoretical possibilities.

   1. The "negative phase" is an avoidable, pathological complication of normal development, and we ought to seek to eliminate it altogether (the way that we would seek to eliminate adolescent drug addiction, teenage pregnancy, and youth suicide).
   2. The "negative phase" is an unavoidable, inseparable part of normal development, and we must seek to understand its positive features as an indispensable precondition to further development (the way that birth, teething, and baby babble are necessary if somewhat stressful preliminaries for what follows).
   3. The "negative phase" is an unavoidable, inseparable part of normal development, but it is still pathological and we should seek to ameliorate, attenuate, and palliate the inevitable suffering it entails (the way that we might palliate the pain of a terminal cancer patient).

Vygotsky disagrees that weak symptoms or absent symptoms are a positive sign, and he denies that children can avoid the symptoms of the crisis under socialism but not under capitalism. In this way, Vygotsky emerges with a very strong version of position 2 above: The "negative phase" is an unavoidable, inseparable part of normal development, precisely because it is not a negative phase at all, but rather a crisis, with its own positive contribution to make to development. Vygotsky now takes up the task of defining that positive contribution and showing its relationship to the next age period.

III. **Splitting and Merging.** The crisis at 13 is a crisis of restructuring: this explains its "fateful," life-changing character for the child, as well as its macroscopic scale but relative lack of completely new mental content for the observer. This relative lack of any completely new intellectual content, according to Vygotsky, is largely an illusion; the child has been using the same words as the adults in the surrounding environment since roughly age three, and adults have not yet perceived the big difference in the nature of the underlying abstraction and generalization of the word meaning. Vygotsky traces the history of the idea of "dissociation" back to Herbart, who argued that forming concepts, like forming any other representation, is a process of splitting up some "original" representations and re-merging them into other more "complex" ones. He points out that this is where the Freudian idea of complexes originates: they are representations held together by affects, which must be split up and remerged, as when the child splits up the erotic attachment to the parent and then remerges it in an erotic attachment to a partner. Vygotsky tries to square Herbart's idea of the complex with more contemporary writers: Freud, Piaget, Bleuler, Kretschmer, (Vol?)kelt, and "Bleder." But all of these treat dissociation as essentially pathological; Vygotsky argues that in at least some cases, this is the opposite of the truth, since some psychotics treat everything as mysteriously linked to everything. If, however, we treat normal adolescence as essentially schizoid (or "schizothymic") in character, we approach answers to two questions.

1. What is the central neoformation of the crisis at thirteen? Vygotsky introduces Lewin, who points out that the whole of structural psychology on which our understanding of the crisis at thirteen as a crisis of restructuring is really based has an oversimple idea of structure. We have been thinking of "structure" as merely fractal, with the same structure being produced at every level, like a matruschka doll-within-a-doll or an egg-within-an-egg. Lewin distinguishes between inter-structure relations and intra-structural ones, and points out they cannot be the same, just as intrapersonal relations cannot simply be copies of interpersonal ones (and social relations in a nation, even a dynastic autocracy, are not simply copies of social relations in a family, even an authoritarian patriarchy). But, Vygotsky points out, for them to be different, they must be broken up and restructured, and this appears to be what is happening in the crisis. The crisis is the "optimal period" for the development of the child's ability to dissociate. Not even perception, Vygotsky points out using Rubin's vase, is immune from being broken up and subjected to volition in this way. It is this development of dissociations that accounts for the apparent awkwardness (spiritual, intellectual, and even physical) we often observe in the teenager. This awkwardness and its underlying dissociation is the central neoformation of the Crisis at Thirteen.

2. How is this central neoformation linked to those of school age and adolescence? Vygotsky points out that an inner conscious life, inner speech, critical thinking, introspection, and voluntary memory are the great accomplishments of school age. But these great accomplishments of the school child come with a real contradiction pointed out in Piaget's work: the child is now capable of inner life, but that inner life is one of actions: the school child's thinking is flighty (in that everything is linked to everything else through actions), but it is also wingless (in that experiences are not abstracted and systematized). For systems to be formed, the link with action has to be broken up. In this process, dissociation has the same relationship to structuring the personality that proto-speech had to speech proper, that hypobulia had to play with roles and rules, and to grammar. In each case, it was not simply that the previous structure had to be dismantled, it was that the critical neoformation played a subordinate but still positive role in the next zone of development.

IV. **Two Words.** In this very brief conclusion (Vygotsky says "two words," although it is rather more than that), Vygotsky looks back. He notes, not for the first time, how pathogenesis has pointed the way for understanding ontogenesis. In particular, he describes how adolescence sometimes appears in the guise of a kind of volitional autism (this may be evidence that "Osbergen" really is Asperger), and he says that the autistic singling out of *perezhivaniya* is a clear example of how critical neoformations play positive roles, for example, in the construction of narrative in later life. Similarly, other apparently negative symptoms (e.g., asthenia, blank affect, angst, mood swings) may also have a complex structure that includes highly positive moments. But just as concepts cannot be formed without the breaking up and merging of qualities, personalities cannot be formed without the dissociation and relinking of these complex structures into the even more complex structure that is the child's emerging personality.

Chapter 14: The Negative Phase of the Transitional Age

Today, we should address together a question related to what is called the negative phase of the transitional age, or the crisis at 13, as several researchers have called it. However, this crisis at 13 was empirically discovered earlier than it was theoretically understood and comprehended, and so the history of the discovery of this crisis is substantially different from the history of the discovery of all of the other critical ages. The uniqueness consists in this. This crisis, to all appearances unfolding in an extremely overt form, was noted very long ago, almost from the very beginning of the scientific study of the transitional age. And yet somehow it was not recognized as a crisis confined within a well-defined period of this age but instead transferred to the entire age as a whole. Thus, it needs to be said that in relation to the remaining critical ages, the difficulty of its discovery lay in this: if any crisis in the course of development proceeds smoothly, then in relation to this crisis we must say that here we have the opposite situation—a rapid and sharp manifestation of a crisis going well beyond into the stable age. So regarding the child's transitional age—a critical age in a range of handbooks—there is the teaching that the entirety of the transitional age is a crisis. At present, the majority of researchers have arrived at a common agreement in two domains: first of all, that the crisis in the strict sense of the word, that which can be empirically observed, cannot but be defined as localized within a certain period, preceding the epoch of sexual maturation. From this has emerged the teaching of a negative phase of the transitional age. In the second place, the features of criticality that inhere in the whole of the period of sexual maturation should, in essence, be considered exclusively in the light of this: that the process of the transitional age as a whole consists in the transition from the state of childhood to that of maturity.[1]

In this way, we may speak of a crisis of a transitional age in two senses: first of all, of the critical phase which distinguishes the transitional age from the school age, and, secondly, the whole of the transitional age in the sense of its relation to the state of (the age of) maturity, a transition to what should be regarded as a certain parallel age, during which the child goes through a mutable transitional age.[2]

By itself the transitional stage, of which we spoke yesterday, does not represent a critical age in the narrow sense of the word. If you remember, we spoke in relation to the basic traits of the critical ages and those traits we found in this: during the critical period of development for a duration that was relatively short, usually a year or somewhat less, there were concentrated a range of very decisive changes and a break in the structure of the child's personality.[3]

---

[1] Note that here, and elsewhere (e.g., the title), Vygotsky is accommodating the most common usage of his time, the usage that his audience must become familiar with. Thus he is not using his own terminology. So "phase" is used, as per the common usage of the time, to mean the first "stage" of the transitional period of adolescence and not, *as per* Vygotsky's own usage in Chap. 2 of this book, to mean the moments of a crisis that precede and follow its peak.

[2] The parentheses around "the age of" are in the original manuscript and they are not noted as additions by Korotaeva. Note that maturity is considered as in some sense "parallel" to childhood rather than intersecting it. This is consistent with Vygotsky's view that pedology is the science of the child—and only the child—and that therefore adult development must obey other laws (see Léopoldoff-Martin, 2014, pp. 287–288). Socio-cultural maturity—the socially conferred and recognized ability to reproduce your own labor and even your body—cannot always coincide with either general-anatomical maturation (bone growth continues until age 25) or with puberty (which has been coming earlier and earlier over the last century).

[3] As we saw in Chap. 2, Vygotsky distinguishes critical from stable periods in several ways. First (1998, pp. 191, 195), stable periods have definite boundaries (the crises) but no peaks, while crises have definite peaks but no boundaries. Secondly (pp. 191–192), stable periods involve an incremental growth in capabilities, while crises involve "introvolution" or "withering away" of some interests and a decrease in capacity for some pursuits. Thirdly (pp. 194–195), stable periods involve neoformations that last (such as speech, will, concepts), while critical neoformations persist only as subordinate, dependent features of stable periods (such as proto-speech, hypobulia, dissociation).

The transitional age as a whole lasts for several years. The break that takes place at this age occurs slowly, with the exception of rare cases of what is referred to as accelerated sexual maturation. The process of sexual maturation itself, as you know, is relatively slow. With regard to the pre-adolescent and the stable age, they gradually pass from one into another,[4] so that neither the biological process itself, as a process of maturation, nor the process of restructuring the personality as a whole takes on a character that is critical, rapid, uneven, or sharp. In this way, the question is carried over into the preceding epoch, which distinguishes the transitional age from the school age.[5] With regard to this, there are different points of view.

In the German literature, it is usual to talk precisely of a phase, and this has in view, it seems to me, the sound idea that this phase is very close to the process of sexual maturation and captures the course of this process. Individual researchers, such as V…, believe that the crisis does not always stand on the boundary between latent and overt sexual maturation. What do we mean by latent sexual maturation? Such is the usual term for the period preceding overt sexual maturation, which consists in the maturation of the rudimentary glands, which must produce overt sexual maturation and change of the whole organism.[6]

Other authors, and in particular the Americans, say of the critical age that they believe it is correct to call a certain period of the whole age epoch a phase, but it seems to me that from the point of view of the general classification into ages, this is not correct. Consequently, it is hard to talk about a negative phase in the sense of a critical age preceding the epoch of sexual maturation, since we know different authors will refer to it differently. The Germans will say that it differs from other ages not because the child acquires something positive, but rather that it is distinguished by the negative features in the development of the child at this age, which is transitional to the age of adolescence. It stands to reason that this novelty is incompatible with scientific principle.[7]

Others speak of a negative phase in the strict sense of the word, in that the process of reverse development is included in the whole course of development. In the

---

[4] That is, the stable preadolescent stage gradually passes into the stable stage of adolescence.

[5] That is, primary school age, which in the USSR was 4 years from around seven or eight to eleven or years of "passport" age. See Chap. 13, Footnote 15.

[6] Korotaeva notes that "B…" is how the individual researcher is referred to in the stenogramme, so it appears the name was unfamiliar to the stenographer. Perhaps a German scholar with a long name that starts with the sound /v/ is meant, since the Russian letter B... is used to transliterate the German sound /v/ into Russian. It is possible, since the subsequent discussion centres on the Gestalt school, that the name is Wertheimer, who founded the Würzburg school and Gestaltism.

[7] The "Americans" referred to are probably William James, Arnold Gesell, and especially G. Stanley Hall, who considered the whole period of adolescence as a period of "storm and stress." Vygotsky rejects this, both because the actual period of "storm and stress" associated with transitional neoformations (e.g., dissociation) is much shorter, and because the neoformations of adolescence (e.g., sexuality, concepts) are permanent ones. The "Germans" referred to here include Ernst Kretschmer, Adolf Busemann, and the Bühlers, who see the "negative phase" as destructive. From Vygotsky's point of view, to characterize any age period, even a critical one, by what it lacks is not consistent with scientific principles (Vygotsky, 1984/1998, pp. 199, 259).

crisis, this appears with exceptional clarity, but it never constitutes the basic content of the process of development in itself. According to one researcher, to call this phase negative would be just as wrong as if the phase of tooth change were called the phase of tooth disappearance. Of course, we are dealing precisely with a loss of the milk teeth; however, it is obvious that the history of development as a whole consists in the loss of some [things – Trans.] and replacement by others—not just losses, not just negative phases.[8]

As we agreed, this should be our approach to all of the critical ages. There is the assumption—not a scientifically probable assumption—that in the transitional period of the critical age we are dealing precisely with a neoformation, that is, not with the splitting off of something new, but with the formation of some special place, precisely with neoformations that do not appear in the process of maturation during the critical age before us. This means that every development goes into the construction of the personality, a result of the previously accomplished … epochs and this or that line that has been laid down in the personality.[9]

One researcher has said that the development and the structure of the personality are related the one to the other like the growth of a tree and the addition of annual rings to its trunk. In each period of development certain formations are laid down in the structure of the personality—this is completely clear. Consequently, when we speak of the neoformations of the basic stable ages it is then that they are laid down in the structure of the personality as the neoformations that the child will retain in the structure of his personality for life. For example, a child acquires speech in early childhood, and he retains it for the rest of his life; it has become a chief part of the personality structure.

The neoformations of the transitional ages are different. They are transitional formations, and they are called neoformations of a transitional type. We may take examples from widely differing ages, for example, the autonomous speech of children or the hypobulic child will of the 3-year crisis, etc.

As a result, even for the transitional period of thirteen, we ought, before anything else, to seek out a positive viewpoint on this crisis. That is to say, we must attempt to connect it to a neoformation of the transitional type which forms the core, the

---

[8] The researcher referred to is probably Vygotsky's friend and colleague P.P. Blonsky, (1884–1941) who developed a scheme of periodization around teething that Charlotte Bühler discusses critically. Vygotsky also rejected the idea of using a single physical characteristic (whether teething or sexual maturation) in order to divide childhood into periods. But here he strongly agrees with Blonsky's view that the periods cannot simply be characterized by absences and disappearances; they must include some positive contribution to development.

[9] Korotaeva does not comment, and the ellipsis is not explained. It seems likely that the omission is on the part of the stenographer, who may have missed a word or two. Vygotsky seems to be making two points with this paragraph. First of all, he is arguing that there has been an incorrect assumption that neoformations appear in place at the beginning of an epoch. But if neoformations appear in place at the beginning of an epoch, this must mean that they belong to the development that took place in a previous epoch. Secondly, he is arguing that critical neoformations, unlike those of stable periods, do not lead an independent life but are subordinated to the neoformations of the following stable period.

center, of this crisis, and find its relation to the subsequent stable age into which it is sublated, in the way that, for example, autonomous speech is sublated into speech proper. Thus, we ought to be able to find its neoformation, its destiny.

In order to address this, I shall permit myself a few preliminary remarks. I will not discuss the symptomatics of the negative phase, because these were presented in your review materials and in the studies of Zagorovsky himself, and so everybody knows about them. There is a condensed symptomatics of those traits, which usually propagate throughout the whole transition period, when we consider them in the spirit of the old romantic school in relation to the psychology of the transition period. The traits of this negative phase are more or less well known and I will not linger over them. I will dwell on the factual side of the matter.[10]

Even now there are researchers who dispute the very substance of a negative phase, that is, some maintain that the negative phase exists, but only as a certain complication of the normal course of development. Consequently, it may occur and may not. Other researchers contend that it is inevitable and necessary that it should occur. Thirdly, and finally, it is held that it must inevitably occur, but as a certain complication, and like any complication, it may be mitigated.

In order to resolve this question, first of all one must address factual observations and not speculative constructions. These factual, experimental, observations appear to leave no doubt that if we observe from year to year the growth of the school child, then we note, as a mass phenomenon, that at a given period somewhere between 11 and 13 years of age, at different times for boys and for girls, a certain decrease in the degree of school performance begins. If we undertake mass observations, some difficulties along the lines of school behavior in the child commence, difficulties that coincide with those in the child's family life, and these changes and difficulties of an internal order are revealed as soon as you have established even a minimal contact with the one you have under observation.

If we take up any documentation that we might have to hand (I am thinking, especially, of diaries that may accompany a negative phase), you will not find much in such a document to suggest that the crisis proceeds indistinctly and unremarked by the author keeping the diary, with the exception of fragments from one particular diary or another. In other cases, we see everywhere clearly and distinctly a natural break in the period of school age. And I may put it even more plainly: I know of not a single practical work which has been done on the plane of development, no matter what partial function it might be concerned with, not a single factual study that

[10] Pavel Leonidovich Zagorovsky (Павел Леонидович Загоровский, 1892—1952) was a professor of education and psychology at Voronezh State University and at the pedagogical institute for teacher training in Voronezh. Vygotsky probably knew him personally, through their mutual friend Osip Mandelstam, the poet. Zagorovsky too was a poet. The "old romantic" school is probably a reference to "Storm and Stress" literature, for example, "The Sorrows of Young Werther," as well as to the school of G. Stanley Hall (Hall, 1907). This is why Vygotsky contrasts the romantic school to the factual side of the matter. Zagorovsky seems to be one of many Soviet pedologists who believed that puberty was not a crisis but merely a "negative phase" of adolescence, and that it was more acute in capitalist countries. Vygotsky is apparently referring to "О так называемой негативной фазе в подростничестве" ("On the so-called negative phase of adolescence," 1928),

would demonstrate that school age has an immediate transition into adolescence. Everywhere, between the symptoms characterizing school age and the symptoms characterizing adolescence—we find a wedge, where we are dealing with moments relating to the action of the memory.

Nevertheless, several authors have said that they have observed a negative phase in a range of cases. It seems to me that the source of this controversy consists in this. First of all, in the majority of pedological work there persists a symptomatic approach to the study of the process of development, that is, the process of child development is identified with the symptoms in which the crisis is revealed, but when these symptoms are sought they are either feeble in form or nonexistent, and then it is concluded from this that either the crisis is progressing weakly or it is altogether absent, forgetting that the symptoms of any process, of course, manifest the process of development of the personality itself under the given circumstances, that different variants of the course of one and the same segment of development can be found in different symptoms, and the symptoms themselves require meticulous analysis in order to understand which of them are of the essence in their occurrence and which are accidental, auxiliary, symptoms which color the crisis in a concrete situation, depending upon the circumstances and which do not in any profound way determine the course of child development but only impart to the formalization of this process a more plastic character.

I think that the opinion of Zagorovsky is not entirely right, so I do not entirely agree with him. He is right on the plane upon which he posed the question. He seized upon the symptoms and, dooming himself to purely empirical verification, he performed his research by interviewing parents, monitoring the children, and seeing if such symptoms occurred or not. He concluded that they occurred in such a quantity and such a percent. Does this matter? It matters because it shows the external, symptomatic picture the crisis gives us. This is so for those children that Zagorovsky observed, but it also goes for those children that Bleder[11] observed. However, the importance of his conclusions lies in this: he shows in general that the symptoms do not simply match immediately the processes which lie behind them. And as a consequence the task lies in this: to define theoretically the nature of this crisis, and as a result to distinguish essential symptoms from symptoms and traits that may be

---

[11] For Zagorovsky, see above. "Bleder" doesn't appear to be a Russian name at all and it is also not obviously a German one. Leopoldoff-Martin and Schneuwly, who also had access to the versions printed in Vygotsky's lifetime, assume that Bleuler is meant, and they substitute "Bleuler" for "Bleder" without any comment.

But the stenographer also cites Bleuler by his proper name. It seems odd, though not impossible of course, that the stenographer can spell the name correctly in some paragraphs and not in others. Another possibility is that "Bleuler" written cursively in German (but not so much in Russian) can look a lot like "Bleder." In this case, it might be a problem transcribing the names for publication (done by Korotaeva and her students and colleagues).

Eugen Bleuler (1857–1939) was a Swiss doctor and later a psychiatrist; a student of Charcot and the teacher of both Jung and Piaget. He developed the whole concept of schizophrenia. For a while he was close to Freud, but broke with him around 1911 because he believed Freudianism was becoming too cultish, too much like a religion or a political party.

more or less accidental. That is why Zagarovsky was wrong when he concluded from the presence of these symptoms the absence of the crisis or from the feebleness of these symptoms the absence of these symptoms. What does this feebleness, however, really mean? Precisely where there are feeble symptoms, child development turns out to be distorted and uneven, but there where they are not feeble, development may proceed normally.

Why then is the measure of the crisis difficulty in upbringing? This is a generally incorrect point of view—regarding the given period from the negative point of view and holding that the more painfully the critical age proceeds, the more difficult the child becomes at this age, and vice versa.

Approaching the crisis as an illness, the purely negative approach, it seems to me, is not correct here.

And so I think that the task of researchers lies in analyzing these crises and, as I think, that the very posing of the question as to whether the crisis is the mandatory inheritance of the bourgeois adolescent and whether it should be altogether absent as a period of development in our own adolescents—such a posing of the question has little foundation and little persuasiveness. I could understand stating the question as one regarding the difference in the course of the critical period over here and over there, as one concerning the difference in the nature of these respective critical periods. If we knew more intimately how the processes of development as a whole were organized and constructed in this or in other age epochs here and there, but to hold as a correct notion that in general the transition from one age epoch to another proceeds smoothly and without a break, this appears to me something that contradicts the very nature of development and is theoretically implausible. No one, of course, knows the factual side of the matter. Theoretically, this notion appears implausible to me.[12]

Now, with your permission, we will move on to a very brief attempt to define the central neoformation of the transitional crisis at 13 years of age and its relations to neoformations of a positive character which arise during the transitional age in the future. I think that we correctly approach this neoformation when we take into account not only the growth of invol…(sic--GSK) symptoms, which point to the process of changing relationships, to antagonisms, to changes in school grades and the increase of inner difficulties, when we take account not only those processes which show a dying away that occurs at this age, but also those symptoms of a positive character with which we are confronted here. If we grasp these, we cannot fail to see that like all of the critical periods, but most especially here, in a critical period that occurs with a sufficiently developed consciousness, with sufficiently developed abstract thinking, where there is a differentiation of the inner and the outer aspects of the personality, the crisis cannot but take place without a re-evaluation of the

[12] The idea that crises in general, and the crisis at 13 in particular, only occur under capitalism, with poorly managed and poorly guided bourgeois upbringing, was later promulgated by Leontiev (Leontiev, 1981, pp. 398–399). Karpov argues, contrariwise, that crises are avoidable under liberal capitalism with permissive parenting (Karpov, 2005, pp. 226–227). One cannot help but suspect that in both cases, an ontogenetic crisis is being used as some kind of metaphor for a sociogenetic one. In any case, Vygotsky would reject both.

whole, a rebuilding of the entire structure upon which the personality of the school child has hitherto been founded.[13]

I told you yesterday, and this idea seems to me to be empirically correct, that in the critical ages the changes in development are, in the main, macroscopic in character, noticeable to the unaided eye: the child changes from week to week, and, when we are following entries in a diary, sometimes a day may play a decisive role; if it happens to co-occur with some minor happening, successful or unsuccessful, some explanation by somebody, you can have a simple day as a watershed moment. This is what in the contemporary descriptions of the crisis and in the analysis of diaries and commentaries on them has become known as the fateful days, because of a light-hearted description of an adolescent calling them fateful days. And in truth, we are dealing here with a decisive rupture.

Osburgen, a psychopathologist working with children and adolescents, takes the point of view of normal psychology, but it appears to me that he is profoundly right in this: if we compare the period of the negative phase and the changes which go on in this period with changes that go on in the remainder of adolescence, or in some other age, that is, a stable one, then we cannot but notice that here before the very eyes of the researcher a transformation is taking place and in this sense the changes in the adolescent in the negative phase are dissimilar to the microscopic psychic changes in the age of adolescence, which become noticeable after several months, in half a year; but here before our very eyes occur changes in the personality, here is a rapid process of change, which we might see with the unaided eye, such that you are left with the impression that the process of change consists not of minute internal accretions, not of minute internal constructions, but instead of vast formations that have been laid down, layers of the personality, which are shifting in relation to one another. If one takes a stable age, one will never find anything that is analogous to this, to what is observed in the process of the relatively rapid restructuring of the personality at a particular psychological moment.[14]

---

[13] Korotaeva notes that the stenogramme said не только инвол.. .("only invol…"). Leopoldoff-Martin and Schneuwly insert the word "involutionary" without any comment (Vygotskij 2018, pp. 185); this reading is certainly justified by the next sentence, which speaks of processes "dying away." "Involution" was J.M. Baldwin's term for the withering away of certain functions, for example, vestigial tails in humans. Vygotsky uses "involution" to mean the "withering away" of certain behaviors or psychological functions, for example, the loss of baby babble when children begin to speak, and the "withering away" of sociodramatic play when preschoolers start going to school and learn games with rules.

[14] Léopoldoff-Martin and Schneuwly were unable to locate any "Osburgen" or "Osbergen" in the literature of the time (2018, p. 185). It seems possible that the stenographer heard the name Asperger, in which case it refers to the Austrian child psychopathologist Hans Asperger, who had already begun his studies of autistic and "schizophrenic" children in Vienna in 1932 when this talk was given. But Asperger had not yet published much of anything yet, and certainly "Asperger's syndrome" was not yet called that. Vygotsky was very familiar with German researchers in Vienna through the work of Karl and Charlotte Bühler and Hildegard Hetzer (e.g. Bühler, 1931; Bühler, 1922; Bühler, 1928).

Asperger himself appears to have been a somewhat autistic child and in 1938 he began to write of the special talents of autistic children. Asperger was a conservative Catholic, but he worked in a

So in the crisis at thirteen, we are dealing with major changes, macroscopic and tumultous ones, in which vast strata, great formations of the personality, come to be involved, rather than tiny microscopic cells, the structure of which change predominantly in the stable ages.

What are these changes? As we know, we have a whole series of attempts to explain the specific features of a whole series of neoformations of the negative phase and we have different theories depending on [approach to – T] this negative phase. I won't dwell on these in detail; I will merely mention that various authors consider that the substance of this crisis lies on the plane of which we spoke yesterday, that is, that sexual maturation is underway, although perhaps incompletely so at the beginning of the crisis; in the general course of development the adolescent remains biologically unconscious but latently functioning, from this arises imperceptible irritations, excitements, and other incomprehensible *perezhivanie* for the adolescent. That is, there is the fact that the adolescent finds himself changed. His very being is sending out signals to him to which he has been up to now unaccustomed.

This is what many researchers, and even the majority of contemporary researchers, place at the foundation of the so-called negative phase of the transitional age. Others, for example V…, say, in relation to the crisis, that autonomy appears—that the relatively violent passions which here engulf the adolescent, which in this sense are something like a parallel to all of the other crises, and that the crisis of 13 years old is when empirically the end of dependence upon adults is finally completed: as Rousseau says, the age of adolescence is like a second birth, when the umbilical cord which attaches the child to his parents is at last cut, and when all of these moments come to the first plane. And so too with a whole range of other propositions. And nevertheless, as you can see, we do not have, to speak of the substance, any theory of the negative phase which would be in the true sense of the word persuasive, about which we might say that this indeed deals with the substance of the matter, because not one of these theories can demonstrate what is most important, what is persuasive for all theory—they do not show how the neoformation necessarily follows from what existed in school age and how it necessarily implies that which will exist at a later age. And since there is no link between the one and the other, then the whole theory linking up the different moments in the right way and providing theoretical coverage of the age cannot be entirely right.

I myself not only do not have an independent and sufficiently worked out point of view, but still cannot, from what I have been able to study and to read, come to an adequately confident conception concerning this crisis. Nevertheless from all that I have perused and thought over, I have a conception regarding one group of theories, one group of observations, which has been often repeated and which in the

unit run by ardent Nazis, and it appears that Asperger referred at least some of his patients to the Nazi T4 program which exterminated thousands of autistic children and removed their brains for study. There is some debate about whether he took part in order to try to save some of his own patients (the same debate occurs with Hetzer, with Pötzl, and with many other German psychiatrists.

end must be reckoned with, which should be engaged with in any case, in order to imagine the actual nature of these neoformations of the critical age. I have in mind unceasing indications of a schizothymic character in the adolescent, the similarities between the schizoid temperament and the temperament of the adolescent, etc. It must be said that all of these remarks, widely employed in the literature, that lie at the foundations of a theory of the transitional age, have recently revealed a tendency to limit the force of this statement only within the framework of a negative phase, that is, to say that these schizothymic changes in the personality which we meet in the transitional age in a wide variety of directions are characteristic not for the entire transitional age, but for the negative phase as such, and that the more it proceeds in line with such schizothymic personality change, the more typically the negative phase turns out to unfold.[15]

I think that no matter how wrong the old theory that calls youth schizophrenia itself may be…as well as the new theory which says that between the sudden gush of sexual maturation and its gentle flow…there are not adequate boundaries and transitions, no matter how wrong it is to attempt to define the essence of the negative phase from the pathological point of view, nevertheless there are hidden therein some true observations which have merely been incorrectly generalized. And it appears to me that if we think it over correctly, if we attempt to compare it with what we have in the school age and afterwards, it seems to me that we can come to the proposition which I worked out for myself and by which I was guided when I tried to think and understand the problem of this age, namely, the proposition that the schism, or the emergence of a divided personality structure, constitutes the central neoformation of a transitional type that we encounter in the negative phase of the transitional age. In order to fill out this definition with some definite content, we

[15]Vygotsky takes the term схизотимного (schizothymic) from Kretschmer (see below). We have taken from the same source the modern notion of the "schizotypal personality disorder" The DSM (the diagnostic and statistical manual of mental disorders used by most psychiatrists today) defines the schizotypal personality disorder as: "A pervasive pattern of social and interpersonal deficits and marked by an acute discomfort and decreased capacity for close relationships as well as by cognitive or perceptual distortions and eccentricities of behavior beginning by early adulthood and present in a variety of contexts and as indicated by five or more of the following:

(a) ideas of reference (everything that is happening is personally significant)
(b) odd beliefs or magical thinking that influences behavior but is inconsistent with subcultural norms (personal beliefs)
(c) Unusual perceptual experiences including bodily illusions
(d) Odd thinking and speech that is vague, circumstantial, and metaphorical
(e) Suspiciousness or paranoid ideation
(f) Inappropriate, constricted affect
(g) Behavior or appearance that is odd or peculiar
(h) Lack of close friends or confidantes other than first degree relatives
(i) Excessive social anxiety that doesn't diminish with familiarity and tends to be associated with paranoid fears rather than negative feelings about the self."

Of course, these characteristics do not occur exclusively during disorders, and it would be unusual for a perfectly normal adolescent not to experience at least one and possibly even all of these.

need to dwell on the psychological understanding of what lies behind this term "schism," how it occurs in development and how it is embodied in the further course of such development.

It must be said that the concept of dissociation was introduced into psychology long before it had become a byword in psychopathology, that is, in the study of mental illness. Observations of the normal psychological life of humans have led to the identification of this concept of dissociation as one of the necessary functions without which consciousness cannot act. It was Herbart who originally had this idea, although it was only later that the representation of his thought became completely clear—that two basic functions are preconditions of consciousness as a whole, so that psychic life can be explained and understood—and that these functions are merging and dissociation.[16] You know the Herbartian system overall consists in this: it is in the mechanics of representations and complex relations between individual representations emerge the variety of psychic activities. According to this view, separate masses of representations can merge together, forming as a result of such mergers mass representations that act *en masse*, rather than as a single representation; on the other hand, in order for the formation of these complex conglomerations of representations to take place, it is necessary that representations, as Herbart says, be split up, just as we might smash up some kind of rock, so that what we call an abstraction of the activity of consciousness may arise. In order for complex representations of objects that have one shared trait to arise, it is necessary that this one shared trait should be able to act as a selected quality and be split away from the general current of conscious processing.[17]

In this way, for the first time, psychology affirmed the concept of dissociation as a function fundamental to consciousness which, alongside constitution, or unification, makes up a necessary type of the inner activity of consciousness without which the normal organization of conscious life is inconceivable.

---

[16] Vygotsky uses the term расщеплении to translate the Herbartian term, "Dissoziation von Komplexen (dissociation of complexes)." This Russian word means something like "dividing" or "cleaving," as in splitting up wood or cleaving an apple in two more or less equal pieces. We will respect the German source and translate it as "dissociation." Later, however, Vygotsky uses a different Russian word, отщепления, to translate the Freudian term "Spaltung," the splitting of consciousness into unequal parts as a result of conflict. This Russian word means something like "splintering" or "chipping," as in removing a smaller piece of wood or stone from a larger one. Here we will use the term "splitting up/off". Note that Léopoldoff-Martin and Schneuwly reject the term "dissociation" because of its psychoanalytic baggage and instead use the term "destructuration." They believe that Vygotsky adopted the term from Bleuler (Bleuler, 1911/1926/1964).

[17] Johann Friedrich Herbart (1776–1841) is best known as an educator today: he helped to found the "Realschule." These taught real skills, but they also eschewed "readers" and made-for-class textbooks and advocated teaching real literature. Herbart's system of moral and ethical education was based on five principles: freedom, perfection, kindness, justice, and equity. He was also a philosopher (he took Kant's old job in Königsberg) and, as Vygotsky says, developed a system of deriving higher representations from the conglomeration and abstraction from lower ones. This system, related to the stages of Hegelian logic, is visible in Vygotsky's experiments on concept formation (Herbart, 1895).

Thus, dissociation was understood as some not completely defined and only theoretically determined activity of consciousness, the essence of which was reduced to this: in consciousness there appeared some discontinuous orders which in one way or another were distributed but which had, originally, been represented as one in consciousness. If you take the speculative stage in the development of psychology and the whole of the Herbartian system, then along with the positive content of Herbartian psychology this doctrine has evolved and has been confirmed in the psychopathology of Freud in the doctrine of complexes.

You know that this doctrine, like the whole of Freud, presents an attempt to resuscitate in the psychology of consciousness the Herbartian point of view. All of the Freudian terminology, such as "condensation," "repression," "transference," and "dissociation" are terms of Herbartian psychology, Herbart's mechanics of representations. Freud restored this Herbartian doctrine of dissociation under the rubric of splitting off, and by "complex" Freud refers to a group of representations linked to a given affect, but pinched off of the general mass of consciousness and thus becoming subconscious, not having any communication with other systems of consciousness as if living in a foreign body.

For example, when an organism is penetrated by a foreign body, it continues to live without entering into contacts linked with all of the processes which permeate all of the living tissues of the organism. We know that Freud, like Piaget, is completely correct in holding the point of view that speech plays an important role in the act of conscious awareness. And of course the more we can see what is going on and tell others about this, the more clearly we ourselves are consciously aware. By communicating with others about our environment, we are consciously aware of what is happening to us. We have, from Herbart, the formula that speech is not only a way of understanding others but also a way of understanding ourselves.

Now, following in the footsteps of Freud, Bleuler introduces the concept … not applied to the schism….[18]

Here Bleuler wished to express two basic ideas in combination. He wished to show that in this psychic state, the dissociating of consciousness occupies the first plane. He had in mind a break in the associative series; in an associative series there is no smooth transition from one association to another. And Bleuler gave an extreme interpretation…schizophrenia, that is, he wished to point out that with this psychosis as many personalities arise in the patient as he has complexes. In him there arise

[18] Once again, there is clearly some missing text, and there is no note from Korotaeva, so we may suppose that the stenographer missed some words. Leopoldoff-Martin and Schneuwly suggest that what Vygotsky wishes to say that Bleuler has introduced the concept of autism rather than schizophrenia. That is possible, but according to Vygotsky it is precisely with autism that Bleuler diverged from Freud, since Freud believed that autism was primordial and Bleuler found it to be late arising (see Vygotsky's critique in Chapter Two of *Thinking and Speech*.) Bleuler did, however, accept many other Freudian concepts: repression, complexes, latency, and Freud's general theory of the unconscious mind.

a vast quantity of representations that have been dissociated from the general line of consciousness.[19]

In this way, the concept of splitting up began to be cultivated and to be developed principally in the field of psychopathology. From here it came into proximity with the age of adolescence, not without recalling its original roots in the doctrine of the psychological nature of splitting. However, from the various sources of contemporary psychopathology, we have come to see that splitting should not be understood as a function of a diseased consciousness but as a function of any normally organized consciousness. This came about in two ways. First, Kretschmer expounded a series of human features and compared them with the features we confront in psychosis. From this a whole school grew up which called this "experimental doctrine of types." In this school, Kelte (Volkelt?—Trans.) and others demonstrated experimentally that dissociation is a function of a normally organized consciousness, and that it is in the same measure necessary for volitional attention, when we pay attention to something and leave all else unattended; in the same measure necessary for abstraction, when forming concepts, and in the same measure manifested in the dissociation of mental life, as we observe in mental illness.[20]

In this way, what became clearer was the idea that in the normal activity of consciousness, in the functions of voluntary attention, in the functions of abstraction, in the functions of concept formation, an adequately developed dissociation was a necessary precondition for the actual emergence of these formations. In this given case, Bleder (Bleuler?—Trans.), in opposition to the experimental doctrine of Freud, came to the position that he formulated in a well-known article devoted to the transition age. Bleder (Bleuler?—Trans.) concluded that schizotomy presents in

[19] For Bleuler schizophrenia (which he viewed as physical and not psychological in origin) is a form of dementia, and it is caused by the break-up of the associations and its replacement by complexes. In neither case is there the kind of logical hierarchy, the logical ranks, we see in conceptual systems. Note that "Bleuler" is referred to correctly here, and not as "Bleder."

[20] Ernst Kretschmer (1888–1964) was a Nazi psychiatrist today best known for his theory of constitutional "typologies": a rather crude holism which associated body type with personality type in indissoluble unities. For example, fat people (pyknic) were jolly, and thin people (asthenic) timid; good Germans, of course, tended to the powerful athletic sort. In personality, he saw two constitutional groups, the "schizothymic" (schizotypical, or polar) and cyclothymic (manic or depressive). As a Nazi, he was also interested in the "psychology of great men." Vygotsky uses some of his early work on the "blocks" of the brain in his first lectures and he is particularly taken by the laws Kretschmer formulated for the "transfer of brain functions upwards," that is, the ability of higher blocks of the brain such as the cerebrum to take over the functions of lower blocks (the midbrain and cerebellum) where the latter have been damaged. He was one of the signatories of "vow of allegiance of professors to Hitler" and he supported the extermination of the mentally ill.

We cannot find any references to "Kelt" and suspect the stenographer actually means Hans Volkelt (1886–1864) who is very often cited by Vygotsky in conjunction with Kretschmer and the Leipzig school. Vygotsky also cites Volkelt's experiments that show that infants and even spiders are capable of certain forms of abstraction and deduction (so for example an infant can be taught that only a square blue bottle contains milk, and a spider will run away from a dead fly but eat a live one). Volkelt was the son of a famous philosopher (Johannes Volkelt) and a student of Wundt and of Spranger. He was a specialist in early years and founded the journal "Kindergarten." He was a Nazi party member and like Kretschmer an early signatory of the vow of allegiance to Adolf Hitler.

itself not an experimental topo-human (i.e., a *topoi*, a *locus communis*, a standard theme? Restricted area?—Trans.) feature of a particular distinct group of people but rather a psychological mechanism which in different degrees inheres in all people and which appears in the negative phase of the transitional age and appears with particular distinct force in psychosis.[21]

In this way, the very approach to understanding splitting in psychosis has been transformed. In particular, a range of researchers have discovered two extremely important sides of this affair. The first consists in this: with schizotomy, mesotomous psychotic splitting does not stand out as the umbrella or predominant form or result of the patient psyche. On the contrary, along with dissociation, the changes stand out in psychosis as a counter-symptom, that is, as an insufficiency of this dissociation. The isotomic (sic—GKS) not only breaks down what is merged as such, but it merges that which for us remains completely distinct. For example, the memories of distant childhood and what he read in the book—everything is connected with everything for him.[22]

In this way, the correct psychopathology of mature mesotomic psychosis consists in this: let us imagine that we are dealing here not with dissociation as such but with a dissociation changed by disease, such that what is dissociated merges and what is merged dissociates. This idea of Bleder's (Bleuler's?—Trans.) that in the negative phase of the transitional age we are faced with the maturation of the dissociative mechanisms seems to me to be extremely close to answering two questions. First, the question of the nature of the central neoformation of the transitional age and secondly, in the sense of what lies really, it seems to me, at the genetic basis in order to properly map out… Hence all of these propositions about the schizoid character of the adolescent.[23]

I will cite one more body of work, the work of Lewin. He belongs to the representatives of the young structural psychology. Lewin defends, both theoretically and experimentally, a single idea: that structural psychology began by interpreting the

---

[21] Korotaeva has replaced the word обретает "acquires" wth появляется "appears." For "schizotomy" see Footnote 16 above. It is not clear today what Vygotsky means by топочеловеческ ("topo-human"). Perhaps he means topographically human, that is, restricted to a particular area or a restricted *topoi* or group. It appears to be counterposed to universal or general.

[22] Again, it is not clear what "mesotomous" might mean in this context; it appears to mean something like "mid-level" or "moderate" as opposed to a high-level, or metastatic dissociation. A mesotomous disorder would be a schizotypal personality disorder rather than a psychosis. Korotaeva (GKS) notes that Изотомия (istomiya) is "thus in the manuscript," so she clearly does not know what it means either. In Greek it means branching, as when you cut a plant stem and it bifurcates; perhaps Vygotsky means that dissociation cuts the 13-year-old off from others, and this "bifurcates" the child's personality in some way. As the DSM said, one of the symptoms of a schizoid disorder is the sense that everything is personally relevant: "Everything is connected with everything."

[23] Some of the text is missing, and there is no note from Korotaeva, so it appears to be another stenographer's lapse. Vygotsky appears, on the basis of the next paragraph, to mean something like this. Assuming that dissociation really is the central neoformation of the crisis, how does it enter into the next zone of development, namely, the stable structure of stable period of adolescence? To answer the second question, he looks at Lewin's critique of "structure."

very principle of structure in a vulgar way. In particular, Lewin experimentally put forward the polemic against the first work of V... who had argued every separate (single) perception is structural, that structure itself represents the relationship of perception to will, to affect, to thinking, etc.; structure represents the whole person, taken as a whole. Lewin countered this point of view that the structural principle can spread like.... (missing—Trans.). He pointed out that if the whole of psychic life is subjected to the structural principle, we arrive at an absurdity; we arrive at the conclusion that we can merge everything with everything. Everything is structurally linked to everything, and in all the parts are parts of some whole, and the human personality presents a kind of toy egg, in which there is a smaller shell enclosed within a larger, and a series of such whole shells makes up the extremely primitive structure. Therefore, Lewin in all of his works has begun to pay attention not only to the unified structure but also to the structural boundaries of the psyche. He has advanced in theory a correct and sound notion that for the normal existence of the whole structure it is necessary not only that it should be a whole unto itself but also that it should be delineated from other structures. This doctrine of delineation, of communication between structures, has become the central idea of his work. He holds that the relationship between one structure and another structure is in principle different from the relationship that exists within a structure. This relationship between structures he proposes to call communication, that is, the degree of sharing of these separate structures between themselves.[24]

In his research on affect and will, Lewin put forward a rationale for differentiation, the independence of orders of consciousness from each other and the emergence between them of links of a different type than those which exist within the structure and its elements. This is one side, the necessary principle of organization of consciousness, but the other side is the principle of psychological analysis and

[24] Korotaeva notes that "V...." is "Так в стенограмме" (thus in the stenogramme). Since we are talking about structural psychology, this is probably Max Wertheimer, as we suggested previously. Kurt Lewin (1890–1947) was an important Gestaltist: important for Vygotsky as well as for psychology quite generally. Lewin was the student of Carl Stumpf, Max Wertheimer, and Wolfgang Köhler and the teacher of Sarah Fajans, Tamara Dembo, and Bluma Zeigarnik. His early work, which Vygotsky cites in his pedology of infancy (Lewin, 1931), is about the idea of "fields" and "affordances"—that is, the elements of a situation that are "irresistible invitations" (Packer, 2017) in early childhood.

He was also a progressive, close to the Frankfurt Institute for Social Research (Theodor Adorno, Max Horkheimer, and Walter Benjamin). All of them had to leave Germany when Hitler came to power—Benjamin died in the attempt. Lewin went to the USA and joined the war effort. He founded "action research," the "change laboratory" (which Yrjö Engeström has adapted very successfully to Finnish post offices, hospitals and businesses) and sensitivity training to combat racism. Lewin also developed methods for treating post-traumatic stress disorder (PTSD, or "shell shock") in soldiers.

Of all the Gestaltists, Kurt Lewin was probably closest to Vygotsky's own views (as we shall see, Lewin even shares Vygotsky's sense that the Gestaltists have taken the notion of "structure" a little too far). A personal friend of Vygotsky, he was the only foreign psychologist to contribute to Vygotsky's obituary when Vygotsky died.

research, because otherwise we are faced with that universal structure of which I spoke with which, as in the twilight, all the cats are sulfur-colored.

If all of this is accepted, then we obtain some theoretical grounds for imagining what kind of neoformations we have to deal with in the negative phase. The features which characterize the negative phase of the transitional age are various. We will not delineate them now, but one can hardly be questioned, as it has been singled out by almost all researchers as the basic feature of the crisis at thirteen.

Suppose we say of the child who is experiencing the crisis at 7 that the main impression that such a child gives consists in this—that he has lost his childish immediacy and that therefore from a simple communication with the child you may take away some impression of whether the crisis at seven has begun or not. Then of the 11–13-year-old crisis what can be said is that the child produces the impression of a spiritual unease, and such unease we also observe in his motorics, and in his physical development, that is, some awkwardness, disproportionality, disharmony, dissonance, some contradictoriness in all of his expressions, that shows up in all the complaints and all the indications that the adolescent has begun to behave in ways that are contradictory in relation to the well-defined way in which he had behaved. He has lost all his definite guidelines and he gives you the impression that there is no longer a whole consciousness before you.

I think that when Klern (Klein?—Trans.) says that the essence of the negative phase consists in the absence of adequate wholeness, then this expresses in other words the same thought (all of you have seen these children); in the negative phase, the more or less integral coherent personality that you met in a schoolchild before this period and the clearly expressed one you will meet in the transitional age is not there. The very presence of negative symptoms speaks to this: here we are dealing with the emergence of a series of differentiated *perezhivanies*, relatively separated from each other, which have not yet been brought together into a new unity.[25]

We may imagine, along with Bleder (Bleuler?—Trans.), that in the negative phase we have all of the symptoms which demonstrate that here we are dealing with the maturation of the splitting mechanism, and in consciousness it begins to play a leading role. What data speaks for this? The first group of facts: purely psycho-experimental. Actually, if you begin to study the history of the development of voluntary attention, your attention will be drawn to something extremely interesting: in itself the function of attention—the capacity to divide the state of consciousness

[25] It is possible that this is another transcription error, since the name "Klein" looks a little like "Klern" if you are not writing carefully on a blackboard. If so, Vygotsky is referring to the work of the Freudian child psychiatrist Melanie Klein—we know that Vygotsky was indeed following her work closely and that he refers to it critically in his correspondence with Luria. In 1932, the year before this talk, Klein was living in London and Leonard and Virginia Woolf's Hogarth Press had just published her book "The psychoanalysis of children," which contained two studies on adolescents: Ilse, a girl, and Felix, a boy. She does speak of a lack of integration and dissociation, as Vygotsky mentions (Klein, 1975).

Leopoldoff-Martin and Schneuwly (2018, p. 189) say that the note we have translated as "all of you have seen such children" is a note added by the stenographer's hand. It does appear to be in the wrong place.

into parts, that which is the focus of our attention and that which lies on the periphery of attention—this inheres in the earliest forms of consciousness. This primitive function of consciousness is called, at the suggestion of Vol'steyn, the function of figure and background.[26]

It consists in this: every perception is a structural disarticulation of perception. One part stands out as the figure, the other as the background. He gave a number of experimentally composed figures: the figure and the background may exchange places.

For example, if you pay attention to the black in this drawing, then this you have two people in profile on a white background. If you pay attention to the white, then the black appears as background, and so on, that is, in other words, what you direct your attention to is what appears; what you are trying to see is due to splitting it off this way or that, and what you see is structured—almost all of this inheres in the very early steps in the development of consciousness.

But producing the highlighting of the figure and the ground, that is, the function of volitional attention, with the ability to direct attention to moments of perception which are structured in order to attract attention to themselves—this develops late; it is at the end of the school age that we meet for the first time the drastic increase in this function of disarticulation. Bleder, whom I mentioned and who is the finest researcher of the school age, showed the dependency of memory upon this attention with a curve.

We know very well that attention plays a constitutive role in perception, that even famous experiments upon the memorization of nonsense words have long been the subject of controversy. Binet showed that what they attest is not so much the power of memory as the power of attention, and the question of the correct interpretation of these experiments is not yet resolved, because the questions of attention and memory are closely linked to each other.[27]

Brunsing (Brunswik?—Trans.) raises this problem and shows that the role… (Text missing—Trans.) at the border of the transitional age in the negative phase has increased to an extreme degree. We are dealing, as he expresses it, with the preferred phase for its development. We know that in general that every function has a

---

[26] We have been unable to find any other references to Vol'steyn. But the idea of "figure and ground" is usually associated with the Danish psychologist Edgar Rubin, and Vygotsky does cite Rubin elsewhere. In the next paragraph, it appears that Rubin's vase is what is meant. The example is important for Vygotsky because it suggest that even perception is susceptible to volition—we can choose to see the Rubin vase as one thing or as another.

[27] Alfred Binet (1857–1911) was a student of Charcot and of hypnotism, and he also did studies on the expertise of chess players. Today, he is best known for his work with Simon on intelligence testing (the Binet-Simon test, which was the source of the problems that Vygotsky refers to in his famous description of the ZPD, as well as the notion of "mental age" on which it is based. He also wrote philosophical works (e.g., *Mind and Brain*) and did a diary study of the development of his own two daughters (the "objectivist" and the "subjectivist") which formed the basis of the notion of psychological types (Binet, 1907). For a critical look at what his work did and did not mean to Vygotsky, see "Leaving the Stage" in *L.S. Vygotsky Pedological Works Vol. 1*.

phase of development which is pre-eminent, that period in which the maximum development of this function is concentrated.[28]

Regarding the process of abstraction and the formation of concepts, this idea is not my own, and it does not rest upon my research alone, but it is, strictly speaking, an old idea, one accepted in pedology and psychology until the last decade, the idea that by the end of school age we encounter a new wave in the development of abstraction and the beginning of concept formation. Recently, a certain tendency to attribute the formation of concepts to an earlier age has begun to emerge, but this tendency has impoverished the concept itself. If we regard the concept from the point of view of formal logic as the singling out of any general trait, then we can attribute the formation of concepts to an early age. My work was only trying to rehabilitate an old empirical opinion based on quality material, only to bolster it scientifically against a number of contemporary currents which have tended to reduce the period of concept formation and attribute it to an earlier age, something which is, in essence, excluded in my idea. All other authors have pointed out that any generalization which requires an actuality mastery of concepts, always, in all countries, belongs to that age that falls at the beginning of the period of secondary school, the negative phase. In this way, we deal with a range of experimental data which demonstrates that the form of psychic activity in which the dissociation function is most clearly manifested matures in the negative phase. This is one of the most important arguments that Bleuler made.[29]

Let us take up all of the negative symptoms of this phase, all of the symptoms of purely contrarian moments which we encounter. These, as we know, also constitute indirect indications that in the system of consciousness of the adolescent there has taken place a kind of differentiation, a kind of distinguishing, a kind of exceptional singling out of different groups of *perezhivanie* which, as Bleuler has observed, are in a state of migration, still wandering, not settling, and which do not, after postponement, turn into this or that character trait of the personality, this or that property or feature, which, depending on the movements of these migrations, may lend an awkward appearance to the behavior of the adolescent.

---

[28] It is possible that this refers to either Cécile or Léon Brunschvicg. Léon Brunschvicg was a Spinozist philosopher who believed in the leading role of judgment. At the Sorbonne, he supervised the MA thesis of Simone de Beauvoir. Cécile Brunschvicg was feminist militant, later undersecretary for education in the socialist government of Léon Blum (1935–37).

But given the inaccuracy of the stenographer, it could also refer to Egon Brunswik (1903–1955) whose work Vygotsky may also refer to elsewhere (see Выготский, 2001, p. 270, where "Brunowich" is one of the main researchers into schools in Vienna).

Brunswik was indeed working with Karl and Charlotte Bühler on school psychology at that time. Later, he became a functionalist psychologist, and still later a historian of psychology, whose ideas are mostly used today in the psychology of decision making (especially in the work of Douglas Hubbard).

[29] Volkelt has argued that the spider which eats a live fly but runs from a dead one already has a functional concept of "prey," because the concept of "prey" is not based on a concrete object but rather on an idea. As Vygotsky points out, this greatly impoverishes the idea of a concept (and in fact it is easy to make spiders "eat" anything by putting it on the web and vibrating the web to simulate a fly).

Finally, if we take on the most convincing argument—that is, in the relationship of the neoformations: the school and the transition period—we then derive an argument which speaks still more in support of this thought. What is one of the most essential neoformations of the school age? No matter how it is looked at theoretically, there is always a basis for believing that the formation of inner speech, the formation of the ability to think for oneself, the formation and emergence of introspection, of self-observation, the formation of an inner form of activeness and ideational memory, the formation of voluntary attention, memory, and attention, which is dependent upon inner process of thinking—this represents one of the essential features of the development of the child at school age. That is to say that, in general, inner life is somewhat differentiated from (…) occurs (…) at school age after the age of seven.[30]

It seems to me that there is a vast quantity of consideration and factual material to reinforce this on all sides. Thus, at school age, in the first period, we have the formation of the inner life of consciousness relatively differentiated from the external side of behavior. Naturally there emerges the idea that <… > (missing—Trans.) school age, this inner life appears extremely amorphous. The work of Piaget brilliantly confirms this <…>. Piaget demonstrates how a contradiction grows (I do not have in mind a dialectical contradiction, a driving contradiction—I am speaking of a factual contradiction) between the fact that the schoolboy is a thinking being who is self-conscious and has a relatively developed inner life, but in this inner life he behaves as a preschooler behaves at one moment, that is, whenever this inner life is separated from concrete reality, and then he falls into a series of difficulties which are not specific to that inner life as such but instead specific to the vicissitudes complicating his behavior. What I mean to say is that a thought which is split away from an action but in which the logic of action still rules—this is an internally contradictory system.

When Piaget discovers the limits of the school age, poised upon the cusp of the negative phase, he says that the child comes to the end of school age with inner thinking which is already well-formulated and broad in its functioning, but it is thinking which is flightless, for in it the logic of action dominates. He comes hither with a kind of inner life which dominates but which is not differentiated, not ordered, because in it everything is linked to everything. However, Piaget in his latest work draws some general conclusions, that the whole of inner life is realized to a large degree in an uncritical way, that is, the child of school age is aware of his experiences in the same way as an early preschooler is aware of external reality, that is, the

[30] Vygotsky speaks of идеологической памяти, which is literally "ideological memory," and it is possible that he has in mind more or less what we have in mind today—a memory for ideologies such as religion, capitalism, and communism. But the Russian equivalent for "ideology" was also used (e.g., by Volosinov) in a quite literal sense, to mean the study of ideas. What seems more likely that he is referring to the research reflected in Chap. 13, which compared memories for structure, for images and for thoughts. We have chosen to translate it as "ideational memory," since the idea of speech as an "ideational" can be found in the work of the Moscow Linguistic Circle, whose members Vygotsky knew.

school child does not differentiate between them and everything is merged with everything else—with all of his many psychological experiences.

The whole sense of his work leads to this: that the proximal steps which should take place in development—these are some kind of split in spiritual life, some kind of differentiation, some emergence of the spiritual, psychological system of which Lewin speaks, but this emergence is on the basis of the disintegration of the immediate singular unity of spiritual life with the emergence of a number of relatively specific systems, which then enter into a certain co-relationship with each other. If we know that which transpires during the transitional age, then once again we can, together, depending upon this or that theoretical approach to the transitional age, formulate the neoformations, which we will encounter in some different way, but if there is one thing which is beyond these doubts, it is this: the personality in the sense of a more or less defined structure of consciousness as a whole and its relation to reality, and to the self, arises in this transitional age.

How did this notion emerge, that this dissociation, this crisis, with which we are dealing in the negative phase of the transitional age, is the necessary prerequisite for the structuration of the personality? It stands in the same relation to the neoformations of the transitional age that autonomous speech does to stable speech, to speech proper; that the hypobulic reaction of the three-year-old does to really volitional actions which emerges in games with rules. The fact that the three-year-old negates and the five-year-old acts according to rules, that a one-year-old child speaks in autonomous speech and the five-year-old uses grammatical and syntactic structures—these facts are linked together genetically. In the same link, we find dissociation during the negative phase: this schizoid thread in the line of development of the personality of the adolescent and the future structure of that personality, a dissociation without which the personality could not emerge.

In this way, considering the symptoms of the negative phase, considering the experimental data and that which we encounter in the school age and in the transitional age, leads to this idea: that the original seed (i.e., the "grain of truth"—Trans.) in the doctrine of the schizoid character of the transitional age consists in this: in the negative phase what is really substantial is an inevitable inner stage of development; as Bleuler says, it is the maturation of the functions of the dissociation in consciousness, that is, some disarticulation, some differentiation of the unity of the child's inner life which predominated in the preceding ages as a prerequisite for the emergence of a differentiated personality in relation to the specific psychic systems within it. Thus, we obtain some idea regarding whether this neoformation co-occurs with all of those traits with the requirements that we are used to making for any neoformation of the transitional age. It presents on the one hand, a real neoformation by itself, and on the other hand, it presents in itself a neoformation that, as such, is not deposited in the structure of the personality, which passes by, but which constitutes a prerequisite for this very splitting off, one to be preserved in the differentiated and integrated structure of the personality which is formed in the future.

In two words, I wish, for the sake of completing the exposition, to express the idea as follows: it can be especially shown in what a close link with genetic continuities the functions of dissociation and concept formation stand to one another. As the formation of concepts constitutes merely a moment in the history of the transitional age, so too the function of the split seems to me to be a basic change in the negative phase.

Let me focus our attention on one [word, one point—Trans.]: What is going on in the child [when concepts are not formed—GSK]? What is going on in the child is a syncretic linking of everything with everything else, what is going on in the child is [a merging—Korotaeva's addition] of things which are strictly delineated in concepts, and a non-merging of things which are connected in unified concepts, that is, every state in the development of concepts, in the development of meanings (…) involves assumes certain limitations to unification and therefore definite degrees, definite characteristics of splitting or of dissociation. Consequently, in my opinion, the link between dissociation and the function of concept formation which has been experimentally confirmed constitutes, to my eyes, one of the most compelling indications or arguments in favor of the schism, or dissociation, as the central neoformation of this phase.[31]

It remains for us to linger a moment over the idea that this may show us in what way in this central neoformation the essential features that characterize the negative phase can be identified. In this regard, we owe a great deal to the psychopathological analysis of Kretschmer and his colleague psychopathologists, as well as to the experimental analyses of Lewin, which established an extremely important fact, namely, the complex formation that occurs on the basis of dissociation.

For instance, we have shown, roughly speaking, that autism—that is, the emergence of the capacity for an adequately isolated inner life as a whole or in different parts—autism in this sense presents a necessary link in any developed personality. I cannot consider myself or you autistic (but there was one person who did not talk about anything with anyone).[32] However, each of us has an obligatory autistic function in the sense that there is part of one's preceding life, part of one's previous experiences, that allows for restricted communication, or, conversely, about which we may not speak. Both the external degree of consciousness and different degree of inner innermostness of experiences belong to the most basic features of the structure of the personality. This comes to us, in this sense and in the proper sense of the word, during the transitional age. With an earlier age, we do not yet possess that which we may not say.

We make this remark not only about the transitional age. We are dealing with the emergence of an autistic singling out of *perezhivaniya,* in the sense of a great inner proximity to what constitutes the remote, that which is hidden within the personality. In this sense, the autistic function inheres in each of us as originality and as reverie. This does not mean, nonetheless, that every person is a fantasist or a dreamer who spends his whole life in a daydream.

[31] Leopoldoff-Martin and Schneuwly note that the 1996 edition of Korotaeva's book attributes the additions we have marked GSK to the stenographer. They are not so marked in the 2001 edition we have used.

[32] Vygotsky appears to be referring to a quieter student, perhaps jokingly, as a way of encouragement?

Here as well, it is thus. Autism is not something contrarian or pathological. It is one of the forms which in different varieties but within certain limits we encounter in any healthy and normally organized personality. Contrariwise, in a number of mental illnesses we have such cases where this capacity disappears and we are dealing with painful manifestations of the autistic side of the personality.

This autism, as research demonstrates, has an extremely complex structure. I do not intend to give the history of the development of autism in the age of childhood. What is important for me is to give a history of the development of autism that shows an unmediated dependence on the function of dissociation, and this is more or less clear from the facts of which I have spoken. It is more or less clear that this demands a certain dissociation within consciousness such that we may stand in some way or another close or distant in relation to other systems, which in one way or another will act immediately.

Other formations, which we speak of as features of the transitional age when we speak of asthenia … about … the proportions, when an excess of sensitivity or some dullness of emotion alternate with each other when we speak of the reverie of a personality in the transitional age, of the new turmoil in child fantasy, etc. All of these features, naturally, arise from the basic assumption that we laid down at the very beginning.

In this way it appears to me that this idea is fruitful and plausible in this respect: that complex formations of the transitional age may be explained and may be identified by assuming that the basis of the transitional age lies in this function of splitting off.

It seems to me that in this way before our eyes it is as if the ends meet in that old controversy, and I think that the grain of truth which is constituted in the doctrine of the convergence of the transitional age with the schismatic transformation of the personality, to all appearances, lies in the recognition that in the negative phase we are dealing with the maturation and development of the function of dissociation, on the basis of which we have a number of macroscopic changes in the spiritual life of the child, and, linked to this appears a range of symptoms of the negative phase complex in character, but which on the other hand, makes up a prerequisite for the emergence and the development of the real inner structure of the personality, which emerges during the transitional age and which could not emerge without the basis of dissociation, that there can be no direct transition from the inner linking of everything and everything in the schoolchild and the disarticulated state if there is no transitional phase, the basis of which is the inner function of dissociation in the consciousness of the adolescent.

References

Выготский, Л. С. (2001). *Лекции по педологии*. Издательский дом Удмуртский.
Binet, A. (1907). *The mind and the brain*. Kegan Paul, Trench, Trübner and.

Bleuler, E. (1911/1926/1964). Analectes – Dementia praecox ou groupe des schizophrènes. : Théraplix.

Blunden, A. (2017). The germ cell of Vygotsky's science. In C. Ratner & D. N. H. Silva (Eds.), *Vygotsky and Marx* (pp. 132–145). Routledge.

Bühler, C. (1922). *Das Seelenleben des Jugendlichen: Versuch einer Analyse und Theorie der psychischen Pubertät*. G. Fischer.

Bühler, C. (1928). *Kindheit und Jugend: Genese des Bewußtseins*. Hirzel.

Bühler, C. (1931). The social behavior of the child. In C. Murchison & J. E. Anderson (Eds.), *Handbook of child psychology* (pp. 392–431). Oxford University Press.

Hall, G. S. (1907). *Adolescence* (Vol. I and II). Appleton.

Herbart, J.F. (1895). *A text-book in psychology: an attempt to found the science of psychology on experience, metaphysics, and mathematics.* (Margaret K. Smith Trans.). New York: D. Appleton and Co.

Karpov, Y. V. (2005). *The neo-Vygotskyan approach to child development.* Cambridge University Press.

Klein, M. (1975). *The psychoanalysis of children.* (Alix Strachey Trans.).; rev. in collaboration with Alix Strachey by (H. A. Thorner. Rev. ed.), New York: Delacorte Press/S. Lawrence.

Leontiev, A. N. (1981). *Problems of the development of the mind.* Moscow.

Léopoldoff-Martin, I. (2014*) La science du développement de l'enfant: La conception singulière de Vygotskij* These No. 561. Genève: Université de Genève.

Lewin, K. (1931). Environmental forces in child behavior and development. In C. Murchison & J. E. Anderson (Eds.), *Handbook of child psychology* (pp. 94–127). Oxford University Press.

Packer, M. (2017). *Child development: Understanding a cultural perspective.* Sage.

Vygotsky, L.S. (1984/1998). *Collected works* Vol. 5, (Volume 4 in Russian). Plenum. (Moscow: Pedagogika in Russian).

Revealing Some Patterns

At the outset of this volume, we suggested that Vygotsky's keen interest in this problem of age was both an interpersonal interest, which developed out of his clinical work with "difficult children" and a much broader sociocultural interest, which developed out of a bold social experiment in consciously planning upbringing, education, and human resources as part of a society—including an economy—which was designed rather than evolved. We also said that, *mutatis mutandis*, both of these concerns still hold our interest today. Here we will try to show how these four strands—interpersonal and more broadly cultural-historical, on the one hand, and past and present, on the other—interweave and form a design.

But perhaps "form" and "design" are not quite the right words. Exactly halfway through this book, at the very end of Chapter Seven on the crisis at one, Vygotsky suddenly remarks:

> The transitions which arise during the critical ages and in particular autonomous child speech, are endlessly interesting, for they present in themselves portions of child development in which we see the dialectical laws of development made bare.

As we noted in the postface of *Foundations of Pedology*, the term "law" has gone out of fashion, perhaps because it would seem to imply a divine law-giver or perhaps because it is really something of an overgeneralization. After all, nature is not made up of laws in the same sense as the criminal code is, nor is the criminal code the sort of law we find in a grammar book. Although the term "pattern" has also been overgeneralized, it does seem preferable to speak in this conclusion of patterns or even rhythms, where instead of slow, steady, linear growth, there is repetition with variation, a cycle of variable wavelength or even a spiral including movement along a completely different axis altogether (e.g., autonomous speech and eventually speech).

L. S. Vygotsky, *L.S. Vygotsky's Pedological Works. Volume 2.*, Perspectives in Cultural-Historical Research 10, https://doi.org/10.1007/978-981-16-1907-6

Very well, there may be laws or rhythms or patterns to be laid bare—but why bother to call them "dialectical?" They are dialectical in the old Greek sense: based on human lines of question and answer rather than mechanical lines of action and reaction, or lines of cause and effect. These patterns will be dialectical in a more nineteenth-century German and even twentieth-century Soviet sense too, in the sense that it will lay bare some notions of Hegelian and Marxian dialectics—rising from the abstract to the concrete, taking conflicts as causal, recognizing chains of negation, and, finally, the nonfinality of change. But perhaps the best thing is not to tell but to show; perhaps it would be best to allow all these patterns to reveal themselves in the weaving—that is, in the asking and answering.

The questions we will try to ask and answer below—interpersonal vs. sociocultural, past vs present—are the following. First, was Vygotsky personally able to use the concepts in this book, including the zone of proximal development, in his own professional work? If so, how so, and if not why not? Second, what would it really mean to use a zone of proximal development in classroom settings today? Third, was his understanding of periods in child development and "optimum times of instruction" really a feasible way of structuring the Soviet curriculum of his time? Fourthly, is there a place for this kind of periodization scheme in cultural-historical theory today?

Did Vygotsky Use These Concepts in His Own Work?

Zavershneva and van der Veer, in the insightful annotations they have made to their fine translations and invaluable selections from Vygotsky's notebooks, express some surprise that pedologists of Vygotsky's time subscribed to a "Continental" and specifically German, clinical approach (in Vygotsky, 2018: 437f). In this approach, patients were interpersonally treated in a holistic way, with careful attention to school achievement and family relations, but somewhat less attention to the kind of class factors that party intellectuals in the USSR insisted on and to the workings of sexual repression and the unconscious that the Freudians were so interested in. In the notes that Zavershneva and van der Veer have selected, Vygotsky does indeed express a keen interpersonal interest in his patients. For example, when an adolescent girl who has previously attempted suicide after receiving poor grades suddenly has a marked improvement in her grades, Vygotsky visits the school to reassure himself that the girl's teachers are not simply inflating her grades to prevent another suicide attempt (Vygotsky, 2018: 451–452). But perhaps what is most surprising is not Vygotsky's attention to the German tradition, but his inattention to his own ideas; in the clinical notes he makes, there are far more references to social class and to Freud, Adler, and syndromes like hysteria than to the development of higher psychological functions, their neoformations, and the most proximal zones of their development. Did Vygotsky doubt his own theory?

First of all, we should not be too surprised that in a clinical setting Vygotsky would turn to what was then the state of the art in patient care. As a speaker of

German, he had privileged access to the very latest literature from what was then the most advanced center for clinical psychology in the world. Secondly, of course, Vygotsky was self-critical, open to everything but convinced of nothing, and this omnivorous but pan-critical intellectual attitude was far too productive to deny to his own ideas.

While the notebooks contain very rich critical appreciations of German writers as diverse as the Nazi doctor Otto Pötzl (Vygotsky, 2018, pp. 425–427) and the socialist professor Kurt Lewin (pp. 403–412), the notes in them are above all a forum for refining his own work, sometimes in the light of other theories (p. 474), but more often in the light of Vygotsky's own experiments (p. 369), his clinical practice (pp. 376–379), and even his parenting (pp. 237–242). So we should also not be too surprised that Vygotsky's clinical work seems to have served him as a source of empirical data rather than as an arena for theory testing.

In this, Vygotsky was following the great example of Darwin. In the famous article "The Mozart of Psychology" which launched the great "Vygotsky Boom," Stephen Toulmin (1978) argues that Darwin hesitated to apply his 1859 theory of natural selection to humans for 20 years for fear of being thought a materialist. But surely this is only part of the story behind Darwin's reticence. As Halliday (2002, p. 162) points out, far more horrifying ideas linked to evolution were already in the air, and many of these are still with us. The poet Tennyson was already in 1849 contemplating, with some equanimity, Mother Nature's imminent extirpation of the whole human species: "And he, shall he," Tennyson writes in part LV of his poem In Memoriam "Man, her last work, who seem'd so fair (…)"

Who loved, who suffer'd countless ills
Who battled for the True, the Just,
Be blown about the desert dust,
Or seal'd within the iron hills?

In contrast to the poet, Darwin (1979) wanted conclusions to emerge well supported from a vast compendium of empirical data. The immense power of the *Origin of Species* depended not on the well-known and widely acknowledged theory and the large body of empirical evidence that supports it today, but instead upon the 450 preceding pages of dense argumentation and detailed evidence. Vygotsky, for his part, had no fear of being thought a materialist; in the end, it would be the opposite accusation of idealism, stemming from the central role he assigned to speech, that would be used to bring down his theory and suppress his legacy (Leontiev, 1936?/2005; Rudneva, 1937/2000). Moreover, Vygotsky had all of Tennyson's keen appreciation of poetry, and retained to the very end of his days a sense that art and science were not opposed but complementary ways of seeing the one-ness—the unity and the uniqueness—of a life. Nevertheless, Vygotsky shared Darwin's desire for conclusions that emerge inexorably on a solid base in data and he probably hesitated to practice what he preached out of sheer humility.

In his notes on an internal conference in late 1932, Vygotsky remarks (Vygotsky, 2018: 398) that there are really only two empirical bases supporting a law he calls "superseding in development." This is an instance of sublation, or *Aufheben*, the tendency of a factor that was once first in importance (e.g., heredity) to be superseded by one that was once merely secondary (e.g., the environment) while being, at the same time, preserved in a subordinated or attenuated form. The first basis for "superseding in development" was the comparative studies of dizygotic and monozygotic twins that Vygotsky spends nearly an entire lecture on in *Foundations of Pedology* (see Chapter Three in Vygotsky, 2019). Vygotsky pointed out that even functions like perception, memory, and attention radically change in the extent to which they can be predicted from heredity as they become complex; higher, meaning-making, functions subject to factors like speech, thinking, and volition acquire a very different relationship to the environment by being mediated through language. Vygotsky likewise pointed to other aspects of development, such as that of psychosexual identity, that appear to move in the opposite direction, from something more mediated by the social environment to something more biological in origin. This understanding of sexual identity is now the mostly widely accepted account and "Born This Way" has become the basis of pop songs and legal arguments on gay marriage.

The second basis for "superseding in development" was the curious case of post-encephalitic children. In 1917, alongside the better known "Spanish Flu," there was yet another pandemic—a mysterious sleeping sickness called encephalitis lethargica, whose origin remains a mystery to this day. The disease was Protean in the symptoms it presented, and the severity of the disease seemed highly sensitive to the age of the patient. Around 18% of patients suffered flu-like symptoms, about 30% of the patients were struck down by acute lethargy which could last for decades (well documented in Sacks, 1973), and about 19%, particularly young patients, experienced hyperactivity, which could in turn range from a loss of motor control similar to Parkinson's disease to what was then called "moral insanity," for example, children who boiled cats, cut rabbits up with scissors, and indulged in precocious hypersexual behavior such as frequent and/or public onanism (Foley, 2018, p. 134). The reason why the latter behavior was referred to as "moral" insanity is that unlike other forms of insanity, intelligence and thinking were relatively unimpaired. Vygotsky notes that the traditional account, which located the soul deep in the sub-cortical area of the brain and accordingly offered an organic explanation of the syndrome (i.e., a virus or an autoimmune response) could not explain this, any more than it could explain why symptoms seemed to vary widely with developmental age. Nor could the traditional approach offer even the rudiments of an explanation why two of the post-encephalitic children Vygotsky examined, referred to in the notes as Sterligov and Kolya Terekhov, exhibited symptoms that were the very opposite of moral insanity: an "ideal child" syndrome and sterile "hypermoral" behavior.

Vygotsky's principle of "superseding in development" did account for all of this: for children at a given moment of personality development, to wit, adolescence, organic factors which dominated in the early stages of the illness were superseded by environmental factors in later stages. Vygotsky says, in his remarks on these two cases, that pedology and pathology have both had a tendency to break down into elements an as-yet-unnamed unit of analysis of healthy and unhealthy development (Vygotsky, 2018: 398). This analysis, of which Sterligov and Terekhov are already a part, might offer a path to treatment, seeing these two children as two instances of compensation, two moments of indirect and circuitous development. But in clinical work, the stakes are high, and there are knotty ethical issues to untangle which are very familiar to us today. Does the possible harm of a novel treatment outweigh the potential benefit for the age cohort as a whole, and does the potential individual benefit of combining novel treatments with extant best practices outweigh the loss of generalizability of a study?

So it is not so surprising that Vygotsky strove to combine his boldest theorizing with cautious "best practices" in his clinical work. Perhaps it is neither true to say that he directly applied his own views on the development of the higher psychological functions nor that he entirely ignored them in his clinical work. Instead, his theoretical work and his practice made up a unit which is only un-named today; Vygotsky and his colleagues knew it by the name of dialectical unity of theory and praxis. Such a unit, of course, does not rule out contradictions and even periodic cracks and crises; on the contrary, development must bountifully include them. A case in point: clinical work almost presupposes a one-to-one form of interaction which is atypical of a classroom setting, even today. Classroom interaction, on the other hand, permits, or at least once permitted, the formation of collectives which are quite impossible in a clinical setting. Some researchers have argued strenuously that interaction with an adult on the one hand and interaction with a band of comrades are simply two different ends of a continuum that begins with the "ideal form" in the environment and ends with "inner speech" (e.g., Veresov, 2017; Guk & Kellogg, 2007). But is this realistic? If so, can we say that they are using one and the same "group" zone of proximal development? If not, what does that suggest about Vygotsky's underlying periodization scheme?

What Would It Really Mean to Use the ZPD in a Classroom Setting Today?

In clinics and classrooms, as we publish this book, one of the most concrete, practical, and immediate realities is a worldwide pandemic of a novel coronavirus known as SARS-COV-2, which causes a sometimes severe and occasionally fatal infectious disease called Covid-19. While no age group has been spared by the disease, it does appear that the symptoms, spreadability, and the immune response are all, as with encephalitis, sensitive to age periodization. Because children and younger people generally risk spreading the disease to their families, SARS-COV-2 has fundamentally changed the climate in which we live, learn, and teach, and like many recent changes, the tendency appears to be toward greater inequality and ultimately toward crisis. On the one hand, online teaching has made universal education (including universal tertiary education in the most remote corners of the earth) a real possibility. On the other, it seems to have reinforced rather than alleviated the divide with which Vygotsky was chiefly concerned in Chapters Twelve and Thirteen of this volume. Sometime in late school age, there comes a moment where interpersonal meanings made in face-to-face affordances have to be replaced by textual meanings made in school settings. These are, from an interpersonal point of view, impoverished, but from a broader sociocultural point of view, much enriched, and the gap between the two is a good measure of the child's next zone of development at school age.

Writing nearly two decades ago, Seth Chaiklin noted that the zone of proximal development was designed to address this moment and also answer questions such as how resources available for education may be allocated to the goals that education can attain, and how the goal of learning is related to the goals of human development. As such, he noted, the concept was "more precise than the common reception or interpretation (2003, p. 39)." These questions were historically specific to Vygotsky's time and place when he raised them, but they are hardly irrelevant today. To continue to answer them in our own time and place, his theory must allow delicacy, and with every quantum of precision, we can expect new ambiguities. To be both historically specific and generally relevant, it must be made both unrefined and refinable; it must become—to put it as an oxymoron—indefinitely precise. Yet here, in *The Problem of Age*, there seems to be a more delicate distinction to be introduced, between the immediately interpersonal and the more abstract social and cultural.

Chaiklin distinguishes two types of ZPD. One is an individual, "subjective" ZPD—"the extent to which a child's currently maturing functions are realizing the structure of the next age period." This subjective ZPD exists, according to Chaiklin, because imitation is only intelligible and practicable when functions have partially matured. Take, for example, negation, the great neoformation of the crisis at three. Negation is an immensely powerful function of everyday speech—it controls access to all kinds of forbidden pleasures, thwarts the will of child and caretaker alike, and sounds splendidly assertive and supremely confident in argumentation, all of which make it an attractive acquisition for a 3-year-old child. But negation is not something the child can directly assimilate. Semantically, negation does not mean the observation of a presence but rather the experience of an absence. Grammatically, it can require some sophisticated analysis to function at higher levels (e.g., indicatives and interrogatives); in English, it requires analyzing the verb phrase into Finite and Predicator, and thematizing the wh-word, and this has created a whole industry of "movement" rules in Chomskyan linguistics. Even at lower speech levels, imitation requires a partially matured function. For example, the negation of a major clause requires all of the wherewithal of the minor clause and more. At the higher levels, for example, those of the major clause, negation will require mastery of all of the lower levels as well as a leap in the dark. Perhaps this is true of higher forms of behavior quite generally: they require the creative, inventive solution of completely novel problems which has only been prepared for but not fully resolved on previous levels.

The second kind of ZPD Chaiklin distinguishes is the "objective" ZPD. This is the zone of which Vygotsky speaks in the first paragraph of Chapter Nine on the crisis at three, where he says that the task of his lecture is to establish the future and fate of the crisis—not the fate of an individual child, but the future of the critical epoch in general. Within epochs, this objective zone exists because neoformations arise only at the end of a developmental period and not at the outset (see the last three paragraphs of Chapter Three). Perhaps it is worth noting that with the examples Vygotsky gives in Chapter Four—two children who have a developmental age of eight according to their scores on the Binet-Simon test—Vygotsky describes zones of 1 year and 5 years. Since both children are only eight, neither zone necessarily includes the next epoch, the crisis at thirteen, so it is left somewhat ambiguous whether a zone of proximal development is ever capable of leaping over the boundaries between epochs. As Chaiklin points out, the objective zone of proximal development inheres in the social situation of development itself: it represents the distance to be travelled from the present social situation of development to the next central neoformation and thus to the next social situation of development, and it is objective in the sense that it is shared by all the children of a given age cohort in a given culture. In much the same way, the epochs of "preschool" and "school" are experiences common to all the children of a given culture (or at least a given culture that has compulsory schooling). Similarly, the crisis at seventeen may be expected to unfold very differently in a society like Korea, where school-leaving and the choice of a job or course of study happens much later than in a society like the USSR (Выготский, 1931), where it happened around seventeen years of age; this apparently external quality, linked quite directly to the job environment and not immanently to the inner pace of development, may go some way to justify the curious circumstance noted earlier that the crisis at seventeen seems to interrupt a stable period which then continues apparently unaffected after the crisis is over! But if there is both an objective and a subjective zone of proximal development, which zone of proximal development does a teacher use today?

Both. A psychological line of development and a sociological one are not to be thought of as separate substances, but rather as two viewpoints: macroscopic and microscopic, on the same phenomenon. So too the objective and the subjective ZPD have to be taken as two different views, afforded by two different instruments with two different degrees of granularity, of the same basic phenomena of development. In this book, Vygotsky has concentrated on the grand panorama; in practical work, the teacher will concentrate on the up close and personal. In the end, however, the pedologist, the parent, and even the passerby who asks how old a child is will find it necessary to shunt between the two perspectives, as when we think about weather against the background of climate, or text against the background of the language system. So too with Vygotsky; in Chapter Three, he insists on theoretical categories like the social situation of development and the neoformations and then, in Chapter Four, shunts to calculating the ratio of the subjective zone of the individual child measured through imitation to the objective zone given by the child's age and by the child's next epoch of development. But then what is the difference between a ZPD and an IQ—which is also a comparison between what the child can do on a test and the child's age and equally a ratio between the child's performance and that of others in the child's age cohort? For that matter, what is the difference between a ZPD and asking how old a child is and comparing the answer with what we would expect from the child on the basis of his or her behavior, speech, and thinking?

First of all, because the subjective zone of proximal development is "objectivizing"—because it makes maturing functions which are normally impossible to observe visible and even measurable—the subjective zone allows much more access to thinking than we would normally get from testing or simply asking and observing—and thinking is, as Vygotsky makes very clear in the penultimate chapter of this book, a central line of development in the school child. Secondly, because the objective zone of proximal development inheres in a social situation of development—because it is linked to goals which are not merely learning skills but immanent to the development of the child's personality, intrinsic to the process of enculturation, and at the base of consciousness itself—the objective zone will allow us to make precise statements about the relationship between particular forms of learning and more general developmental goals like self-control, mastery of speech, and intellectualization of functions, the results of which are generally not observable in the classroom. But thirdly—and most importantly from a practical point of view—this method of testing, relating the subjective zone to an objective one, constitutes a direct attack on the separation of assessment and instruction, and thus a full frontal assault on the central purpose of testing today, namely gate-keeping. As Chaiklin notes, Vygotsky is simply not very interested in standardizing the forms of assistance offered the child so that we can compare the size of child ZPD—exactly one of the most fraught issues with applying the ZPD in the classroom today. This is easy to explain. Vygotsky's purpose is not competition, but diagnosis; the ZPD is not an aptitude test, a job interview, or even a school sports field day. The ZPD was designed to be more like a public health checkup.

Did Diagnosing Development and "Optimum Periods for Instruction" Really Offer a Way to Structure the Soviet Curriculum?

But then, as now, diagnosis—precisely because it frames development as a public health issue—turned out to be an easy issue to politicize. Then, as now, without mass testing, there would be no risk of embarrassing results that point inexorably to government neglect. So even before Vygotsky's death—indeed, while the lectures in this book were being given—Vygotsky and his colleagues in pedology came under attack.

Andy Byford (2014) gives us the external view of these attacks. The "complex" form of education associated with post-revolutionary labor schools was abruptly abandoned for "education in concepts." The push to complete the first five-year plan in 4 years (1928–1932) involved, for the first time, a serious effort to guarantee universal primary education in practice. But the scanty resources for this at first sincere effort almost inevitably resulted in a tracking system that advantaged some schools over others. In particular, schools that could promise immediate results got resources while those which required large investments had to wait—for resources which somehow never quite trickled down. So pedology which, under the leadership of Blonsky, Zalkind, and Vygotsky himself, had at first supported the egalitarian "complex system" was suddenly enlisted by teachers and functionaries to provide testing services in support of the tracking system.

Kellogg (2019) offers an inside view of the same tumultuous change, arguing that the zone of proximal development represents an adroit tactical maneuver as well as an astute strategic move: the zone could offer both a decisive advance from teaching in complexes to a curriculum based on conceptual knowledge and a way of combating the inevitable inequalities that must result from tracking children. One way it could do this was by diluting the gate-keeping individual performances with various forms of collaboration. Vygotsky hoped to use the diagnosis of development to structure the Soviet curriculum into optimal periods for instruction along the lines suggested in this book, that is, imaginative play and written speech in preschool, narrative and fiction at seven, general representations and abstract preconcepts in primary school, and sex education in secondary school, about which more below (and much more in future volumes of this series). But for that to have happened, the attacks on pedology would have to have been well-meant criticisms intended to refine Vygotsky's proposal for reforming the Soviet syllabus in a practical way.

This was always unlikely. Pedology had been, almost from its inception, allied with Lenin's widow, Nadezhda Krupskaya, who had joined the Leningrad opposition to Stalin. Zavershneva and van der Veer (in Vygotsky, 2018, pp. 311–216) offer us harrowing selections from Vygotsky's notebooks that give us a heart-breaking view of Vygotsky's side of the story. Two purge commissions, one in Moscow and one in Leningrad, were set up to investigate the work of Vygotsky and his colleagues. The Moscow commission seems to have chiefly targeted not Vygotsky's pedological proposals but rather his book proposal for *Thinking and Speech*. The chief objections seem to be that Vygotsky paid insufficient attention to the biological basis of historical development in the human brain (Kolbanovsky), that Vygotsky was undertaking "individual studies outside time and space," and that, as a consequence, his work lacked "the class aspect and the progressive aspect" (Gershonovich). The work on concept formation consisted of laboratory experiments far removed from practice so that it could not show the real process of concept formation (according to Vvedenov). In general (again according to Gershonovich), "one does not feel dialectical materialism in the analysis" and "there is no dialectic in the definition of thinking" (2018, p. 313). The commission at the Herzen State Pedagogical Institute, where the lectures in this book were mostly delivered, seems to have arrived at similar conclusions: Vygotsky's views were dismissed as "idealist and bourgeois theory" based on an "anti-Marxist" conception. Vygotsky's response, to the director of the Herzen State Pedagogical Institute, was that these conclusions were founded on the hearsay of commission "collaborators," "based on misunderstandings" that did not "correspond with reality," and so the commission was not yet in a position to discuss his work (2018, p. 315).

With this book, we are at last in a position to discuss it. We noted at the outset that, at the end of Chapter Seven, in his discussion of the future and fate of the proto-speech that Eliasberg has misleadingly called "autonomous," Vygotsky remarks that this transition to speech proper, and indeed all the transitions in all the critical ages, lay bare the dialectical laws of development. As if an answer to a question, the stable neoformation arises only with the apparent cessation of the transitional form. However, just as a question finds a certain echo in the wording of the answer, the subordinate form of child proto-speech does not disappear altogether but instead finds itself transformed, obeying that law of superseding, into a subordinate part of a more complex formation, for example, as intonation, stress, and above all, childly semantics. So too with the crisis at three: the negation of the negativism of the 3-year-old is not its obliteration but more like the negation of a negation, and the older child's ability to say "no," for example, to sexual predators, owes something to the "seven stars" Vygotsky explores in Chapter Nine. With the crisis at seven, the child's acting out, acting up, and apparent self-absorption are all likewise a question to which the complexes of generalization, the abstractions of potential concepts, and the self-esteem of the school child are the answer. In all this, as Vygotsky says, the dialectical laws of development are laid bare.

And all of this is the prologue to the very real questions that confront 13-year-olds, to which the "transitional period" of adolescence is the answer. Careful readers of Vygotsky's *Thinking and Speech* will already have noticed the curious circumstance that Chapter Five of that book, ostensibly about adolescents, actually precedes a chapter that is ostensibly about school children. Careful readers of this book will find the reason, in Chapter Thirteen on Thinking in School Age: Vygotsky replaced the whole Chapter Five system of complexes and potential concepts that was now in disfavor with the Chapter Six "measure of generality." This clever tactical move allowed Vygotsky to omit the mention of the complex system of education associated with the discredited labor schools (though it is interesting that Vygotsky's notebooks, including the notes taken at the commission meetings, still use this very system). But it was also an astute strategic move which allowed Vygotsky to provide for the generalization of generalizations that the child has already made instead of starting over from scratch with each new complex. Vygotsky had, as he remarks in his notebooks, been criticized for underestimating the external line of development, that is, the effect of the social environment and the new socialist order; his response, however, was to criticize himself for underestimating the internal line of development and ignoring the child's own powers of generalization!

By introducing the zone of proximal development, Vygotsky could now include, at one end of the zone, the generalized representations and potential concepts that are the main line of development for children in elementary school, and, at the other end of the zone, the introduction of true concepts from the child's next epoch of development, namely adolescence. Yet, Vygotsky did not flinch from a struggle against the Stakhanovite adventurism that was plunging the country into famine and the educational system into chaos. We saw that he ended Chapter Thirteen with a clear and timely warning: the child's ability to master concepts had been overestimated and exaggerated in the rush to complete the five-year plan in 4 years. Vygotsky even singled out for special criticism the social science curriculum, which we know from *Thinking and Speech* involved teaching concepts like "revolution," "planned economy," and "socialism" to second and fourth graders (Выготский,

1934, pp. 163–259). The child's ability to assimilate and communicate real scientific generalizations remained unrealized, because the bridge to true concepts—the child's preconceptual generalizations—has been burnt before the child could cross.

We might dismiss all this as over-canny maneuvering, on the one hand, and the uncanny courage of despair, on the other. We might assume that Vygotsky's project for diagnosing development and teaching concepts at optimal moments for instruction was doomed from the very inception; we might have asserted with some confidence at the very outset of this section that the answer to our question—whether diagnosing development and teaching during "optimum periods of instruction" was a feasible proposition in the long term—must inevitably be no. But that assertion would itself have been both over-canny and despairing. Victory for Vygotsky might have been unlikely, but it could not have been ruled out in advance: people who would make history cannot know all that the historians who will write about it will know. Van der Veer and Valsiner (1991, p. 374) argue convincingly that it is "facile" to write off hostility to Vygotsky's ideas as a mere political football of the Stalin period. In any case, all these negations of Vygotsky could be themselves negated, and in the fullness of time, they would be.

Is There a Place for This Kind of Periodization Scheme Today or Not?

Another reason that van der Veer and Valsiner consider it too simplistic to dismiss the Stalin-era criticisms of Vygotsky—and indeed devote a whole chapter to taking them seriously—is that both periodization and testing are considered at best necessary evils even today. Joseph Glick remarked, in an introduction to the fourth volume of the Vygotsky *Collected Works* in English, that one of the things that greatly attracted readers to Vygotsky was the conviction that he was not constrained by Piaget's structure dependency. So readers hoped that the "zone of proximal development," despite its name, would not involve periodization (see Vygotsky, 1997, pp. ix–x). There were at least three good reasons for this hope.

The first was very much shared with the Soviet critics of Vygotsky's own time: the recognition that periodization schemes have the effect of privileging one sort of culture above another; establishing a hierarchy of culturally shaped forms of thinking exist is only one short step from naturalizing them, and that is one short step in turn from imposing the natural order by man-made means such as gate-keeping. The second is the growing recognition that child development as a process is far too complex to be uni-dimensional; even Vygotsky, after assigning a "dominant" function for early childhood (affective perception) and preschool (memory), seems to give up on the idea that one period has only one dominant and abandons the task of establishing a single central line of development and a single central neoformation for each age. Because a neoformation is now confronted with the well-defined and well-differentiated functions of previous ages, the differentiation of new functions no longer passes through a period of its dominance. But a third reason for resisting the periodization that is, after all, Vygotsky's central purpose in this book of lectures is completely practical: for thousands of years, education in families must have largely dispensed with age stratification and looked after many different ages together; this historically successful model of upbringing is still widely used today at the bookends of childhood, for example, in daycare facilities and in graduate schools.

When we carefully consider these three reasons why readers resist the idea today, we notice that all three reasons, pursued to a certain point, appear to negate themselves. If we ask, for example, why periodizing childhood has historically led to a hierarchy of forms of behavior that is then naturalized and imposed on children by artificial means, we are compelled to answer, as Vygotsky does at the outset of Chapter Two, that these historical periods are the result of a great deal of human and even non-human experience with the raising of offspring. If we accept, as we surely must after reading this book, that complex functions do not spring readymade from the brain like Athena from the head of Zeus, we must likewise accept that the different components of a complex function must appear in a sequence which corresponds to definite periods, and the interpersonal, and ultimately sociocultural, inequity produced by this process can only really be eliminated if it is first thoroughly understood. As for the argument that the process is too complex to be considered unidimensional, this is not an argument against periodization; it is only an argument against univariate periodization—against considering development as growth or mere increase in child ability and thus against reducing the zone of proximal development into a zone of proximal task learning. The antiquity and continued existence of a period of education in the home, where the older child's zone of actual development functions as the younger child's ideal form and creates his or her zone of proximal development, is itself a kind of periodization: children of different ages creating zones of proximal development in autonomous and adult speech, affective and semantic perception. "Role and rule play" is itself a periodization scheme, particularly if we see development not as increase merely, but rather as a process of differentiation. The very process of ontogenesis may be—and historically has been—differentiated into a relatively undifferentiated period of family schooling and one in which instruction can and indeed must be made more age specific.

So in addition to following a best practice central to the pedology of his own time, Vygotsky had his own theoretical reasons for periodizing childhood (e.g., explaining the nature and inevitability of crises) as well as his own practical ones (e.g., deciding when and how to intervene to change it under the grim conditions of the post-revolutionary inter-war period in the USSR). And in addition to all of these, he had other reasons we can easily share, reasons we set out at the very outset: comparing the development in health and vitality of a particular child with the health and vitality of other children his or her age. It is hard to see how these can be accomplished without solving the problem of age and understanding the process of ontogenesis as a process of pattern formation. Therein lies the value of this book.

Finally, Non-finality

All patterns, including those revealed here, are not rules and regulations to be imposed at the outset, but rather designs to be laid bare in the data. But the simple pattern we set out to weave here—past and present, interpersonal and more broadly sociocultural—has already revealed at least four basic conclusions.

First of all, we have seen that Vygotsky's own clinical work involved him in a "rise to the concrete"— instead of seeing the particular and the individual case as an embodiment of a Platonic idea, Vygotsky, like both Marx and Darwin, insisted that it was the intersection of an indefinite number of concrete patterns, regularities, and lines of development that created the particular and the individual case and can render them comprehensible to us. But for Vygotsky the task was not to impose those concrete patterns on the data of experience but rather to discover them in his clinical work. Secondly, we have seen that "rising to the concrete" involves construing conflicts with the environment and with others as a moving force, not merely in conversations between human voices but throughout human history—including the histories of the individual children that grew up and made it. In the latter histories, the zone of proximal development which allows us to measure the distance between the child's actual state of development and that of the next developmental epoch actually requires us to distinguish the interpersonal and the sociocultural—the subjective and the objective zone of proximal development. Thirdly, we have seen that the pattern of children's lives at any given moment in history and even in history taken as a whole must involve negation and even negation-of-the-negation—as every 3-year-old discovers, a double negative must eventually yield, like it or not, an alternative, an affirmative way forward. So each stable period is negated by a crisis, which is then negated in turn by the succeeding stable period. Finally, we have seen that weaving the pattern of development culminates in novelty but also in nonculimination, that is, in endless nonfinality.

Nonfinally, we said, at the outset of this book, that it offered little more than a tantalizingly distinct but ultimately unattained end. Surely we are now in a better position to appreciate how very promising that little bit more that Vygotsky offered us toward that end was; surely, we are now in a worse position to reconcile ourselves to the excruciating frustration of not attaining it. Now nearly nine decades separate us from the historical context of these texts. Yet, the misgivings we have about Vygotsky's words today are really not so distant from the ones that the Soviets themselves had, and Vygotsky can still, at least partially, answer them for us. If our doubts about periodization are not entirely laid to rest by the answers that Vygotsky has given us here, perhaps this is simply because that doubt is how all human voices develop other human ideas. Like our less articulate ancestors, we and all of our theories and understandings of our world are also things of nature most beautiful and most wonderful—things of nature which, as Darwin described in the closing paragraphs of *The Origin of Species*, have been and are being evolved. So when we try to explain and describe development, there is never really any good time to say "the end."

Nikolai Veresov
Monash University, Melbourne, Australia

David Kellogg
Sangmyung University, Seoul, Korea (Republic of)

References

Byford, A. (2014). The mental test as a boundary object in early 20th century Russian child science. *History of the Human Sciences*. https://doi.org/10.1177/0952695114527598
Chaiklin, S. (2003). The ZPD in Vygotsky's Analysis of Learning and Instruction. In A. Kozulin, B. Gindis, V. S. Ageyev, & S. M. Miller (Eds.), *Vygotsky's educational theory in cultural context* (pp. 39–64). Cambridge University Press.
Darwin, C. (1979). In P. Appleman (Ed.), *Darwin: A Norton critical edition*. Norton.
Foley, P. B. (2018). *Encephalitis lethargica: The mind and brain virus*. Springer.
Glick, J. (1997). Prologue. In L. S. Vygotsky (Ed.), *Collected Works* (Vol. 4, pp. v–xvi). Plenum.
Guk, I.-J., & Kellogg, D. (2007). The ZPD and whole class teaching: Teacher-led and student-led interactional mediation of tasks. *Language Teaching Research, 11*(3), 281–299.
Halliday, M. A. K. (2002). *Linguistic studies of text and discourse*. Continuum.
Kellogg, D. (2019). The storyteller's tale: Vygotsky's 'vrashchivaniya', the zone of proximal development' and 'ingrowing' in the weekend stories of Korean children. *British Journal of Educational Studies, 67*(4), 493–512. https://doi.org/10.1080/00071005.2019.1569200
Leontiev, A. N. (1936?/2005). Study of the environment in the pedological works of L.S. Vygotsky. *Journal of Russian and East European Psychology, 43*(4), 8–28. https://doi.org/10.1080/10610405.2005.11059254
Rudneva, E. I. (1937/2000). Vygotsky's pedological distortions. *Journal of Russian and East European Psychology, 38*(6), 75–94. https://doi.org/10.2753/RPO1061-0405380675
Sacks, O. (1973). *Awakenings*. Random House.
Toulmin, S. (1978). The Mozart of psychology. *New York Review of Books, 25*(14).
van der Veer, R., & Valsiner, J. (1991). *Understanding Vygotsky: A quest for synthesis*. Blackwell.
Veresov, N. N. (2017). ZBR and ZPD: Is there a difference? *Kul'turno-istoricheskaya psikhologiya = Cultural-historical psychology, 13*(1), 23–36. https://doi.org/10.17759/chp.2017130102
Vygotsky, L. S. (1997). *Collected works* (Vol. 4). Plenum.
Vygotsky, L. S. (2018). *Vygotsky's notebooks: A selection* (E. Zavershneva & R. van der Veer, Ed. and Trans.). Springer.
Vygotsky, L. S. (2019). *Vygotsky's pedological works* (Foundations of pedology) (Vol. 1) (D. Kellogg & N. Veresov, Ed. and Trans.). Springer.
Выготский, Л. С. (1931). *Педология подростка. Задание 9–16*. Государственное учебно-педагогическое издательство.
Выготский, Л. С. (1934). *Мышление и речь*. Соцэкгиз.

Author Index

L. S. Vygotsky, *L.S. Vygotsky's Pedological Works. Volume 2.*, Perspectives in Cultural-Historical Research 10, https://doi.org/10.1007/978-981-16-1907-6

Subject Index

L. S. Vygotsky, *L.S. Vygotsky's Pedological Works. Volume 2.*, Perspectives in Cultural-Historical Research 10, https://doi.org/10.1007/978-981-16-1907-6

Q

R

S

T

U

V

W

Z

The manufacturer's authorised representative in the EU is Springer Nature Customer Service Centre GmbH, Europaplatz 3, 69115 Heidelberg, Germany. If you have any concerns regarding our products, please contact ProductSafety@springernature.com

Printed and bound by CPI Group (UK) Ltd, Croydon, CR0 4YY
30/09/2026
02225246-0016